SELECTED ESSAYS OF ANDREY BELY

SELECTED ESSAYS OF

ANDREY BELY

EDITED, TRANSLATED, AND
WITH AN INTRODUCTION BY

STEVEN CASSEDY

UNIVERSITY OF CALIFORNIA PRESS
Berkeley Los Angeles London

University of California Press
Berkeley and Los Angeles, California
University of California Press, Ltd.
London, England

Printed in the United States of America
1 2 3 4 5 6 7 8 9

Library of Congress Cataloging in Publication Data

Bely, Andrey, 1880–1934.
Selected essays of Andrey Bely.

Translated from Russian.
Includes index.
Contents: Symbolism as a world-view—The magic of words—The emblematics of meaning—[etc.]
1. Symbolism (Literary movement)—Soviet Union—Addresses, essays, lectures. 2. Russian poetry—History and criticism—Addresses, essays, lectures.
I. Cassedy, Steven. II. Title.
PG3453.B84A23 1985 891.71′3′0915 84-23919
ISBN 0-520-05273-0

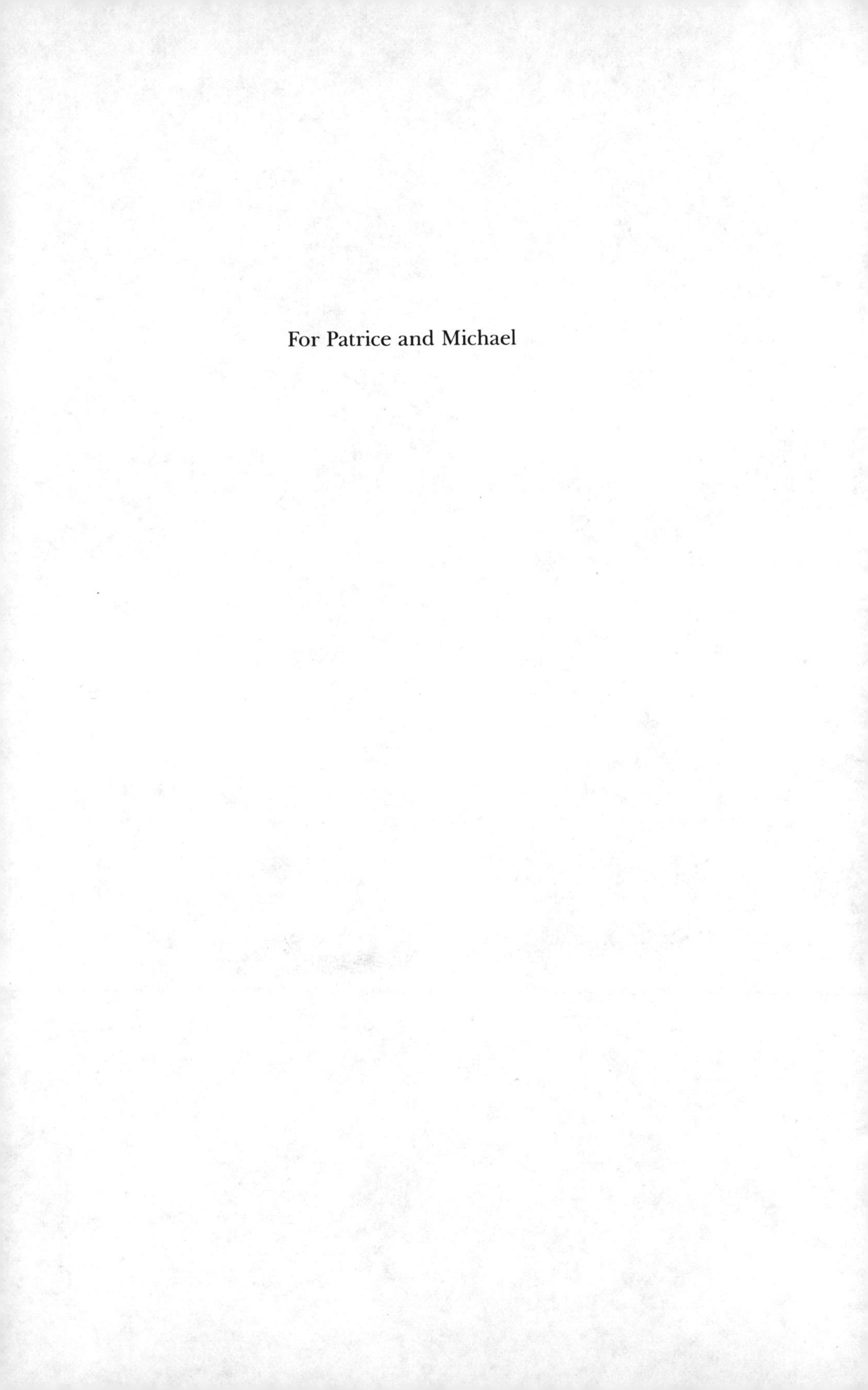

For Patrice and Michael

CONTENTS

PREFACE

None of the essays in this volume except one has ever appeared in English translation before. The one essay that has is "The Magic of Words," which was translated by T. G. West and included in his anthology *Symbolism* (London and New York: Methuen, 1980), pp. 120–43. My decision to issue my own translation of this essay for the present collection does not represent any sort of judgment of Mr. West's work, nor is it meant to imply that I think my translation should supersede his. I simply felt that "The Magic of Words" absolutely needed to be included in a collection of this sort, and I used my own translation so that the terminology in this essay would be consistent with the terminology in other essays I selected, particularly "The Emblematics of Meaning."

In preparing this collection of Bely's essays for the English-speaking reading public I faced two problems of audience. First, given the obvious difficulties of Bely's theoretical writings—the frequently esoteric nature of his subject, his frequent and arguably superfluous displays of erudition, the equally frequent lack of clarity in his exposition (more often than not the result of haste and carelessness)—was it necessary, I wondered, to present each essay in its entirety? A dedicated but perhaps small group of readers with a keen interest in aesthetic theory would wish to read the essays unedited. But the risk, I feared, was of losing the less patient readers. The solution would have been to provide "tidied-up" versions of Bely's writings, that is, suitably shortened and suitably purified of all material I deemed dispensable or hopelessly arcane.

And second, given that much of what Bely says implies a context that a reader not specializing in Russian or Russian symbolism might be unfamiliar with, did I, as editor, hope to have something to say and present that would be instructive to both the specialist and nonspecialist? Should I assume that only readers without Russian would be reading my book? For specialists it would be necessary to provide certain notations and bibliographical references that would probably be meaningless to the reader without Russian, while for nonspecialists it would be necessary to leave out a good deal of material that Slavists could profit from.

Two important considerations affected the choice of materials. All but one of the essays I selected had appeared in Bely's 1910 collection *Symbolism*. After Bely compiled this volume he added to the more than four hundred pages of text almost two hundred additional pages of notes and commentary. Almost none of the material Bely added, however, was directly relevant to his text. Many of his notes are little more than long lists of books (some in languages Bely did not even know) supposedly bearing a relation to a point he has made in the text. Others launch into a lengthy excursus only marginally pertinent to the subject. In some cases the notes to an essay exceed the essay itself in length. Rarely does Bely use footnotes to clarify a point or to provide truly useful information that, for one reason or another, does not fit well in his original argument. Since including some or all of these notes would have greatly increased the length of my own book, and since the notes really do constitute an entirely separate body of writing from the essays themselves, I decided that I would be risking little by leaving them out altogether. This is what I have done. In a few instances Bely has placed brief, explanatory notes at the bottom of the page. These I have included, with a notation in square brackets to indicate they are Bely's.

The second consideration of this sort concerned the essay "The Emblematics of Meaning." In the "Translator's Introduction" below I point out the difficulties associated with this essay. It is anything but clear, it is extremely long, it is carelessly written, and that is just the beginning. Including the entire essay required an explanatory section in the "Translator's Introduction" virtually half as long as the essay itself. Since no one has yet published an analysis of "The Emblematics of Meaning" that in my view is both satisfactory and complete, I felt an adequate explanation to be a necessary condition for including the essay. The question, then, was this: given the essay's length, given the length of the explanatory section, given the wealth of statements in my introduction that fault Bely for his excesses and obscurities, would I not be undermining my own presentation, inadvertently demonstrating that the foolish thing is simply too long and too much trouble to read?

Here, I have to say, I was willing to take the risk. My true purpose in producing this book, I reasoned, was to introduce a major modern thinker to a public that knows virtually nothing about him. Bely's theoretical writings now receive precious little attention in his mother country, and, as a consequence, if they are going to be read at all it is going to be in the West. Introducing Bely the theoretical thinker to the English-speaking world is thus almost the same thing as just introducing him. Let us assume, I said to myself, that the essays are successful in attracting attention. What was it I really wanted from this encounter between the West and an erratic Russian thinker?

What I really wanted, I decided, was for Bely finally to be taken seriously. I wanted his writings to generate the kind of discussion and controversy that surrounds the writings of other great (and especially other difficult) thinkers. My purpose would be truly accomplished, I felt, if one day another writer came along, read my translation of "The Emblematics of Meaning," and wrote an analysis of it that entirely superseded mine. For this reason I decided it would be unfair for *me* to decide where Bely's argument was needlessly unclear, where it could afford to be cut, what was truly essential in it. That way I would be stacking all the cards in favor of my own interpretation and commentary, and I would effectively be building in a device that would forestall, rather than encourage, discussion. Imagine, for example, what the reaction of the reading public would have been if the editors of a recent collection of previously untranslated essays by Bakhtin (who, like Bely, was often long-winded, repetitious, and unclear) had taken upon themselves to trim Bakhtin's writings down to a "manageable" size! No, I felt it was better in the end to leave all these judgments to my readers, and this is why I decided to include not only the entire "Emblematics of Meaning," faults and all, but my lengthy analysis, too.

The problem of how to address an audience both Russian reading and non-Russian reading largely concerns the use of Russian words and names. The final essay in this collection, "Lyric Poetry and Experiment," contains a system of verse analysis that is applicable to Russian verse alone. The reasons for my decision to include this essay will become clear from my remarks in the "Translator's Introduction." But in order for Bely's system to make sense to the nonreader of Russian it was necessary to include at least a transliterated version of the original texts Bely analyzes. In the

"Translator's Introduction" I outline the general principles of Russian versification, and I provide additional guidelines for reading these passages in a footnote to the essay itself.

This brings me to the question of transliteration. Since I was aware that this book would likely be used by readers of Russian, I felt it necessary to adopt a policy that would place as few encumbrances as possible in the way of those without Russian, while still providing the readers of Russian with information they might like to have. For this reason I decided to use the international scholarly system of transliteration for bibliographical entries in the footnotes, for verse passages in "Lyric Poetry and Experiment," and for the occasional Russian word or phrase taken from Bely's original. Everywhere else, I have used a more familiar and readable system. I would have been the first to recoil from the possibility of seeing hundreds of occurrences of the author's name spelled "Belyj!"

I would like to thank the University of California, San Diego, for awarding me a summer grant in 1982 to enable me to work on this project, and for assisting me financially in the preparation of the manuscript. Thanks are also due to Michael Flier of the University of California at Los Angeles for identifying a quotation from *The Russian Primary Chronicle* in "The Magic of Words," and to John P. Van Mater, Librarian of the Theosophical Library Center in Altadena, California, and his staff for identifying a quotation from Mabel Collins in "The Emblematics of Meaning." My editors at the University of California Press, Doris Kretschmer and Jeanne Sugiyama, have been so encouraging and helpful from the beginning of my association with them that my first experience with a book manuscript has, I fear, left me with a severely lopsided and hopelessly illusory view of the world of book publishing. It has been a pleasure and a privilege to work with them.

And finally, a word of gratitude to Vladimir Alexandrov of Harvard University, who first introduced me to Bely's writings when we were graduate students.

TRANSLATOR'S INTRODUCTION

BELY AS THEORIST

At one time my hope was that by the time a volume like the present one was published, it would be no more necessary to introduce Andrey Bely than it has been to introduce, say, Roland Barthes each time an English translation of one of his books has been issued in the last fifteen years. The day would surely arrive, I assured myself, when even a casual student of literature and literary criticism, browsing in a bookstore and seeing the title, *Selected Essays of Andrey Bely*, would exclaim, "At last! Bely's essays have finally been translated!" The realization that I was setting myself up for a disappointment, however, took hold increasingly each time a colleague or student, on hearing Bely's name, would affect that characteristic, knowing attitude that is a trademark of the academic profession and, reducing the Russian symbolist to an object more likely to be found behind the counter of a New York delicatessen, ask whether any of the New Critics were familiar with the work of . . . Bialy!

Andrey Bely (1880–1934) *is*, in fact, becoming better known in the English-speaking world as a key figure in early twentieth-century modernism. A series of recent translations is one indication of this. The new translation of the novel *Petersburg* in 1978 by Robert Maguire and John E. Malmstad was a major step in this direction.[1] Since then a number of Bely's works have appeared in English translation for the first time: *The First Encounter*, translated by Gerald Janeček, a collection of short stories translated by Ronald Peterson, and the essay "The Magic of Words," translated by Thomas West.[2] The attention the appearance of the Malmstad-Maguire *Petersburg* received in the press when it first appeared, together with the by now famous judgment of Bely by Nabokov in *Strong Opinions*, where the author firmly places Bely next to Joyce, Kafka, and Proust as the writers of the four greatest (in his own view) works of twentieth-century literature, indicates that Bely's reputation has indeed begun to take hold in the English-speaking world.[3]

The fact remains, however, that this reputation, such as it is, rests almost exclusively on what has been translated into English, and what has been translated into English consists almost exclusively of Bely's prose fiction. *Petersburg* (1916) was available in English as long ago as 1959, and Bely's other best-known novels, *The Silver Dove* (1909) and *Kotik Letaev* (1922), have also existed in English translation for a decade by now.[4] But what many readers do not realize is that these works represent only a small portion of Bely's production in the single area of prose fiction, and an even smaller portion of his entire corpus of writings. In fact, many readers will likely not even be aware of Bely's astoundingly large output not only in prose fiction but in verse, in a literary form that he called the "symphony," in memoir literature and correspondence, and, most of all, in criticism and aesthetic theory. In an attempt to fill the void in this last area for the English-speaking reader, I chose to bring out the present volume.

Bely's production in this area was enormous, running to over three hundred individual items.[5] His critical and theoretical writings are as wide ranging in subject as they are ample in quantity. Bely seems to have wanted to embrace everything, to absorb and systematize all areas of knowledge, either bit by bit or all at once. His theoretical writings reflect this desire. Many items in his bibliography are simply short essays on one or more works of a single author. Many early writings are devoted to the elaboration of a theory of symbolism. Others confront the problem of establishing a "scientific" aesthetics and propose various systematic models, drawn from contemporary theory in mathematics and the natural sciences, for an understanding of the analysis and the creation of artworks of all kinds. Still others can only be described as attempts to formulate a complete world view, a system (or "prolegomena" to such a system, as Bely terms his effort in "The Emblematics of Meaning") that will essentially explain, or begin to explain, the entire world as it is both revealed to, and concealed from, man. Bely's last published book, *Gogol's Craftsmanship*, is an essay in practical criticism in which the author set himself the task—unrealistic by most standards, but modest next to the ambitious program of elaborating a world view—of coming to grips with a purely literary problem that had plagued him throughout his entire career as a writer: "defining" Gogol's fictional world.[6]

Of this vast production only two short items, to my knowledge, have been translated into English until now: "The Magic of Words" (by Thomas West, mentioned earlier) and an essay on Gogol written on the centennial of that author's birth.[7]

The essays in this volume have all been selected from Bely's early, "symbolist" period, that is, from the period that saw the publication of his three most important collections of theoretical and critical writings: *Symbolism* (*Simvolizm*, 1910), *The Green Meadow* (*Lug zelenyj*, 1910), and *Arabesques* (*Arabeski*, 1911).[8] With the exception of "Symbolism as a World View" (which appeared in *Arabesques*), all the essays in this volume were taken from *Symbolism.*

In light of the title of the volume from which most of the essays were selected, it seems necessary to say a few words about symbolism as a literary movement in Russia. The symbolist movement in Russia is customarily divided into two distinct "generations": the founding generation, including such poets as Valery Bryusov (1873–1924), Konstantin Bal'mont (1867–1941), Dmitry Merezhkovsky (1865–1941), Zinaida Gippius (1869–1945), and Fedor Sologub (1863–1927), who found inspiration primarily in the French symbolists; and the second generation, including Vyacheslav Ivanov (1866–1949), Aleksandr Blok (1880–1921), and Bely, who turned instead primarily to German idealism for a theoretical foundation to their aesthetics. The division is, of course, somewhat arbitrary, since many poets within a "generation" have as little in common with each other as they do with members of the other group. But this historical context contributes little to an understanding of Bely. What a nonspecialist really needs to know is simply that there *was* such a thing as a symbolist movement in Russia, that it grew from its original form as a cult for poetic techniques associated primarily with the more vulgar practitioners in France (Mallarmé, for instance, was *not* widely read by the Russians) to a far more metaphysical and idealist system during Bely's time, and that Bely was intimately connected with it.

And what really matters for an understanding of Bely's theory is Bely's theory. Bely was never one to toe the party line, regardless of the party, and orthodox symbolism was no exception. His system remains his own and is not rendered immediately more understandable by placing it in the context of his contemporary, fellow symbolists. In fact, as Bely points out in his memoirs, much of his theoretical writing was either conceived as a polemic with his contemporaries or else invoked the wrath of these same contemporaries for its failure to adhere to orthodox tenets. At one point, for instance, Bely says, "Open my books: *Arabesques, Symbolism, The Green Meadow.* Fully half of what is in them is polemics; and two-thirds of the polemics are directed against Vyacheslav Ivanov, Blok, Chulkov, Gorodetsky, the theatre of Komissarzhevskaya, Anton Krainy (Z. N. Gippius), that is, precisely against those with whom the press of that time aligned me."[9] Later in the same collection of memoirs Bely recalls the response of one contemporary to the publication of "The Emblematics of Meaning" in *Symbolism*: "Andrey Bely," he had said, "has drowned symbolism in neo-Kantian scholasticism."[10] And while this specific remark may or may not be strictly true, the point is still that Bely always imparted his own distinctive hue to whatever he chose to confront, and, moreover, that he did so to such an extent as to render the "original" virtually unrecognizable. To the degree, then, that Bely really was writing "theory of symbolism," where "symbolism" is to be understood as a contemporary literary and artistic movement in Russia, he transformed his model into something entirely different from what it was for his peers.

If Bely was not writing exclusively, or almost exclusively, as part of a movement, and if the world of literary scholarship has survived until now in the West without an English translation of his essays, or without *any* major acknowledgment of Bely's theoretical writings, why bother with them now? Can one claim that they are worthy of our interest for any other reason than that they will fill a gap in our knowledge?

I think one *can* make such a claim, and my reasons should become clear in my examination of the individual essays. For the moment, however, let it suffice to mention two important features of Bely's work as a theorist of literature and aesthetics. The first is that Bely's more "idealist" writings (as I will classify them shortly) give us a version of a modernist aesthetic that shows some astonishing affinities with other, better known modernist aesthetics in the West. "The Magic of Words," for example, shows the same kind of pressing concern as one finds in Mallarmé or Valéry for retrieving the mythical lost linguistic paradise where the constituents of language (that is, words), by virtue of their own intrinsic properties, exist in a *necessary* relation of intimacy—even identity—with their designated objects. The same essay also draws a distinction—standard in modern literary aesthetics—between the intrinsic properties of poetic language and those of ordinary language. As it happens, there are some good (and related) historical reasons, which I will discuss below, both for Bely's concern with these issues and for their prominence in modern literary criticism. For this reason alone it is important to know about Bely.

The other feature is Bely's status as a precursor to many of the techniques employed by the Russian Formalists in the study of versification. I am speaking here of the methods developed in the essay on metrics included in this volume: "Lyric Poetry and Experiment." The Formalists were certainly not overly eager to acknowledge a debt to the likes of Andrey Bely: he was, after all, a "symbolist," consequently concerned with considerations that the Formalists viewed as extrinsic and irrelevant to the study of literature. Still, it is worth pointing out that even a Formalist critic as hostile to Bely as Zhirmunsky readily acknowledged Bely's position as an innovator in the modern study of poetics. In an article on the Formalist movement written (in German) in 1925 for a German periodical, Zhirmunsky credits the symbolists, including Bely, with providing a new orientation to the study of literature, one that emphasized the "intrinsic value" (*Eigenwert*) of art instead of the social utilitarianism that had characterized literary studies of the latter nineteenth century.[11] Later in the same article Zhirmunsky explicitly recognizes Bely as the founder of the formal method in Russian "science" and refers specifically to Bely's essays on Russian meter.[12]

A much kinder and, I think, more sober and objective judgment comes from an authority less ideologically committed to the Formalist movement: Roman Jakobson. The fifth and final volume of Jakobson's *Selected Writings*, entitled, *On Verse, Its Masters and Explorers*, contains an essay called "Retrospect," in which the author, writing towards the end of his life, surveys the history of the modern study of verse, meter, and rhythm as it developed during his own lifetime (and, of course, through his own efforts).[13] It is no small measure of Bely's importance in the history of modern criticism that Jakobson's essay opens with a reference to *Symbolism* and the essays on rhythm and metrics. If no one other than Jakobson had ever seen Bely's essays, Bely's place in modern criticism would still be assured, since it was he who apparently launched Jakobson on his own course of investigation into the science of metrics: Jakobson tells how, as a young man in 1911, he attempted to apply Bely's methods to a study of the eighteenth-century Russian poet, Tredyakovsky.[14] Jakobson also identifies Bely as an important seeker in the question of the relationship, specifically the mutual constraints, between ordinary and poetic discourse. Once again it is the essays on rhythm and metrics that are cited.[15]

But perhaps the most compelling reason for studying Bely's theoretical essays is simply that the thought in them is so utterly fascinating. Bely was not only uncannily erudite and prolific as a writer, he was also what the Russians call a *chudak*, that is, a quirky, odd fellow who has peculiar ideas of his own and who follows them with the sort of pertinacious, unquestioning confidence that suggests that the idea of their peculiarity has never entered his mind. Bely was at least aware of his status as a *chudak*, as he indicates in the title of a book of memoirs written in 1922, a title, incidentally, that was borrowed from Gogol: Gogol had written "Zapiski sumasšedšego" (Diary of a Madman); Bely wrote *Zapiski čudaka* (Diary of a *Chudak*).

Bely's ideas were peculiar, but they were also extraordinarily varied and diverse. He was capable of approaching almost any problem from a number of different, and often potentially conflicting, viewpoints. Later I will discuss the problems relating to Bely's diverse approaches to the study of aesthetics. But this is only one broad example among many. Turn to any essay in this collection, and it will immediately become apparent that the desultory character of Bely's thought not only emerges from subject to subject or from essay to essay but appears locally as well, even on the level of the sentence. All of which is merely a way of saying that the essays should speak for themselves.

ON THE ESSAYS THEMSELVES

If one thing can be said about Bely the thinker it is that he loved systems. His biography can almost be viewed as a series of infatuations with different philosophical systems. Bely's father was a well-known mathematician and the Dean of the University of Moscow, and Bely's own university education was devoted to the natural sciences. Natural science, or "exact" science, as he calls it, thus became one of Bely's systems. In "The Emblematics of Meaning," Bely proposes to elaborate a world view by first presenting a critique of several alternative systems, and the first system to be considered—and rejected—is exact science.

But exact science is only one of many systems. By the time Bely was in his early twenties he had already gone through a period of infatuation with Nietzsche, Schopenhauer, and Vladimir Solov'ev (1853–1900), whose combination of Orthodox theology and mystical idealism appealed strongly to the entire second generation of symbolists. Bely's *Symphonies* (1899–1908) are pervaded with a (rather juvenile) brand of Nietzscheanism, and the early essay "Symbolism as a World View" is essentially devoted to Nietzsche and his thought.

In the first decade of this century, Bely studied Kant and a host of neo-Kantian philosophers, especially Heinrich Rickert and Hermann Cohen. He became a devotee of the theosophists, Helena Petrovna Blavatsky (1831–1891) and Annie Besant (1847–1933), and made extensive forays into a tremendous number of Eastern religious systems. The footnotes to *Symbolism*, running to almost two hundred pages and consisting primarily of long digressions and displays of erudition, show at a glance how widely read Bely was in the most diverse areas of religion and philosophy. Although it is certainly difficult to believe that Bely actually *read* all the books he cites in these notes, the long lists of works included there still serve to indicate an extensive familiarity with the scholarship in the many fields he touched on. From theosophy Bely turned to the newly formed science of anthroposophy, the science that took theosophy as its point of departure but redefined the center of the universe as man, instead of an external, transcendent absolute. But the anthroposophy episode, as well as Bely's post–Revolutionary flirtation with the strict Soviet ideology of materialism, takes us into a period subsequent to that in which the essays collected here were composed. The point is simply that Bely's desultory nature remained with him permanently.

In spite of the variety and diversity of the systems of philosophical thought to which Bely subscribed at various moments of his life, it can still be said that the fundamental characteristic of his thought is its idealism and what I call its iconicity. Bely remained at heart a Kantian (although in a somewhat modified form) in his approach to epistemological problems and an idealist in the broader sense in his approach to practically all problems, from metaphysics to aesthetics.

The dominant notion in his thought is the existence of a transcendent order that is accessible to man only indirectly. In theory of knowledge this means, as it did for Kant, that the world of "reality," as Bely calls it, is merely a world of appearances ordered and interpreted according to a preexisting pattern by the categories of our understanding.

In metaphysics and theology it means, as it does for Russian Orthodoxy, that all creation is an iconic *emanation*, a "humiliation" or concrete manifestation, of a transcendent order that is inaccessible to men under ordinary circumstances. The world is thus a collection of symbols or emblems that, like icons in the Orthodox tradition, exist as dualities: they are concrete objects, consequently partaking of the nature of "real" objects in the natural space-time manifold, but at the same time they partake to a limited extent of the essence of a higher order of things that transcends space and time. This is what I mean by the "iconicity" of Bely's thought. I will discuss this notion later in the section entitled, "Symbolism and the Iconic Imagination in Bely."

Finally, in aesthetics, idealism and iconicity mean, as they did for the symbolists, that any aesthetic object exists as a symbol for a higher truth not directly accessible to men through concrete means of representation. Consequently, art objects in general enjoy the same status as icons, or as all God's creation in the Orthodox view: they are emanations of a type of experience that is presumably not communicable in its purity through other than mystical, or transcendental, means.

Even in his creative work Bely exploits the notion of a world existing in a state of dependence on a transcendent realm. The novel *Petersburg* is filled with suggestions that the world as we perceive it is merely a creation of what Bely calls our "idle cerebral play"; but this idle cerebral play, which generates illusions and fantasies of all sorts, is merely a mask from behind which emerges the "incursion into the brain of forces unknown to us."[1] The incursion (*vtorženie*) and the unknown (*neizvestnyx*) are both important for Bely. What interests him is not only the normally inaccessible truth behind the façade but also the means by which it becomes accessible (makes its "incursion") and the deformation it undergoes in the process.

I have divided the essays in this book into two sections to reflect two apparently diverging areas of interest for Bely: the more "idealist" concern, as reflected in essays on modern art and theory of symbolism, and the more scientific and formalistic concern, as reflected in the essays on form and metrics. The "idealist" essays are those that take Bely's theory of symbolism as their point of departure and either elaborate that theory into an all-embracing world view, or else assume as a premise the existence of such a world view. The "scientific" essays take a variety of methods from modern science as their premise and attempt to use these methods to address particular problems in the area of aesthetics.

MODERN ART AND THEORY OF SYMBOLISM

"Symbolism as a World View"

"Symbolism as a World View" (1903) is among Bely's earliest writings. The title is somewhat misleading, since it implies that the focus of the essay is theory of symbolism and its implications for a philosophical system of some sort. This *is* in fact a topic treated in the essay, but it is not the only one or, for that matter, the principal one. Bely would have done better to entitle his essay "Nietzsche," or "Nietzsche's Role in the Formation of the Modern Consciousness, with Remarks on Why his Accomplishments Closely Resemble Those of the Symbolist Movement in Russia," for "Symbolism as a World View" is really an essay on Nietzsche. Nietzsche had died in

1900, and it was only fitting that Bely pay tribute to the author of *Zarathustra* who had had such a profound impact on him.[2]

Still, if Bely sees fit to pay tribute to Nietzsche, it is certainly not a coincidence that he views Nietzsche's worthiness of a tribute as deriving precisely from the affinity between Nietzsche's philosophy and the aesthetic philosophy of symbolism as it developed in Russia (by which Bely means his own thought). There are several reasons for the affinity Bely has in mind. One is simply Nietzsche's rejection of traditional scholastic rigor in a philosophy that as a result came to resemble a form of literary artistic creation rather than a systematic philosophic world view. Art has effectively replaced philosophy in the modern age, as Bely says, and it is no doubt largely to Nietzsche's credit that this is so. Bely will return to this thought later in section 6 of "The Emblematics of Meaning," where he states that, in the modern age, theoretical philosophy has increasingly become a theory of creation and that the day will come when artist and philosopher will find themselves traveling the same road forever. Another reason for the affinity between Nietzsche and the symbolists is the cult of music, seen as the supreme form of artistic creation by the symbolists and as a fertile realm of intersubjective and irrational creativity by the author of *The Birth of Tragedy*.

But there is a more subtle reason for this affinity, and the first part of "Symbolism as a World View" is devoted largely to elucidating it. First I should point out that there is perhaps yet another misnomer in Bely's title. To the extent that this is an article on symbolism, Bely is not concerned precisely with a *world view*, in the sense of an all-embracing system of knowledge: this will be the object of "The Emblematics of Meaning." Instead, Bely is thinking simply of symbolism as a philosophy in a more modest sense. His argument runs something like this. In speaking of symbolism it is actually proper to speak of a theory of knowledge or a theory of cognition. Art, after all, says Bely, is "genial cognition." Symbolism, he says, is a "method that unites the eternal with its spatial and temporal manifestations," because symbols are things that mediate between man (under normal circumstances incapable of direct access to the transcendent) and a timeless realm of Ideas. The province of symbolism, consequently, is artistic cognition, which is to say, cognition through revelation, which is to say, religious cognition. The notion of cognition in art, incidentally, will be a crucial one for Bely, who develops and considerably modifies the ideas presented here in "The Emblematics of Meaning."

But if the province of symbolism is some form of cognition, then are we not speaking of a philosophical discipline? The study of cognition, after all, forms an entire branch of traditional philosophical investigation, namely epistemology, or theory of knowledge (called either "theory of knowledge" or "theory of cognition" in Russian). Thus symbolism may be viewed as a philosophy.

If symbolism is to be regarded as a philosophy that not only investigates but also provides the method by which to *create* things that mediate between man and the hidden depths of transcendent truth, then it is a philosophy directly in line with that of Nietzsche. For Nietzsche, says Bely, unlike thinkers and writers of a more classical turn of mind before him (for instance, Goethe), created a philosophy (or art form) that directly brought the "depths" to the surface, where they could be seen and experienced by all. "The aim of the new art," says Bely, "lies not in the harmony of forms [as for classical artists], but rather in the visual actualization of the depths of the spirit."

Nietzsche has accomplished this "visual actualization of the depths of the spirit." For this reason virtually anyone, not just an initiate with special training, can understand the depths of *Zarathustra,* Bely claims. This is why Nietzsche's writings have provided such an important contribution to modern art. And finally, as Bely says in an observation of truly admirable insight, this is the reason for the democratic quality of modern art. Modern art, like Nietzsche, makes accessible to all what formerly had been intended for only a select few.

This accessibility is the subject of the second part of the essay, where Bely points up the common ground between Nietzsche, symbolism, and the theurgy of Vladimir Solov'ev. Theurgy, like Nietzscheanism (as Bely sees it) and symbolism, is concerned with the process of making the eternal concrete: it is, in its original sense, the neo-Platonists' method for magically conjuring, for *making present,* gods. Thus Bely has been able to show how symbolism unites a great number of philosophical traditions, both pagan and religious. The beauty of both Nietzsche's thought and the theory of symbolism, it appears, lies in their ability to rely heavily on a form of cognition, a world view, whose orientation is essentially religious but whose content is not overtly religious. And this serves Bely's purposes just fine, since it affords him a world view that is at once idealistic and religious in character. Bely has managed to preserve the distinction between the world of appearances and the world of essences, while holding in reserve a possible means of access between the two.

"The Magic of Words"

"The Magic of Words" (1909) is perhaps the best known of Bely's critical essays, the one most commonly cited in discussions of his theory of symbolism. It is easy to see why this should be so: not because it contains a more cogent exposition of Bely's theory, but simply because its style is so representative of the visionary rhetoric in which Bely indulges in his more mystical moments. Apart from the beauty of Bely's style and the fervor of his tone, however, historical reasons make this essay an important document in modern criticism. If one sets apart the mysticism, the theurgy, the magic, what one finds in this essay is a strong contribution to the question of the distinction between the language of poetry and the language of everyday discourse. Bely thus places himself firmly in a Russian tradition that effectively begins with the great Russian philologist, Aleksandr Afanas'evich Potebnya (1835–1891), and continues through Viktor Shklovsky and the Formalists, and beyond.

Bely clearly acknowledges his debt to Potebnya in "The Magic of Words," both through frequent references to his works and through the wholesale borrowing of virtually all the material in the second part of the essay from Potebnya's *Notes on the Theory of Literature*.[3] Bely also devoted an entire article to Potebnya's theory of language in the same year *Symbolism* was published.[4]

In Potebnya's conception, the poetic word, or poetic language, consists of three elements: the articulate sound (*členorazdel'nyj zvuk*), the representation (*predstavlenie*), and the meaning (*značenie*).[5] The articulate sound is the external form, the simple series of sounds that constitute a word and that by convention render the third element, the received meaning of a word or utterance. The representation is the crucial element for Potebnya. This term, more prominently called the "image," is what gives the word its newness, its freshness, in short, its ability to call up what it represents in a vivid and real manner so that the listener can truly perceive it as if it stood in front of him. In another schema designed to elucidate the poetic word from the point of view of the speaker producing new meanings or the listener perceiving new meanings, Potebnya distinguishes the following constituents of the poetic word: that which is cognized for the first time (*vnov' poznavaemoe*), that which has already been cognized (*prežde poznannoe*), and a sort of *tertium comparationis*, which is responsible for objectifying the meaning of the word.[6] This last element corresponds to the representation or image in the first schema.

Just exactly what the image is, that source of the objectification of meaning in the truly poetic word, is never entirely clear. It appears to be a quality distinct both from the perceiver's previous experience in general and from his experience with the *word* in question, with its conventional significance. In any case, the idea leads to extensive and elaborate discussions of images in poetry (understood in this specialized sense) and of imaginal (*obraznyj*) and nonimaginal (*bezobraznyj*) words, hence Bely's frequent use of these terms.

The image also has to do with another, more fundamental notion in Potebnya: the inner form (*vnutrennjaja forma*) of words, the inner quality that lends (specifically poetic) words their peculiar ability to impart meaning vividly and effectively. Bely's discussion of the relation between image and inner form follows Potebnya exactly, as does the assertion that "a change in the inner form of a word leads to the creation of a new content in an image."

More important than a simple borrowing of terminology, however, is the distinction that both Bely and Potebnya draw, on the basis of Potebnya's categories, between poetic and prosaic language. As Potebnya asserts, the distinction between the poetic and the prosaic word rests entirely on the presence or absence, respectively, of that element variously called the "representation" or the "image." Potebnya maintains that one may observe a continual transformation of one type of language into the other. Poetic words become prosaic as they lose the intimate connection between image and meaning through continued use. Prosaic words become poetic as soon as new life is breathed into them and as they adopt a fresh image that had not previously been there.[7]

Bely develops a similar notion in "The Magic of Words" in his distinction between "living, imaginal speech" and abstract terms, or, as he also calls them, "word-terms." The difference lies, as for Potebnya, in the presence or absence of that living element, the image, that gives the word vividness and calls the listener's attention to it *as a word*. Word-terms are dead; their meaning has come to rely exclusively on a timeworn convention. Imaginal words, as Bely tendentiously points out, are the province of poetry, whereas word-terms are the province of science and everyday discourse.

All of this should sound quite familiar to anyone who has read the Formalists, particularly the early writings of Viktor Shklovsky. The distinction Bely makes, following Potebnya, is really the same one Shklovsky makes between automatized and deautomatized or defamiliarized (*ostranennyj*) language. Shklovsky's "The Resurrection of the Word" (1914), for instance, is devoted precisely to the problem of how words, through continued and habitual use, lose their vividness and become "dead," or "petrified." The way to the "resurrection" of the word lies precisely in those techniques that call attention to the word as such: by using the word in a new and unfamiliar sense, by resuscitating an archaic and forgotten sense, by creating new words that give meaning either through their sound or through a new combination of constituent parts native to the language in question.

This distinction is part of what might be called an aesthetic epistemology that gives rise to all the basic terms and tenets of Formalism and that one can find in virtually identical form in "The Magic of Words." The self-valuable word for Shklovsky is the one that, on the strength of its own properties and through its very *form*, renders a clear and vivid meaning. Such words are the province of poetry; "dead" words are the province of prose. As Shklovsky says, poetic or artistic perception, as opposed to the perception occasioned by prosaic language, is "that perception wherein the form itself is experienced."[8] The emphasis on perception in this passage is significant, since it is this orientation that subsequently gives rise to the notion of *ostranenie* in "Art as Device" (1917). If this notion of *ostranenie*, or defamiliarization, where the author assumes a point of view foreign to the one he implicitly ascribes to his reader and thus "renders strange" the phenomenon described, became prominent in Formalist writings, it was because defamiliarizing devices in art were seen as the proper response to the type of automatization that Shklovsky decried in "The Resurrection of the Word" and that Bely had discussed in "The Magic of Words."

Many of Shklovsky's ideas seem to have been derived from Potebnya. In fact, Shklovsky attacks Potebnya in a number of contexts that only draw attention to the author's debt to his predecessor.[9] But Bely must be placed in this line of filiation as well. Shklovsky and his fellow critics were certifiably familiar with Bely's critical writings, and even if it cannot be unequivocally demonstrated that they *derived* their theory of automatization and deautomatization from him, it remains true that his contribution is there and consequently must be considered alongside both those of his predecessor in Potebnya and those of his successors in the Formalists.

Another point is worth mentioning, since it has major implications for Bely's aesthetics, in particular his notion of the nature and existential status of the literary aesthetic object. I am speaking of his belief in the *theurgic* nature of the poetic word. Theurgy, as

I mentioned above, is the magical conjuration of gods, an idea brought into prominence in the early neo-Platonist tradition by the third-century philosopher, Iamblichus. The central concept for Bely is that of producing, through magical means, a direct effect on the temporal world. The specific effect that Bely has in mind is calling-into-existence, or creation. Thus when Bely refers to the creative power of words it is clear that he means this in a most literal sense. Words not only assert the existence of the objects they name, as Bely states in the very opening of the essay, they not only have the power to subjugate and subdue phenomena, they actually have the power to call new things into being:

> For in sound there is recreated a new world within whose boundaries I feel myself to be the creator of reality. Then I begin to name objects, that is, to create them a second time for myself. In attempting to name everything that enters my field of vision, I am in essence defending myself against the hostile, unintelligible world that presses in on me from all sides. It is the sound of the word that enables me to subdue the elements. The process of naming spatial and temporal phenomena with words is a process of invocation. Every word is a charm. By charming a given phenomenon I am in essence subjugating it. Thus connections between words, grammatical forms, and figures of speech are in essence charms. By calling the frightening sound of thunder *grom*, I am creating a sound that imitates thunder (*grrr*). And by creating this sound, it is as if I were beginning to recreate thunder itself.

Thus Bely's title is not to be understood in any banal or purely figurative sense. The emphasis is on *magic*, and the title means "The Magical Powers That Words Possess." In an earlier essay entitled "Apocalypse in Russian Poetry," Bely had stressed the qualitative proximity of poetic creation to religious creation.[10] This is the reason he uses the term *magic*. He returns to the theme at the end of "The Magic of Words," drawing a parallel now between poetic creation and what he calls "mythic creation." Bely borrows the terms of his discussion from Potebnya's theories of metaphor and poetic images and makes the following striking statement concerning the status of the poetic image or symbol:

> The independence of the new image *a* (the finished metaphor) from the images that engendered it (*b* and *c*, where *a* results from the transference of *b* to *c* or *c* to *b*) may be seen in

> the fact that *creation endows it with ontological being independently of our consciousness*. The whole process occurs like this: the goal (metaphor-symbol), having received being, turns into a real, active cause (cause from creation); thus the symbol becomes incarnation. It comes to life and acts autonomously. [my emphasis]

Bely's ideal poetic language is thus a kind of Edenic discourse where words are endowed with the same degree of ontic reality as their referents and are consequently virtually coterminous with them. This idea places Bely firmly in a tradition going back, in the modern period, at least as far as Mallarmé. Mallarmé, in "Crise de vers," had evoked with nostalgia the mythical state where language "par une frappe unique" had been able to *render* its objects through a direct and necessary correlation between sound and sense.[11] Mallarmé, too, had found compensation for the lost linguistic paradise in a poetics that valorized the word as such (as well as its mutual resonances with other words). The point for him, as for Bely, was that poetic words must become objects in their own right and call attention to themselves *as poetic words*, instead of behaving as mere mediators for conventional meanings that, once retrieved, render words superfluous.

By implication, then, either the literary aesthetic object or the world created by it (and there is a strong suggestion that they are the same thing) enjoys an ontic status of phenomenal reality analogous to that of real objects in the natural world. The poet seems to have the same power as God in the logology of Eastern Orthodoxy: by pronouncing the Word (Logos), which then becomes incarnate, he (He) is creating a concrete "world" reality that exists as a hypostatic emanation of his (His) own being. This is a point that Bely will make in "The Emblematics of Meaning" (see section 13 and my commentary).

"The Emblematics of Meaning"

By far the most ambitious of Bely's theoretical essays in scope as well as in pure length is the long and exceedingly difficult essay, "The Emblematics of Meaning," subtitled "Premises to a Theory of Symbolism." In his introductory footnote to the essay in *Symbolism* Bely describes the aim of "The Emblematics of Meaning" in primarily negative terms.

> In this article I am in no way attempting to provide a theoretical foundation for symbolism. A theoretical foundation

> for symbolism is altogether too crucial a task. Such a foundation lies in the context of a critical reappraisal of the basic epistemological premises concerning reality, and in my deepest convictions the time has not yet come for constructing a system of symbolism in this manner. In the present age all that is possible are the prolegomena to such a system. But I do not regard my article even as "Prolegomena to a Theory of Symbolism." Perhaps, instead, it might be characterized as "Prolegomena to Prolegomena."

Bely's task, as he sees it, is much more limited: simply to clear up certain misconceptions concerning symbolism in general and symbolism as a specific movement in contemporary culture. Fulfilling this obligation involves pointing up "the connection that becomes clear between the evolution of several philosophical tendencies in the area of *transcendental empiricism* and *mystical realism* on the one hand, and the evolution of several conceptions concerning the essence of artistic and religious creation in the literary school of the so-called modernists and symbolists on the other hand."[12]

Many years later, Bely wrote about "The Emblematics of Meaning" in his memoirs and, for reasons pertinent to the age in which he was writing, took an even dimmer view of the article. He makes the almost incredible claim that the article was written in a single week, and the much less incredible claim that it was never even corrected. For this reason the article "showed no real program; the epistemology in it was of a rudimentary quality: it was there, but half-baked and straight out of a critique of [Heinrich] Rickert. In the end the article turned out to be an emblematics (although in a different sense), sketching out the psychology of my earlier errors and exposing them as a dialectic of approaches to a theory whose contours became clear only later."[13]

There is good reason to treat Bely's denigrating tone in the memoirs with considerable mistrust, given that he was writing in the early thirties and that one of his main purposes in these memoirs was to reinterpret his early thought in a way that would make it acceptable to the current dogma of rigid materialism in Stalinist Russia. Thus in speaking of a piece of writing as obviously and thoroughly antimaterialist as "The Emblematics of Meaning," Bely is probably not even to be trusted in his version of the amount of time he took to write it.

Nevertheless, considering the complexity of its subject, "The Emblematics of Meaning" was written in haste, and this is one of the major difficulties in interpreting it. In the few mentions of this article in the secondary literature on Bely, the tendency has been to assume that the difficulty arises not only from poor writing and organization but also from Bely's own lack of clarity concerning his terms and arguments. My own view is that the first shortcoming is by far the dominant one. Bely leaves out essential steps in his arguments; he assumes too much knowledge on the part of his reader; he fails to define terms that he introduces for the first time in untraditional senses; he quotes passages from a host of learned works without identifying his source or stating the significance of his quotations; he overloads his writing with ostentatious displays of erudition that add nothing to his argument. The list could go on and on.

But in spite of all these sins, and in spite of the trouble they create for the reader, Bely still does have something to say, and what he has to say is coherent, comprehensible, and significant, more significant, in fact, than Bely himself intimates in the two passages I have just cited, or, for that matter, in his subtitle. Even the first passage, with its talk of defining the connection between a limited number of philosophical and cultural trends, does not quite get at what Bely is after in "The Emblematics of Meaning." What Bely is really attempting is nothing less than the foundation for a new world view. Several important things are true of this world view: (1) its central subject is meaning, the acts by which meaning is created and conferred on things, and the way meaning universally constitutes experience; (2) it is formally idealist (hence Bely's embarrassment over it in the thirties); (3) it takes Bely's version of contemporary symbolism as a point of departure, hence Bely's implicit assertion (as I will explain later) that all meaning is *emblematic*; and (4) it is approached through mapping a schematic strategy, a determined set of steps that human understanding must take in order to arrive—at some distant time in an ideal future—at the perspective from which this world view is possible. As Bely's article shows in its most important section, this strategy serves as a model for the process by which the ordinary human subject constitutes and confers meaning. It involves an ascent through a hierarchy of increasingly transcendent levels of human activity until the summit is reached at what Bely calls the Symbol Embodied (*Simvol voploščennyj*) and a subsequent descent through increasingly immanent levels of human activity for the purpose of infusing these levels with the supreme, absolute Value of the Symbol Embodied.

The path Bely follows in order to arrive at the center of his argument is long and tortuous, but the argument is essential to an understanding of his final point. Because of the faults of Bely's writing and the absence of any extended treatment in the critical literature, I have attempted to trace Bely's argument step by step to restore what underlying simplicity there is in it. What follows is intended as a kind of reader's guide and might best be read in conjunction with a reading of the essay itself, section by section.

Section 1

Since Bely's concern is to promote his own theory of symbolism as a world view, that is, to make the apparently unnatural leap from what most readers would understand to be at best a current theory of art and art criticism, to an all-encompassing system of knowledge, his first task is to make a plausible case for seeing symbolism as more than just an aesthetic theory. The most persuasive argument Bely finds in the circumstance that Russian symbolism—indeed all modern art: Maeterlinck, Nietzsche, Knut Hamsun, for example—is no mere passing caprice generated by the immediate needs of a specific moment in contemporary history. Symbolism and modern art are distinguished above all by the enormous degree to which they *contain* essentially all past culture. "It is as though we were reliving in our own age the entire past: India, Persia, Egypt, as well as Greece and the Middle Ages rise up and pass before us, just as epochs closer to us pass before us." The simple existence of this broad cultural-historical base is sufficient to demonstrate that symbolism is more than just a passing moment in one restricted area of human activity.

Section 2

The question, then, is where to look for a foundation for the all-encompassing world view Bely has in mind. We all know that the answer to this question lies in Bely's theory of symbolism, but we do not yet know how or why. Bely reserves this issue for later in the essay and proceeds now to exclude those areas of knowledge that either have served as the basis for world views in the past or might seem appropriate at first glance for such a role. The first of these areas is exact science. After all, as Bely says, exact science is the "basis for any positive information about reality," and if we assume that positive information about reality is the same thing as reality, then it is only natural that we should extend the province of exact science to include the entire universe in all of its aspects. But exact science is not qualified to serve as the basis for a world view because it has consistently failed to offer a point of view that is both fundamental and universal. The individual sciences have failed in this regard for the simple reason that each science is constructed on its own logic and is thus incapable of ever extending its domain beyond the concepts peculiar to it. An example of this failure may be seen in the effort of physicists to confer universal status on their science by locating the underlying essence, what the medieval scholastic philosophers would have called "substance" (*substantia*), in the concept of energy. But this attempt failed, as Bely says, because the resulting explanation of the universe as a closed system of forces left the notions of both universe and force entirely unclear. The individual sciences are thus incapable of supplying a world view, because the fundamental concept in each case is ultimately pertinent only to the science in question.

The prospect of finding the basis for a world view in a larger *system* of sciences proves equally fruitless, and for similar reasons. With the individual sciences, the first step was to search for the underlying, fundamental concept; with a system of sciences, the first step is to search for the underlying method or science that is fundamental to the system. This fundamental science can only be epistemology, as Bely says, because the problem in unifying a group of sciences is reconciling their different logics, and this is the domain of epistemology. Thus, since epistemology seeks universal and necessary forms of reason, a world view based on it would be a universal and necessary metaphysics. But Bely asks us to accept his unsupported assertion that epistemology has simply never been able to elaborate such a metaphysics, and so, he concludes, science can never give us a world view. All it can give us are "emblematic" concepts, which is to say, false copies of things.

But the real reason that exact science cannot give us a world view is much simpler than the foregoing critique implies. The real reason is that the aims of science are essentially different from those of a world view. After all, scientific knowledge is not really knowledge at all, it is merely "the capacity for establishing and utilizing functional dependences." The knowledge we are after, on the other hand, is the kind that will "console us and explain the puzzles of our existence to us."

Sections 3 to 5

The foregoing argument takes care of exact science—almost. In the next three sections Bely turns to a matter he had touched on in the preceding section: theory of knowledge. His purpose here is first to present a critique of Kant's epistemology by demonstrating its inadequacy for establishing a world view and by identifying the concept of value as the missing element in Kant's system. Bely then turns to the value-based epistemology of the neo-Kantian philosopher, Heinrich Rickert, very much in vogue in intellectual circles in Russia at the turn of the century, and critically examines this philosophy, too, but with the intention of salvaging several ideas that will then form the cornerstone of his own theory.

Kant's theory of knowledge falls short because it is dualistic and tautological. It is dualistic because it places an ultimately invincible barrier between the laws governing our knowledge of the world and the actual material, the "unformed content," of that world. It is tautological because it presents a view of knowledge wherein the raw, unformed material of experience is ordered and systematized according to the formal laws of our consciousness, but where these formal laws are motivated by nothing beyond themselves (Bely maintains). Consequently, Kant's system can never refer to anything beyond the laws of pure logic, which for Kant meant the laws of mathematics and Newtonian science, and we have already seen why *these* offer no prospect for establishing a world view.

The Kantian distinction Bely discusses first is that between what he calls the "cognitive forms" on the one hand, and the unformed material of knowledge or cognition on the other. The cognitive forms are simply the a priori laws by which our understanding orders experience, and, in Kantian terminology, they embrace both the Categories, or Pure Concepts of Understanding, and the pure forms of sensible intuition, namely space and time. This is why Bely is able to apply the term both to causality, one of Kant's twelve Categories, and, a few pages later, to space and time. (The three-part classification of the a priori functions of the mind—time, space, causality—comes from Schopenhauer.) But these subtleties are not important to Bely's argument. What is important is the distinction between the cognitive forms and the "unformed material," which is to say the material not yet subjected to the "forming" powers of the cognitive *forms*.

This much is clear and readily comprehensible. To confuse matters, however, Bely has already introduced a terminological distinction in the original text that casts doubt on the consistent use of the two terms in question and that also bears a questionable relation to the rest of his discussion. This is the distinction in Russian between *poznanie* (usually translated as "cognition") and *znanie* (usually translated as "knowledge"). *Poznanie* is the term generally used to denote the faculty of acquiring knowledge, of coming-to-know, of ordering the sense data of raw experience into meaningful contents of consciousness. In philosophical usage it corresponds roughly, like the English "cognition," to the German *Erkenntnis*. It is the subject of epistemological inquiries, what in German is called *Erkenntnistheorie* and what in Russian, when precision is sought, is called *teorija poznanija* (literally, "theory of cognition"). (This theory is also, more loosely, called *teorija znanija*; Bely uses both.) *Znanie*, on the other hand, is the already formed content of consciousness, that which, in Kantian terms, is present, residing in the mind after being subjected to the systematizing efforts of the cognitive faculties. It ordinarily translates the German *Wissen*, although the parallelism between the *poznanie/znanie* and *Erkenntnis/Wissen* pairs is not absolute.

Thus Bely's statement that "cognition [*poznanie*] is not simply knowledge, it is, so to speak, knowledge about knowledge [*znanie o znanii*]" is puzzling. *Poznanie* in its ordinary sense is not knowledge about knowledge: theory of knowledge is knowledge about knowledge (or more accurately about cognition). And when Bely, a few sentences later, states that "cognition is . . . beyond the limit of knowledge," what he says is true. Our cognitive faculties, Kant would agree, are not something we can "know" in the same way we can "know" an object or a fact of nature: they can be understood only by a process of transcendental deduction, that is, inferred logically from an examination of the a priori workings of the understanding. But the same may be said of theory of knowledge, for this, too, strictly speaking, is "beyond the limit" with respect to ordinary knowledge: theory of knowledge is derived from *transcendental* thought processes, or thought processes whose object is *transcendent* (beyond the limits) with respect to ordinary knowledge.

What Bely seems to be talking about here is simply the critical capacity of the mind in a general sense. Whether he really means to say "theory of cognition" when he says "cognition," or whether he has altered the accepted understanding of the term *poznanie*, it is nonetheless clear that here, too, he is distinguishing the faculty by which the mind examines itself, examines its own laws of understanding and coming-to-know, from what simply resides in our consciousness as content. Whatever Bely's point is, it clearly is intended to call attention to the wedge that critical philosophy drives between being and consciousness.

Thus the cognitive forms of critical philosophy present Bely with two major problems. The first is the radical dualism that this notion creates between being and consciousness. "Knowledge is embraced on all sides by cognitive forms" in the critical view, as Bely says. The consequence of this is that reality, as it presents itself to us in Kant's conception, becomes infused with the properties of these forms. Thus, since causality is one of the cognitive forms (one of Kant's twelve Categories), reality for us becomes a *causal* reality. But reality itself, or being, is something we can never know: it is as though the form of reality were a "closed sphere whose surface is the form of cognition," that is, *true* reality and our understanding of it are two entirely separate realms that merely share a common dividing wall. The form of cognition, says Bely, "exists outside being." But the problem is that the concept of *truth* is associated with something outside the reality that our cognitive faculties give to us, with the result that "either truth is not real, or reality [as given by our cognitive faculties] is not the same thing as being." Truth, that is to say, must have something to do with being, but being is forever cut off from us by the boundary of our cognitive faculties.

The second problem with the cognitive forms, or Categories, is that they are always examined purely from the perspective of objects of knowledge and never in and for themselves, Bely thinks. And this is what explains the unmotivated quality of the whole system: the forms are never ordered in any normative fashion either with respect to themselves or with respect to the realm of experience that they are meant to systematize. A true theory of knowledge worthy of its name will not only examine the forms that determine knowledge but supply a *norm* by which these forms may be ordered. Finally, it will establish between the cognitive form and its content "a relation that is independent of the paths [of knowledge] for which the given form is an extra-experiential premise," which is to say, once again, that it will supply a transcendent (that is, outside knowledge) principle by which cognitive forms and the contents of knowledge are related. The ultimate tautology of Kant's system is that it offers no such principle: all it gives us is a list of forms, or Categories that are there for the purpose of ordering reality and of whose existence we are aware precisely because reality is ordered according to them. The transcendent principle (transcendent and consequently *outside* the closed system of Kant's circular logic) that is missing is a *value* principle, or *norm*, and the philosopher who filled the gap in Kant's theory of knowledge is Heinrich Rickert.

Rickert (1863–1936) was a neo-Kantian of the so-called Freiburg school, a school that distinguished itself by its acceptance of Kant's a priori functions of the understanding on the one hand and by its attempt to integrate practical reason into pure reason on the other. The work by Rickert that interested Bely primarily, and the one to which he refers in "The Emblematics of Meaning," is *Der Gegenstand der Erkenntnis* (The Object of Cognition), published originally in 1892 as a short monograph of ninety-odd pages and bearing the subtitle, *Ein Beitrag zum Problem der philosophischen Transcendenz* (A Contribution to the Problem of Philosophical Transcendence). The book saw a number of expanded and revised editions, but the one that Bely read and that was translated into Russian was the first revised edition, which appeared in German in 1904 as *Der Gegenstand der Erkenntnis: Einführung in die Transzendentalphilosophie* and in Russian translation the same year.[14] In his memoirs Bely dates the period of his greatest infatuation with Rickert from 1907, describing how he freed himself from a previous preoccupation with Kant like a fly from a spider web, only to become entangled in the web of Rickert. Not until 1913 was he able to free himself from both.[15] Elsewhere in the memoirs Bely alludes briefly to the significance of Rickert's philosophy for "The Emblematics of Meaning," describing this essay as one whose way was "paved by Rickert," but that was "in essence anti-Rickertian."[16]

Since the foundations for Bely's system as he outlines it in "The Emblematics of Meaning" rely so heavily on terms and concepts from *Der Gegenstand der Erkenntnis* (usually without acknowledgment of their source) and since Bely's own system is in essence a critical adaptation of Rickert's theories, a brief summary of Rickert's argument is in order.

The motivating question for Rickert's inquiry is whether a reality exists that is independent from the cognizing consciousness and that is also an object of cognition (*Der Gegenstand der Erkenntnis*, p. 10). This way of posing the question, as well as Rickert's eventual affirmative answer to it, was bound to appeal to Bely, since the concern for both Bely and Rickert was to escape from the inevitable closure of Kantian epistemology by finding a proof for the existence of an independent (that is, not merely conceived by the laws of the cognizing consciousness itself) object of *all* knowledge, scientific or not.

But first, Rickert insists, it is necessary to specify what is meant by "object," and this necessarily requires a clarification of the distinction between subject and object. As Rickert points out, one important reason for the solipsism of Kant's system is that Kant persists always in treating the subject pole of the subject-object opposition as the individual consciousness. What is needed for a true theory of knowledge (*Erkenntnistheorie*), says Rickert, is a much more limited notion of the subject, and this Rickert finds in what he calls *das Bewusstsein überhaupt* or *das unpersönliche Bewusstsein* (absolute consciousness or impersonal consciousness). This concept is arrived at simply by restricting, or narrowing, the concept of the subject to its absolute limit, to the point where the pure "limiting concept" (*Grenzbegriff*) of subjectness is reached. "Subject" as a limiting concept cannot contain any component of physicality, individuality, or immanence. As a result, it is obvious that it will be an impersonal concept, one that is valid, in other words, for *all* individual cognizing subjects. The object that corresponds to this view of the subject will be, by definition, everything that is not *subject*, or everything that does not form part of the content of consciousness (*Bewusstseinsinhalt*), where consciousness, once again, is understood as absolute, impersonal consciousness. This object is termed by Rickert the "transcendent object." The distinction is essential to Rickert's system, as we will see presently, since it alone enables him to attach universal validity to his concept of value in cognitive judgments.

Once these principles and definitions have been established, Rickert turns to the central task of his book, which is to prove that cognition encompasses practical as well as pure reason. Rickert's book, as he explains in the preface to the first edition, arose from investigations into the nature of judgments (*das Urteil*, p. iii), and it is upon this basis that he constructs his theory of knowledge. For truth, says Rickert, is not to be sought in representations (*Vorstellungen*), as Kant had maintained. Such a conception inevitably drives an artificial wedge between reality as it is represented to our senses and some other inaccessible, "true" reality. It also confuses the individual, corporeal subject with the true cognizing subject, which for Rickert is impersonal and incorporeal. Truth is instead to be sought in judgments (*Urteile*) and in judgments of a specific type: those consisting in an affirmation (*Bejahung*) or a denial (*Verneinung*). Thus any act of cognition is based on a judgment that affirms the truth of the subject's perception. Any positive judgment contains an implicit "Yes" in answer to the question of the truth of that judgment (a negative judgment contains an implicit "No" to a falsehood). From a strictly logical point of view then, the two statements, "The sun is shining," and "Yes! The sun is shining," are identical, since the "Yes" is implicit in the former (p. 98).

Cognition is thus inseparable from judgment. Judgments, containing as they do an implicit affirmation or negation, are based on an act of willing (*das Wollen*), a kind of will-to-truth. But all acts of willing or feeling, continues Rickert, imply a value (*Wert*), something, that is, whose worth is recognized by the subject's judgment. Here is where the ethical or practical element makes its appearance in Rickert's theory of knowledge. The existence of a value as an implicit component of pure theoretical cognition implies a practical orientation to Rickert's theory, as he states (p. 106). For pure theoretical cognition is the act of "adopting a position relative to a value" ("ein Stellungnehmen zu einem Werte," p. 106). Cognition (*das Erkennen*) is thus, in actuality, *re*cognition (*das Anerkennen*) of what is either affirmed (*bejaht*) or denied (*verneint*). What is affirmed or denied is *value*. Thus cognition is recognition of a value.

The true extent of the infusion of practical reason into pure reason becomes evident in Rickert's concept of the "transcendent Ought" (*das transzendente Sollen*). In treating the question of the (logical) necessity of cognitive judgments (*Urteilsnotwendigkeit*), Rickert asserts that any logical judging (*logische Beurteilung*) is ultimately based on a feeling of certainty (*Gefühl der Gewissheit*), and that this feeling is the source of the necessity of cognitive judgments. But the necessity we are talking about, says Rickert, is not to be confused with physical or causal necessity, nor is it to be confused with the sort of obligation that is based on external constraints (*Müssen*). The necessity here is an ethical necessity, a *Sollen*, or "Ought," "an imperative whose justification we recognize in judgments, and that, to a certain extent, we assimilate to our Will" (p. 115). This is why truth, in the end, is a value concept (*Wertbegriff*), and why the very notion of *being* must be redefined to include the notion of ethical necessity. For that-which-is (*das Seiende*) is really only a name for "that which is judged as being this or that" ("das so oder so seiend Beurteilte," p. 120). Being is not that about which we pronounce judgments, it is that which is *asserted* (*ausgesagt*). Thus it is that we arrive at the identity of the true object of cognition promised in the title of Rickert's book. The true object of cognition is the *Sollen*, or "Ought," which obliges us to affirm or deny the truth of what we perceive when we cognize something: "the Ought that is proclaimed through the feeling of the necessity of judgments" (p. 124).

If all this is true, how is one to escape the charges of relativism and subjectivism that so many philosophers were leveling at each other in the many treatises on the foundations of pure logic in Rickert's day? [17] How, in other words, is the "feeling of certainty" on which cognitive judgments are based to attain universal validity for all subjects? This is where Rickert returns to his notion of the subject in cognitive acts as "absolute judging consciousness" (*das urteilende Bewusstsein überhaupt*). The charge of relativism can be made only if we understand by subject, "individual subject," that is, the individual, corporeal being who confronts the world of experience with his cognitive faculties. Only in this case does one arrive at a chaotic multitude of subjective "judgments" from which it would be hopeless to attempt to extract any sort of universal validity. The *true* subject of cognition, however, is absolute, timeless, impersonal, and incorporeal. It is the limiting concept of everything that can in no wise be construed as an *object* of cognition. Once this is understood, it becomes clear to Rickert that cognition as an act of practical and pure reason is in a position to lay claim to the same universal validity that Kant had sought in the Categories and the a priori forms of sensible intuition. The transcendent Ought becomes the very condition of existence for Rickert (as the Categories and the a priori forms of sensible intuition had been for Kant): the Ought, together with its recognition, is conceptually *prior* to immanent being. Thus Rickert has found a purposive element for cognition that is independent of cognition (thus transcendent) and that also orders the workings of the cognitive faculties in a meaningful way.

Bely's remarks in section 4, where he explains in Rickertian terms the insufficiencies of Kantian epistemology, should now be clear. Consciousness, says Bely, must have a norm, that is, it must be purposive. Otherwise cognition appears as merely "an arbitrary complex of forms of activity," rather than as a harmonious, self-enclosed world with a transcendent norm, which is the Ought of Rickert.

Section 5 of "The Emblematics of Meaning" pursues the distinction between Kantian and Rickertian epistemology and establishes the supremacy of Value for Bely's own system. Pure Kantian, theoretical cognition is termed by Bely "existing cognition," and the value-based cognition of Rickert is termed "true cognition." Although Bely often uses his terminology in confusing ways, he is essentially saying the same things as Rickert. Thus "existing cognition" is said to be defined by a "methodical arrangement" that *forms* the material of cognition. Its functions are mechanical rather than purposive. True cognition, on the other hand, is normative and purposive. Under this conception it is *value* that determines cognition.

The most important thing about value is that it is irreducible. It is neither a psychological nor an epistemological concept. In fact, it is not a *concept* at all. "It is, as it were, an emblem of an emblem."[18] It is "the absolute limit to the formation of epistemological and psychological concepts," that to which all other so-called limiting concepts, such as the thing-in-itself (Kant), the Spirit (Hegel), the Will (Schopenhauer), may be reduced.

Here Bely arrives at his own angle in the lengthy and often crabbed epistemological discussion that has occupied virtually the first quarter of the essay. Value, for Bely, as the ultimate, irreducible limiting concept, now comes to be associated with Bely's own supreme principle, the one in relation to which all forms of human activity, creative or cognitive, are mere hypostases: the Symbol. "Value is symbol," Bely says here and then hints briefly at the reason for the identity: both are irreducible notions and thus express unity. The symbol expresses unity specifically because the word, in its Greek roots, contains the idea of a uniting, a "throwing together," but where this "throwing together" results in an organic, rather than a purely mechanical and accidental, union (as is the case with "synthesis").

The full consequences of this association will be explored later in the essay, where Bely turns to his mystical pyramid, which is crowned with the terms *Value* and *Symbol Embodied*. What is important for the moment is Bely's neat conclusion to his foray into speculative philosophy: just as science has proved in modern times to be untenable as a foundation for a world view, so is theoretical philosophy, by which is meant the philosophy that proposes a purely theoretical, formal (Kantian) cognition as the basis of its logic and its theory of knowledge. Once theoretical epistemology has given way to a value-based outlook, however, the resulting world view becomes a creative one, and philosophical systems become symbolic. Why creative? Because when the very acts of perception by which we interpret our world are founded on value and obligation, then it is clear that we, as subjects, are contributing something vital, something creative, something outside the closed system of Kantian Categories, to our view of reality.

Section 6

This is the point Bely develops in section 6, clearly one of the more hastily written sections of the essay, to judge by the incoherence of the argument. Bely's aim is to distinguish the neo-Kantian position of Rickert from the strict Kantianism of Rickert's predecessors. What Bely seems to be saying is this: Kantian theory of knowledge entails for the object of knowledge a dual position of dependence on, and independence from, the cognizing faculties. The recognition of a certain unknowable material of cognition as preceding even the laws by which the Kantian subject gives form to what he *does* perceive ultimately places the subject in a position of dependence on that material, and the cognitive faculty becomes a "deduction from this material, its product." Kantianism, however, wishes to maintain a strict line of separation between cognition and object and accordingly refines the notion of an object into something unknowable, a mere negative limiting concept. But, says Bely (in a passage where he leaves it to the reader to guess that he is making a transition from something he regards unfavorably to something he regards favorably), all that is needed is to take one additional step into critical philosophy, to allow the thing-in-itself simply to vanish from one's purview, and at that point, *being* actually becomes a form of thought, a judgment (*Urteil*). The truth of a judgment has nothing to do with any external "object." Instead, truth lies in a norm of *practical* (not pure) reason.

This is where theory of knowledge can best escape the tautology of Kantian epistemology, because it is the *norm*, the value-based goal of cognition conceived as the *object* of cognition, that stands outside all the Categories and a priori laws of objective cognition traditionally understood. But even more important than the autonomy of this new object of cognition (the norm) is that it is not something that is merely passively received by the subject after the subject's cognitive faculties have exercised their functions on it; this new object is a product of *creation, of an active process in which the subject participates*. This is where Bely finally identifies the true point of departure that Rickert's philosophy represents for him, acknowledging, of course, that the leap from the idea of *norm* to that of *creation* is one that Bely has had the kindness to make for Rickert.

But the leap is crucial, since it also allows Bely now to jump from creation to a yet more important idea, namely that of the symbol-forming activity. For, says Bely, "cognitive value is contained in the creation of idea-images, and it is in identifying these idea-images that one forms objective reality itself. Cognitive value, then," he concludes, "lies in the creative process of symbolization." Thus a theory of creation, as derived from a value-based theory of knowledge, must also be a theory of symbolism. And in order to bolster his view of a symbol-based world view, Bely now introduces all the baggage of mystical terminology from Kabala to theosophy as a way of suggesting an outlook based on the presupposition that the universe has meaning, that man is no stranger in his world.

Section 7

Before proceeding to his notion of the dialectic of cognition and creation, Bely first insists on some additional critiquing, this time turning his attention to various philosophical and religious systems of the past that have gone astray in their understanding of the relation between norms (based on values) and reality as they represent it. The traditional error consists in a hypostatization (although Bely does not use the term) of the norm in question and the consequent emergence of a divinity or other First Principle on the basis of the norm. This is how past religions have integrated the notions of value and being. But all this is not without its significance for Bely, because these systems do "represent for us different methods of symbolizing the world of Value," and that is a start. In addition to giving us a clue about the process of symbol formation, these systems also serve as evidence of the work of *creation* in forming a world view.

Section 8

Now here is the problem, as Bely goes on to set it forth in section 8: It is clear from what he has already said that two necessary components of any world view will be cognition and creation. We have even seen how the two may, to a certain extent, be integrated into a single model, in the value-based epistemology of Rickert. The question, then, is first, whether by successive stages of idealization or, put more simply, removal from the purely empirical and phenomenal, the various human disciplines associated with cognition on the one hand and those associated with creation on the other can ever lead us up to the absolute, eternal quality we have been seeking as the First Principle of our world view; and second, whether the two lines of cognition and creation show any possibility of intersecting. In order to conceptualize Bely's argument in this section it is necessary to consult figure 1, the triangle, which the author through an apparent oversight has failed to mention at this point (see p. 145). The full implications of this diagram, which is essential for the mapping of Bely's strategy for symbolist understanding, do not emerge until section 16, but a few preliminary words of explanation are in order here.

What concerns us here are the broad divisions of the diagram. The terms appearing inside the small triangles of the diagram, with the exception of "Value" at the top, refer to traditional fields of human activity that generate and organize meaning. For the sake of simplicity I will call them "fields." The vertical altitude of the triangle represents the line of demarcation between those fields of activity associated with cognition (or *science* in its etymological sense—that is, fields concerned with knowledge and knowing), which appear to the left of the altitude, and those fields associated with creation, which appear to the right. A cursory glance at the diagram will also reveal that Bely has arranged in a hierarchy the fields whose names appear inside the subtriangles, from primitive and empirical at the bottom, to sublime and ideal at the top. Finally, one will observe that, as one reads across the diagram at any given level, the mirror image of any field from the cognitive side is that field's creative analogue. Thus metaphysics corresponds to theurgy, since metaphysics involves *knowledge* or *cognition* of the transcendent, where theurgy involves *creation* of the transcendent. Similarly, *theory of knowledge* corresponds to *creation of dogma*, since the former involves *knowledge* of knowledge, while the latter involves *creation* of knowledge.

Bely's point in section 8 is simple: he merely wants to show that the "ladder of cognition" (the ascending series of fields on the left side of the triangle) and the "ladder of creation" (the ascending series of fields on the right side) taken by themselves lead nowhere. Why? Because, even though the two areas at times intersect, and even though, when they do, the common ground is a form of value (this is a good sign, because the absolute we are seeking will have to include cognition, creation, *and* value), they are continually finding themselves in a position of mutual relativity with no hope of escape. For example, "cognitive" fields like metaphysics and epistemology on the one hand and "creative" fields like theurgy and religious creation on the other find a common ground in value-based norms. It may be seen from the diagram that epistemology on the Rickertian model, and metaphysics in general, will be oriented towards the *knowledge* of a norm, whereas religious creation and theurgy on the other hand will be oriented towards the *creation* of a norm and its representation in an idealized Image (*Lik*, see note 41 to "The Emblematics of Meaning"). But the problem is that the norm for each of these fields is restricted by being strictly cognitive or strictly creative and by being pertinent to that field alone. This will become clear in section 16.

Even the field of ethics, which occupies a central position on Bely's diagram, straddling the territories of cognition and creation, lacks an absolute norm and thus can provide no absolutes for either cognition or creation. As a consequence, cognitive fields and creative fields, even when they overlap, do so in an area that provides no escape from their mutual dependency. What is truly needed, as Bely asserts in the remainder of this section, is an uncognizable unity to transcend the whole system; this unity will have to be a symbol, a value that lies "outside of being, outside of cognition, and outside of creation." The meaning of the term *symbol* in this usage will become clear later.

Section 9

In section 9 Bely gives a preliminary explanation of the logic of figure 1. Any single field of the diagram has a logical primacy over all fields beneath it, which are seen as predetermined, or governed, by the superior field. Thus the area of epistemology, for instance, governs the entire triangular region at whose summit it stands, from mechanics in the lower left to being in the lower right. Although Bely does not explain yet why the diagram works in the way it does, he uses it now to draw some conclusions in advance of a full account. For instance, he explores the ways in which the collection of "governed" fields beneath various analogous fields (a cognitive field like epistemology, say, whose creative mirror image is religious creation) overlap in certain fields but not in others. The most important observation to be made, however, is the way the diagram serves to map the logic by which we arrive at the absolute unity that is to have primacy over all, namely the Symbol Embodied at the apex of the whole triangle. For the moment, the diagram is meant to indicate that one may arrive at the notion of pure Value (the apex of the field of Value is the Symbol Embodied) by proceeding upward through the converging set of disciplines represented in the diagram, and that, furthermore, the ascent to Value and the Symbol Embodied brings us to a point where the dichotomy between cognition and creation is finally reconciled. Bely also points out here, in a historical note, that, since even the penultimate level of the diagram has not been reached in our age (that is, reading across immediately below Value: metaphysics in the pure cognitive area, theurgy in the pure creative area, and theosophy in between), the prospect of attaining Value is a future one.

Section 10

In section 10 Bely derives the notion of *emblem* from the notion of what he calls relative concepts. The problem, he says, is this: If, as the axiomatic proposition at the head of this section asserts, "Unity is Symbol," the unity we are seeking is to be found in the supreme Symbol (capital *S*), and if, as our common sense tells us, a symbol (in the general sense) is thought of as something removed from reality, is merely "relative," to use Bely's terms, then a symbol can certainly not pretend to give us any truth. There are two kinds of concepts that we may ideally press into service in our efforts to make sense of our experience: real concepts and relative concepts. Real concepts are those that directly give us their object (truth being defined as the coincidence of representation and represented object). Relative concepts are those that do not directly give us their object.

Incidentally, the entire discussion on this point is extraordinarily naive, especially in light of Rickert's theories on the subject of concepts and concept formation, theories with which Bely was intimately familiar. Rickert had argued forcefully for the absolute impossibility of what Bely calls "real concepts," since, as Rickert points out, the empirical world is far too complex, its aspects far too diverse for our senses and understanding ever to "know" it completely; and if we draw a distinction between the empirical world and some transcendent world beyond the range of our knowledge (the Platonic Ideas, the Kantian thing-in-itself), then clearly the best we can ever do here is to furnish ourselves with concepts that are mere *copies* of that transcendent reality. Now it is possible that Bely meant for his terms to allow for some of these complexities, but if so, he never makes this clear. In any case, he simply wishes it to be accepted that there are concepts that directly coincide with their objects.

Bely's next point, presented in a rather convoluted and confusing passage, is that the distinction between real and relative concepts is at best artificial, at worst, downright wrong. After all, what is a relative concept? A relative concept is, for instance, a methodological concept that serves to order the collection of real concepts making up an individual science. Or it is simply a concept that bears an indirect relationship to its object. It is wrong to maintain that such so-called relative concepts bear no relation to their object: in both cases they are simply further removed from reality than are real concepts. Methodological concepts thus serve to order concepts that do bear directly on reality, and other relative concepts are simply concepts that are separated from reality by a series of transitional concepts, and these transitional concepts are real.

Here is where the notion of emblem comes in. Relative concepts have a bearing on reality but also reflect an aspect of our perceiving consciousness (since *we* use them in order to interpret our experience). This is the definition of an emblematic concept. The emblematic concept is one in which "the givenness of the world of reality and that of the world of consciousness combine to unite reality and consciousness into an image of immanent being." The essential point is that emblems are always *concepts* and thus, as the epistemological intermediaries between reality and understanding, always have one foot in the world of immanence.

The notion of emblem is crucial to the derivation of the idea of the Symbol, which Bely sketches out briefly at the end of section 10. It is also important for an understanding of the idea of symbols (lowercase *s*) in general. As Bely will show in section 16, symbols stand in relation to emblems as images do to concepts. The logic of Bely's diagram will also show that symbols are consequently the *creative* (right side of the diagram) counterpart to emblems, which, because of their conceptual base, are associated with the *cognitive* pole of human activity. The point for now, however, is that emblems are derived from the Symbol (capital *S*). In fact both emblems and symbols are derived from the Symbol, but Bely restricts himself here to treating emblems. If one takes the essential idea of an emblem, Bely argues, which is *unity*, and then takes one additional step from all the different kinds of emblematic concepts (real, relative, allegorical) back to a unity that is no longer tied to the immanent component of concepts, back to an emblem of an emblem, so to speak, then one arrives at the notion of the Symbol, that is, the ideal unity that logically precedes all concept formation, all operations of consciousness whose purpose it is to *unify* experience. Thus the truth of the statement with which Bely began section 10: "Unity is Symbol." The idea of the Symbol as the supreme limiting principle from which all emblematic and symbolic activity is derived will be fully developed in section 16, and I will reserve discussion of it until my treatment of that section.

Section 11

In section 11 Bely seeks to prove the contention that the way to the absolute Symbol necessarily lies through the field of metaphysics (a contention that is clear from figure 1). He begins the section with another axiomatic statement, "Symbolic unity is the unity of form and content," makes two basic points relative to this statement, and once again has recourse to the language of Rickert.

His first point is something like this: Form is understood in the sense of the "forming" faculties of cognition, those that give order and sense to our experience. Content seems to be understood here as *formed* content, that is, knowledge that has been subjected to the "forming" operations of cognition. Since the forming operations are provided by the subject and the formed content is what the subject knows, Bely identifies form with subject and content with object of cognition. But the true subject in Rickert's view is the absolute consciousness, which transcends individual consciousness. Thus when Bely says that "the supra-individual subject emerges in the reasoning consciousness," he refers to the way the operations of the individual consciousness reflect the operation of the ideally conceived absolute consciousness. It is as if the supra-individual consciousness had performed an act of self-limitation, restricted its own essence to appear as an individual consciousness.

Thus it is that we, as individuals, appear as products of a form of activity, namely the self-limiting activity of the supra-individual consciousness. And thus when we individuals perform the cognitive activity of "forming" reality, of transforming the *products* of our forming faculties into *contents* of cognition, or objects, we are, in a sense, raising ourselves to the level of the supra-individual consciousness, since every act of cognition reflects hypostatically the ideal operation of the supra-individual consciousness. This is what Bely seems to mean when he says, "Our development consists in a process of raising ourselves to the level of supra-individual consciousness by means of the transformation of products into objects."

But Bely's principal point in this section is to demonstrate why it is that the path to the Symbol lies through the realm of metaphysics, and this is where both his Rickertian and his anti-Rickertian positions come in. What is truly important in an act of cognition is that its formal laws are purposively predetermined according to a moral imperative, as Rickert had said. Where Bely departs from Rickert, however, is in speaking of the moral imperative as a metaphysical entity, a position that appears to make sense on the surface but one that Rickert had forcefully denied. For Rickert goes to great lengths to draw a sharp distinction between *Erkenntnistheorie* (what *he* writes) and metaphysics, claiming that his own theories elude the latter category because they do not posit the existence of an unknowable world accessible only through appearances. But for Bely there is an aspect of Rickert's view that *is* metaphysical, which is to say that it is metaphysical in the way Bely chooses to understand this concept. For Bely the existence of an ethical moment in the process of cognition, the value-based norm of cognition, implies metaphysicality. And since it is this ethical moment that serves as the unity-giving force in Rickert's theory, since unity of form and content is an attribute of the Symbol in Bely's view, then it serves Bely's purposes to regard Rickert's view as metaphysical. And although Bely has his reasons for denying traditional, scholastic metaphysics as the ultimate repository of truth, he hereby recognizes the necessity of passing through it to attain that truth, ultimately, in the Symbol.

Section 12

Bely now turns to the problem of unity and its relation to the notion of symbolization as this notion emerges from a variety of logical operations on figure 1. The point to be made here is that unity as a concept is always derived from triunity. This is true, to begin with, in a judgment-based philosophy such as that of Rickert, Bely points out. In Rickert's system truth is always contained in judgments. The judgments that contain truth consist of four elements: a subject, a predicate, a copula, and a categorical imperative. But the proper arrangement of these terms places the first three in a relation of subordination to the categorical imperative, since the categorical imperative (Rickert's "Ought") is the vehicle of value, and since value is the supreme principle of unity for both Rickert and Bely. Thus subject, predicate, and copula represent a triad grouped around the unitary principle of value, a principle that subsumes the three elements and is thus not to be taken as a separate, fourth element of the same order.

A similar principle can be used to order the various fields represented in figure 1. But first a preliminary word of explanation about a separate feature of this diagram that comes into play in this section but whose meaning does not become clear until section 16. Each triangle in Bely's drawing not only contains the name of a field of meaning-generating activity (the top triangle, of course, is an exception, since Value, as the absolute principle, is in a different category from such fields as metaphysics, theosophy, theurgy, and so on), but also has a term inscribed at each of its three angles. In section 16 Bely explains that this term stands for the *norm*, or highest goal, of the field named inside the triangle. For now, a glance at the diagram will be sufficient to suggest that this is so: thus the norm of ethics is the "ethical norm," the norm of epistemology is the "norm of cognition," the norm of Value, the "Symbol Embodied," and so on.

More important than this for the moment, however, is the relation between fields. For we see that between fields of meaning-generating activity a relation holds that is analogous to that between Rickert's value-based categorical imperative and the three components of judgments. Any triangle in the diagram is seen as both subsuming and unifying the three triangles lying in a row beneath it. The most significant example of this is the uppermost triangle, the triangle of Value, which subsumes and unifies metaphysics, theosophy, and theurgy.

But there is more to it than this, and here is where Bely's diagrammatic strategies come in. Bely now has his reader rearrange the diagram in order to clarify the relations among fields (the inside areas of triangles) and norms (the summit points). The operation can best be described by referring to Bely's example, which involves the four triangles at the top of the diagram: Value, metaphysics, theosophy, and theurgy. The operation consists in taking the two outside triangles (metaphysics and theurgy in this case) of the three that appear in a row beneath the principal triangle (Value, here), spinning them a half-turn about their altitudes so that the norm term originally at their common base angle point (ethical norm in this case) now appears on the outside (it is also retained in its original position), and finally spinning them upwards on their summit points so that each now shares a side with the principal triangle. As figure 2 shows (p. 159), the result is a large inverted triangle with ethical norm at all of its points and with Value now surrounded by the three fields that had lain beneath it. The point of all this is that each of the surrounding triangles is a kind of hypostatic form, with its own orientation, of the central triangle. Thus there is absolute Value at the center, but there are also the three types of diluted value that turn up in metaphysics, theosophy, and theurgy (metaphysical value, theosophical value, and theurgical value). All three outside triangles represent, depending on one's point of view, either paths to the center, or emanations from the center (the distinction is important, as section 16 will show). Bely defines the relation, as one proceeds from the inside out, as one of *symbolization*. Each of the surrounding fields represents a means for symbolizing (for providing a hypostatic emanation of) Value or, to be more precise, for symbolizing the *norm* of Value, which is the Symbol: "The Symbol is expressed in symbolizations, and, in the present case, metaphysics, theosophy, and theurgy are such symbolizations." Figure 3 (p. 160) is simply meant to show that one can perform an operation similar to that performed on Value in order to generate figure 2 on each of the triangles surrounding Value in figure 2. Figure 3 then displays metaphysics, theurgy, and theosophy surrounded by fields appearing beneath them in figure 1. Bely's discussion of figure 3 is extremely confusing and incomplete, but the significance seems to be that, with Value at the center, each new addition of an outlying triangle (taken from increasingly low positions on figure 1) represents a further step towards increasing symbolization and away from the pure essence of Value (and its norm, the Symbol). The same point will be made in section 16, with reference only to figure 1, and for this reason it is doubtful that figure 3 serves any truly useful purpose in Bely's argument.

Section 13

Bely now moves on to examine the concept of unity as it is found in Leibniz's *Monadology* and the idea of the symbol as it is found in Hinduism. As usual, Bely's displays of erudition do not really advance his argument significantly. The real point of this section comes in the last few paragraphs, where Bely clarifies the notions of *S*ymbol and *s*ymbol, as well as the distinction between them. "The Symbol cannot be given without symbolization. This is why we embody it in an image. The image embodying the Symbol is called a symbol only in a more general sense of the word. God, for example, is such a symbol, when seen as an existing something."

When Bely speaks of *embodying* things and when he likens the common conceptualization of God to the process of what he calls symbolization, he is borrowing language, concepts, and a whole style of thinking from Eastern Orthodox theology. A word of explanation is called for, since the concepts in question will prove to be fundamental to Bely's entire system and to his own way of thinking, which, as I will argue later, is rooted in the logic of Eastern Orthodox theology.

The essential concept, the one that appears to have logical primacy over all others, is kenosis. I will define this concept in some detail, because both the logic of the definition and the terms associated with it are essential to Bely's own thought. Russian Orthodox theology places an enormous emphasis on the act by which Christ, the God-man, came into being. This act is described as a kenosis, the Greek word for "emptying," since Christ is seen as having "emptied" himself of His divine nature in order to appear on earth as a man and, thus, in a form accessible to the experience of men.[19] The significance of this act of kenosis cannot be overstated. For Christ must be conceived of as an earthly, concrete *embodiment*, or incarnation, of the divine, since the divine is entirely beyond the experience of corporeal beings, but He must at the same time be seen as still possessing the attributes of the divine. Thus, to the extent that the God-man is *man*, the miracle is that He can be experienced by other men. But to the extent that He is God, He allows men the possibility of a limited means of access to the divine: limited because we, being corporeal, can experience only corporeally. The God-man consequently offers the closest approximation to a direct experience of the divine.

The importance of this type of thinking for Bely's system lies in the ramifications it has in other areas. Of these, iconology is by far the most significant. The image on an icon (Christ, the Mother of God, various saints, or any of the other traditional subjects) enjoys a status entirely analogous to that of the God-man. Just as Christ is a concrete embodiment of the divine, a kenotic or "humiliated" emanation of God the Father, the saintly Image (*Lik*) on an icon is seen as a concrete emanation of Divine Grace, or to put it more accurately, the *beauty* of the saintly image, rather than inspiring a purely aesthetic pleasure, serves as a concrete, kenotic emanation of Divine Grace. This means that icons have the same dual nature as Christ: they are concrete and capable of being sensuously experienced, but their status as embodiments, as kenotic emanations, allows them to give the same approximate, limited experience of divinity as Christ the man.

All of this is important for an understanding of Bely's symbolism because the term *symbolization* as he uses it is clearly the same thing as kenosis (humiliation or hypostatization): both terms describe an act or process by which a relatively transcendent quality is embodied, becomes concrete, while still containing the essence of the transcendence that it embodies.

From the passage cited a moment ago it is clear that the symbol (lowercase *s*) for Bely stands in relation to the Symbol (capital *S*) as Christ stands to God, or as iconic beauty stands to Grace, or, to use Bely's example, as our conception of God "seen as an existing something" (a necessarily *symbolic* conception) stands to God Himself. This means two things, as Bely will illustrate in section 16. It means, first, that if we think of the Symbol, as we think of God, as simply an absolute something, invisible, impalpable, inconceivable in any concrete sense, then any attempt on our part to *represent* it will give us only an approximation several removes in transcendence from the Symbol Itself (as the iconic image of the Saint is several removes from the Grace he enjoys). But it also means that, if we wish to *arrive* at the notion of the absolute Symbol, starting from the other end, then we may take the notion of symbolization, which is to say, the process by which concrete emanations of transcendent entities are formed, perform a regress back towards transcendence and away from concrete representation, and imagine the extreme limit of this regress. The theoretical point at which all immanence disappears, where all is transcendence and Value, where representation is no longer possible, is the Symbol. This is perhaps the central truth of the entire essay.

At the end of section 13 Bely returns to the theological dimension of his argument to distinguish between *being*, seen as an absolute, divine state that is never manifested but that simply *is*, and created reality, which is to say the concrete reality that we perceive. This created reality is a symbolic reality, because, though it never manifests *being*, or God's *true* reality, it nonetheless gives us a symbolic approximation of that reality. Bely confuses his point considerably when he says that "one cannot say that this [symbolic] reality is the same thing as being, for in saying this we would be regarding the Ought as predetermined by being, whereas theory of knowledge leads to the opposite view." I think Bely has simply mixed up his terms in this sentence. What he appears to have meant is, first, that the Ought (which is the ethical moment in our judgments concerning reality) predetermines reality (understood as concrete, immanent, "symbolic" reality); and, second, that equating being with reality would be the same thing as saying that the Ought predetermines *being*, which is false, since in the present, religious context, being is not caused by anything: it is the same as God.

Section 14

In section 13 Bely hinted at the two different approaches to the notion of Symbol: one that begins with the Symbol as an absolute, indefinable entity, working *down* to successive layers of symbolization, and one that starts from the idea of symbolization and works *up* to the idea of the Symbol as an ideal, limiting concept. In section 14 Bely continues with the second approach, which we might term here the genetic or constitutive approach, since it is an account, from the human point of view, of how we arrive at or *constitute* transcendent notions.

Immanent reality may be viewed as a series of individual instants, or complexes, each of which is a unity unto itself. Certain experiences, however, may stand out for an individual person as he concentrates on them, with the result that one experience may come to dominate over the other experiences of not only an individual but also an entire group. When this happens, the single, dominant experience is said to become "a sort of norm for a whole series of experiences." Similarly, an individual member of a group who has had an experience of this type may become a norm, or a symbol of value. In this manner, Bely says, "the eternal 'I' is experienced in the personal 'I' [that is, of the extraordinary individual]," which is to say that the individual who has become a symbol of an eternal value now serves as an approximation of that eternal value and through himself allows the other members of his group to come close to the experience of the value itself. This is essentially the description of Christ or a saint in Russian Orthodox theology. But this account is given from the point of view of theory of knowledge and is really a faithless account of how the idea of Christ or a saint would be *constituted* epistemologically in the absence of any prior belief in the existence of such a being. Bely is careful to point this out when he says: "Thus religion, *when examined from the point of view of theory of knowledge*, is experience in immanent being of the supra-individual. God thus becomes a symbol for the subject" (my emphasis).

Section 15

"The Symbol is the limit of all cognitive, creative, and ethical norms: the Symbol is, in this sense, the limit of limits." Once again, Bely is interested in the genetic approach to the Symbol, seen as the limit to the regressive movement through increasingly transcendent stages of symbolization. Without saying so, Bely is referring here to figure 1, where the various fields appearing on both the cognitive side of the triangle (epistemology, for example) and those appearing on the creative side (aesthetic and religious creation, for example) are now seen as types of symbolization, as activities, that is, to which the Symbol may be seen as a norm and absolute limit.

Section 16

This is the most important section in the entire essay. In it Bely finally lays bare the entire logical foundation of his system, and he does this through an elucidation of the structural workings of his pyramid in figure 1. For it becomes clear that the Symbol as an ideal, absolute form, is something that must be approached through a strategy of reasoned steps on the diagram. The genetic, or constitutive, approach to the Symbol, the movement of regress that *derives* the ultimate limiting concept, Bely's version of a "transcendental deduction" by which he arrives at an all-embracing world principle, is now presented in full.

Bely begins the section by describing the movement of ascent along the triangle. We begin by ascending the left side of the triangle (the cognitive side) up to a point immediately beneath Value (see figure 1). Then we start at the bottom of the right side (the creative side) and ascend to the same point beneath Value. Here it is, says Bely, that we face our final choice: the choice between denial (proclaiming "No") and affirmation (proclaiming "Yes"). This is the point at which Bely most clearly betrays his underlying Rickertianism at the same time as he reorients Rickert's ideas to reconcile them with his own. By proclaiming "Yes" we land ourselves in the realm of Value. Earlier I pointed out the connection existing in Rickert's thought between affirmation and value. But Rickert's program was purely epistemological. Bely's is much broader. Thus, in keeping with his underlying Kantian tendency to view theoretical thought as ultimately directed towards the establishment of ideal, limiting concepts, Bely has extracted the essential principles from Rickert's thought and constructed a system that proposes those principles as absolutes.

This completes only half of the strategy. The second half consists in descending through the very same fields—first on the cognitive side, then on the creative side—and infusing them with the Value attained at the summit of the pyramid. From the top, everything below had seemed still and dead, Bely says, but now, as we descend, everything comes to life, and "right is restored." Another feature of the diagram emerges clearly for the first time: the significance of the terms appearing at the points of the small triangles in figure 1, as well as the relation between them. In this section Bely applies the expression "emblem of value" to these terms.

This is a convenient place to clarify the terms *emblem* and *symbol*. In section 10 Bely used the expression "emblematic concept," which he defined as a concept in which "the givenness of the world of reality and that of the world of consciousness combine to unite reality and consciousness into an image of immanent being." Later on, in his memoirs, Bely refers back to "The Emblematics of Meaning" and to the distinction he made between emblems and symbols. His discussion, much clearer than that in "The Emblematics of Meaning," shows that the choice of the word *image* in the passage just quoted ("image of immanent being") is a careless one. In the memoirs Bely mentions how the means we employ to speak about reality are themselves determined by reality. He then goes on to say this: "And for this reason all our determinations [concerning reality] by means of concepts are emblems, whereas all our reflections of this reality by means of images are symbols."[20]

Symbol and *emblem* are thus analogous concepts. Each designates a means for representing reality in a way that combines a component of transcendence and a component of immanence. Why? Because, as the passage on emblematic concepts had implied, these concepts combine reality and consciousness into a single, immanent entity. But consciousness must always be understood as the value-based consciousness that Rickert had proposed and that Bely had accepted as a model. Thus an emblem presents a moment of value (from the Rickertian ethical consciousness) and a moment of concrete reality in a *concept*. A symbol presents the same two moments, but in an *image*.

When Bely speaks of the emblem of value of a given field, he means the concept representing the type of (diluted) value peculiar to that field (as illustrated in figure 2, where each of the fields appearing beneath Value had its own diminished form of value). But the value belonging to each field must of necessity represent the highest point of striving in that field, since it is the portion of the field closest to Value itself. Consequently, the *emblem of value* will be a concept representing the *norm* (or point of highest striving) of the field in question. Thus as we descend from Value to metaphysics (see figure 1), we create an emblem of value for metaphysics; according to the diagram, this emblem of value is "metaphysical unity," in other words, the norm, or goal, of metaphysics. As we descend another step to epistemology we create an emblem of value for this field, too: the "norm of cognition." As we proceed down the side of the triangle, we create a new emblem of value for each field.

In addition, each emblem of value appearing at the summit of a small triangle stands in a special relation to the terms at the base angles of that triangle (each of which, of course, is also the summit of another, lower triangle, except for the terms appearing at the very bottom of the diagram). In each case the upper term is said to "break down" into the two lower terms or to "predetermine" them. The point is that if, in our descent, we take Value and *its* norm (the Symbol Embodied) as an absolute, First Principle, logically prior to everything beneath it, then each new emblem of value predetermines the two terms below it in the sense that it is logically prior to them. The superior term is also, of course, closer to the top of the diagram, thus closer to absolute Value, so that the process by which it breaks down into its two component terms represents a further step towards immanence and away from the transcendence of Value and the Symbol Embodied. Bely illustrates how this principle works in each of the outlying small triangles on figure 1.

One further detail should be pointed out. Bely has explained the individual *upright* triangles and the logic of the terms appearing at their angles. What remains to be explained are the *inverted* triangles. A glance at the diagram will show that a field appearing in an inverted triangle stands in relation to the field of the triangle whose base it shares as a kind of obverse that is an additional degree removed from transcendence: a primitive image of that field. Thus psychophysics is an obverse of psychology, because it deals with cruder, more physical data than does psychology. Mythical creation is an obverse of aesthetic creation because it is more primitive, and so on.

This, then, is how things stand. The supreme principle is Value. This Bely has taken from Rickert's theory of knowledge, where Value provided the unitary principle for all truth. The norm of Value is the Symbol Embodied, defined as the ultimate principle of all unity. "Symbol is Unity," as Bely says repeatedly. By the logic of the pyramid, either we may derive Value and the Symbol Embodied from the various fields of human endeavor, or we may derive the various fields of human endeavor from Value and the Symbol Embodied. For the notion of the Symbol as the highest principle of unity is not arbitrary; it is truly a *derived* notion. The primary concept here is that of *symbolization*, the representation in relatively more immanent form of something that is relatively less immanent (and thus *more transcendent*). If we take any example of symbolization, say, for example, the representation of Christ in an iconic image, perform in our mind the regress that takes us back to the ideal *original* of that image (remembering that this image is the product of symbolization), then we have an example of the process by which we may arrive at the Symbol. For, in order to arrive at the Symbol, all we have to do is take any form of human endeavor that involves symbolization, perform the same regress to derive the next, more transcendent field, and repeat this process until we reach an ideal concept that stands as the limit to the entire process: the Symbol. Since it represents an ideal limit and, accordingly, cannot be further broken down into immanent/transcendent components, the Symbol also represents unity. Similarly, in order to arrive at any field of human endeavor, having started with the Symbol, one merely descends towards increasing levels of symbolization, which is to say, increasing levels of immanence.

Thus the notion of symbolization, and the logical origin of this notion in the idea of kenosis and hypostasis, is the fundamental idea in Bely's whole system. This is the idea that supplies the logic of the pyramid and the strategy by which we derive the supreme principle of unity from human experience, or human experience from the supreme principle of unity. It is at the heart of an "emblematics of pure meaning," or theory of symbolism, as Bely explains at the end of section 16.

This paraphrase of the title of the essay at the end of the most important section of the essay is crucial, because, particularly in light of what we have learned in section 16, we are now in a much better position than previously to understand what Bely means when he says "The Emblematics of Meaning." Bely, in fact, intends two things in his title. The first is simply to show that the central subject of his essay is *meaning*. This is important, because it will become clear by the end of the essay that all human experience is a function of our capacity for generating and organizing meanings. This is also the key to the proposed all-encompassing universality of Bely's theory. Bely's second intention is to state that all meaning *is* emblematic (or symbolic, as the case may be), which is to say that meanings, significative activities, and human signifying objects all have a status similar to that of icons: they may be formally conceived as containing a component of transcendence (Value) embodied in a more or less concrete form in accordance with the schematic pattern of Bely's triangle.

If all experience for Bely is a function of the meanings we give it, if the universal property of all meaning is that it is emblematic, and if the formal principles of emblematism are ultimately derived from those of the theology of icons, then it should be clear why Bely includes such frequent references to the Logos, to iconic Images (*Liki*), and to the Trinity (as, for example, early in section 12). For each of these theological terms implies a notion of hypostasis, of a distancing from essence and a move toward immanence, concretion, materiality. The Word made Flesh is perhaps the fundamental example of the concretion of divine essence. The three members of the Holy Trinity are hypostases within divine unity and stand in the same relation to that unity as the fields of metaphysics, theurgy, and theosophy stand to Value in Bely's triangle or as the parts of a judgment stand to the categorical imperative, as Bely has maintained earlier in the essay. And the Image (*Lik*), whether understood in the sense of the image of a saint's face on an icon or as the Person of our Savior (*Lik spasitelja*), contains the notion of a hypostatic distancing from pure essence: the beauty of the image on a holy icon is an earthly approximation of Divine Grace, just as the Person of our Savior (Christ) is a humiliation, a kenosis or "emptying," a concrete earthly embodiment of an essence that is beyond the concrete experience of men on earth.

Section 17

Bely could almost have finished his article with section 16, since he has already said most of what he has to say. The remaining sections primarily amplify previous points. In section 17 Bely shows that modern epistemology, that is, epistemology understood in the value-based, Rickertian sense Bely discussed at the beginning of the essay, must necessarily be a metaphysics. Why? Because the moment an ethical element, namely the Ought that is recognized (*anerkennt*) in Rickertian judgments, is introduced into a simple act of cognition, one passes beyond the boundaries of traditional epistemology (viewed as the study of purely scientific knowledge and as independent from any categories of willing or feeling) into a realm that at least overlaps with metaphysics. As Bely puts it, pure givenness, whose equivalent in a judgment is the verb *to be*, becomes normative because of the implicit presence of the affirmation. Epistemology thus acquires an ontological element, where ontology is clearly understood as the study of what ideally is or should be, and thus comes under the heading of metaphysics. Before restating his central point at the end of this section, Bely sees fit to demonstrate that the modern science of psychology, no matter how it is understood, fails to incorporate the principles of modern epistemology.

Section 18

Here Bely continues to explore the notion of a metaphysical epistemology (or epistemological metaphysics, as he calls it). The question is the relative position of the three fundamental ideas: truth, the Ought, and Value. The answer is that all judgments (judgments, we remember from Rickert, form the basis of our cognitive faculties) possess *symbolic* (or emblematic) being and consequently a form of being infused with value (since any symbol contains a component of transcendent Value, as we have seen). This is why the being of a judgment, as Bely says, is transcendent (because value is a transcendent idea) and also why an epistemological judgment may be said to be metaphysical (because the moment it contains a transcendent idea, like Value, it passes from the realm of traditional epistemology, understood as the study of pure scientific understanding, into the realm of metaphysics). Having established this, Bely concludes that Value as a concept is logically prior to the Ought, which is *contained* in the concept of Value. This, once again, is because the symbolic mode of being of all judgments implies necessarily that they contain a component of Value. Thus Bely establishes the hierarchy (in order of decreasing logical primacy): Symbol, unity, value, ought, truth.

Section 19

Bely's task now is to show how his world view actually allows for the all-important reconciliation of the cognition-creation duality, which appears as one of its most basic principles. A clue to this reconciliation may be found in the philosophy of Rickert. Rickert, and the entire school of philosophy of which he was a part, in introducing the (transcendent) notion of a norm into the (empirical) notion of *givenness* or ordinary, empirically perceivable reality, is proposing a view of cognition that is creative (because the subject contributes something in the form of willing or feeling to his cognition of "givenness"). By extension, Bely says, the Freiburg school "finds itself propounding the metaphysical doctrine of the Logos." This is the essential message of section 19. Bely returns at some length to the philosophy of Rickert, explaining once again how the purely scientific and the metaphysical are combined in Rickert's use of the concept of methodological and constitutive forms of cognition. Following this, Bely adopts the rhapsodic tone of "The Magic of Words" to describe the creative force of words in what he views as the true means for reconciling the cognition-creation dualism: namely, the metaphysics of the Logos, by which man *creates* reality through the act of naming it.

Section 20

Bely now turns to the Symbol and draws a distinction between it on the one hand and concepts and images of the Symbol on the other. The Symbol, as Bely says, is the "limit of all possible acts of cognition and creation." This much has already been established. But Bely now says a very puzzling thing, one of the most puzzling, in fact, in the entire essay. In distinguishing the Symbol from concepts and images of the Symbol, Bely says that "with respect to these symbols [that is, concepts and images of the Symbol] the Symbol is an embodiment." Until now, everything Bely has said on this subject has led to the belief that the Symbol stands in relation to symbols and emblems (or images and concepts) as God to the embodied Christ: as an absolute that appears to men only in a humiliated or embodied form. Here, however, Bely suggests that the Symbol itself is embodied, a conception that not only confuses the picture as it has existed until now, but also leaves Bely's entire system without an undiluted First Principle. For if the Symbol is an embodiment, what is the thing or idea it embodies?

The only explanation I can offer is that "embodied" must be understood in the same sense as the word *Symbol* itself. The word *symbol* in its general sense implies the representation, in concrete terms, of something that does not otherwise appear in concrete terms (because it is a transcendent quality or essence). The Symbol, on the other hand, represents the extreme limit of the notion of symbolization in the direction of increasing transcendence: the point where the symbolic actually ceases to be symbolic since all concretion has been refined out of it. By the same token, embodiment would be understood in connection with the Symbol as the *extreme limit* to the process of embodiment. This limit would then represent the point at which all embodiment vanishes, since all that is left is, once again, pure essence, Value, Symbol. This would also explain the term that appears at the summit of Bely's figure 1: the Symbol Embodied. This term would signify the extreme limit of an embodied symbol: once again, that is, the point where concretion (the "body" of em*bodi*ment) disappears. In fact, the term *embodied* is, in the end, a redundancy: it is already contained in the general concept of a symbol. Thus to say "symbol embodied" or just "symbol," "Symbol Embodied" or just "Symbol" is really the same thing.

Bely concludes the section with a comparison between religious and artistic creation, one that he had already drawn in section 14.

Section 21

Having established the unitary nature of the Symbol, Bely now develops the idea of an aesthetics of unity, an aesthetics, he says, that is to be found in the theory of symbolism. He begins by demonstrating that form and content in art cannot be separated and that traditional aesthetics, which (he implies) has always made such a distinction, always leads to one-sided views of art and the art object. For this reason the symbolist school must "seek its basis elsewhere than in aesthetics."

What distinguishes the aesthetics of a theory of symbolism? Bely chooses at this point to introduce a "nomenclature" for his system, but since the terms and definitions he now presents come in what is essentially the last section of the essay to say anything of substance, it is not clear that they truly further the reader's understanding of the global system that is the subject of "The Emblematics of Meaning." However that may be, Bely now turns to the problem of artistic creation seen from the artist's point of view and the transformation of his experience into artistic symbols. The *symbolic image of experience* thus appears to be an experience that presents itself as a unity and forms an image in our mind. It may remain in this state, in the mind, or it may be given form through a means of representation, in which case it becomes part of an *artistic symbol.* This means of representation Bely calls *style* (without elaborating on the term). The final term is the *emblem*, which Bely now presents clearly as the member of the symbol-emblem pair that is associated with cognition (the symbol being associated with creation). The theory of symbolism, for this reason, may be applied to either cognitive or creative fields. When it is applied to cognitive fields, it proposes an "emblematism of all the different cognitive methods and retains for each one the right to be what it is." When it is applied to art and religion, on the other hand (both fields located on the right, or creative, side of Bely's triangle), theory of symbolism becomes a theory of creation.

The remainder of the section is spent clarifying a number of terms from Bely's system. Since the meanings of these terms should be evident to the reader by now there is no need to discuss them further.

Sections 22 and 23

The final two sections offer some rather disorganized speculations about the characteristics of a "future system of symbolism." The central problem in the task of forming such a system, as Bely sees it, will be to come to terms with one of the fundamental questions in "The Emblematics of Meaning": the resolution of the antinomy between cognition and creation. Bely has already proposed an answer to this question (or what might be more properly regarded as the prolegomena to an answer) in the form of a system, based on principles borrowed from Rickert, that integrates moments from the cognitive and the creative realms of human activity. He now meditates on how this problem will be worked out in the future, complete system of symbolism.

Bely concludes his essay by pointing out the universality of the symbolist school, which refuses to confine itself to any single artistic canon, such as that of romanticism, classicism, or realism, but instead emerges as the expression of a "single creativity." And finally, if symbolism is (ideally, at any rate) universal with respect to artistic canon, it is also, above all, universal with respect to time and history. This is Bely's final point and one he also made at the very beginning of the essay. Symbolism, as a specific contemporary movement in Russia, expresses an experience of "*all* ages and *all* nations." It is the power of the "single creativity," the universal generative force on which symbolism both as an aesthetic movement and as a world view is based, the force that in the future will overcome all time and permit men to experience past, present, and future all at once.

"The Art of the Future"

This short essay appears at the very end of *Symbolism*. It bears the date 1907 and consequently precedes the major theoretical thinking of "The Magic of Words" and "The Emblematics of Meaning." In fact, as the reader will notice, there is relatively little of substance in it, both because it is short and because it is largely an exercise in rhetoric. We find the concern, by now familiar to us in Bely's writings, with the ideal future where art will have come into its own. We find the familiar distinction between cognition and creation. But most of all we find rhetoric, and this is the reason I have included this essay in the present collection.

There is a special style of tendentious writing associated with Bely's programmatic statements on symbolism, and "The Art of the Future" is a perfect example of it. One could hardly find a more typically Belyan message than this:

> Now, in the rock, the paint, the sound, and the word, a process of reforming the life that was once living but is now dead has been accomplished. Musical rhythm is the wind blowing across the sky of the soul. And as it courses through this sky, which languishes warmly in expectation of creation, musical rhythm, that "voice of delicate cold," has already thickened the clouds of poetic myths. And myth has veiled the sky of the soul, begun to sparkle with a thousand colors, and fused into stone. The creative flow has created a living cloud myth. But the myth has hardened and disintegrated into colors and stones.

One finds here resonances from Bely's poetry, filled as it is with images of sparkling colors, comets, and fireworks. Bely's poetry does not represent his best work. But, to the degree that the style so pervasive in his poetry has crept into and infused his prose, both creative and theoretical, we can see how for Bely it was really all part of the same thing. Clearly Bely never separated the different areas as markedly as one might have expected. For him, literary production was ideally seen as deriving ultimately from the same source, regardless of the specific genre (lyric, poetic prose, theoretical prose) in which he was writing.

THE SCIENTIFIC AESTHETIC

"The Principle of Form in Aesthetics"

"Science simply proceeds from one form of ignorance to another: it is nothing more than a taxonomy of every conceivable kind of ignorance" ("The Emblematics of Meaning"). It may seem odd in light of Bely's fundamental assault on the natural sciences in "The Emblematics of Meaning" that he should have devoted a number of essays precisely to the problem of establishing an "exact science" of aesthetics. In fact, even without an overt statement like the one cited above, it is difficult to imagine that the same man should have authored both the essays grouped in the first section of the present collection and those grouped in the second. Later, in my discussion of "Symbolism and the Iconic Imagination in Bely," I will show that Bely's point of view in the "idealist" essays is not essentially different from that in the "scientific" essays. For the moment, however, let us examine what Bely means by aesthetics as an exact science.

As Bely explains in the first few pages of "The Principle of Form in Aesthetics," there are two points of view from which one might construct a scientific aesthetics. "An aesthetics constructed in accordance with the first point of view," he says, "will be an empirical aesthetics. It will limit itself to elucidating and classifying the given forms of art. An aesthetics constructed in accordance with the second point of view, however, will seek the laws by which the given forms are of necessity constructed and derived from the necessary elements of space and time." An empirical aesthetics, Bely has already suggested, is simply one that follows an inductive method: the investigator gathers his data and derives empirical laws from them. The second point of view is different. Bely defines it further in these terms, choosing the specific example of the art of painting: in adopting the second point of view, he says, "I will direct my attention to the necessary, a priori conditions of the art of painting, that is, the spatial elements that give the paint the capacity to represent reality on a plane surface." If the first point of view seeks empirical laws as its goal, the second point of view seeks a "'plan' that predetermines each form of art and that cannot be determined by that form."

Each art form (by which Bely means what we would probably call "medium": painting, sculpture, poetry, music, and so forth) must have a set of laws that predetermine it, logically precede and govern each individual example of that form (that is, say, an individual painting, a particular sonnet or symphony). By the same token, Bely says, there must also be a universal law that predetermines even the art forms. This law would be the "universal norm of creation," and the various art forms would be "restrictions" (*ograničenija*) to that norm, which is to say, restricted, individual examples.

What Bely has in mind is a kind of Kantian transcendental schematism of aesthetic creation: a logically preexisting, categorial set of laws governing the form that every contingent manifestation, or example, takes. This is the method he proposes to follow in "The Principle of Form in Aesthetics." It is also the superior of the two methods mentioned, for, he says, "only in the latter case can aesthetics free itself from the various encroachments on it from all sides. . . . Only then can aesthetics become an independent, formal discipline whose sole task is to preserve creation from both principled and unprincipled encroachments."

All of this sounds very interesting as long as Bely remains on the level of theoretical speculation. The notion of a preexisting norm of creation as the "natural order governing the arrangement of existing art forms" is intriguing as a theoretical ideal. As soon as Bely begins to offer concrete suggestions for carrying out his program, however, his ideas begin to sound comically naive, and what value they have is often vitiated by flaws in Bely's arguments (as well as by sloppy editing).

Bely has taken principles from chemistry as the source for the "laws" defining aesthetic creation. I have explained Bely's terms in my notes to this essay. The central principle that Bely borrows is the law of conservation of energy. The logic of the argument seems to be this: if, by the principles of modern chemistry, mass is a fixed quantity, something that can be neither created nor destroyed, then there must be a corresponding fixed quantity in aesthetics that can also be neither created nor destroyed. This Bely calls the "material" of artistic creation. But Bely has already posited the existence of a hierarchy of the different art forms: one that places music, the most time-oriented of the art forms, at the top. The reason that temporality becomes a criterion in ranking art forms, as Bely has already pointed out with a bizarre tip of the hat to Kant, is that time is the "form of inner sense," and the forms based on it will thus communicate more profoundly with us.

If all this is true, then, in speaking of the "material" of artistic creation, one fails to emphasize the dynamic (time-oriented) quality in art. And here it is that our analogy with the physical laws of chemistry is completed. For, argues Bely, if there is a dynamic principle in art (time), then there is also one in nature (energy). And if matter is nothing more than "resistant" energy, then those art forms that contain a greater component of spatiality, or materiality, are nothing more than "resistant" forms of the supreme art form, music.

The correlation between time and energy in Bely's two models would undoubtedly strike a physicist or chemist as rather strange, especially since time is an independent factor that plays its own part in laws relating precisely to matter and energy. And naturally one could also point out the difficulty of establishing experimentally the existence of a universal norm of creation using the analogy of a physical constant governing the relation between mass and energy. Bely's later arguments are self-explanatory (except in cases of errors and inconsistencies, which I have pointed out in the notes), and the objections that might be raised to his ideas are quite obvious. It is difficult to say whether Bely took his proposal seriously at the time he wrote this essay. One almost hopes not.

Still, there is an important point in the essay that almost renders the question irrelevant (although one prefers to think that Bely was proposing his model purely as a hypothetical ideal). As Bely's remarks in section 4 of this essay suggest, he is not on a quest for mathematically expressible, exact quantities that describe the process of artistic creation. The science of aesthetics Bely has in mind is a science of *forms*. Bely draws another analogy here to illustrate what he means. The medieval philosophers distinguished between *substantia*, or the underlying, eternal form of a thing, and *accidens*, or the actual, contingent manifestation of that form as a thing in the world. In art, too, it is proper to speak of form on the one hand, as the underlying principle, and content on the other, as the contingent manifestation. Aesthetics as a science of forms, then, would have as its purpose to seek those forms that stand behind individual works of art, so to speak, and determine their various characteristics. And if in science and philosophy it is energy that unites *substantia* and *accidens*, then in art it is the *symbol* that serves the analogous function of uniting form and content. For energy, as Bely has already pointed out, is the dynamic principle in the world of nature, and time is the dynamic principle in the world of art. Thus symbolization, which is the same thing as artistic creation, is equivalent to the capacity of an artistically created object to return to the condition of music, or pure time.

This is where Bely concludes his essay. In this way he has managed to bring the entire discussion around to an exposition of symbolism. The central principle in setting the terms of such an exposition is that of the underlying transcendent form presented through concrete means. As I will explain in my discussion of "Symbolism and the Iconic Imagination in Bely" below, this is not only the essence of symbolism for Bely, it is also the unifying factor in his entire outlook.

"Lyric Poetry and Experiment"

Where Bely had approached the problem of an exact science of aesthetics from what might be called the "schematic" point of view in "The Principle of Form in Aesthetics," in his essays on metrics he adopts the other point of view he had mentioned: the empirical one. In the early pages of "Lyric Poetry and Experiment" Bely draws a distinction between an "exact" aesthetics and a "metaphysical" aesthetics. "The goal of an exact aesthetics," he says, "is to analyze artistic monuments and derive rules that define and determine those monuments. The goal of a metaphysical aesthetics is to discern the one, true purpose and end of beauty and, by means of it, to probe the aesthetic experience of mankind." The problem with a metaphysical aesthetics, Bely says, is simply that it is unrealizable in our times. Aesthetics as a human science is thus impossible. Aesthetics as an exact science, on the other hand, *is* possible. The task of such a science is "the derivation of principles that will provide connections between the empirical hypotheses of aesthetic investigations. Its hypotheses will result from a process of induction from empirical laws."

This takes care of the method. The material of this new science remains to be defined. Bely says that the material of an exact aesthetics will be "the form of the arts." In the case of lyric poetry this means "no more than words that have been arranged in particular phonetic, metric, and rhythmic combinations and that constitute a certain combination of means of representation." The choice of rhythm as a subject for inquiry thus appears to be almost arbitrary, to judge by what Bely says. One might just as well have chosen other aspects of the way in which words have been arranged if one's sole purpose were to demonstrate the *method* of exact aesthetics. This, in fact, is what Bely does in his analysis of an extract from a poem by Nekrasov. Here Bely approaches his object of study in a variety of "exact" ways for the express purpose of demonstrating his method. Only later does he point out that a definition of rhythm is, in its own right, "the most urgent task facing researchers in the area of Russian poetry."

Thus Bely's essay appears to have two purposes. The first is to demonstrate the validity of the proposition that an exact aesthetics, understood as a science of artistic form, is indeed possible. The second is to provide, through the methods of this new science, a definition of rhythm. Bely has shifted his definition of form from what it was in "The Principle of Form in Aesthetics." There it was a kind of schematism governing the manner in which works of art came into being according to necessary laws. Here Bely has returned to a much more traditional sense of "form" as simply the vehicle that conveys content. Still, a distinct similarity in methodology persists between the schematic and the empirical approach: both are founded on a process of what might be called recovery, or retrieval. If the investigator's task in "The Principle of Form in Aesthetics" was to retrieve the set of schematic laws lying behind any art form or actual manifestation of an art form, then his task in "Lyric Poetry and Experiment" is roughly the same. The only difference is that the thing to be retrieved is not transcendent and logically preexisting, but rather a set of formal laws particular to a single work of art. The investigative method for the empirical aesthetician consists of a process of decomposition followed by a reorganization of the analyzed material into a new whole. Bely's own analyses in this essay and in the other essays devoted to the empirical study of metrics do, in fact, conform to his methodological prescriptions, as we will see.

But before we turn to Bely's findings, a few words about Russian prosody and versification are in order. Russian verse, like English, is *syllabo-tonic*, which means that meter is established on the basis of both syllabic count (number of syllables per verse) and stress (regular pattern of accented syllables). Traditional Russian verse has, like English, followed the various forms handed down from Greek and Latin prosody: iambic, trochaic, dactyllic, anapestic. The most common metric form used in traditional Russian verse is the iambic tetrameter, although Russian poets have readily used a greater variety of meters than English, including forms that are quite rare in English, like the amphibrachic foot (short-long-short).

The problem that forms the point of departure for Bely's study of rhythm in Russian poetry arises from a simple attribute of the Russian language. Russian words, in principle, contain no more than one accented syllable each. At the same time, as a new student of Russian knows all too well, many Russian words are quite long. Thus one quite often encounters in Russian utterances, series of consecutive unaccented syllables numbering more than the maximum that would occur naturally in a regular example of any of the meters listed above (this maximum of two would occur in the three-syllable meters: dactyl, anapest, and amphibrach). In fact, it has been established that the average proportion of unaccented to accented syllables in Russian prose is 2.8 to 1.

As a consequence, it is relatively rare for an entire line of verse to conform perfectly to any chosen meter. Instead, although one usually finds only unaccented syllables occurring in positions that are meant to be unaccented, one quite frequently finds unaccented syllables occurring in positions that are meant to be *accented*. The first two verses of Pushkin's *Eugene Onegin* are a perfect example of a regular and an irregular verse. The meter is iambic tetrameter:

Moj djádja sámyx čéstnyx právil,
Kogdá ne v šútku zanemóg, . . .

[My uncle of most steadfast principles,
When he took seriously ill, . . .]

I have marked all stressed syllables with an accent. The reader can easily see that the first line is perfectly regular: the second syllable in each foot is accented as the meter requires (the final, unaccented syllable is a "feminine" verse ending). The second verse, however, departs from the regular scheme, since the meter requires an accented syllable on the sixth syllable (*za-* in *zanemóg*). But, since *zanemóg* is a three-syllable word accented on only the last syllable, and since that last syllable corresponds to the final, accented position in the line, the sixth syllable of this verse remains unaccented. The result is a pyrrhic foot (short-short), which Bely calls either an "acceleration" (since the lack of emphasis has the effect of speeding up the verse) or a "half-accent" (since, in deference to the meter, one tends to give a slight accent to such unaccented syllables when they fall on metric positions that by rights should be accented).

Such deviations as these are just what interests Bely. Pyrrhic feet serve as the basis for the entire aesthetic principle governing Bely's study of rhythm as well as for the fundamental distinction between *meter* and *rhythm*. Bely uses a graphic method to represent visually the patterns formed by deviations from regular meter. His first example is the ode by Fet appearing in figure 5 (p. 251). The method is quite simple: Bely has drawn a grid on which every metric foot is represented by a single box. For every foot in the poem that contains a half-accent, Bely places a dot in the corresponding box on the graph. He then draws lines to connect any two dots that occur either in the same line of verse or in two consecutive lines. The result is a series of geometric figures.

Each geometric figure bears its own rhythmic meaning, as Bely points out. For example, an upright triangle is formed when a verse containing a pyrrhee on the second foot is followed by a verse containing a pyrrhee on both the first and third feet. Since the second verse contains an additional "accelerated" foot, the effect that the upright triangle represents graphically is that of a *ritenuto* followed by an acceleration. By the same token, an inverted triangle serves as the graphic representation of an acceleration followed by a *ritenuto*.

These observations lead Bely to one of his most important positions in his essays on rhythm. "The relation between the figures and the intervals between them (standing for regular iambic verses)," he says, "as well as between the figures themselves, marks the rhythmic individuality of the poet within the bounds of a given metric form." Thus the geometric figures give us a rhythmic "signature" for any given poet. And this is because of the fundamental distinction between meter and rhythm that I mentioned a moment ago and that Bely adumbrates shortly after the passage just cited. For it appears that meter is the *regular* succession of accented and unaccented syllables dictated by the poet's choice of one of the classical patterns: iambic tetrameter, amphibrachic trimeter, and so forth. Rhythm, on the other hand, is no more than the pattern formed by the *deviations* from the prescribed meter. This is the distinction Bely has in mind when he speaks of metric verses, graphically represented as "empty," as opposed to rhythmic verses, graphically represented as "containing dots." He expresses the distinction more clearly at the beginning of another essay on rhythm, "Towards a Characterization of the Russian Iambic Tetrameter," where he says: "We will define rhythm as a certain unity [discernible] in the sum total of deviations from a given metrical form."[21]

It quickly becomes clear that Bely's distinction between meter and rhythm is not merely descriptive. It is normative as well. Bely now goes on to distinguish between what he terms "poor" and "rich" rhythms. The sole important criteria in determining richness of rhythm are the number and complexity of geometric figures generated by the graphic representation of a poem, and, by definition, the sole criteria in determining number and complexity of geometric figures are the number and complexity of deviations from regular meter. Hence Bely's mathematical definition of rhythmic richness as "being in inverse proportion to the average number of half-accents required to generate a geometric figure."

The same principle is also at work in the distinction between living and dead speech in "The Magic of Words." The unstated premise of "Lyric Poetry and Experiment" is that all aspects of a work of art that prevent a fixed, automatized response are intrinsically valuable. In "The Magic of Words" it became evident that the very poeticality of poetic language comes directly from the use of words in unconventional ways. Similarly, in "Lyric Poetry and Experiment" rhythmicality is based on *deviations* from the regular pattern established by a set of rules implicit in "metric form." Thus Bely once again places himself in the tradition that the Formalists made famous with their ideas of deautomatization and defamiliarization.

One purpose of Bely's essays, as I mentioned earlier, is to prove the validity of the scientific method in aesthetics. And Bely actually achieves some startling concrete results. For instance, table 2 (p. 253) is a graphic indication of what Bely calls a "rhythmic revolution in Russian poetry": one that begins with Zhukovsky and continues through the group of poets who are contemporaries of Pushkin. The scientific fact that distinguishes the earlier group from the later is a drop in the frequency of half-accents on the second foot in iambic tetrameter.

The objection can be raised that not only is an observation like this trivial, but it also has a certain circularity. Since the fact itself is not accessible to the ordinary perceiver until he has learned and applied Bely's method, the conclusion derived from that fact must be of dubious value if it is based on data that are themselves accessible only through the application of Bely's method.

But this objection turns out to be unfounded. Bely's scientific observation concerns a phenomenon that any student of Russian poetry would have noticed on a superficial level, namely, that there is a distinct change in the style and rhythm of Russian poetry that occurs around the time of Pushkin. Bely's analysis has given a scientifically verifiable foundation to an observation otherwise based on purely subjective criteria. Furthermore, after finding a scientific expression for the popularly acknowledged change in Russian poetry, Bely uses his method to date the change more precisely than popular knowledge had been in a position to do before he made his findings. In "Towards a Characterization of the Russian Iambic Tetrameter," Bely points out that the true revolution in Russian verse occurs not with Pushkin, as had been popularly assumed, but before him, with Zhukovsky (1783–1852) and Batyushkov (1787–1855).[22]

Other observations have the same effect of validating Bely's method by confirming scientifically a "truth" recognized in popular literary knowledge. The most obvious example is the strong correlation between rhythmic richness, as defined scientifically by Bely, and "good" poets, as defined by popular taste. Another good example occurs in Bely's discussion of rhythmic affinities between older poets and poets of Bely's own generation. Such an affinity, he says, exists between Bryusov's poetry of the period of his collection *The Garland* (*Venok*) and the youthful "Lyceum" poems of Pushkin (so called because they were written when Pushkin was a pupil at the Imperial Lyceum in St. Petersburg). Bely points out that the date of composition of Bryusov's collection (1906) renders such an affinity plausible: Bryusov at this time was working on a study of Pushkin's Lyceum poems. More important than this, however, is that the statistical charts bear out the observed affinity by showing the same characteristics in Bryusov's collection as in Pushkin's Lyceum poems. Here, once again, Bely's method has apparently been successful in using scientifically measurable phenomena to validate an observation originally made on the strength of purely subjective criteria.

The essays on rhythm and metrics, more than any others, were responsible for establishing Bely's reputation as a critic. The Formalists above all, as I have already mentioned, betrayed a significant debt to just these essays. But, although many succeeding critics who borrowed heavily from Bely's methods of statistical analysis were willing to acknowledge his position as a discoverer and an initiator, relatively few treated his results with unqualified praise. The kindest assessment of Bely's work in this area by one who used Bely's methods in the years immediately following the publication of *Symbolism* was made by Jakobson, as I pointed out earlier.

Others were not so lenient. Earlier I referred to an article by Zhirmunsky that identified Bely as the founder of the formal method in Russian literary scholarship. In the same year as this article appeared, Zhirmunsky published his *Introduction to Metrics* in which he included a critique of Bely's method.[23] The critique contains the following points: (1) Bely's graphic method takes into account only accentual absence and leaves *supplementary* accents (accented syllables falling on unaccented positions) entirely out of the picture. Furthermore, the representation of a poem on a continuous, uniform graph overlooks the possible effects of division into strophes. (2) Bely's sample of 596 verses for each poet as a means for establishing the relative frequency of certain accentual patterns is too small to be statistically meaningful. (3) Bely's judgments concerning the significance of his rhythmic figures are arbitrary and subjective (a charge whose possibility, incidentally, Bely acknowledges). Zhirmunsky also points out that, in his distinction between meter and rhythm, Bely is confusing two different senses of rhythm: namely, rhythm as the expression of the natural melodiousness of the poet, and rhythm as any deviation from "meter." Furthermore, Zhirmunsky states that the second definition of rhythm is too restrictive, since it denies the possibility of any rhythmic value to verses that *do* follow their prescribed meter. (4) Bely's terminology is vague.

The validity of Zhirmunsky's critique cannot be denied. To his first, second, and fourth points one could reply that Bely viewed himself as a pioneer staking out new territory and that he never claimed to provide definitive solutions to the problems he was confronting. But the third point does present a real difficulty for Bely. In identifying the situation that leads to the existence of pyrrhic deviations, Bely rightly points out that there *is*, for example, no pure iambic rhythm in Russian. He cites two "iambic" verses from Tyutchev in order to show that Tyutchev's rhythm hesitates between iambic and amphibrachic, but is not strictly either one. He then goes on to say this:

> Is it possible that we have here a combination of metric forms? Certainly. But what is the point of introducing into our study of metrics forms that are meaningful only relative to Greek prosody and that make true rhythmic sense only in a language whose poetry is musically constituted in iambs, trochees, amphibrachs, and so on? In Russian prosody the only meters that are formally permitted are the iamb, trochee, dactyl, anapest, and amphibrach. But an artificial cultivation of, say, the trimeter, does not always create a natural impression on the ear of the listener. Demonstrating the rhythmic modula-

> tions of the iamb by speaking of "paeons" is only using metrics to compound the problems of metrics, since in so doing one forgets that the metric form itself expresses a rhythm that has become crystallized.

What is one to make of this perfectly persuasive passage in light of everything that follows? For, after asserting the inappropriateness of applying Greek metric categories to a language as rhythmically different from Greek as Russian, Bely then goes on to found his entire system on the implicit recognition of Greek metric forms as the norm in relation to which all variations are defined. And when one considers once again the aesthetic of deautomatization that is fundamental to Bely, then it appears that the system of Greek metric forms is not being posed as an arbitrary standard by which to construct a new and more appropriate system. No, the implication is that, to the ordinary Russian listener, this very same system is the complacently accepted, automatized norm, and that this norm provides the pattern of regularity against which all violations stand out.

Still, the fact remains that Bely's studies in metrics, for all their flaws and inadequacies, were a pioneering venture and one that was to prove most influential on the work of subsequent investigators. Bely's influence may be seen in the work of Tomashevsky, for instance, in addition to other Formalist critics already mentioned. One might also mention, among more recent works in this area, Boris Unbegaun's *Russian Versification*, the standard English book on the subject, in which the author identifies Bely's metric studies as forming "the starting point for all subsequent studies of the iambic metres in Russian."[24] And Nabokov, in his *Notes on Prosody*, originally included in the introduction to his edition of *Eugene Onegin* and then published separately, not only mentions Bely's essays but uses essentially the same system in his own metric analyses of Russian verse.[25]

SYMBOLISM AND THE ICONIC IMAGINATION IN BELY

The essays assembled here constitute what I consider to be a representative selection of styles and subjects from Bely's theoretical writings. The reader will undoubtedly have noticed the almost contradictory divergence of goals that Bely has pursued in the different essays. When one juxtaposes, say, "The Emblematics of Meaning" with an essay like "Lyric Poetry and Experiment," when one compares this with an essay like "The Principle of Form in Aesthetics," one can hardly believe, apart from the uniformity of the style, that the same person wrote all of this material. The contrast is all the more amazing when one considers that "The Magic of Words" and "The Emblematics of Meaning" were written in the same year as the essays on rhythm and metrics.

To take just one example already mentioned, how is one to view Bely's pursuit of an exact science of aesthetics, whose possibility was meant to be demonstrated by his essays on rhythm, in light of the fundamental attack on exact science in "The Emblematics of Meaning?" To be sure, when Bely attacks exact science in that essay, his specific purpose is to deny its possibility as the basis for an all-encompassing world view. Thus in theory at least, science might still have some validity in its more limited applications. Still, it is difficult to find room for even such limited applications in a field that has been qualified as "nothing more than a taxonomy of every conceivable kind of ignorance."

One cannot help wondering, then, if Bely's thinking followed such a desultory course that he lost sight of earlier interests and pronouncements as he turned to new ones, or if there really is a unified view behind the disparate interests he showed. After all, one thing that all the essays assembled here have in common is that they are all either exclusively or in part devoted to questions of aesthetics. Perhaps, then, the real question is whether *aesthetics* for Bely is simply a collection of essentially unrelated but interesting areas of investigation, or whether there is a common factor uniting efforts like those in "The Emblematics of Meaning" and those in the essays on form and metrics.

I believe there is, and I believe the key to a unified picture in Bely's aesthetics lies in what I call iconicity, or the iconic principle. Earlier, in my remarks on "The Emblematics of Meaning," I referred to the iconic nature of Bely's system in that essay and pointed out its origin in the idea of kenosis. The underlying principle of iconicity is fundamental to Russian Orthodox theology. Bely recognized this source only obliquely in "The Emblematics of Meaning," through his use of theological terminology. The principle has enormous implications in theology, covering the whole nature of the relation between the Godhead and the concrete reality in which man moves. Since it pervades Bely's whole system of thought, it is really the clue to what is most essentially Russian about a man who might otherwise appear to have imported from abroad more than he produced at home.

Russian Orthodoxy draws a sharp line of separation between the experience of corporeal beings and the direct experience of divinity. As any reader familiar with the teachings of Father Zosima in *The Brothers Karamazov* will remember, the truly faithful do not rely on miracles, which is to say material manifestations of divinity, to bolster their faith. Miracles are few and far between, and their true sense is to bring added joy to those who already believe. This is the truth brought home to Alyosha Karamazov as he sleepily prays over the body of his mentor and listens to the priest read the story of Cana of Galilee.

How, then, does man find access to the divine? The best illustration may be found in the idea of Christ Himself. For, according to the tenets of Orthodox theology, Christ came into being as the God-man specifically through the act of "emptying" (*kenosis* in Greek) that I mentioned earlier. In assuming the form of a man, Christ "emptied" Himself of His divinity so that He might appear in the humble guise of other corporeal beings. This is the sense of the key passage from the Scriptures: "But [Christ] made himself of no reputation, and took upon him the form of a servant, and was made in the likeness of men: And being found in fashion as a man, he humbled himself, and became obedient unto death, even the death of the cross" (Phil. 2:7–8). The phrase "made himself of no reputation" translates the Greek verb that means "emptied himself." The idea, then, is that, in assuming a fundamentally different nature, Christ made Himself accessible to the experience of men, who, as corporeal beings, can experience only what is corporeal. The specific way in which Christ's experience becomes available to men is suggested in the phrase "humbled himself." The true mark of Christ's kenosis was His capacity to suffer physically. If Russian Orthodoxy places such a strong emphasis on the notion of humiliation and suffering, it is for this reason: it is the only means available to men by which we can approximate as much as possible (given the limitations imposed on us by our fleshly nature) the experience of Christ.

But Christ, in spite of the "humiliation" by which He assumed the nature of men, remained the Son of God. As a consequence, His being contains two components: an immanent (corporeal) one and a transcendent (divine) one. The same principle operates in the art of iconography, as I pointed out before. The images of the standard subjects of icons (Christ, the Mother of God, saints) are not mere imaginative renditions of what the icon painter believed to be the physical appearance of those subjects. On the contrary, the *likeness* is meant to be absolute, since every icon painter is meant to paint his subject so that it will resemble previous renditions of the same subject, and the archetype for all previous renditions is an actual visual perception of the subject in question (Christ, the Mother of God, a saint) by a contemporary of that subject. But, if the likeness ideally is absolute, it is still not because the physical being of the subject is rendered in an icon. The concrete image of the icon stands in relation to its original as the kenotic or humiliated Christ stands in relation to His divine origin. This means that the original of an icon is not a physical being at all, but a divine, transcendent essence. Thus the original in the case of an icon representing Christ is Christ's divinity. The original in the case of an icon portraying a saint is the Divine Grace that the saint enjoyed.

As a result, the icon has the same dual existential status as the God-man: it is a physical entity that, although fundamentally of a different nature from that of its transcendent original, still partakes to a limited extent of the essence of that original. Furthermore, it allows corporeal beings a limited form of access to that essence. Just as, through the *physical* experience of Christ, we can approximate His divine experience as closely as is possible for us (given, once again, that we are only corporeal beings), so, when we experience the beauty of an icon, we are partaking in an approximate fashion of the Divine Grace for which that beauty stands. The final example of the principle of humiliation—the *original* example—is God's creation. The concrete reality in which mortal men move is actualized through a humiliation of God's Being. That is, by the Word that became Flesh, God created a corporeal realm of existence different in nature from Himself.

It is this peculiar existential status that is the key to the unity of Bely's aesthetics. For, just as religious objects (Christ, iconic images, God's creation) have a dual status, containing a component of transcendence and a component of immanence, so symbols and emblems for Bely have a dual status, as the scheme elaborated in "The Emblematics of Meaning" shows. In fact, if one examines the triangle in that essay, it becomes clear that Bely has effectively adopted the entire iconic system of Orthodox theology and simply replaced the religious First Principle (namely God the Father) with his own First Principle: what he calls the "Symbol Embodied." As his explanation of the diagram indicates, all fields (as I have termed them) of human meaning have the status of symbols, which is to say that they, and presumably their products, possess a component of transcendence (proximity to the Symbol Embodied at the top of the diagram) and a component of immanence, or concretion.

Thus any field of human meaning, or object produced by that field, has the peculiar characteristic of being concrete and phenomenal but at the same time merely serving as a kind of façade, or front, for a transcendent essence that lies, so to speak, behind or above it. Now one such field, occupying, incidentally, a rather humble position on Bely's triangle, is aesthetic creation. This field lies on the right, or "creative" side of the triangle, indicating that its products are symbols, rather than emblems. Thus an aesthetic object has the status of a symbol, which is to say that, like an icon, it is the concrete embodiment of a relatively transcendent essence.

In order to conceptualize what I see as the principle of unity in Bely's system, it is necessary to view the aesthetic object, this iconic symbol, from the point of view of the perceiver and the act by which he apprehends it. That act is essentially like the act by which one experiences Christ's nature or Divine Grace in an icon. It is an act of reaching beyond the concrete presence of the object and seeking the transcendent essence that it symbolizes. Similarly, the task facing the perceiver of an art object is one of reaching beyond, to retrieve the essence behind it. This, in a word, is what symbolism is all about for Bely.

So much is relatively clear from "The Emblematics of Meaning," which is designed to propose a program for a theory of symbolism. But what about the "scientific" essays? If we recall the underlying principles in these essays we will see that Bely was being entirely consistent with his theoretical beliefs as they appear in "The Emblematics of Meaning." In "The Principle of Form in Aesthetics," as I pointed out earlier, Bely's intent is to discover what I likened to a transcendental schematism governing the manner in which aesthetic objects are actualized. In the essays on rhythm and metrics his purpose is to discover sets of inductive laws particular to individual artworks. Here is the crucial passage from "Lyric Poetry and Experiment:"

> What does it mean to describe a work of literature? To describe means to give a commentary. Every lyric work demands a basic commentary. In commenting on a poem we are decomposing it, as it were, into its constituent parts and looking carefully at the means of representation, at the choice of epithets, similes, and metaphors in order to characterize the content. . . . In thus reorganizing the analyzed material into a new whole, we often can no longer recognize a familiar poem at all. Like the phoenix, it arises anew out of itself in a more beautiful form, or, conversely, it withers away.

What happens in both cases is that the perceiver or the investigator, in approaching the poem, views the concrete aesthetic object as merely a front for something else that lies *behind* it, that is to be retrieved, and that then effectively replaces the concrete object. In "The Principle of Form in Aesthetics" this something is a set of schematic laws, a kind of preexisting mathematical abstraction. In the essays on rhythm and metrics it is geometric patterns. In each case, Bely has approached the poem as a front behind which there lies a hidden correlate for the concrete literary object. The rhombuses, baskets, roofs, and right triangles are the "phoenix," risen anew from the ashes of the concrete object, to use Bely's own figure of speech: they are the visual correlates of the abstraction that Bely calls "form."

Thus in the scientific essays Bely is as much of a symbolist as he is in "The Emblematics of Meaning" or "The Magic of Words." The iconic act, wherein the subject, through his experience of a concrete *perceptum*, strives to approximate (but can never actually attain) direct experience of the transcendent, is everywhere present in Bely's theory. It is always a question of retrieval, of looking beyond the concrete to the essence that lies behind it. In Bely this essence is generally not transcendent in the metaphysical sense of lying beyond the realm of ordinary knowledge. It is usually a purely formal quality, like a geometric pattern or the epistemological abstraction, "Value." But the act by which symbolic or aesthetic objects like poems are apprehended is formally the same as that by which iconic objects are apprehended. With this principle in mind the reader will perhaps be able to approach Bely as somewhat less of a *chudak* and somewhat more of a systematic thinker than he might have appeared to be at first glance.

THE ESSAYS

MODERN ART AND THEORY OF SYMBOLISM

SYMBOLISM AS A WORLD VIEW

1

Not long ago it was thought that the world had been thoroughly investigated. All the hidden depths had disappeared from the horizon, and only a vast, flat plane stretched away into the distance. All the eternal values, which previously had revealed new perspectives, had become a thing of the past. Everything had lost its value. But the urge to seek faraway things had not disappeared from men's hearts. At a certain point the desire arose for new perspectives, and the heart of man began once again to inquire after the eternal values.

It was then that a yawning chasm opened up between feeling and reason. A tragic terror of discord rose up from the depths of the unconscious to the very surface of consciousness. An unprincipled skepticism appeared as the consequence of man's inability either to retain the eternal values or to do without them. The philosophy of Schopenhauer bore the traits of a great negation, and many were attracted by it in its time. As the spirit of pessimism became prominent, it became increasingly easy to acknowledge openly all the terrors of being. Being became spectral, illusory. Only a black gloom peered through it. Feverish tension then gave way to a spirit of contemplative inactivity. The waters in life's channel parted, and with a thunderous roar the chariot of philistine insipidness came galloping across.

Still, there was a peculiar value in this contemplativeness. Once pessimism had been elevated to the status of a principle, it was able to blunt the sting of disaffection. Man, after diverging from the path of life, sank into a gloomy reverie, enchanted by the grandeur of his own tragedy. But in this state of inactivity, man's wasted forces began to gather, and his depressed personality began to spread its wings. It was in this imperceptible evolution from passivity to activity, from pessimism to tragedy, that the first rumblings, the first beating of the wings, were heard.

A man lulled to sleep by visions and apparitions has the semblance of death. But his sleep is of the kind that restores his strength. The passion of European society for philosophical pessimism was precisely this kind of somnolent oblivion, and it was fraught with serious consequences. And thus it was, as darkness closed the eyes of the impassioned pessimists, that one from among them called out in words with a strange ring to them: "The time of the Socratic man is over: crown yourselves with ivy, take up the thyrsus staff, and wonder not when the tiger and the panther lay themselves caressingly at your knees, [. . .] for ye must be redeemed. Ye must accompany the pageant of Dionysus as it proceeds from India to Greece! Arm yourselves for harsh strife, but believe in the wonders of your God!" (*The Birth of Tragedy*).[1] These words rang out with extraordinary effect. Who could understand them? Perhaps it was from this moment that the air became alive with presentiments of future revelations. A gentle breeze began to blow across the faces of the sleepers. Visions appeared, still and enticing, sweet and sleepy. Day had begun to break.

Pessimism turned out to be a crucible in which the spirit of philistine insipidness was scorched. Schopenhauer, through his distinction between the visual, contemplative, intuitive form of cognition on the one hand, and the thinking, abstract form on the other, as well as through his preference for the first form, not only founded the symbolic method as a counterpoise to the logical, but also paved the way for assigning exclusive meaning to the symbolic method in the future. If philosophy must live entirely under the sway of abstract cognition, then Schopenhauer represents the last philosopher. In him we see the beginning of the end of philosophy. As soon as the source of all sparkling essences was revealed, the airy castles of thought faded away.

The reduction of all philosophical questions to nothing does not, however, imply a victory for scientific positivism. What we have before us is not a complete edifice, crowned with a cupola, but rather a many-storied structure of walls without a roof, disfigured by the presence of a scaffolding surrounding it.

For centuries people had complete faith in the ability of science and philosophy to resolve all questions of being. How many Titans erected strongholds on which to climb! Is it that the age of struggles between gods and Titans was being repeated, or had the Titans once again been cast down into Tartarus? Where is our past? Why has the earth shaken beneath us? What is the reason for these involuntary tears? Cherished names, sacred delusions! It is like sitting comfortably in a fisherman's cabin before setting out on a journey. You can hear the sea. The wind and driving rain are blinding. You stand before the old fisherman one last time, and one last time you press his callused hands. You are about to depart, never to return again. The time has come to set out.

Schopenhauer was the summit to which those seeking to rise above the somnolence of life ascended. He represented the crossing point of two directions of thought, both inflamed with eternal vitality. The two came together only to part once again immediately thereafter: philosophical rationalism, which had become a kind of religious, abstract pantheism, and empiricism, which had turned into a form of individualism with mystical, prophetic overtones. Thus both directions turned up on the other side of critical philosophy, on the very border of symbolism.

Nietzsche and [Eduard von] Hartmann[2] both passed through Schopenhauer, crossed paths and then separated for good.

In examining the principle of appearance (representation), Nietzsche opposed to this principle the orgiastic principle, which destroys illusion (will). The confluence of these two principles in tragedy eliminates the Schopenhauerian antinomy between will and representation in the personal principle of man. Hartmann's unconscious lies deep in the nature of man, and it never errs. It is in the unconscious that Vladimir Solov'ev sees the link between God and man. It is also the place of confluence between the metaphysical will and the world of phenomena. Historical process, according to Hartmann, is not aimless, but has a definite end, and that is the unfolding of the all-embracing spirit. Nietzsche proposes the appearance of the one and only personality, or superman, as the end of historical evolution. The question of the appearance of the all-embracing spirit in the personality is what points history in the direction of Godmanhood.[3] Solov'ev, in defining the [Universal] Church as the organization of Godmanhood, was seeking a reconciliation between science, philosophy, and religion. The aims of the science of theosophy are roughly the same as those of Solov'ev, although one could argue about individual tenets. One cannot overlook the general trend of this science, since it is now a fully established current of thought that has recently been revived and that has developed far beyond its original form.

Cognition of the formal, logical kind, having come full circle in its development, gave symbolism its freedom. In Schopenhauer's conception, cognition as it operates in the process of symbolization must be of the genial type. After the crisis in thought, it was inevitable that art should come forth to take the place of philosophy as the guiding beacon of mankind.

The idea is a step in the objectivization of the will. The will is the most profound principle of being. But if this principle is that which, having revealed itself in the depths of the spirit, draws us out to the starry expanses, discloses the black gulfs of the spirit, illuminates empty places with all its radiance, if this is so, then any attempt to define this most profound principle of being as *will* is fruitless. For such an entity is necessarily distinct from our will, something that flickers in the will only from time to time: it is a will within our will, as it were. By thus confusing the personal will with the world will, Schopenhauer hypertrophied the personal will. That which comes and goes, lights up and goes out in the will is [not will, but] essence. On the other hand, that which, remaining unilluminated from without, oppresses us with all the elemental force of chaos, is not essence, but rather the very boundary of the world of appearances, the negative definition of essence: in a word, the personal will. The suprapersonal generic principle conditions personality. This world principle must be absolute and unconditional, and, as such, it embraces all the forms of cognition. If the most general form of cognition is the division into subject and object, into representation and will, then the absolute and unconditional covers both will and representation. This is its formal definition, and it corresponds to the unconscious of Hartmann.

An idea is not a concept. Representing the emergence of the unconscious into the visible world, the idea abolishes the relative division between volume and content. In the case of a concept, any increase in volume results in a decrease in formal content. For the idea, however, this is not so. Defining the idea in relation to the concept, we can say that the idea changes the indirect proportion of volume to content (which holds for the concept) into a direct proportion. The idea constitutes a limiting force on the absolute and unconditional. If the absolute bears the character of unity, then its emergence into the visible world is limited by the multitude of steps involved. This is the reason for the existence of a multitude of ideas. One may speak of generic and specific ideas. In this relation generic ideas are more intensive than specific ideas. With the elimination of the opposition between volume and content, generic ideas become distinguishable from specific ideas by virtue of their degree of intensity. Intensity may be expressed as the degree of influence they have on us.

In order for the cognition of ideas to take place, a representation is necessary. If time is the form that systematically organizes representations of inner sense, then the contemplation of temporal ideas has a more intensive influence on our mind [than the contemplation of spatial ideas does]. One may therefore speak provisionally of a greater intensity of temporal ideas. Temporal ideas are thus generic with respect to spatial ideas. Now the content of art consists in the cognition of ideas. The temporal art forms consequently provide a more essential cognition, and this is why musical ideas are essential symbols.

Musical ideas are generic with respect to the ideas of all the other arts. This is why one may speak of images that are musical but not the reverse. An "imaginal" music does not add anything to the images expressed in it. This is why one may speak of the musical origin of all the arts. One may speak of the spirit of music in sculpture, but not the reverse. It is in music that the depths of the spirit approach most closely the surface of consciousness.

The entire essence of a man is grasped not through events, but through *symbols of the other*. Music ideally expresses the symbol, and for this reason the symbol is always musical. The transition from criticism to symbolism is unavoidably accompanied by an awakening of the spirit of music. The spirit of music is an index of this transition in consciousness. It was not to drama alone but to all culture that Nietzsche addressed his exclamation: "Crown yourselves with ivy, take up the thyrsus staff, and wonder not when the tiger and the panther lay themselves caressingly at your knees. . . . Ye must accompany the pageant of Dionysus as it proceeds from India . . ."[4] Contemporary humanity is troubled by the closeness of internal music to the surface of consciousness. Mankind can be grasped, not by the event, but only by the symbol of the other, and until this other is embodied, the symbols troubling us in contemporary [artistic] creation will remain unclear. But only those afflicted with myopia in questions concerning the spirit seek clarity in symbols. In such people the soul has no resonance, and they are incapable of knowing anything.

What existed before time and what will exist in the future—this is the province of the symbol. Music gushes forth from the symbol.

Music passes right by consciousness without stopping. He who is not musical understands nothing.

The symbol arouses music in the soul. When the world enters into our soul, our soul begins to resonate. When the soul becomes the world, it will exist outside the world. If it is possible to influence objects over a distance, if magic is possible, we know that it is all from music. For magic is nothing other than the musical resonance of the soul increased to an exorbitant degree. Only the soul that is musically attuned has the power to charm, for in music is sorcery. Music is the window from which the bewitching torrents of Eternity flow into us and magic gushes forth.

Art is genial cognition. Genial cognition has the power to expand the various art forms. In symbolism, seen as a method that unites the eternal with its spatial and temporal manifestations, we encounter the cognition of Platonic ideas. Art must express ideas. Each of the arts is in essence symbolic. Every symbolic act of cognition is ideational. The purpose of art, understood as a special type of cognition, remains the same in all ages. All that changes are the means of expression. For instance, the development of philosophical cognition through proof by contradiction places art in a position of dependence on cognition through *revelation*, or symbolic cognition. Man's attitude towards art thus changes with a change in the prevailing theory of knowledge. Seen in this light, art ceases to be a self-sufficient form. But it cannot, on the other hand, be made to serve utilitarian ends. Instead, it is becoming the pathway to a more essential type of cognition, namely religious cognition. Religion is a system of consistently unfolding symbols. This is its most basic superficial definition. The change that takes place in the means of expression for symbols in art corresponds to a transition in man's consciousness. We must now examine the nature of this change.

The characteristic trait of classical art is the harmony of form. This harmony places a seal of restraint on the expression of insight. Goethe and Nietzsche were often after the same thing. Where the former as it were would accidentally lift a corner of the curtain, revealing the depths behind it, the latter attempted to cast up the depths to the surface, thus forcefully underscoring the phenomenality of their revelation. Classical works of genius always have two different sides: a façade, where the accessible form is presented, and an interior. Concerning the latter there are mere hints that only a select few can understand. But the vulgar mob, content with the clearly comprehensible phenomenalism of action, of poses, and of psychology, never suspects the existence of those internal traits in a work of art that serve as a background for the phenomena represented. These traits are accessible to only a few. This is the sort of aristocratism so characteristic of the finest examples of classical art, which, by disguising itself as ordinary and commonplace, is able to protect itself against any incursions by the vulgar populace into its secret depths. Artworks like these are source, depth, and surface all at once, so that both the masses and the elite few can be satisfied. This duality inevitably arises from the duality in critical philosophy itself and also from the unwillingness of genius to see its symbols serve as a subject for the dogmatic prattle of rationalism, utilitarianism, and similar systems.[5] Thus the artist's contempt for the "little ones," the aristocratic irony towards the blind, who, though they do not see, continue to praise nonetheless, and the coquetry towards the spiritual elite.[6] *Faust*, for example, is comprehensible to everyone, and everyone will unanimously declare it to be an artistic work of genius. And yet the theosophical depths of *Faust* are often hidden from even those present-day readers who appreciate "depth" of all sorts, that is, the adherents of the new art. Still, these adherents of the new art understand perfectly well the depths of *Zarathustra*, which shatter the contours of images and the clarity of thought. In this respect the new art is more democratic, since it is able to mediate between the deeper understanding of a few and the superficial understanding of the masses. The aim of the new art lies not in the harmony of forms, but rather in the visual actualization of the depths of the spirit. This is why the new art cries out, proclaims, plunges us into deep thought, where classical art simply turned its back on the "little ones." This change in the means of expression is linked to a change in theory of knowledge, namely the one that led to the conviction that cognition of the eternal, in a temporal mode, is no longer an impossibility. If this is accepted as true, then it becomes the duty of art to teach us how to see the *Eternal*. The heretofore irreproachable, petrified mask of classical art has been torn off and broken. From out of the cracks there come crawling profound meditations that saturate images and then shatter them, once their relativity has been apprehended. The images become a method of cognition rather than something self-sufficient. And their purpose is no longer to arouse a feeling of beauty, but rather to develop the observer's capacity to see for himself the prototypical meaning of these images in the very phenomena of life. Once this goal has been achieved, the images cease to have any significance. This explains the democratic sense of the new art, an art to which the near future undoubtedly belongs. And as soon as this future has become present, art, having prepared man for what he must do, must then disappear. The new art is less art than a kind of token or precursor.

The change in means of artistic expression is occurring gradually. Contemporary art has often proceeded gropingly during the change, and many have stumbled. The Artesian waters have burst through to the surface, spreading mud and grime. Only later will the sun light up the purity of crystalline water with millions of rubies. One must not be too hard on those who have led the way, in fact it is on their wounded bodies that we tread as we continue on our own way. Let there be thanks for them, and pity as well! Let those who would detract from them be silent! For Nietzsche himself is among them. And besides, how could we help automatically lowering the hand that had been raised over the body of the martyr, when his deathly pale head, bearing drooping mustaches and a crown of thorns, with the mark of terror on its brow, all illuminated, suddenly began to nod reproachfully and bitterly? How could the sufferer help opening his eyes in order to pierce with his clear glance the soul that had gone mad? How could the crimson flash of "the crucified Dionysus" fail to scorch us, and how could the panthers, caressing and fondling him at first, fail to tear him limb from limb?

We must look trustingly at the deceased one, in order that the panthers may turn into gentle, tame kittens. But his image gazes on us so pensively and sadly from those immortal distances! His childish glance speaks to us of childish happiness, of the white isle of children, awash with azure radiance.

Hush! for this is a holy grave.

2

The diamond patterns of constellations are motionless in the black delirium of the world, where everything rushes about and where nothing that exists is to be found. The earth whirls around the sun, which in turn hurtles towards the constellation Hercules! And where does the constellation Hercules hurtle? It is all a mad dance of the bottomless world!

Whither are we flying? Over what spaces will we cross as we fly? Will we cross paths as we fly? What will fly towards us out there?

Here and there, confirming certain strange thoughts, golden dots light up in the heavens. They light up and go out in the ethereal-aerial folds of the great earthly veil. They light up, expire, and fly and fly away from the earth through endless realms of nonbeing, to light up once again after millions of years. You feel a desire to cry out to the momentary acquaintances you make out here: "Greetings! . . . Where are you flying? . . . Send my regards to Eternity! . . ." All this happens at an unattainable height. A spark slipping by in the sky does not break the thread of the conversation. Only an involuntary sigh, perhaps, escaping from your breast, will reveal that the soul has not forgotten where the cardboard surfaces of being are immersed.

But when lightning flashes across the cloudless sky, and a bright, crimson star hovers over the heads of the terror-stricken, lighting up their pale faces with a fiery delirium, and then slips away leaving a shower of sparks in its trail, the general cry, "A meteor! . . . So low! . . ." will interrupt all conversations. For all will sense that the incursion of Eternity has taken place far too close, that next to it the bases of our own existence, capable of covering over the depths only now and then, are far too insignificant. The conversation is renewed, but everyone becomes thoughtful.

Nietzsche was just such a meteor. He brought depths to us from immortal distances. And even though the friendly battle over the traveler to Eternity has not subsided, we are all somehow more serious in his wake than we were before. We no longer have the shortsighted naiveté we had before. For even if that explosive charge of eternal fire has streamed by so close to us today, nothing can preserve us from the eternal perils. A certain indelible new mark has been left on us all in the wake of the wise Nietzsche.

Wisdom is a loophole through which to peer out from the "blue prison" of three-dimensionality.[7] Man comes into the world and immediately begins knocking at the door of the nonworldly. Here it becomes clear that thought, bolstered up by an immense store of proofs and expressed verbally to the greatest possible degree, is like a frog, ever hopping ahead out of reach and drawing the wise man on to seek more and more enlightening thoughts. The wise man grows to prefer the swiftly darting swallow to the frog, for he knows that even though swallows may founder and disappear in a great sea of azure, the frog will only lead him into a swamp. He would much rather lose himself in an azure reverie than in a swampy one. The wise man is the keenest, the subtlest of madmen, a merry and cheerful person who is, however, serious and sombre for all those who are incapable of combining wisdom with lightheartedness. Thus he freezes, as it were, into a hieratic pose. He is perhaps distracted, but not from thought: he thinks perfectly freely. His thought darts about at will. This is music. Only for a select few does the silk curtain of indifference fall from around the wise man. An expression of ardent power and superhuman tenderness flickers like lightning across his shining face, and then once again the face becomes stonelike. A man who is not deprived of the spirit of music is like an eternally gushing fountain in whose spray the sun and moon are reflected. The man who is devoid of inner music is a stagnant puddle, full of worms and reflecting nothing. The most important attribute of the wise man is his attitude towards the content of his own views, that accompaniment of the soul to his words. The essential distinction between the wise man and the fool is that the fool, too, says intelligent things, but appears stupid. The wise man, on the other hand, in uttering stupidities, fools no one save, perhaps, fools themselves.

Nietzsche is not a philosopher in the earlier sense of the word but rather a wise man. His propositions are often purely symbols. God only knows which way to go after him—so many walls of granite simply melted away before his childlike eyes! Reality itself assumed a glasslike transparence with Nietzsche. He was like a box containing the other. The only blunder one can make with Nietzsche is to demand a religious revelation from him. For religious revelation is a system of regularly unfolding symbols. Such, at any rate, is its superficial definition. And if the symbol is a window looking out on Eternity, then a system of symbols cannot be continuous in the same way as the systems of dogmatism and critical philosophy can, where everything is connected by logical form. Instead, it is an interrupted series of images, all revealing different facets of a unity. For Nietzsche, symbols are not brought together into a system. Formal, logical systems could never have satisfied him, for he had taken the great step from critical philosophy to symbolism, and this is why we find in him such a confusing array of methods of cognition. One often finds him saying the very same thing more than once, but in different languages, and even though this increases the number of apparent contradictions in his thought, it nonetheless sheds a certain light on the fate he suffered. For was not Nietzsche's eventual madness the result of an inability to distinguish between symbolism and critical philosophy? Critical philosophy, after all, will inevitably lose its strict clarity with an incursion of blinding images that divert thought hither and thither instead of concentrating it. But wisdom gives rise to *values*, whereas criticism is not in a position to give rise to anything. Is this not why those bright, salamander colors are often imbued with poison for Nietzsche? Even medicinal substances are often poisonous.

The [literary] form Nietzsche used most of all is the aphorism. The aphorism allows one to take in any horizon, no matter how broad, at a single glance, and at the same time to observe in a single moment the relation between all the different parts that make up one's field of vision. The aphorism is the most compact form of communication between an author and his readers, provided, of course, that the author expresses himself skillfully and that the reader skillfully grasps the author's meaning. The aphorism is an open door to a path that may be followed independently in a terrain where the author has merely placed occasional signposts. From one good aphorism one may extract more pearls than from a whole ponderous book. The surface of the sea conceals more than one monster in the watery depths below. The aphorism is a point of departure from which the entire road ahead is already visible. Those who do not see in the aphorism the best possible means for gathering a rich harvest in their nets, in spite of its superficial unpersuasiveness, are naive indeed. For what good is a trap if it can be seen from miles away? An aphorism is either higher or baser than strict, logical thought: everything depends on the author. For is it not true that the aphoristic style of thinking has so many enemies because the great majority of those who choose to express themselves aphoristically encounter nothing but fiasco? As they pounce furiously upon the aphorism they are undoubtedly holding up before their eyes samples of their own wares.

The symbol, defined superficially, is an aphorism that has been strained to the utmost. An aphorism is thus a bridge leading to the symbol. This is the bridge Nietzsche crossed as he passed from critical philosophy to symbolism. In certain of Nietzsche's aphorisms one can see that the inner core is symbolic, whereas the exterior belongs to reason. There is no reason why this should appear strange. After all, the only thing that distinguishes [Nietzsche's type of] mad-genius cognition from rational cognition is an expansion of forms. The symbol is the ideal of the aphorism. Nietzsche's aphorisms are frequently quite far from being ideal, but then Nietzsche was not altogether a symbolist. One may speak provisionally of Nietzsche's ideas as being systematic, but only as long as the systematic quality is viewed as merely an external phenomenon: from the inside it is all symbols; only from the outside is it [systematic] ideas. Often, on analysis, these ideas turn out to be quite shaky and are not intrinsically so convincing as to obviate the need for proof. Approaching these ideas, in fact, requires jumping back and forth between symbolism and philosophy. Nietzscheanism, like any doctrine with inroads into symbolism, contains several different zones of understanding connected by an inner path. We will touch briefly on just two stages of Nietzschean understanding: the tragic and the theurgic.

A great chasm opens up at our feet the minute we tear the mask off phenomena. We are terrified by the abyss separating us from the sleepers on the other side. We are terrified by the great difference between appearances and being. We withdraw, alone, many millions of miles, but we are powerless in the face of the chasm. The deceptive veil of phenomena, the reasoning by opposites concerning the nature of essence—all this discourages the spirit in our encounter with the great depths. And as the great depths ingratiatingly approach our trembling heart, we suddenly find ourselves turned head over heels by our glimpse into the great yonder. For what has been revealed to us is so far from the ordinary that it terrifies us. We begin to have the impression that we have aroused some hitherto slumbering monsters of our spirit. The smooth surface of the sea conceals more than one monster in the watery depths below. Chaos begins to call out. At first it is only the gentle mewing of a kitten—then it becomes the roar of the elements. With a shrill whistle, the chaos bursts out of the aperture we have created and into our life. In order to control the mounting pressure of essence (which appears to our unaccustomed eyes as chaos), we draw an artificial curtain over our windows into the depths. With horror we watch as the veil is puffed out by the whistling tempest below. This is the source of our drama. No matter how much we cover the chaos over, we remain eternally standing on the boundary between it and life. This blending of essence (the spirit of Dionysus) with the visible world (the spirit of Apollo) is our tragedy, that movement of the hand to the eyes as a blinding light takes away our sight and circles before our eyes become monsters, which we take for the *real* representation of essence. A time will certainly come when we can remove our hand from our eyes, when we will renew our faith in the mask of appearances, that is, renew our faith in the external. But it will never be possible to forget what we have seen. One may only turn away. Turning away is a form of terror for *us,* whereas turning toward the depths is a form of terror for those around us. Both forms of terror guard us in our position on the border between pessimism and tragedy, criticism and symbolism.

This is the first stage in Nietzsche's world view.

The rainbow colors that run together in *Zarathustra* are colors that shimmer in the turbid waves of chaos. A motley-colored spider web will suddenly burst into a thousand colorful shreds, and Eternity will bare its teeth. Its jaws will open wide, threatening to swallow everything. The dazzling golden splendor of Nietzscheanism, that treading along the mountain tops, has something wild, ancient about it, something that seems to summon up the Titans from Tartarus. The whole of Nietzscheanism seems to consist in savoring that "Stillest Hour" of Zarathustra, when something, neither a "he" nor a "she," but some horrible "it" whispers fearful things to him:

> Then it spoke without voice to me: "*Dost thou know it, Zarathustra*?"
>
> And I cried in terror . . .
>
> Then it spoke again without voice to me: "Thou knowest it, Zarathustra, but thou sayest it not!"
>
> And I answered finally, like an obstinate one: "Yes, I know it, but I do not wish to say it!"
>
> Then it spoke again without voice to me: "Thou dost not *wish* to say it, Zarathustra? Is this true? Conceal thyself not in thine obstinacy!"[8]

Nietzsche himself begins to resemble a man living in his own private apartment who hears the door being forced. People he has never seen before finally break in, but, assuming that they are merely friends playing a prank on him, the beleaguered inhabitant as a last hope screams, "I know you, you jokesters!" He tries hard to smile. At this point Nietzsche resembles the apocalyptic star, about which it is written, "And the fifth angel sounded, and I saw a star fall from heaven unto the earth: and to him was given the key of the bottomless pit. And he opened the bottomless pit" (Rev. 9:1–2). And yet, at the same time Nietzsche is pure delight: that fount of wit, the play of thoughts, of gushing streams—these are the skips and jumps of a giant from mountain top to mountain top. But try to slake your thirst at this spring, incline your parched lips towards the water, and all you find is froth and foam, which can be neither drunk nor caught in a vessel: it simply fizzles, sputters, and slips away.

If we do not lower our eyes in front of Nietzsche, if we are able to endure the terror of his images, an unexpected, refreshing breeze, velvety and caressing, sad and soft, wafts over us with a timid hope.

The roar of chaos settles into the velvet of pleasing song. What previously had terrified us, threatened to scorch us with fire, shower us with debris, and inundate us with lava, now appears as merely a passing storm. Only the silent sheets of lightning,

> Like demons deaf and dumb
> Carry on a conversation with each other.[9]

Three ideas dominate Nietzsche's philosophy: the relativity of the moral law, the superman, and the eternal recurrence.

In every religion, the moral law appears not as an end in itself, but rather as the means for attaining an end, namely eternal values. To fulfill the moral law is to behave in such a fashion as to clear for oneself and for others the path (that is, morality) leading to this end (deification of the person). At the summit of the law stands paradise. Paradise contains both the law in all its plenitude and something above the law. This is the point of contact between any morality and the religious symbolism that governs morality. There is no such thing as a single morality: there are only *moralities* that are subordinated to higher principles. In Christianity, morality outside of Christ means nothing, since Christ embodies morality. "For the law," says the Apostle Paul, "having a shadow of good things to come, and not the very image of the things, can never with those sacrifices which they offered year by year continually make the comers thereunto perfect" [Heb. 10:1]. "But when the fulness of the time was come, God sent forth his Son" [Gal. 4:4]. "But before faith came, we were kept under the law, shut up unto the faith which should afterwards be revealed. Wherefore the law was our schoolmaster to bring us unto Christ, that we might be justified by faith. But after that faith is come, we are no longer under a schoolmaster" [Gal. 3:23–25]. "Now are we the sons of God," says the Apostle John, "and it doth not yet appear what we shall be: but we know that, when he shall appear, we shall be like him; for we shall see him as he is. And every man that hath this hope in him purifieth himself, even as he is pure" [1 John 3:2–3]. "To him that overcometh," says the Lord, "will I grant to sit with me in my throne, even as I also overcame, and am set down with my Father in his throne" [Rev. 3:21]. Every morality, given a full awareness of man's dual nature, is ultimately grounded in phenomenality. It cannot extend to the very end of our path towards God, where Christ's freedom is absolute. In Christianity the source of morality is Christ Himself, and everything is defined in relation to Him. In Nietzscheanism it is the superman. Christ *was*, therefore we possess a criterion of morality. The superman *will be*, therefore what will favor his appearance is moral. This is the source of Nietzsche's split with Christianity. Nietzsche's morality has its peculiarities, but it is a morality nonetheless, for, by the very fact of its reappraisal of values, it presupposes the existence of those values. In fact, it is a path towards them. Both the Christian and the Nietzschean morality stand in opposition to theories of morality in its own right, which omit God and this path.

A critique of Nietzschean morality inevitably leads the problem of moral values into a comparison between the figure Christ and that of the superman. This question can only plunge us into a bottomless pit of cavils concerning various psychological, mystical, and dogmatic details. And this is where we begin to see that secrecy that surrounds every mystical system—a secrecy predicated on a certain propensity towards, and predilection for, mystico-psychological methods of investigation.

If we reject every idea that has occurred through the ages concerning the repetition of existence, if we dismiss that completely peculiar feeling that seizes us when we contemplate phenomena that appear to have occurred before at some time, then all arguments in support of the idea of Eternal Recurrence are for naught: there are none. It is another matter altogether, however, if we examine the idea of Eternal Recurrence and the idea of irrevocable passage as two different sides of our being, two different ideas concerning our existence and having equal rights on our psyche.

It is fitting that, if irrevocable passage may be symbolized by a straight line, the Eternal Recurrence should be symbolized by a circle, the "ring of recurrence."[10] The straight line and the circle come together in the ellipse. Furthermore, the path of a point traveling along a straight line or along a circle is infinite, especially if the radius of the circle is equal to infinity. A straight line is the same thing as the circumference of a circle whose radius is infinite. But it is the *spiral* that truly gives us the combination of the straight line and the circle. If something can be symbolized by a straight line, it can also undoubtedly be symbolized by a spiral. If we analyze movement along a spiral of a larger order, we observe that such movement is circular but also defined by a straight line. Now if we conceive of this straight line as a spiral of a smaller order, then this spiral, too, may be analyzed into a straight line and a circle. Extending this process to infinity, we obtain a graphic depiction of both a straight line and a series of circles strung one on top of the other. Can we not see the same thing in this diagram as provoked the irrepressible cry from Nietzsche: "Oh, how should I not yearn for Eternity and for the nuptial Ring of Rings—the Ring of Recurrence!"[11]

Shestov[12] has eloquently called attention to the inexpressibility of everything in Nietzsche concerning the idea of Eternal Recurrence, for the Eternal Recurrence is an ideal symbol, a focal point towards which the rays of Nietzscheanism converge. Any explanation of this idea is nothing more than a bridge leading to an immediate fascination by it. Shestov has also shown that the emphasis should lie on the concept of eternity, not on that of recurrence. The Eternal Recurrence in this light, then, is the recurrence of Eternity, of those ages about which Maeterlinck says: "In a distant era in the history of India the soul must have approached the surface of life [to a degree that it has never attained since]. . . . A time will come perhaps when our souls will perceive each other without the mediation of our senses."[13] In the spiral journey of the soul through time there are periods of proximity to the surface, that is, a periodic recurrence of Eternity. This is the "day of great noon" of which the Apostle Paul says, "But when the fulness of the time was come, God sent forth his Son" [Gal. 4:4].

All three of Nietzsche's ideas, or symbols, unwittingly touch on religious, mystical questions. The confusion in Nietzsche surrounding methods of cognition prevented him from seeing where his bridge from critical philosophy would lead him. He simply remained standing in the middle of the bridge, at an equal distance from critical philosophy and the shadowy contours of the shores of the promised land: the isles of children in the midst of the azure.

When Nietzsche looked at religious truth he did so through the prism of distance. Distance can alter truth and create in its place a phantasmagoria. But Nietzsche rose up against this phantasmagoria. He took religion for something that in fact had overshadowed it. He abandoned the eternal truths only to arrive back at them later: having described a circle, he simply came upon them from the other side. The course he followed was the inverse of the one that theosophy follows. Having rejected the eternal, blue temple, he arrived at the blue temple of Eternity. In fact, he even unwittingly strengthened the foundation beneath it. Having undermined all the old dogmas, he simply set out to create new ones. In Nietzsche's unfinished labor, the sharp eye eventually begins to see the same contours over and over. In the very depths of the old dogmas there is an infinity of new features that are gradually revealed to "these little ones."[14] It is written in Revelation, "Behold, I make all things new" [Rev. 21 : 5]. "To him that overcometh will I give to eat of the hidden manna, and will give him a white stone, and in the stone a new name written, which no man knoweth saving he that receiveth it" [Rev. 2 : 17]. Nietzsche wanted to taste of the hidden manna and call out the new name. For this purpose he separated himself from everything. In fact, he was able to create only to the extent that he separated himself from the common, philistine banality that surrounded him. But he was never able to discern the eternal truth behind the layer of dust. Only in accepting that truth may we come close to the hidden name. Nietzsche, however, never called out the hidden name.

Religious dogmas have a way of fixing those experiences that bear the character of revealed truth. Christianity has assembled within itself all that is most significant in these experiences. Christianity is thus a material, not just a formal, synthesis. European culture, once having taken this valued fruit, has often been incapable of comprehending the boundlessness of Christianity's symbols. It became necessary either to disavow Christ or else to pervert religious understanding itself. And many of those who sought to disavow their own lack of understanding ended up by disavowing the truth itself. This is where the error lay, but it is also where great strength lay.

One would have expected a material change to have occurred in our attitude towards religious questions. A fruitful period of development in European culture began at the moment of return to paganism, that is, at the beginning of the Renaissance. And yet this same culture, once it had come to naught, began to turn its gaze to the East. And so the doubt remains: either religion is incapable of satisfying mankind, and a turn towards religion is simply an indication of despair, or else serious errors have crept into our understanding of religious truths.

Vladimir Solov'ev had a special term to define the union of the summits of symbolism in art with mysticism: he called it "theurgy." For the Lord says, "I will dwell in them, and walk in them; and I will be their God" [2 Cor. 6 : 16]. Theurgy is what raised up the prophets and put into their mouths the word "that breaketh the rock in pieces."[15]

Nietzsche's wisdom at his most profound level of understanding, that is, at the level comparable to that of tragedy, may be defined as a striving towards theurgy. Certain aspects of this wisdom, in fact, betray a certain theurgism. If we can see in symbolism an initial attempt to manifest the eternal in the temporal, then in theurgy we can see the beginning of the end of symbolism. For here one hears of the incarnation of Eternity through the transfiguration of the resurrected person. The person is the temple of God in which God dwells: "I will dwell in them, and walk in them" [2 Cor. 6:16].[16]

Schopenhauer rejected all the dogmatism of Christianity, whereas Nietzsche rejected the worldly art of living. The Christian theurgists—who assert the notion of the *person* as a vessel containing the Godhead and the notion of dogma as a circle traced from the outside and containing an endless path, who refuse to sever their ties with Nietzscheanism, though striving all the while to overcome Nietzsche *from within* as Nietzsche overcame Schopenhauer—continue to hope for the imminent approach of the new glad tidings, an indication of which may be found in the Scriptures. The solution to the great mysteries of being is thus relegated to the yonder side of Nietzscheanism. The land mine finds itself sitting on top of a counter mine. But even here there is terror, enough to take one's breath away. For right behind Nietzsche there is a precipice, and, aware of the hopelessness of continuing to stand on the brink, aware also of the impossibility of returning to the lowlands of thought, one finds oneself hoping for the miracle of flight. Before flying machines had been improved, flight was an extremely dangerous affair. It was not long ago that Lilienthal, the famed aeronaut, died.[17] It was not long ago that we saw the unsuccessful flight (unsuccessful in the eyes of many, at any rate) and death of another aeronaut: Nietzsche, that Lilienthal of all culture. The theurgists' conception of Christianity has always been unwittingly striking. For either it is a final act of cowardice before crossing the boundary to fearlessness—a true leap (since only a goat made of stone will jump into the abyss)—or it shows the prophetic boldness of neophytes who are confident that, at the moment they begin their fall, wings of salvation will sprout to carry mankind up above history. The task of the theurgists is quite complex. They must soar through the air in places where Nietzsche had stopped. At the same time, however, they must take into account the theosophical interpretation of the great questions of being while avoiding any split with the historical church. When this task is accomplished perhaps the horizons of Nietzsche's visions, the ones that he himself was unable to reach, will come together. For Nietzsche simply bore too heavy a burden in the face of it all. His path was far too long. In the end, all he was able to do was to arrive, weary and exhausted, at the shore of the sea and, in a beatific stupor, contemplate the glowing reflections of the clouds as they moved by in a twilight flood of radiant emeralds. He could see the sunset only in a reverie, where it looked like boats of fiery gold in which one must float:

> Oh my soul, over-ripe and heavily laden art thou,
> a vine with swollen udders and brown-gold grapes
> full to bursting:
> full to bursting and weighed down with thine
> happiness. . . .
> See, I smile myself . . .
> until the boat, the golden wonder, shall glide
> over still, yearning seas.[18]

Did Nietzsche float on the wine-dark sea? He no longer appears on our horizon. Our bonds with him have been sundered. But we, too, stand now on the shore, and the golden boat rocks and splashes at our feet. We must climb in and float away. We must drift into the azure and sink.

There are some among us whose gaze is turned to the past, where the ancient gold blazes in the name of torrents of sunlight. In their eyes is the fleeing sun, and they weep, perhaps for the burning gold.

> The ether will light up with gold,
> and burn brightly with passion.
> And over the sea there settles
> a fleeting shield of sunlight.
>
> And on the sea
> golden fire-tongues from the sun tremble.
> Everywhere is the sheen of golden pistoles
> in the midst of the sea's mournful splashing.
>
> Cliffs rose up like breasts
> in the quivering sunlight-cloth.
> The sun set. The cry of albatrosses
> was filled with sobbing:
>
> "Children of the sun, once again the chill of impassivity!
> It has set—
> the golden, ancient bliss—
> the golden fleece!"

Others, showing their endless faith in the miracle of flight, might answer:

> The Argonauts summon their guests
> to a sun feast,
> trumpeting the sound into the gold-glowing world.
> Hark! Hark!
> Enough suffering!
> Don your sun-fashioned
> armor!
>
> All the sky is clothed in rubies.
> The sun's sphere has gone to rest.
> All the sky is clothed in rubies
> above us.
> Up on the mountain tops
> our Argo,
> our Argo,
> Preparing to fly,
> has begun to beat its golden wings.[19]

1903

THE MAGIC OF WORDS

1

Language is the most powerful instrument of creation. When I name an object with a word I thereby assert its existence. Every act of cognition [*poznanie*] arises from a name.[1] Cognition is impossible without words. The process of cognizing [*poznavanie*] is the establishing of relations between words, which only subsequently are related to objects corresponding to them. Grammatical forms, responsible for the very possibility of the sentence, are themselves possible only where there are words: only then can the logical articulation of speech be fully accomplished. When I assert that creation precedes cognition, I am asserting the primacy of creation, not only because creation is epistemologically superior, but also because it is prior in actual genetic sequence.

Imaginal speech consists of words that express the logically inexpressible impression I derive from the objects surrounding me.[2] Living speech is always the music of the inexpressible. "The thought, once spoken, is a lie," said Tyutchev, and he was right, assuming that by "thought" he meant something that can be expressed through a series of terminological concepts.[3] But the living, spoken word is not a lie. It is the expression of the innermost essence of my nature, and, to the degree that my nature is the same thing as nature in general, the word is the expression of the innermost secrets of nature. Every word is a sound. The flux of spatial and causal relations outside me first becomes intelligible to me by means of the word. If words did not exist, then neither would the world itself.

My ego, once detached from its surroundings, ceases to exist. By the same token, the world, if detached from me, also ceases to exist. "I" and the "world" arise only in the process of their union in sound. Supra-individual consciousness and supra-individual nature first meet and become joined in the process of naming. Thus consciousness, nature, and the world emerge for the cognizing subject only when he is able to create a designation. Outside of speech there is neither nature, world, nor cognizing subject. In the word is given the original act of creation. The word connects the speechless, invisible world swarming in the subconscious depths of my individual consciousness with the speechless, senseless world swarming outside my individual ego. The word creates a new, third world: a world of sound symbols by means of which both the secrets of a world located outside me and those imprisoned in a world inside me come to light. The outside world spills over into my soul. The inside world spills out of me into the break of day and the setting sun, into the rustling of trees. In the word and only in the word do I recreate for myself what surrounds me from within and from without, for I *am* the word and only the word.

But the word is a symbol. It is the intelligible union of two unintelligible essences: space, which is accessible to my vision, and that inner sense vibrating mutely inside me that I provisionally (formally) call time. In the word, two analogies are created simultaneously: time is represented as an external phenomenon—sound—and space too is represented as the very same external phenomenon—sound. But the *sound of space* is already an internal recreation of space. Sound unites space and time, but in such a way that it reduces spatial to temporal relations. This newly created relation liberates me, in a certain sense, from the power of space. Sound is the objectivization of time and space. But every *word* is a *sound* before it is anything else. The original victory of consciousness lies in the creation of sound symbols. For in sound there is recreated a new world within whose boundaries I feel myself to be the creator of reality. Then I begin to name objects, that is, to create them a second time for myself. In attempting to name everything that enters my field of vision, I am in essence defending myself against the hostile, unintelligible world that presses in on me from all sides. It is the sound of the word that enables me to subdue the elements. The process of naming spatial and temporal phenomena with words is a process of invocation. Every word is a charm. By charming a given phenomenon I am in essence subjugating it. Thus connections between words, grammatical forms, and figures of speech are in essence charms. By calling the frightening sound of thunder *grom* [thunder], I am creating a sound that imitates thunder (*grrr*). And by creating this sound, it is as if I were beginning to recreate thunder itself. This process of recreation is at the same time an act of cognition. What I am essentially doing is invoking thunder.

The combination of words, the sequence of sounds through time is necessarily a form of causality. Causality is the union of space and time. Sound is at once a symbol of spatiality and a symbol of temporality. It is in this sense that sound, which is externally determined, combines space and time. The utterance of a sound requires a moment of time. Sound invariably must resonate in a *medium,* since it is itself a *vibrating medium.* In sound, space and time come together, and this is why sound is the root of all causality. The connections between sound emblems invariably imitate those between phenomena in space and time.

The word thus always gives rise to causality. It creates causal relations, which are cognized only subsequently.

In the initial stages of mankind's development a causal explanation of something would simply have been the creation of words. A wise man, then, was simply one who knew more words than the others, one who spoke more, and who consequently invoked. It is no accident that magic recognizes the power of the word as it does. For living speech itself is unbroken magic. With a successfully created word I can penetrate far more deeply into the essence of phenomena than I can through the process of analytic thought. All I can do with thought is distinguish a phenomenon, whereas with the word I can subjugate, subdue a phenomenon. The creation of living speech is always a struggle between man and the hostile elements surrounding him. The word ignites the gloom surrounding me with the light of victory.

This is why living speech is the very condition of existence of mankind itself. It is the quintessence of mankind. This is why, in the beginning, poetry, the process of cognizing, music, and speech were all one and the same. This is also why living speech was magic, and people using it were creatures who bore the imprint of communion with divinity itself. It is no coincidence that so many ancient traditions refer to the existence of a magic language whose words were able to subjugate and subdue nature. Nor is it a coincidence that every one of the sacred hieroglyphs of ancient Egypt had a triple meaning: the first meaning went with the sound of the word, and the sound gave a designation to the hieroglyphic image (time); the second meaning went with the spatial inscription of the sound (the image), that is, with the hieroglyph itself; the third meaning was contained in a sacred number symbolizing the word. Fabre d'Olivet is successfully attempting to decipher the symbolic meaning of the designation of the Jewish divinity.[4] It is undoubtedly no coincidence that one hears the myth of a certain sacred dialect called *Senzar*, in which all the highest revelations were given to mankind.[5] The natural deductions as well as the myths of a language express, independently of the degree of their objectivity, an involuntary tendency to symbolize the magic power of the word.

Potebnya and Afanas'ev cite a number of curious instances of popular lore where the course of thinking is conditioned by the sound of words.[6] For example, May 11 marks the founding of Constantinople [*Tsar' grad*]. In the popular mind the conception arose that one must not work in the fields on this day, "lest Czar Hail [*Tsar' grad*] beat down the grain."[7] On June 16, which is Saint Tikhon's Day, "The sun goes more quietly [*tiše*, comparative of *tixij*], and the songbirds quiet down [*zatixajut*]" (Dahl).[8] On November 1, [Saint] Koz'ma with a nail shackles [*zakuet*] (the frost) (Dahl). February 2 is Candlemas [*Sretenie*], when winter and summer meet [*vstretilis'*] (Dahl). "Vladimir founded a city on this river bank, and called it Pereyaslavl', because this youth had won glory [*pereja slavu*] there."[9]

Mankind's purpose lies in the living creation of life. The life of mankind presupposes a form of communication among individuals.[10] But communication of this sort exists in the word and only in the word. Every act of communication is a living, creative process, where souls exchange secret images that depict and create the mysteries of life. The aim of communication is to kindle, through contact made between two inner worlds, a third world that is indivisible for those communicating and that unexpectedly deepens the individual images of the soul. In order for this to happen, the word through which communication takes place must not be an abstract concept. For the abstract concept is something that, in a determined fashion, crystallizes already past acts of cognition. But the goal of mankind is to create its own objects of cognition. The goal of communication is to kindle the signs of communication (words) with the fires of ever newer processes of creation. The goal of living communication is a striving towards the future. This is why abstract words, when they become signs of communication, cause communication between people to revert to something that has already existed in the past. When we hear living, imaginal speech, on the other hand, it kindles our imagination with the fire of new creations, that is, with the fires of new word constructions. And a new word construction is always the beginning of the acquisition of new acts of cognition.

Poetic speech is speech in the true sense of the word. Its tremendous significance lies in the fact that it does not actually prove or demonstrate anything with words. In poetry the words are grouped in such a fashion that their totality gives the image. The logical significance of this image is entirely indeterminate, as is its visual clarity. Instead, we ourselves must suffuse living speech with cognition and creation. The perception of living, imaginal speech impels us towards creation. In every truly living man this speech inspires a whole range of activities. The poetic image can be successfully created by anyone. Imaginal speech engenders images. Every man becomes something of an artist in hearing a living word. The living word (a metaphor, a simile, an epithet) is a seed that germinates in the souls of men. The seed contains the promise of thousands of flowers. In one person it sprouts forth as a white rose; in another, as a blue cornflower. The meaning of living speech does not lie in its logical significance, for logic itself is a creation of speech. It is no accident that a condition sine qua non of logical assertions is the [implicit] creative command to consider them logical assertions for specific ends. But these ends by no means cover all the ends of language as an instrument of communication. The most important purpose of speech is to create new images, to infuse people's souls with their glittering splendor in order that this splendor may cover the entire world. The evolution of language is certainly not a process whereby words are emptied of all imaginal content. It is a word thus emptied that becomes an abstract concept. The abstract concept represents for man the end of the process of subjugating nature. It is in this sense that mankind, at certain stages in its development, erects monuments of cognition out of living speech. There is another requirement that makes its presence felt in creation. The seed-word, having departed into the depths of the unconscious, swells and bursts its dry casing (the concept), sending forth a new shoot. This animation of the word represents a new organic period in a culture. The feeble old men of yesterday's culture, under the sway of new words, abandon their temples and go out into the woods and the fields, so that they may charm nature anew and prepare her for new conquests. The word sheds its concept-casing and then sparkles and glitters with a virgin, barbaric display of colors.

Such epochs are accompanied by an incursion of poetry into the domain of terminology and of the spirit of music into poetry. The musical force of sound is resurrected in the word, as we are once again captivated, not by the meaning, but by the sound of words. In this state of enthusiasm we unconsciously sense that the deepest vital meaning of the word—namely, to be a *creative* word—lies hidden in the sound and image level of expression. The creative word creates the world.

The creative word is the word made flesh (the word is flesh), and in this sense is real. Its symbol is the living flesh of man. The word-*term* is merely a skeleton. Now no one will deny the importance of the field of osteology (the study of bones). From the practical standpoint the study of osteology is indispensable in our lives. A knowledge of anatomy is above all one of the preconditions for treating illnesses (since it is necessary to be able to correct humps and set dislocations). At the same time, though, no one will pretend that the skeleton is the central axis of culture. By assigning the terminological meaning of a word a position of primary importance, instead of an accessory, ancillary position, we are killing speech, that is, the living word. In the living word there is an uninterrupted exercise of the creative forces of language. By creating sound images and then combining them, we are in essence exercising certain forces. It might well be said that such exercise is a form of play, for is not play the same thing as exercise in creation? All the concrete diversity of forms has its source in play. Play is the very instinct of life. It is in sportive play that the muscles are exercised and strengthened, for armed struggle requires this when one encounters the enemy. The creative force of the spirit is exercised and strengthened in living speech, since this, too, is required in moments of peril that threaten mankind. This is why the exercise of the spirit as it appears in the sound combinations of words is so enormously important, ridiculous though it may seem to the undeveloped ear. For it is precisely by creating words, by using sounds to assign names to phenomena unknown to us, that we subjugate, captivate these phenomena. All of life is contained in the living force of speech. Outside of speech we have no direct signs for communication. All other signs (even living gestures or abstract emblems) are merely accessory, auxiliary methods to speech. Next to living speech they are nothing. Living speech is an eternally flowing, creating activity, always raising up great numbers of images and myths before our eyes. Our consciousness finds strength and confidence in these images. They are the weapons with which we penetrate the darkness. But once the darkness is conquered, the images decompose and the poetry of words vanishes. At that moment we already begin to identify words as abstract concepts, but this is not to convince us of the idleness of the images of language: we decompose living speech into concepts in order to tear concepts away from life, crush them into thousands of weighty tomes, lock them up in the dust of archives and libraries. This is the point where life in all its vitality, deprived of living words, becomes madness and chaos for us. Space and time begin once again to threaten us. New clouds of the unknown sail up to the horizon of the familiar and menace us with fire and lightning, inciting men to strife and threatening to wipe the human race from the face of the earth. Then the age of so-called degeneracy sets in. Man begins to see that all his terminological distinctions have failed to save him. Blinded by the oncoming doom, man in his terror begins to conjure the unknown dangers by means of the word. To his own astonishment he sees that only the word holds the true means of conjuration. And now, from under the crust of eroded words, a luminous torrent of new verbal meanings begins to emerge. New words are created. The period of degeneracy gives way to a period of healthy barbarism. The cause of degeneracy had been the death of the living word. Now the struggle with degeneracy is carried out in the creation of new words. In all periods of cultural decline the ensuing revival has been accompanied by a particular cult of words. The cult of words has always preceded the revival. The cult of words is the active cause of new creation. Limited minds have invariably confused the cause with the effect. The cause (the death of the living word) that provoked the effect (the opposition to death in the cult of words) is what is always confused with the effect itself. The creative cult of the word has invariably been linked to the revival. But the reverse is true: revival is the *consequence* of the extinction of the word. The cult of the word is the dawn of revival.

The word-term is like a beautiful but dead crystal, formed by the completed process of decomposition of the living word. The living word (the word-flesh) is a blossoming organism.

Everything that is palpable to my sense organs will decompose when I die. My body will become putrid carrion, giving off a foul stench. But once the process of decomposition is finished, I will appear before the gaze of my loved ones as a collection of beautiful crystals. The ideal term is an eternal crystal that appears only at the end of a process of decomposition. The word-image is like a living human being: it creates, influences, and alters its own content. The common prosaic word, that is, the word that has lost all its sound and pictorial imagery, but that has still not become an ideal term either, is a fetid, decomposing corpse.

Ideal terms are few, as are living words. Our entire life is filled with decaying words, giving off an unbearable stench. The use of these words infects us with a kind of ptomaine, because the [true living] word is the direct expression of life.

This is why the unity to which our vitality binds us is none other than the creation of words. We must exercise our force in the combination of words. Thus do we forge arms for the struggle with living corpses that worm their way into the circle of our activity. We must be barbarians, hangmen of the everyday word if it has become too late to breathe life into it. The word-term is another matter. For the word-term does not present itself as living. It simply is what it is. It cannot be called back to life. But it is harmless: it is as if the ptomaine itself had decomposed in the ideal term to such an extent that it can no longer infect anyone.

But the putrid word that is half-image and half-term, neither entirely one nor entirely the other, is still another matter. It is rotting carrion that pretends to be living. Like a werewolf, it steals into the everyday affairs of our life in order to weaken the force of our creation with slander, as though this creation were no more than an empty combination of words. It strives to weaken the force of our cognition with slander, as though this cognition were nothing more than the empty nomenclature of terms. Perhaps those who assert that the imaginal properties of language are nothing more than the purposeless play of words are right, since we can perceive no palpable meaning in the selection of words, to the degree that the selection is governed purely by considerations of sound and meaning. The purposiveness of such a selection is truly a purposiveness without purpose.[11] What an odd coincidence that a thinker of genius like Kant, who so highly valued works of art, should have defined art in precisely these words when one of the finest music critics, Hanslick, defined music in almost exactly the same way.[12] Thus either Kant and Hanslick are madmen, or their words touch on some entirely real dimension of art. Purposiveness in art has no purpose within the bounds of art, since the purpose of art is rooted in the creation of objects of cognition themselves. Either life must be transformed into art, or art must be made living: only then is the meaning of art revealed and illuminated. If we consider poetry, for example, we can see that this statement is true in the sense that the purpose of poetry is the creation of language. And *language*, it must be borne in mind, is the creation of living relations. The play of words is thus purposeless only so long as we regard matters from a purely aesthetic point of view. But once we recognize that aesthetics is merely a single facet refracting life's creation in its own peculiar way and that, outside of this creation, it plays no role whatever in and of itself, then the "purposeless" play of words begins to appear full of meaning: the combining of words without regard for their logical meanings is the means by which man defends himself against the encroachment of the unknown. Armed with the shield of words, man recreates everything he sees, and, like a warrior, invades the territory of the unknown. And if he conquers, his words thunder, flare up with the sparks of great constellations, shroud his listeners with the darkness of interplanetary space, hurl them onto some unknown planet where rainbows flash, brooks babble, and the colossal forms of cities rise up. And in these cities the listeners find themselves driven, as if in a dream, into a quadrangular space called a room, where they dream that someone is speaking to them. They think that the word of the speaker is actually issuing from the speaker. And this is indeed true. If this is the way things appear to these listeners, then the magic of words has been created, and an illusion of cognition has begun to operate. Then it begins to appear that a certain meaning lies concealed behind the words, that cognition is now separable from the word. At the same time, however, the whole dream of cognition is created by the word. The cognizing subject always speaks either outwardly or mentally. Every act of cognition is an illusion following from the word: word combinations and sound analogies (for example, substituting time for space, or space for time) already have their source in the imaginal forms of speech. And if speech did not take shape in the form of metaphors, metonymies, and synecdoches, then Kant's theory of the Schematism of the Pure Concepts of Understanding could not exist, since this is not really a *theory* or any content of cognition, but a mere verbal exposition and nothing more.[13] He who speaks, creates. If he speaks with confidence, then it begins to appear to him that he is cognizing something, while those to whom his words are directed presume that they are learning something. Strictly speaking, however, there are no pupils and no teachers, no cognizing subjects and no cognized object. For the cognizing subject is always the indeterminate roar of the inarticulate soul, and the cognized object is the opposing roar of the elements of life. Only verbal fireworks, as they occur on the boundary separating two chasms that are too wide to cross, create the illusion of cognition. But this cognition is not really cognition at all, but the creation of a new world in sound. Sound by itself is indivisible, omnipotent, inalterable. But choruses of sound that crisscross each other, the vague sonorous responses stirred up by memory—these are what begin to weave a veil of eternal illusion. We call that illusion cognition, but only as long as our cognition, having once decomposed the sounds into their smallest components, remains something other than a mute word or a mute mathematical sign.

Cognition thus becomes a mere nomenclature of mute and empty words. Mute, because they do not speak of anything; empty, because all content has been removed from them. The basic concepts of epistemology are like this, or, at any rate, this is what they strive to be. For they attempt to free themselves from any kind of psychism. But without psychism there is no sound, no word, no life, no creation. Cognition here becomes ignorance.[14]

In this openly avowed reduction of cognition to ignorance, as in the frank combination of sounds for their own sake, there is far more candor and honesty than in a cowardly adherence to words festering in decomposition, words that are neither openly imaginal nor openly florid. All science, unless it is openly mathematics or openly terminology, leads us into deception, degeneracy, lies. And all "living" speech, so long as it fails to revel in the verbal fireworks of sounds and images, is not living speech at all, but speech saturated with ptomaine.

Let it be said directly: there is no such thing as cognition in the sense of a *verbal* explanation of phenomena. This is why scientific discoveries that are fundamental in experimentation have their source in the creation of sound analogies that are brought to light and put into effect. What is an experiment? It always lies in an action that has a peculiar way of combining various conditions in nature. Take, for example, a magnet (the action) that has been inserted into a coil of electric wires (action). We will witness the phenomenon of electromagnetism (action). Now there are no *words* here. And yet it will be claimed that the phenomenon of electromagnetism is explicable through verbal means. And we will answer straightaway that it is *not*. For the sphere of explanation is the sphere of construction of verbal analogies. The verbal explanation of an experiment becomes an explanation through the use of formulae, and a formula is already a kind of gesture, a mute emblem. The explanation of formulae by means of words is an explanation based on analogies, and an analogy is not the same thing as cognition.

And conversely, even if one can demonstrate the provenance of experiment from the word, that is still not the same thing as demonstrating the provenance of exact science from abstract concepts. Every living word is the magic of conjuration. No one can prove the untenability of assuming that a first experiment engendered by the word actually engenders, or conjures, by means of the word, a phenomenon that has never occurred before. The word engenders action. Action is a continuation of a mythical construction.

The worlds of abstract concepts, like the worlds of essences, whatever one chooses to call these essences (matter, spirit, nature), are not real worlds. They do not even exist without the word. The word is the sole real vessel on which we sail from one unknown to another—amidst unknown spaces (called "earth," "heaven," "ether," "void," and so forth) and amidst unknown temporalities (called "gods," "demons," "souls"). We do not know what matter, earth, heaven, air are. We do not know what god, demon, soul are. There is something that we call "I," "you," "he." But in naming unknown things with words we are creating ourselves and the world. A word is a conjuration of things. It is a summoning, an invocation of God. When I say "I," I create a sound symbol. I assert this symbol as something existing. And only at that moment do I create myself.

Every act of cognition is a firework display of words with which I fill the void surrounding me. If my words sparkle with colors, then they create the illusion of light. This illusion of light is also cognition. No one persuades anyone. No one can prove anything to anyone. Every argument is a battle of words, is magic. When I speak I do so only for the purpose of casting a spell. Parrying with words, something that gives the appearance of being a dispute, is nothing more than filling a void for the mere sake of filling a void. It is an accepted practice to stop the mouth of one's opponent in such cases with putrid words. But this is not the same thing as persuading him. For all the putrid words do is sicken the opponent when he returns home after the argument. In the beginning the void was kindled with the fires of images. This was the process of mythical creation. The word begot the image symbol—the metaphor. The metaphor appeared as something actually existing. The word begot myth; myth begot religion; religion begot philosophy; and philosophy begot the term.

It is better to fire rockets made of words aimlessly into the void than to fill the void with dust. The primary thing is the action of living speech. Second is the action of dead speech. We often give preference to the second. When we do, we are half-dead and half-alive.

2

The whole process of creative symbolization is already contained within the means of representation inherent in every language. In language, as in the activity of life, the means of representation is an organic principle. The means of representation has a direct influence on the formation of grammatical forms. For instance, the process by which an *epitheton ornans* becomes an adjective is imperceptible. Every adjective is, in a certain sense, an epithet. And every epithet is close to one essentially more complex form or another (metaphor, metonymy, synecdoche). Potebnya has demonstrated, and not without justification, that every epithet (*ornans*) is at the same time a synecdoche. On the other hand, he points out cases where the synecdoche also conceals a metonymy. In metonymy we can already see a tendency to create cognition itself. The contents of many of the mutual causal relationships we establish have their source initially in certain metonymic combinations of images (as for instance where space becomes time and time becomes space, or where the meaning of the metonymic image consists in having the cause contained in the effect, or the effect in the cause). Aristotle, on the other hand, regards synecdoche and metonymy as special cases of metaphor.

Potebnya evinces a whole series of typical cases of mental deduction as it occurs in metaphors, metonymies, and synecdoches. I will cite several of these cases (taken from his *Notes on the Theory of Literature*).[15]

In the sphere of metaphor: (1) *a* is similar to *b*. Consequently, *a* is the cause of *b*. Example: *ringing* is a phenomenon of *hearing*. Hence, a ringing in the ears of an absent person is the consequence of a conversation about him. A whistling sound is associated with wind. Hence, a sorceress is able to incite the wind by whistling. (2) An image becomes the cause of a phenomenon. Example: pearls are similar to dew, consequently dew engenders pearls, and so forth. All mythical thinking is constituted under the influence of the creation of language. The image in myth can easily become the cause of an existing visual reality. From here the creation of language passes over into the domain of philosophy. This is the sense in which philosophy is an outgrowth, the ultimate dismemberment, of myth.

The various forms of representation are not distinguishable from one another but overlap considerably. Certain types, in fact, include a combination of many different forms. The epithet, for example, combines metaphor, metonymy, and synecdoche. At the same time, the broadest definition of a metaphor may include both synecdoche and metonymy. In the epithet, synecdoche combines both metaphor and metonymy within itself. And finally there is a good deal of overlapping between the simile and the metaphor. For example, the expression "a cloud is like a mountain" is a typical simile. The expression "heavenly mountain" (in reference to a cloud) is a typical metaphor. But in the expression "the cloud, mountainlike, floats across the sky," we have an overlapping between simile and metaphor. Simile and metaphor coincide in the words, "the cloud, mountainlike." In the following expressions we can see all the stages of transition from epithet, through simile, to metaphor: "terrible eyes," "eyes, like terror," "eyes, terrorlike," "terror in the eyes (instead of in the look)." It is interesting thus to break down the various means of representation from the point of view of the psychological transition in time from the given object to its likeness in an image.

One thing is common among the various forms of representation: the tendency to expand the verbal presentation of the image in question, to make its boundaries unstable, to give rise to a new cycle of verbal creation, that is, to give the customary presentation an impetus in the word, to impart motion to its inner form. A change in the inner form of a word leads to the creation of a new content in an image. And thus full sway is given to our creative perception of reality. An expansion like this can occur even in a case where, from the formal standpoint, we seem to be dealing with the simple analysis of a notion concerning an object. When we say, for example, "the moon is white," we are attributing to the moon one of a number of aspects: the moon can also be gold, red, full, pointed, and so forth. Thus we can decompose the moon into a series of different qualities, but we must not forget that this decomposition of the concept of the moon, seen as a complex of aspects, is only the beginning of the process. For it is as though we were fusing the concept of the moon in order to unite each element of the complex with the fused complexes of various other concepts through just one, two, or perhaps many aspects. Analysis here is thus predetermined by a need for synthesis. By singling out from the many aspects of the moon its whiteness, we dwell on this particular one only because the direction of the creative process is established through it: having chosen the whiteness of the moon as a point of departure, we may group other aspects around this one. Observing that the moon is generally white in the evening when it is crescent-shaped, we define it by adding an additional epithet: *the white, pointed moon*. The concept of the moon is now narrowed, becomes concretized, and we now involuntarily compare the moon with any number of other white, pointed objects (a white horn, a white tusk, and so forth). What we are doing is joining two contrasting objects through just one or two of their aspects: (1) *a white, pointed horn* (belonging to some animal); and (2) the *white, pointed moon* (that is, a celestial object not belonging to an animal). We are thus comparing the moon with a horn: *the moon, like a white, pointed horn*. And thus the shift from epithet to simile is unavoidable. Simile is simply the next stage in the creation of images.

The simile, or comparison of objects through one or several aspects, leads us to a new stage. In the simile we introduce a compound complex of aspects into our field of vision. Thus we have before us two objects, two contending concepts. We saw earlier that there are three possible outcomes to this conflict between concepts, as indicated by Potebnya: *A* is fully contained in *X* (synecdoche); *A* is partially contained in *X* (metonymy); *A* and *X*, without coinciding directly, coincide through a third, *B* (metaphor). In all three cases either a transfer takes place from one awareness of an object to another—quantitative in the case of synecdoche and qualitative in the case of metonymy—or an exchange of the objects themselves (metaphor) occurs. As a result of the conflict, we derive another, double form of metaphor: namely, the epithetic form, where the concept of the compared object is dominant in the object with which the initial object (say, the moon) is being compared: *the white-horned moon*. The epithet "white-horned" is derived from the comparison between the whiteness of the moon and the whiteness of a horn. Compare the following diagram:

(*A*) Moon—(a_1) white, (a_2) pointed. (*B*) Horn—(b_1) white, (b_2) pointed. }	White-horned moon (a_1, b_2, *B*—*A*).

In the first half of the epithet (white-), two similar aspects of dissimilar complexes (moon, horn) are joined together. In the second half of the epithet (-horned), one complex of aspects (horn) becomes one of the aspects belonging to another object (moon). The epithet "white-horned" is by itself a synecdoche, since it identifies the species (white horn) with the genus (horn, which may be yellow, white, or black). But when we add to the epithet "white-horned" the name of an object, "moon," we obtain a metaphor, because the synecdochic epithet "white-horned" is combined with a representation of the moon, which is to say that it is now applied to a new object (instead of, say, "white-horned goat," we have "white-horned moon").

Or else we may obtain another type of metaphor: "The moon is a white horn," or "the white horn in the sky." Here the object with which several of the moon's qualities are being compared has actually supplanted the original object itself. Now the course that the formation of the new image follows may take two directions: either the representation of the white horn in the sky supplants both the traditional representation of a horn (as something belonging to a creature of the earth) and the traditional representation of the moon (that is, not as a mere part of a whole, but as the whole itself), and we obtain a symbol that can no more be "reduced" to the moon than to a horn; or the representation of the white horn in the sky assumes a different form: "the moon-white horn in the sky." The diagram looks like this:

(A) Moon—(a_1) white, (a_2) pointed.	}	Moon-white horn
(B) Horn—(b_1) white, (b_2) pointed.		(A, a_1, b_1,—B).

In the first half of the epithet (moon-) one complex of aspects (the moon) is applied as one of the aspects of the object in question (horn), while in the second half (-white) two similar aspects of dissimilar objects are linked together. The epithet "moon-white" is thus a synecdoche. "Moon-white horn," however, is simultaneously a metaphor and a metonymy (metonymy, because it is a moonlike horn). The *substitution* that posits the process of metaphorical assimilation referring to "horn" indicates (1) the determination of a genus through the species (horn through white horn) and (2) a qualitative distinction between objects (a moonlike horn is qualitatively distinct from any other kind of horn).

The process of depiction is exactly the same as it passes through different phases, appearing to us now as epithet, now as simile, now as synecdoche, now as metonymy, now as metaphor in the strict sense of the word.

Let us express diagrammatically the successive psychological phases of a transition from one set of forms to another:

Moon = A, horn = B; white = a_1 b_1; pointed = a_2 b_2.

Thus we have:

$A—a_1, a_2$
$B—b_1, b_2.$

Complex epithet:

$a_1\ a_2—A$ = white-pointed moon
$b_1\ b_2—B$ = white-pointed horn

Simile:

$A—\mathrm{a}_1\ B$ = moon, like a white horn
$B—B_1\ A$ = horn, like the white moon
But $a_1 = b_1$ (white = white)

Hence the metaphor:

$A = B$ moon—horn
$B = A$ horn—moon

A number of ancillary processes of word formation could be placed in between the simile and the metaphor (for instance, synecdoche and metonymy).

Synecdoche:

$a_1\ B—A$ = white-horned moon
$b_1\ A—B$ = white-moon horn

The last example qualifies also as metonymy.

Metonymy:

$b_1\ A—B$ = white-moon horn

Finally, with the epithetic form *AB* = moon-horned, we have all three forms at once: metaphor, metonymy, and synecdoche, depending on how the epithet is put. By itself the epithet "moon-horned" is a metaphorical epithet. But like any *epitheton ornans* it is also, in Potebnya's view, a synecdoche. Thus in saying "the moon-horned goat," we are not only relating the species (goat) to the genus (any horned animal), but also attributing to one member of that type a certain qualitatively new aspect, namely, by indicating not just that the goat in question is horned, but that his horn bears a certain resemblance to the "horns" of the moon.

From the pychological point of view, then, every word formation undergoes three stages in its development: (1) the epithet stage; (2) the simile stage, where the epithet calls forth a new object; and (3) the allusion (hint, symbolism) stage, where the conflict between two objects produces a new object not contained in either of the terms of the comparison. The allusion stage includes several phases, depending on whether the transfer of meaning occurs relative to quantity (synecdoche) or quality (metonymy), or whether there is an actual substitution of objects (metaphor). In the last case we have the case of the symbol, that is, an irreducible unity. In this sense the means of representation is truly the means of symbolization, that is, the primary creative activity irreducible by cognition.

The creation of a verbal metaphor (or symbol—that is, the combination of two objects in one) is the goal of the creative process. But no sooner has this goal been reached through the means of representation, no sooner has the symbol been created, than we find ourselves standing on the boundary between poetic creation and mythic creation. The independence of the new image *a* (the finished metaphor) from the images that engendered it (*b* and *c*, where *a* results from the transference of *b* to *c* or *c* to *b*) may be seen in the fact that creation endows it with ontological being independently of our consciousness. The whole process occurs like this: the goal (metaphor-symbol), having received being, turns into a real, active cause (cause from creation); thus the symbol becomes incarnation. It comes to life and acts autonomously: the white horn of the moon becomes the white horn of a mythical creature. Symbol becomes myth. The moon is now the external image of a celestial bull or goat that is kept secret from us. We see the horn of this mythical animal, but not the animal itself. Every process of artistic creation is in this sense mythological. Our consciousness has two possible ways of apprehending a "created legend." As Potebnya says: "Either . . . the image is considered objective, thus makes its way entirely into the meaning, and serves as the basis for further deductions concerning the properties of the designated object; or . . . the image is seen as a merely subjective means of transition to a meaning and does not serve as the basis for any further deductions."[16]

Mythical creation either precedes aesthetic creation (the conscious use of means of representation is possible only where myth is in a stage of dissolution) or follows it (in an era characterized by a breakdown of cognition, by general skepticism, by cultural decay), returning to life in mystical brotherhoods and unions, among people who have consciously lost faith in science, art, and philosophy but who still unconsciously conceal within themselves the living element of creation.

This is the kind of era in which we are now living. A religious world view is foreign to us. Philosophy has long since replaced religion, which was experienced in symbols and in the dogmas of metaphysical systems. Science put an end to religion from the other side. Instead of dogmatic assertions that God exists and the soul is immortal, science gives us mathematical emblems expressing the correspondences between natural phenomena in whose mystical essence we believed perhaps only yesterday, but in which we can no longer believe now that we are familiar with the laws of mechanics governing those phenomena.

Poetry is directly linked to the creation of language and obliquely linked to mythical creation. The strength of an image is directly proportional to one's faith (though perhaps not identified as such) in the existence of that image. When I say "the moon is a white horn," I am certainly not asserting in my consciousness the existence of a mythical animal whose horn, in the shape of the moon, I perceive in the sky. But in the deepest essence of my creative self-assertion I cannot help believing in the existence of some reality whose symbol, or representation, is the metaphorical image I created.

Poetic speech is directly linked to mythical creation. The tendency towards the imaginal combination of words is the fundamental trait of poetry.

The real force of creation cannot be measured by cognition. Cognition is always subsequent to creation. The tendency towards the combination of words, and consequently towards the creation of images from new word formations, is itself an indication that the root of the creative assertion of life is alive, regardless of whether consciousness sanctions this tendency or not. Such an assertion of the force of creation in words is a religious assertion. It is indifferent to consciousness.

This is why, in periods of general decay, the new word of life is nurtured in poetry. We revel in words because we recognize the meaning of new, magical words through whose use we will increasingly be able to conjure the gloom of night hanging over us. We are still alive, but we are alive because we hold on to words.

Playing with words is a sign of youth. From beneath the dust of the debris of a decaying culture we can thus invoke and conjure using the sounds of words. We know well that this is the one useful legacy we have to leave to our children.

Our children will forge a new symbol of faith out of luminescent words. The crisis of cognition will appear to them as merely the death of old words. Mankind is alive so long as the poetry of language exists. And the poetry of language is alive.

We are alive. 1909

THE EMBLEMATICS OF MEANING

PREMISES TO A THEORY OF SYMBOLISM

1

What does it mean to speak of an aesthetics of symbolism? What ideological justification is there for such an aesthetics?

Symbolist art of the last decades, considered from the point of view of form, is not fundamentally different from the methods of the great art familiar to us. In one case we encounter in recent trends a return to the forgotten forms of German romanticism. In another, the East rises up before us. In a third, we see before us the rise of altogether new techniques. But then on closer inspection these techniques turn out to be no more than a peculiar combination of older techniques, or simply a more studied application of them.

Nor does there appear to be anything new as far as the ideational content of symbolist art is concerned, in the majority of cases. Thus, for example, the peculiar ideology of Maeterlinck's dramas, their tendency towards the elusive, turns out to be simply the result of the author's study of the old mystics; one need only recall the influence of Ruysbroeck on Maeterlinck.[1] Or, to cite another example, the peculiar charm of Hamsun's pantheism is due, in essence, to a reworking of certain elements of Taoism into a realist world view.

Precisely when there seems to be a great proliferation of new forms of human concerns in contemporary art, it turns out that all we are seeing is some religious ideology that can scarcely be called new, or, as in the case of Nietzsche, an attempt to apply ancient wisdom in a practical way to a contemporary historical period. Nietzsche's teachings on the new man, on the future fate of Aryan culture, the appeal for the creation of an individual personality and the rejection of outmoded moral forms—all this can be found in the philosophical and religious movements of India, and these are as old as the world.

But it is precisely in this unwavering urge to make new combinations from the artistic methods of a variety of cultures, in this impulse to create a new outlook on reality through a reexamination of a whole series of forgotten world views that the entire strength, the futurity of the so-called new art lies. This is the source of the peculiar eclecticism of our era. I do not know whether Nietzsche was right in so completely condemning the Alexandrian period of ancient culture. Indeed, this period, intersecting so many different paths of thought and contemplation, appears to us even today as a firm base, when we gaze into the depths of past ages. By mixing Alexandrianism together with Socraticism into one big illness, one big, degenerate mass, Nietzsche was subjecting his own path of development to a cruel, Nietzschean judgment. For what Nietzsche himself created, and what we like so well in him, is neither more nor less than Alexandrianism. If he had not himself been an Alexandrian to the core he would never have been able to pronounce such prophetic words about Heraclitus, about the mysteries, about Wagner. Moreover, he would never have been able to write *Zarathustra*. In creating something new he always returned to the old.

The thing that is really new and captivating in symbolism is the attempt to illuminate the deepest contradictions in contemporary culture with the multicolored rays of a great variety of other cultures. It is as though we were reliving in our own age the entire past: India, Persia, Egypt, as well as Greece and the Middle Ages all rise up and pass before us, just as epochs closer to us pass before us. It is said that, at the important hours of a man's existence, his entire life passes before his spiritual gaze. Today the life of all mankind is passing before our eyes. From this we may conclude that an important hour has struck in the life of mankind. We have truly touched on something new, but we have found it in the old. For it is in the overwhelming abundance of the old that the newness of symbolism is to be found.

This is why the literary platform of symbolism attempts simply to summarize the individual declarations of artists on their work.

This is why the ideology of symbolism must be a very broad one.

The principles of symbolism must be able to create a firm philosophical system. Symbolism as a world view is indeed possible.

What are the prolegomena to such a world view? What is the creative meaning of such a concept?

2

It is customary to consider the exact sciences the basis for any positive information about reality. In the process of their development, the exact sciences arose from inexact sciences. Philosophy gave rise to natural science; Kabala and magic gave rise to mathematics; astronomy grew out of astrology; chemistry developed from alchemy. If we consider only exact knowledge to be knowledge, then the genesis of this knowledge presents a picture of its origin in ignorance. Ignorance gave rise to knowledge.

How did knowledge arise from ignorance?

It arose as a result of limiting the object of knowledge. Previously, the entire universe had been that object. Afterwards, however, the universe came to be examined from a single, clearly defined point of view. This point of view, then, gave rise to science and developed into a method.

Subsequently, as science split up and branched out, each distinct branch grew into an independent science. The scientific method of investigation split into many methods. The principles of each distinct science subsequently developed into an independent field. They now came to direct the course of development of the individual science. This is how the study of methodology arose. This is also how the individual systems of logic arose in the different sciences.

Until quite recently we still knew what a scientific world view was. A scientific world view appeared to be a synthesis of a great many positive areas of knowledge. At one time it appeared that materialism formed the basis of such a world view, but then it turned out that matter as such does not even exist: one science, namely physics, had completely overturned the scientific world view of its era. For a while a system of sciences was considered the basis of a scientific world view. Auguste Comte proposed one such system, and the system actually passed for scientific. But then the individual sciences developed independently of the scientific systems and world views, and one system after another simply crumbled. Later, an attempt was made to place at the center of the scientific world view the conclusions of just one of the individual sciences (chemistry, physics, mechanics). But then it was discovered that the results of a single science could by no means support a whole world view.

Thus, for instance, at one point some believed that energy, or work, was the essence of every living process. Even today we encounter philosophers who are faithful followers of the energy school. Philosophy, in their conception, can be reduced to energetics. But these attempts to give scientific foundation to a world view turned out to be a complete fiasco. The concept of energy may be defined only in relation to a field that links it to the concept of mechanical work. In a field like thermodynamics one cannot do without a clearly defined concept of energy. But once this same concept is carried outside the limits of its own science, it takes on a great many meanings and becomes completely unclear. For thermodynamics builds the concept of energy from a whole series of formulae and mechanical symbols that have been able to push back the horizons of one science, but that in no wise are capable of clarifying for us the problems of consciousness. And besides, the energy principle is defined exclusively by the formula $K + P =$ Constant, which is to say that P decreases for every increase in K in a closed system of forces.[2] If, then [in our effort to construct a philosophical system on the thermodynamic model] we were to recognize in energy the role of *substance*, so that the closed system of forces then corresponded to the universe, all we would be doing is substituting the concept "energy" for the concept "substance," but without clarifying it through our notion of universe, as [in thermodynamics the concept of energy is clarified] through the concept of a closed system of forces. We would thus be clarifying neither "universe" nor "force." And, what is more, in substituting "substance" for "energy" we are in essence giving the dynamic principle all the attributes of scholastic philosophy, which is exactly what the scientific world view of our day was supposed to replace.

It is clear, then, that a scientific world view is impossible in our day if by scientific world view we understand a world view derived from a given system in the natural sciences. The development of a given science leads to a centralizing of that science in a particular method. The principles of this method form a logic peculiar to that science. The language of this logic is such that it can explain all the phenomena of reality in the language of the science in question. But there are many separate sciences, and there are also as many explanations of reality as there are [scientific] methods. A scientific world view in essence is one in which the world is explained by means of a special image. Thus philosophy, considered a special science, has at various times been transformed into the history of philosophy, into sociology, psychology, and even thermodynamics, and this came about simply because at each of these various times the methods of one particular science were supplying the answers to all the questions about the meaning of life. Naturally these answers were, in the end, inseparable from the methods that gave rise to them, and each answer made sense only when examined in the sphere of the method in question. But the aggregate of all these answers proved contradictory. Thus some were saying, "There is no thought without phosphorus," and they were right in their own way, just as others, who said, "There is no phosphorus without thought" were right in *their* way. For such answers were purely relative, emblematic answers,[3] in which life itself had been replaced by a mere emblem, by a mere "concept of life." Nevertheless, these answers would catch on in a striking way. Not surprisingly, all this simply led from one crisis in world view to another. The most fantastic edifices of the "scientific world view" would rise up and suddenly crumble. From the ruins of materialism, for example, the icy peaks of Spencer's "synthetic philosophy" sprang up—and fell to pieces.[4]

The point is that science is incompatible with a world view. A world view today cannot have as its foundation an individual science or the conclusions of such a science. Nor can a world view have a *system* of exact sciences as its foundation. For such a world view today will only be built from a large aggregation of errors. And this is why in combining various conclusions of scientific knowledge I have no control whatsoever over the investigative paths that lead me to these conclusions. Every scientific discipline follows its own paths. As an example, if I were to use the physiological method in the field of psychology, I could not thus arrive at a result confirming the substantiality of the soul. This is not because the soul does not exist, but because, in applying the principles of physiological investigation, we have replaced the terms relating to spiritual processes with terms relating to physical processes. Energy appears as substance in a dynamic conception of the world, just as the soul does in an animistic conception. As a consequence, the question concerns the notion of substance. It is necessary, then, to find out the genetic origin of the basic concepts of each science. And furthermore one must look critically at the essence of the genetic method itself [that is, the method by which origins are traced] when this method pretends to be able to unify a certain group of sciences.

Only then will the energistic and the animistic interpretations of the processes of spiritual activity appear before us in a more accurate light.

The individual logics of the different sciences require a general logical foundation. But such a task places us in the area of theory of knowledge, and a theory of knowledge is the preface to any sort of world view.[5]

But all too often the aims of a theory of knowledge are understood only in the light of the individual logic of a particular science. Psychology, sociology, the natural sciences have all placed theory of knowledge in a position subordinate to their own logic. More than once in history the logic of one of the sciences has attempted to occupy the place of a logic of science in general. A logic of science cannot be identical to the logic of an individual science.

In subordinating the logic of a science to one of its methods, we inevitably get a one-sided view of a given object of knowledge. And in combining the results of many different methods and calling this combination "a scientific world view," all we get is a melange of concepts that merely smack of sagacity and plausibility. At the base of any genuine world view one must have a classification of the sciences according to their methods, not according to the results of their methods. What must serve as a basis for such a classification is the principle by which these methods are derived, and by which they come to be necessary and obligatory for all cases.

Thus the question of a scientific world view involves the derivation of one science from another. And epistemology may be just such an independent science.[6] But if the aim of epistemology is the discovery of universal and necessary forms of reason, a world view based on these ideas and connections will naturally go far beyond such a simple aim.

Indeed such a world view would be a universal and necessary metaphysics. In our day, theory of knowledge has never elaborated such a metaphysics, and for this reason it would be a comprehensive world view without any limitations on its competence. Below we will attempt to demonstrate that the very way in which a world view is perceived has acquired an unexpected form in the present age.

And if theory of knowledge is incapable of giving us a comprehensive world view, then we certainly cannot expect to find such a world view in science or in systems of sciences. The precepts of the scientific world views are, then, even in the best of cases, no more than utopian fantasies in the style of H. G. Wells or Flammarion.[7] They hint at or state a feeling, but they never speak in clear language.

The precision of science lies in groups of connections. Each group may be extended indefinitely, but there is a great abyss between it and the adjacent groups. All groups are stretched out in a single direction, forming as it were a row of parallel, nonintersecting lines. All the lines lie in one plane, and this plane represents causality. All the scientific-dogmatic resolutions to the problem of causality—where the concept of "cause" is simply replaced by some other concept, like energy, force, atom, will—are utterly ridiculous. For in such cases we explain the whole using just one of its parts. To say that "the cause" is force is like saying that a unit is equal to one-third of itself. Calling a melange of these limiting methodical concepts a scientific world view leads to the heteronomy of each limiting concept.[8] For if we examine these same limiting concepts in the process of their historical formation, we see that, on the one hand, newer and newer concepts are always being added to them. Yesterday's limit has ceased to be the limit, and instead, what had formerly been beyond the limit has now become the limit, both in science and in metaphysics. Some examples: molecule—atom—ion; gravity—force—work; the thing-in-itself—the self—the one—the will, and so on.[9] If, however, we consider these concepts to be derived from rational propositions (that is, premises of experience), then we are subordinating exact science to theory of knowledge.

The same aporia greets us in yet another connection. The plane of scientific concept formation is never intersected by the question of the meaning of such formation. [Our curiosity about] the meaning of life is constantly leading us to the formation of new words, and yet the formation of *scientific* terms is forever repulsing our urge to require that such concepts console us and explain the puzzles of our existence to us.

But this is precisely what the aim of a world view should be.

This is the reason that science is incompatible with the idea of a world view. Any forced union between science and a world view can only be offensive to science. And by the same token, such a union would offend our most hidden need to have a world view that we can both cherish and value.

Is a knowledge of mathematical, dynamic, and other emblems really the same thing as knowledge? Does such knowledge consist in nothing more than the ability to use these emblems in practice?

I am not at all certain whether one can generally call a science "knowledge." The meaning of knowledge has changed through history. The nature of this change is that knowledge has come to mean the capacity for establishing and using functional dependences, but is it possible to talk about the meaning of these dependences? It would be strange indeed to argue here about the meaning of functions, differentials, and integrals. "A differential is a differential": this is essentially the answer science gives us. Science simply refuses to entertain questions about the human meaning of phenomena. All it does is weigh the facts and establish connections between them. One sometimes hears it said that science consists in the ability to predict phenomena. But the meaning of life is certainly not contained in the notion of prediction.

If by knowledge we are to understand knowledge of the meaning of life, then science is not knowledge.

Science simply proceeds from one form of ignorance to another: it is nothing more than a taxonomy of every conceivable kind of ignorance.

3

Critical philosophy concerns itself with the basic problems of cognition.[10] It defines the basic cognitive forms without which thought itself is impossible.[11] But this does not exhaust the aims of critical philosophy. One still has to establish the connections between the various cognitive forms, that is, establish their theoretical place with respect to each other. A systematic description of these forms presupposes a *norm* of cognition. Some epistemologists, for example, Simmel, content themselves with a mere description of cognition.[12] Others, for example, Rickert, see in the theory of knowledge a teleological connection in the distribution of cognitive forms.[13] It is the norm of cognition that systematizes the categories of thought. The connection between cognitive forms, such forms being regarded as the result of a process of division, presupposes a theory describing this division. Such a theory is a theory of knowledge.[14] In defining itself as a theory of knowledge, critical philosophy occupies an autonomous position with respect to the other sciences. For, although in no way limiting the freedom of development of any other science, it shows our reason just what we would expect from any of these sciences. It establishes firm limits for any given scientific method. Any other science, while forever approaching these limits, never actually crosses them. What we have here is the relation of a series of variables, as it were, to their constant.

A theory of knowledge is a constant of all knowledge. Any given science is definable, just as any systematic exposition of knowledge about any given field of knowledge is definable. For a theory of knowledge, however, knowledge itself has become the object.

Cognition is not simply knowledge; it is, so to speak, knowledge *about* knowledge.[15] Knowledge in the primary sense of the word is the domain of science. But it is not against the exact sense of scientific knowledge that the sting of critical philosophy is directed. It is directed rather against the various means for expanding knowledge. As knowledge about knowledge, cognition is, then, beyond the limit of knowledge. Cognition in this sense is rather "post-knowledge." One of the fundamental aims of cognition is to establish definitive boundaries for knowledge. A theory of knowledge in this sense encloses, as it were, whole groups of sciences within one circumference. The relation of such a theory to science is that of an eccentric sphere to concentric spheres. If the paradox will be excused: the conclusions of critical philosophy, which are so eccentric for common sense, are eccentric in a literal as well as in a figurative sense. The limits of this sense fall somewhere between the concentric circle of the sciences and the eccentric circumference of cognition. Ordinary common sense is concentrated in science and becomes eccentric in theoretical philosophy. Common sense does not have its own *Standpunkt*. A theory of knowledge is a hammer raised over common sense. But it is in vain that common sense is concentrated in science, for science turns out to be the anvil. The hammer of cognition strikes knowledge, and common sense does not account for anything at all.

Knowledge is embraced on all sides by cognitive forms. Causality is one of these forms. Its application to the sciences is, of course, universal. The essential characteristic of science, in fact, lies in the establishment of causal connections. The province of causality in being includes being itself. Reality, if reality is understood as identical to being, becomes a causal reality. The different parts of reality determine reality from the point of view of content: we see before us an uninterrupted series of contents of every description. Every act of knowledge turns out to be the subsumption of the various parts of reality under the general form of reality. But this form may not be subsumed under being. In this sense this form [that is, of reality] emerges as a closed sphere whose surface is the form of cognition. This latter form exists outside being. But the concept of truth for us is bound up with something outside reality, so that either truth is not real, or reality is not the same thing as being.

A cognitive form requires a dual form of description. One can describe the form of objects that are subsumed under the cognitive principle. These objects are then the content. Reality is such an object, that is, reality understood as immediately given being.

One can also define a cognitive form in relation to other cognitive forms (space, time). Then it is necessary to establish a connection between the content of these forms. In applying a form to a content, we see that the spheres of application of the forms can become confused or overlap. It is in this way that a relation of subordination or opposition is established and that the connections between the cognitive categories become apparent.

A theory of knowledge may be a discipline whose purpose is to deduce the concepts under which the material of the content [of knowledge] is subsumed. The connection between principles in that case would be established from the vantage point of their formed content.[16] Such, for example, are the laws of the *Transcendental Logic* [in Kant's *Critique of Pure Reason*], which establishes the means for defining the relation between forms on the one hand and elements subject to "forming" on the other. If we understand "cognitive form" as identical to Concept of Understanding, which is independent of experience, and content as identical to the world of experience, then the aims of theory of knowledge may be easily reduced to those of the *Transcendental Logic*. According to Kant, this logic is divided into an *Analytic*, which examines the necessary modes of thinking, and a *Dialectic*, whose aims are defined negatively by Kant as the exposure of the relativity of transcendental judgments. But a negative definition of the aims of cognition as limiting the activity of reason does not exhaust the object of an epistemological investigation.[17] A theory of cognition may examine the forms of cognition, not only from the point of view of objects, but also from the point of view of these forms themselves, considered independently of their experiential content. Such an examination assumes an order among the categories of cognition and views that order as a norm of sorts.

In the course of development of various epistemological conceptions, it is the individual contents of experience that determine the forms of cognition. But theory of knowledge takes the original post-factum and turns it into a logical prius. The change [in emphasis] from experience to its logical premise signals the first period in the development of epistemological notions. In this period the cognitive problem is posed, and quite clearly, but it is not resolved at all. Here we still encounter the dialectical procedure of attempting to approach the limits of the theory of knowledge. But one cannot then take the direction of this approach and make of it a starting point for the formation of theoretical constructs. A given cognitive form, considered either a postulate of an experiential order, or a premise to that postulate, will always turn out to be the inviolable boundary between the formed material of cognition and the cognitive norm. The transcendental problem, then, breaks down into two areas of investigation.

One area of investigation comprises the premises of experience. In this case the course of the investigation may run from experience to its premises or from the premises to experience.

The other area of investigation endeavors to bring together the premises of the investigation of experience into a system, that is, to discover uniformity among the cognitive categories. Only by this type of investigation can the epistemological problem become a true theory of knowledge. In Kant, for example, this kind of theory of knowledge is lacking. We do find it in Rickert, however.

As we wend our way along the tortuous paths of the different contents of the individual sciences, we move from knowledge ever closer to cognition. Cognition in this sense appears as a postulate of knowledge, that is, as something conditioned by content. The form of cognition here is conditioned by content to the same degree that content is conditioned by form. The consequence is a dualism: on the one hand we have the formless material of cognition, which is systematized only in a relative sense by science, and on the other hand we have the form that immediately predetermines this material. The various kinds of methodical investigations, which must be defined as truthful, *define their own definitions.*[18] This is why, when the question is posed in this way, none of them can be reduced to any other.

In one direction, then, there lies before us a series of irreducible forms that cannot be said to be identifiable. In the other direction lies that unknowable material of scientific knowledge that has been conditionally brought together into a system. This is how the problem of cognition is posed by Kant.

In taking as his point of departure the limits of knowledge, Kant arrived at the necessity of a theory of knowledge. But his theory, in the end, is only a problem. Cognition for Kant predetermines knowledge. A theory of knowledge does not exist for Kant as a science, nor can it. For Kant was not interested in first finding a cognitive *norm* from which the necessity of the cognitive forms indicated by him could then be deduced. On the contrary, he took the *forms* as given and from *them* attempted to find the norms determining them. The whole epistemological problem arises out of a dualism: that is, from the dual assumption that the material of experience on the one hand, and cognitive reality on the other, are both given. In overcoming this dualism, the epistemological problem then makes its way into theory. In defining the norm by means of the form, and the form by means of content, we inescapably arrive at some system of realism (naive or mystical). By deducing the form of cognition from its norm, and, further, deriving the content from the form, we inescapably arrive at a system of epistemological idealism. The first path (proceeding from a foundation up to the *norm*) is cut off for theory of knowledge. The second path (proceeding from a foundation up to *content*) is the [only] path for theory of knowledge. In this formulation both the procedure of starting with content and deriving everything else from it [that is, up to the *norm*, or the "first path" mentioned above] and the procedure of building up from the opposite foundation [that is, starting with the norm, or the "second path" mentioned above] so as to *arrive at* content are independent of scientific knowledge. These forms lead us to an epistemological problem that finds its highest expression in theory of knowledge. Furthermore, the relation of cognitive forms to the material of cognition is established as if the forms of knowledge, whose inadequacy gave rise to the whole epistemological problem in the first place, did not even exist. To put it differently, every science undergoes two stages of development: in the beginning its methods develop in a state of complete dependence on its material; then, however, this same material comes to be deduced from the logic of the science. The logic of a given science is but one paragraph to be learned in the mastery of the science.

A theory of knowledge is possible only on condition, first, that it raise itself from the paths of knowledge to the forms that predetermine these paths; second, that it be a norm or link for cognitive forms; third, that it establish between the cognitive form and its content a relation that is independent of the paths for which the given form is an extra-experiential premise. Next to such a theory, Kant's theory of knowledge is merely a riddle to be guessed at, but certainly no solution.

The awareness of the dualism that lay at the foundation of Kant's problem led to various attempts to overcome this dualism: theory of knowledge made this necessary. But subsequent philosophy was unable to overcome the Kantian problem. The revolution Kant had accomplished was simply too great. Pre-Kantian dogmatism, defeated for a short time, joined forces with the general critique of the *Critiques*. The Wolffians now, with the impartial appearance of scientific investigators, started to bury Kant. There is a belief that a paleontologist can reconstruct an entire animal from a single tooth. In the wake of Kant, his books became like a fossilized mammoth tooth. It was necessary to describe the mammoth on the basis of that one tooth, that is, to describe the philosophy of Kant on the basis of the *Critiques*. Subsequent philosophies, desiring to reconstruct the skeleton of Kantianism, were often capable of doing no more than scurrying timidly about the skeleton. But these philosophies were at least serving the purpose of animating a vigorous desire to find a true cognitive principle. The attempt to overcome Kant took two directions: the first, in overcoming dualism, found its dogmatic development in the work of Fichte, Schelling, and Hegel. The other was elaborated in the work of Schopenhauer and Hartmann.[19] In both cases a unity was substituted [for the old dualism]. But this unity turned out to be a metaphysical unity. What was really necessary was to find an *epistemological* unity, or at least to sort out *epistemologically* the methods for constructing all the metaphysical unities, whatever they might be called ("Self," "Spirit," "Unconscious"). Fichte replaced the Kantian dualism with a teleological principle. Schopenhauer attempted in vain to find uniformity in voluntarism, but the form of this unity turned out to be just another duality, namely, the breakdown into subject and object. The subject for Fichte appeared as a teleological norm, having already served as a theme in the Schelling-Hegel variation. But the subject, having already presented to the world of the object four different forms of the law defining it, collapses for Schopenhauer into the abyss of metaphysical will, and from here Kant's epistemological dualism simply becomes a metaphysical split. Schopenhauer's will, however, is a perfect scandal, since it simply turns into its opposite, appearing in the world of representations in the guise of a law of motivation. One of the failures of Schopenhauerian metaphysics lies in the confusion of the object with objective reality.

The unitary principle is permissible in theory of knowledge only when it regards the forms of cognition themselves as an actual descent into the realm of experience. The various stages of this descent then form the cognitive categories and the transcendental forms. In such cases every possible content is deducible from the forms. In Schopenhauer a grain of truth may be found in the recognition accorded the world of representable objects. All the errors, however, arise from the inadequate definition of the subject, both in its relation to the will and in its relation to representation.

In the metaphysics of Fichte, though, while we do not discover the solution to the Kantian problem, we do at least find a program for a solution.

4

Causality in the Kantian sense is a cognitive principle (form).[20] The connection between this principle and the other cognitive principles is normative.

What troubles us is the question whether, on the one hand, acknowledging the existence of a cognitive norm is a necessary metaphysical premise for a theory of knowledge, or whether on the other hand such a norm is a transcendental unity. To put it simply, is this norm transcendent?[21] In the latter case every attempt to overcome the Kantian dualism epistemologically has been metaphysical in character. In the *Critique of Judgment* we can already divine an attempt on the part of Kant to complete his theory of knowledge by means of metaphysics. Today we can see most clearly that an epistemological problem is merely a prelude to a new metaphysics. The metaphysicalness of theory of knowledge may be seen in the fact that [in the epistemology of today] a purely practical imperative serves as the premise underlying any act of cognition. Cognition must be able to realize its purposes: it is purposive, in other words. In what lies the purpose of cognitive activity directed towards a comprehension of itself? Its purpose is that cognition should appear to us not as an arbitrary complex of forms of activity, but as a harmonious, self-enclosed world, where the norm of cognition appears as a unity, and where the cognitive forms appear as the means by which the unity of cognitive activity is defined. Our practical reason takes the relations that exist between the norm and the forms of cognition and gives them the metaphysical form of purposiveness. This moment, where the practical reason intervenes in the activity of theoretical reason, is actually a *premise* for theoretical reason. A certain heteronomy of cognitive activity is inevitable here, so long as we stand at the threshold of an epistemological problem. But once we realize that the problem is a futile one until a theory, that is, a systematic arrangement of the cognitive forms, is brought to bear on it, we will understand that the systematizing norm is a norm of practical reason. In this sense the norm is not a limiting form of cognition, but a translimiting form, as it were: not a transcendental form, in other words, but a transcendent one. The categorical imperative of cognition is an unavoidable premise to cognition. But this imperative prescribes that cognition itself should be purposive. The Ought in this sense, according to Rickert, is a transcendent norm.[22] Purposiveness is a metaphysical condition for theory of knowledge.

From this it is clear that the transformation of epistemology into metaphysics occurs at that fateful moment when we realize that we are introducing an ethical element into cognition.

Fichte was right in proposing a teleology, and this is the reason his epistemology is in essence a metaphysics. He did not, however, demonstrate with sufficient clarity that the transformation of epistemology into metaphysics is grounded in the very essence of the epistemological problem, or that this problem is really an ethical one. As a critique of method, this problem owes its origin to practical reason. Practical reason, then, finds itself involved here in the affairs of science: for, although it does not limit the freedom of development of a given science, it nonetheless limits the degree to which the results of systematic knowledge can be interpreted. Practical reason clearly indicates that without some sort of self-imposed limitation the meaning of human activity is entirely lost. In the process of limiting systematic cognition, practical reason gives rise to a critical philosophy in which, by limiting itself, it appears as theoretical reason.

The meaning of this activity of practical reason has become clear to us following the astonishing efforts of the contemporary philosopher, Heinrich Rickert. The work of both Kant and Fichte is illuminated in the light of Rickert's labors.

The basic problems of cognition appear in a new light in the wake of Rickert's work.

5

What ought cognition to be?

Another question, concerning the value of cognition, depends on the answer to this question. But before we turn to that, what is cognition?

In answer to our question there emerges before us cognition as it exists in a great many systematic series, none of which can be reduced to any other. This "existing" cognition reveals itself to us in the confines of [ordinary] knowledge.

In this same sense, then, "existing" cognition does not exist at all. There is no cognition: there are only bits of knowledge. But bits of knowledge are not the same as acts of cognition. If such bits of knowledge were the same as acts of cognition, then [the faculty of] cognition would never emerge from individual acts of cognition. The sum of these acts of cognition is not equivalent to *cognition* in our sense.

Existing cognition (or knowledge) is not "Ought"-cognition. Instead, it is characterized by various mechanical functions, all of which are carried out by existing bits of knowledge.

Ought-cognition is defined by means of the imperatives of practical reason. In this sense cognition must also have *value*. The question of the value of cognition must be posed regardless of whether this value is actually realized in the given confines of knowledge.

The value of cognition determines the norms of true cognition. True cognition, in defining and realizing its own purposes, cannot be broken down into any systematic arrangement. Any such arrangement made by means of transcendental, normative principles must stand in a subordinate relation to cognitive values. Anything that is dictated to us by our practical reason is defined as having value.

The totality of Ought-norms, if arranged in a purposive fashion, fully delineates the object of true cognition.

True cognition, according to Rickert, is cognition of the Ought and of value.

Does true cognition exist then?

Existing cognition is defined by a methodical arrangement. This arrangement "forms" the material of cognition. The perfection of a methodical arrangement lies in its objectivity, that is, its independence from the sensual influences and volitional impulses of our nature. The material susceptible to being introduced into the methodical arrangement is also an object of methodical cognition. Objects are assumed to be data [of experience], independent of our cognitive faculty, which itself is a datum among other data. At the same time, the laws of this faculty dictate for us the definite direction that our relation to reality will take.

Before we identify the laws of cognitive activity with the norms of true cognition, we must decide whether it is necessary to make such an identification. For if the direction taken by normative cognition is determined by its value, then the value of cognition cannot be identified with its object. And even when cognitive activity itself is the object of cognition, the value of cognition is nonetheless not to be found in cognitive activity. There is something else that determines this value, and this something else is a value for cognition and is consequently in and of itself beyond the limits of [ordinary] cognition. Either Rickert's statement, "Truth is value,"[23] is a synthetic proposition, or "value" is the subject of the proposition.[24] "Truth" in this sense is merely the predicate of "value." Nor can value be identified with the Kantian "thing-in-itself," since the "thing-in-itself" is not at all an object of true cognition.

Objective, empirical reality emerges for us because of our ability to place the intended material into a systematic arrangement. This is also how objects of cognition (things-in-themselves) come to be. But objects of cognition cannot determine the *norms* of cognition. And it is these norms that outline the sphere of transcendent value. This value is not determined by cognition. On the contrary, it is value that determines cognition. In fact, the formation of a concept of value is impossible, for it would have to be our cognitive activity that formed such a concept, but, as we know, *value* forms cognition. In fact, no epistemological concept is capable of determining value. At the same time it must be pointed out that epistemological concepts represent limits to the formation of psychological concepts.

Concepts formed from [empirical] reality are psychological through and through. The class of epistemological concepts is obtained through the use of these [psychological] concepts in an entirely different, and in fact inconceivable, sense. Psychological concepts become emblems for certain other inconceivable concepts. The concept of value can certainly not be a psychological concept in the generally accepted sense of the word. But neither is it an epistemological concept. It is, as it were, an emblem of an emblem. Or, conversely, the Ought is an emblem of value, and the class of concepts pertaining to value, being neither epistemological nor psychological, is related to the class of symbolic concepts.

In what sense can we understand the symbolic concept of value within the bounds of cognitive terminology? We must understand it as the absolute limit to the formation of epistemological and psychological concepts. For every other limiting concept[25] (the thing-in-itself, the self, Spirit, Will, the epistemological subject of cognition) is theoretically reducible to a concept of value. This concept, however, is not reducible to any other. In forming such a concept we are, of course, submitting to the commands of practical reason. And if we make the statement, "Value is symbol," then by this we mean that (1) *symbol* in this sense is the ultimate limiting concept, and (2) a *symbol* is always a symbol of something, and this *something* can be found only in areas having no direct relation to cognition (much less to knowledge). A symbol in this sense is the union of something with something else, that is, the union of the purposes of cognition with something that may be found only outside the limits of cognition. We call this union "symbol," and not "synthesis," for the following reason: the noun *symbol* comes from the verb συμβάλλω (throw together, unite). A symbol is the result of a uniting. The noun *synthesis* comes from the verb συντίϑημι (place together). When I place together diverse elements, it is not established from the outset whether I am truly *uniting* the elements that have been "placed together." The word *synthesis* presumes instead a mechanical conglomeration of the elements that have been placed together. The word *symbol*, however, indicates rather the result of an *organic union* of one thing with another. Now, in using the expression "organic union," I am fully aware that I do so in a figurative sense. But the figurative quality of expressions is something intrinsic to symbolic concepts. Symbolism of expression characterizes the underlying strata of our cognition. But even at the topmost strata we find ourselves having recourse to figurative concepts. In defining the truth of cognition by means of its value, we are using a notion of value as something known to us internally. At the same time, the data of our lived experience defy psychological analysis, because we approach them having long since left any kind of psychological method behind. Wherever symbolic concepts hold sway, neither psychology as a science nor theory of knowledge has any force, for although both disciplines rely on a class of symbolic concepts, they do so in a baffled and uncomprehending way.

What we have pointed out above is that the very way we treat the question of a world view in our day has acquired a rather unexpected form. Having stated the problem in these terms, we can clearly see that the existence of a theoretical world view is impossible. We saw earlier that science is incapable of giving us such a world view. And theoretical philosophy simply takes the question of a world view and substitutes for it the question of the forms and norms of cognitive activity. To be sure, theoretical philosophy has an answer to the question, "How do we construct a world view?" But the very sense of a world view has been lost in this formulation of the question, and all the more since theoretical philosophy is careful to distinguish the method for constructing the various world views from the tenets of those world views. A world view in this guise no longer appears as a vital impulse towards activity, but as a dead principle. Theoretical philosophy will always answer the question, how I am to understand the meaning of my own existence, by saying that, if we understand the meaning in such and such a way (always relatively), then such and such a method of construction is possible. The seeker, hungry for meaning, is given stone instead of bread by theoretical philosophy.

But if we are to define meaning by value, then the strongholds of theoretical philosophy collapse. World view then becomes creation, and philosophical systems acquire a symbolic meaning. In cognitive terms they come to symbolize a notion of value and a notion of the meaning of life. There is no sense in even looking for any kind of theoretical significance in these systems, because theoretical significance is something that belongs only to epistemology. Theory of knowledge in its metaphysical form is the liquidation of the strongholds of pure reason. As a result of this liquidation, world view, as a theory, passes over into the realm of creation.

6

The critical attitude towards the problem of value and the objects of cognition is usually preceded by a dogmatic understanding of the concept of cognizing [*poznavanie*]. Such a concept is often not capable of serving as the basis for a classification of norms and forms. The result of such dogmatism is a self-assured narrow-mindedness regarding the establishment of the limits of cognition: agnosticism, relativism, skepticism, all hospitably received by science (from the rear entrance, as it were), find themselves in the front chambers of cognition. At this point certain talented scholars have recourse to a little trick: they demonstrate the existence of cognition, but their demonstrations do not agree on a single point. Thus, for example, Harald Høffding shows what he sees as the qualitative distinction between static cognition (scientific forms) and dynamic cognition (religious symbols of experience) and bases the distinction on whether we subject the content of knowledge to the relative concepts of science or to the relative images (symbols) of experience.[26] Why, then, not call Høffding's dynamic cognition simply "noncognizing" [*nepoznavanie*]? If we call noncognizing by the name of cognition, then we are simply reviving a doctrine of double truth. So then why all this scholastic rigamarole?

The fundamental problem of cognition lies in the strict differentiation of cognitive value from the object. Objective cognition leads to the acknowledgment of a certain material of cognition (thing-in-itself), which is independent of the perceiving faculties. The material of cognition has been regarded in the history of philosophy as the object. If this is so, then the cognitive faculty, not being wholly able to bring into its field of vision the material given to it (for if this were not the case, the object would not be a "thing-in-itself"), finds itself in a position of dependence on the material of cognition. The cognitive faculty is a deduction from this material, its product. There arises here a whole series of metaphysical theories, which are all conveniently able to interlace their own premises with those of the "scientific world views," and, depending on the specific arrangement of the material, we get materialism, empiricism, positivism, or skepticism.

At the same time, though, objective cognition is distinguished from the object. The cognitive faculty is recognized as given on one side while the object of cognition is given on the other. Any sort of dependence between cognition and its object is seen as premature. This is how the critical problem arises for many of the Kantian philosophers. But deducing experience from its premises deprives the object of cognition of all objective significance, since in such a case the content is being deduced from the form. And, in a similar manner to that in which scientific determinism deprives cognition of all independence, deducing it from simple, objectively given movements, transcendentalism deprives the object of all its recognizable signs, conferring on it instead the right to be an uncognizable "thing-in-itself," that is, conceived negatively, as a limiting concept. Take another step into critical philosophy and the object of cognition appears as nothing more than a mental concept. Thus the objectively given material of cognition simply vanishes into thin air.

The study of the laws by which concepts are formed is at the same time the study of the laws of objective being. Being thus becomes a form of thought. Rickert deserves credit for formulating this position in contemporary theoretical thought. Being, according to Rickert, is the form of an existential judgment. The truth of a judgment, moreover, lies neither in its being nor in its coinciding with an object: the truth of a judgment is rather a norm of practical reason that both predetermines and actually constructs the world of the object. The object, then, is the product of cognitive creation. It is we who have drawn this conclusion, and indeed we cannot escape it, since without it Rickert's whole harmoniously constructed edifice simply crumbles into dust.

Cognitive value cannot be treated as a product of the cognitive process. On the contrary: the cognitive process *comes from* this value. Cognitive value is contained in the creation of idea-images, and it is in identifying these idea-images that one forms objective reality itself. Cognitive value, then, lies in the creative process of symbolization.

It is here that the connection appears between the ultimate conclusion of theoretical thought and the slogans of contemporary innovators of the symbolist school who have placed on their banners the primacy of creation over cognition. Here we also find the most fertile soil for the foundation of symbolism. The artist and the philosopher encountering one another tomorrow will both ask, "Where are we now going? What dazzling horizons are shining forth for us? How are we to measure the depth of the abyss that has opened up at our feet?" And both will agree that their roads, from that day on, are one and the same. Henceforth the artist cannot avoid being aware of the providential mystery contained in his creation. In his creative service he is subject to the command of a duty not of his own making. He cannot help knowing the foundation of this creation in theoretical philosophy. Theoretical philosophy, through metaphysics, is passing more and more into the realm of the theory of creation. The theory of creation so sought after in our age would be, in essence, a theory of symbolism.

The artist and the philosopher, encountering each other along the progressive path of their development, will never again separate from that day on. For they both know that there is no going back. Besides, where could they go if they did go back? To the world of empirical reality? But that world no longer exists today. All that exists are the many different methods of knowledge that deduce the world from indivisible particles, forces, ions, and so on. But all these particles, forces, and ions now necessarily appear before us as products of cognitive activity, and this same activity is a product of value. And where is value to be found? Value is to be found not in the subject, and not in the object, but in vital creation. But at the same time it is revealed to us that this single, unified symbolic life (the world of value) has not been deciphered but appears to us instead in all its simplicity, charm, and diversity as the alpha and omega of all theory. This symbolic life is the symbol of a certain mystery, and the approach to this mystery is an ever-increasing, seething creative urge that carries us, as if arisen from the ashes of phoenixes, on the cosmic dust of space and time. All theories stop short beneath us, all reality flies past like a dream, and it is only in creation that reality, value, and the meaning of life may still be found.

Here we return to activity, that is, to that symbolic unity that our cognition cannot disclose to us. From the objective existence given to our senses, we soar upwards to the crests of cognition, where cognition only dreams of existence, and from there we soar upward once again to symbolic unity. Then we come to understand that even cognition itself is a mere dream of this unity. In our dream we awaken into another dream. One dream after another falls away from our eyes, one meaning is replaced by another, and all the while we are still dreaming. And we know none who are awake until we come to understand that the very process of awakening from one dream into another is an activity unto itself, but a *creative* activity. Something within us creates its own dreams and then surpasses them. What our dreams create is called value, but this value is a symbol. What is created in dreams we call realities. All these realities are colorful and rich. But the laws of all the realities are the same. These realities, as they are perceived through the laws, give us an image of objective reality. But this is true only so long as we are outside of the activity we have mentioned. This activity (understood as creation) establishes a scale of realities in the world as it is given to us. We proceed along this scale, as if it were a long ladder where each new step is the symbolization of a value. When we are below a given step, then the step on which we are standing is an invitation and an urge towards the higher step; when we have reached that higher step, then it becomes reality; and once we have surpassed it, then it looks like lifeless nature.

In returning to activity, we recognize that same reality from which we had drifted away on the sea of cognition. Now we have once again returned to that reality; we have returned to our homeland. And we will, in fact, continue to dwell in this homeland henceforth and for all time, for all the different "steps" [on our scale of realities] are the inexhaustible richness of our homeland, the flowers and fruits on the Tree of Life.[27] Our homeland is a paradise that was lost once upon a time and found again. The heaven of cognition, like the earth of life, is henceforth one firmament in which heaven and earth mingle together as one. Thus Nietzsche was right in exhorting us to remain faithful to the earth. For earth here is the symbolic earth of Adam Kadmon.[28] Hermetic wisdom defines the symbolic composition of this earth: the Moon, the Sun, Venus, and Jupiter are part of it, and the Zodiac gives it its shape. Man himself is Adam Kadmon. Activity forces us to see the mystery in life, where the wandering about in search of meaning strongly resembles the trails of the neophyte, who is subjected to the perils of death on earth, both in water and in fire. Meaning lies in activity. Such activity is irreducible, whole, free, and omnipotent. Pure cognition, when it comes into contact with this activity, endows it with a terminological significance. But the terms associated with pure knowledge and cognition are merely symbols of activity. When, in the midst of these terms, we approach this activity, we can speak about it only in symbolic images, for the activity itself is a living image and cannot be reduced to any term. Still, we necessarily think by means of such terms, and as a result, all of our words about activity are mere symbols.

The very tragedy of our cognition is, as it were, a neophyte's trial, the threshold to the mystery of life. At first we seek the meaning of life in terms pertaining to knowledge—and this meaning subsequently slips away from us. We then look for meaning in cognition—and the meaning fails to emerge. Then we inquire of cognition what the meaning of cognition is—and the meaning is revealed *outside* of cognition. Cognition turns out to be merely one facet of activity. Both the meaning and the value of this activity are to be found in the activity itself. Now if we were to apply metaphysical thinking in its conventional form to activity and ask, "What is the object of this activity?" our activity would reply, "You are that object." And if we were to ask what the subject of this activity is, then the unity of our activity, revealing itself within us, would reply, "I am you." We go out from ourselves, as from an insignificant grain of sand in the desert of existence, and then back to ourselves, as if back to Adam Kadmon, or to a universe where *I*, *you*, *he* are all one, where father, mother, and son are all one, for, in the words of the sacred Book of Dzyan, "father, mother and son were once more one" (first stanza).[29] And this "one" is the symbol of a mystery that never reveals itself.

The conquest of this mystery lies on the path of creative activity. On the path this veil of mystery becomes translucent and begins to shine with a seven-colored light.

And thus it is that the ancient words of wisdom now come to us: "Seek the way by retreating within. Seek the way by advancing boldly without. Seek it not by any one road. . . . But the way is not found by devotion alone, by religious contemplation alone, by ardent progress. . . . Seek it by testing all experience . . . in order to understand the growth and meaning of individuality."[30]

7

Contemporary theory of knowledge is undergoing a crisis. It has already recognized itself as a metaphysics. What is more, contemporary theory of knowledge will either disappear altogether or be forced to become instead a theory of creation.

In light of this crisis, in light of the search for new paths of philosophical thought, artists, philosophers, and scholars have all become concerned with a reconsideration of the relations existing between knowledge, faith, cognition, and creation. These questions truly concern everyone equally in a most vital fashion.

The connection that establishes and normatively fixes these relations cannot, however, take the relation of cooperation existing between religion, science, and art, and turn it into one of subordination [of one of those areas to another]. Nonetheless, naive thinking has done precisely this, and continues to do so. As a result, we are confronted with a whole series of perfectly natural errors, errors that have been crystallized in a great variety of religious and philosophical conceptions. We are now, however, in a position to see the true extent of the foundation on which such errors have arisen.

Naive thinking has replaced the purposiveness that must of necessity characterize any arrangement of cognitive principles relative to one another, with both a biological and a metaphysical teleology. Both Aristotle and Fichte are guilty of this, for [with them] purposiveness is carried over into reality, and the norm of cognition becomes an object. And thus arises a conception of ideas as objective entities independent of any principle concerning our perception of reality. One more step and the naive mind endows these entities with the individual properties of our own nature, or else these entities come to be seen as actually bearing physical forces. This is how a world of gods is formed. It is also how a teleology can suddenly turn into an ontology or a cosmology.

From time immemorial, the object of cognition has been symbolized by a vital, eternally existing principle, namely a divinity. And the product of cognition has always been the world, which has kept God hidden behind a veil. The object of cognition [that is, God] became a cause, while its product [that is, the world] became the effect of that cause. The causal connection was turned around, and we arrived at a teleology: the world became the means for returning to the divinity.

But just as the revelation of the divinity occurs inside us and for us, the deepening and purification of our own personality must be seen as the indispensable condition for the return to the divinity. This is the source of the unavoidably moral tinge to all subsequent religions. The mythological moment in religion gives way increasingly to the mystical. Thus the Vedas, in the classification of Deussen, lead into the Vedantas, and then find completion in the Upanishads, that is, a hermit's collection of rules for living.[31] One more step and the divinity comes to be identified with us: God is I, liberated now from the veil of Maya.[32] Here the adept has become an "Anupadaka," that is, anarchical (torn free from slavery), worldless.[33] At this point metaphysics becomes the foundation for mysticism. The metaphysics of Schopenhauer, for example, can be seen as a theoretical threshold to the Vedantas. The relation between "I" and "not-I" is repeatedly discussed in metaphysics, where "I" is largely identified with the subject and "not-I" with the object.

In Greek philosophy the opposition between value and the world of being was frequently discussed in rather naive terms. The Eleatics, Plato, and the Neoplatonists in particular were concerned with this. For Parmenides and Zeno, this value turns out to be the divine unity of being. In this connection, teleology is replaced by ontology for the Eleatics and by cosmology for the Physicists.

The dependence of the cognitive faculty on the object is refracted variously in the mystico-religious teachings of the Milesians, in the flux of Heraclitis, or the mechanics of Empedocles, Anaxagoras, and Democritus.[34] The object becomes the prime source of both being and cognition, and fire, air, and water are that prime source. Physics here combines with mysticism into a theosophy and a *Naturphilosophie*, arising again later in the philosophy of Schelling. Magic, astrology, and alchemy all presuppose a unity of cognition and being. In Anaximander's "Boundless" one still finds an indissoluble mixture of the metaphysics of cognition and the cosmological illumination of cognition seen as a first principle.[35] The first principle here is less a logical principle than an image of chaos seen as giving birth to gods and humans. And, strange though it may seem, in our own day we see the philosophy of the Boundless resurrected in Hartmann, just as we see Heraclitus resurrected in Nietzsche.

The opposition between the eternal change of appearances (the world of being) and the fixed essence (the object of cognition) is reconciled in the Pythagorean Number, which is at once the measure of things and the measure of the harmony of the world.[36] The opposition of the product of cognition and its object is the philosophical nerve running through all Greek religion: it appears not only in the historical evolution of religion (in the struggle between the chthonic and the Olympian deities) but also in the reconciliation of this struggle through tragedy-mystery.

On the other hand, this same opposition is reflected not only in the concept of value as an ethical norm, but also in the concept of being as a natural law. In fact, the essence of all Socratic thought lies in the subordination of being to a norm. Such a purposive reduction of cognitive forms to a cognitive norm endowed the forms with an independent existence (Plato). The world of being propped up by ideas is the very living image of Platonism. The mode of being of ideas, which separates these ideas from the cognizing subject [*poznajuščij*], is either confined to the unknowable world of the object (thing-in-itself) or identified with objective reality. The first solution to the Platonic question is to subordinate this question to the religious question. The second solution is to advance the significance of empirical knowledge, and with this, Plato is resurrected in Aristotle.

Today we are able to see all the beauty and attraction of such lofty errors. Their strength lies not in their having solved any problems of cognition, but in their status as creative works. All such systems represent for us different methods of symbolizing the world of Value. This is why we can so easily read the symbolic jargon of these philosophemes. This is also why we can easily wend our way into all the nooks and crannies of cognition without fear of getting lost. For the words of wisdom ring true: "Seek the way by retreating within. Seek the way by advancing boldly without." What we are seeking in these systems is a kind of active esotericism, but we must remember that the external form of a given philosopheme, its objective significance, is only its visible outer cover, whereas the true underlying foundation lies in the capacity to disclose, to *show*. Every deduction presented to us in the guise of a dogma is no more than an empty husk of value. We must look not *at* the deduction but *past* the deduction, *through* the deduction. The more formal it is the more valuable. In fact, we would even say that the contentual part of any such deduction in theoretical philosophy constitutes the very impurity of that conclusion. We can see nothing through soiled glass: the glass through which we look must first be wiped clean. Thus in a theory of knowledge if the deductions are formal, and therefore pure, we may convince ourselves of both the completeness and the richness of what is revealed behind the theory. And now, rather than being oppressive, our theory of knowledge frees us from philosophy. After that there is only creation, the way, freedom.

8

The results of our search for pure meaning along the lines of knowledge are significant. In attempting to find meaning we pass certain well-defined zones of cognition, which we might liken to a series of planes arranged one above the other. Each plane reveals to us a path of endless searches, that is, until we realize that meaning is not to be found on that plane. It is as though we were forever forcing meaning off one plane and onto the next, where we will still be unable to find it.[37] In our day the following disciplines constitute such zones of ascent: natural science, psychology, theory of knowledge, metaphysics, ethics. We mount five steps, and no sooner have we landed on each than the meaning slips up to the next. The five fundamental methodical groups turn out to be empty. We have before us, then, a whole tableau of nature that acts upon us and affects us. We wish to discover its meaning, so science analyzes it into a series of objectively given particles. Further on, these particles are broken down into atoms, ions. Beyond this the tableau of nature has already become for us an ethereal mirage. Beyond this, forces become prominent, and then the tableau of nature becomes a product of work (*Sthula Sharîra*).[38] Here we come to a stop, and meaning finally abandons us. Inner feelings (*Linga Sharîra*) remain a criterion for our judgments in what we see: we then realize that we are already standing on the next step. But once we understand that even inner feelings are subject to the formal conditions of time, we realize that the content of this captivating tableau is the result of cognitive forms that have been constituted in a certain way. Our consciousness, reasoning impersonally, has already determined for us, by certain universal and ineluctable laws, the conditions of experience, with the result that we are able to obtain a representation of the tableau of nature. We realize that another plane already stretches before us. But even here, meaning slips away from us. Our reasoning consciousness is predetermined by ethical duty (*Prâna*). Ethical duty is the norm of both theoretical and practical reason (*Manas*). When we realize that value in cognition lies outside of cognition, that value is itself a symbol made real through activity, and that the image of this activity is, in turn, also symbolic, we then begin to understand that the whole power lies in the union of cognition with something else. The ancient wisdom teaches us that love is a symbol of this union. The ancient wisdom uses a special term to designate this zone in the Path: Buddhi.[39] Pure meaning is pushed back out of the cognitive region, forming a pyramid of methods, transcendental forms, categories, and norms. The pyramid of cognition, whose base is the world, appears either hanging in a void or joined at its tip by means of its symbolic, transcendent unity. And only when we disclose this unity do we begin to approach meaning. This unity is not a norm of knowledge. The symbolic unity (value) is, as it were, a norm of norms. A single norm is far more profound than anything we can find in the metaphysics of theory of knowledge. But the discovery of this norm lies in creative activity.

Thus there occurs, as if involuntarily, a sudden change in the theory of knowledge, which now finds itself obliged to become a theory of value. For this purpose the theory must describe and systematize the different manifestations of value. And thus it is that we arrive—again involuntarily—at the study of artworks from the point of view of their form, content, and mutual connections. But even here we encounter a scale, or ladder ascending before us. As we pause on the step of art, we see that everything in it is form and form alone. The meaning of art slips away from its own sphere in precisely the manner we described a moment ago. This meaning turns out to be a religious one.

If we examine the arts from the standpoint of the material that forms them, we are able to establish little more than a law of conservation of energy and a law of resistance of materials in the creative process. The world of the arts appears before us as the product of an energetic process where the act of creation is like the collision of potential energies (the artist and his raw material) that are consequently converted into kinetic energy.[40]

If, on the other hand, we examine the arts from the standpoint of the feelings that may be aroused by us, in our attempts to classify the images of art we find no genuine principles to aid us, none, that is, besides the elements of spatiality and temporality. We recognize, then, that the images of art strive towards harmony. But harmony, it must be remembered, is a musical principle and is subject to [the exigencies of] melody. We further recognize that music is an art of pure movement, subject to time, and time is the form of inner intuition. In this direction, however, there is nothing we can learn.

Any taxonomic classification of forms will make art subject to epistemological principles. But even these principles have been determined in advance by metaphysics. If we turn to the images that occur in the arts and examine them from the standpoint of the unity manifested in them, the lofty peaks of artistic creation will present to us perfect and complete images of mankind, will draw us to the lofty peaks of [ethical] duty [*dolg*].

But even metaphysics crosses over into the domain of theory of value. Value is symbolized by living, individual activity. Emblems of value in art are always images of supermen and gods. Such is Dante's Beatrice, such are the images of Christ and Buddha. Art here crosses over into the realm of mythology and religion. At the center of art there must stand the living image of the Logos, that is, the Image [*Lik*].[41]

A classification of Images should be what crowns any attempt at systematizing the arts. But here we encounter a new question: What is an Image? An Image is a human image that has become the emblem of a norm. Aesthetics here begins to take on the appearance of a kind of ethics. We encounter a heteronomy of creation, just as the ladder of cognition led us to recognize a heteronomy of cognition. In defining the value of cognition, we are obliged to base cognition in creation. In defining the value of creation, on the other hand, we base creation in cognition. Formal ethics then appears as an inviolable boundary between cognition and creation.

We are able to understand how cognition can be conditioned by an ethical norm. We can also understand how the same may be true of creation. There is one thing, however, that we do not understand, and that is how a norm of cognition and a supra-individual object of aesthetic cognition can be united in an ethical norm. The pyramid of cognition, like the pyramid of creation, is split in half by ethics. The norm of ethical principles is a transcendental norm. Our life makes up the content of these principles. If we fail to transform the norm into an ideal, that is, into a transcendent essence commensurate with the norm, then the ethical life appears as purposiveness without purpose.[42] The transformation of the norm into an essence will give us the symbolic Image of this norm. With this transformation we find that we have suddenly slipped into the domains of religion and aesthetics. Meanwhile, the natural limits of religio-aesthetic creation oblige us to reverse ourselves and base the Image in the norm. In doing this, though, we have slipped into ethics, that is, into that same "purposiveness without purpose" that we mentioned a moment ago. In seeking some other perspective on the problem we realize that the solution to this problem is impossible without a critique of the problem of cognition. Furthermore, our ethical norm is placed in a relation of dependence on cognitive norms, and we slip right back into cognition. In a word, we find ourselves in a whole new circle of contradictions.

This time, however, the contradiction apparently offers no hope for reconciliation. The essence of cognition and the essence of creation lie in their meaning. Unfortunately, this meaning is lacking in both cases. Or else the search for the meaning and value of life is simply cast aside—for cognition, into the realm of creation, and for creation, into the realm of cognition. Cognition and creation are continually dragging each other out of the same abyss only to discover that they both remain just as deeply entrenched.

Cognition, then, turns out to be dead. Creation similarly turns out to be dead. The universe becomes a great catacomb in which we are enclosed, like mummies. For this reason all our forays into the transcendent are really fictitious forays, for our aspiration here presents us with a series of focuses, overexposed, as it were, so as to persuade us that our aspiration is quite dead. Here, for the second and apparently final time, the skepticism of the genuine epistemologist is justified in the face of all attempts to resolve the problem of cognition by transcendental realism.[43] Also justified is the reluctance of the genuine artist to acknowledge the primacy of religion in his creation. The artist and the epistemologist oppose any attempt to dupe them, as it were, with empty fantasies about the transcendent. And simple instinct will bear them out on this.

But is this really so?

Various attempts at a monistic solution to the problem of cognition have crowned the Kantian dualism. Similar attempts at a monistic solution to the problem of artistic creation have crowned the resulting aesthetics with religious premises. Both paths lead us to a holistic world view. But as these two world views come into collision above the dualisms they have overcome, they lead us to a new dualism, which ethics is able to reconcile only because it finds itself sitting between two incommensurable abysses. In essence, then, ethics does not unite at all: on the contrary, it divides.

In the depths of the abyss of cognition we encounter a series of metaphysical unities; in the depths of the abyss of creation we encounter a series of universal, supra-individual Images.

The only thing we can do is to arrange these unities and Images in a parallel fashion without any possibility of uniting them. Such a parallel arrangement has occupied the secret doctrines of all ages. In our day it is the domain of theosophy. In theosophy the arrangement of metaphysical unities in order of their transcendence is made to correspond to the arrangement of the central symbols of religion, also in order of transcendence. The correspondence is often taken to be a synthesis. But even here the synthesis is simply a parallel arrangement of two series. For if the dualism does not hold firm here, and if we approach our monistic scheme by deriving the series of limiting creative symbols from the series of limiting metaphysical concepts, then we fall into the age-old heresy of religious gnosticism. Conversely, if we approach the monistic scheme by deriving the metaphysical concepts from the creative symbols (seen now as active, preexisting), then we fall into the heresy of magic and theurgy. In both cases we are terming our approach to monism, deviating as it does from the dualism mentioned above, a "heresy." In speaking thus we do not disparage the significance of gnosticism, magic, and theurgy in any way. On the contrary, contemporary humanity is just now entering a period where the problems of gnosticism, magic, and theurgy are emerging in their full significance. We use the term *heresy* solely for the reason that in both cases we have turned aside from the traditional path on which the solution to the basic problem of value is sought. Theosophy must rise above gnosticism, magic, and theurgy. But, at the same time, theosophy as such does not solve the problem, for it lacks the means. Instead, theosophy must honestly and candidly examine both series of limiting concepts [that is, the cognitive and the creative] and realize that there is no unity capable of joining them, that its gaze is directed into a void.

The loftiest religions in history, rising up to the heights of theosophy, adopted either the form of gnosticism, that is, at the stage where gnosticism begins to make the transition into mystical criticism, or the form of a theurgy that borders on magic. In the former case these religions, in denying the primacy of creation, have had the courage to destroy creation by means of cognition, also denied by them. In the latter case the religions saturate cognition with religious creation in the same way that magic does or else attempt to destroy cognition (as theurgy does) with the help of mysteries. Characteristically, Buddhism has all too often taken on the complexion of mystical criticism, whereas Christianity has adopted the theurgical form of the mysteries in its notions concerning the sacraments.

Theosophy is a taxonomy of taxonomies. It is, as it were, an extraterrestrial view of the world and man's nature. Theosophy can neither change nor overcome anything: its meaning lies in completeness. It gives completeness to senselessness by classifying the whole sum of senselessly emerging images, forms, and norms. Existing theosophy appears to us either in the guise of gnostic syntheses or in the guise of offshoots from various forms of magic, theurgy, and other religious systems that have existed at one time or another. The effectiveness of contemporary theosophy lies precisely in its failure to have risen to the tasks of true theosophy. In the present era theosophy represents merely a threshold to a whole series of tendencies, some old and some new, that have recently been resurrected but that have not yet taken hold in our day. All the more reason to conceal from us its ghastly, soul-chilling meaning and crown the whole system with the drama of our priceless cognition and our meaningless sufferings. Theosophy continues in its progress towards its true kingdom, the kingdom where the eyes close, spirits sink, and the heart stops . . . [Bely's ellipsis].

Having mounted the ladder of cognition, we see that it is replete with the most profound value, though this is only because it defines the quest for this value as located in the Other. But by basing value fundamentally on the Other, we distinguish nothing but creation, and by basing ourselves on the heights of this creative activity, we suddenly find ourselves sliding back down the ladder of creation. Conversely, having mounted *this* ladder [that is, of creation], we see that it, too, is replete with the most profound value, though this is only because it defines the quest for this value as located in the Other. Now if we choose to seek this Other, we arrive at cognition, but we are still without the value we seek, having replaced it with problems of cognition. This is because we are now proceeding in the reverse direction, from cognition to knowledge. Thus we find ourselves in a vicious circle: both ladders preserve their force and value only where they are seen as products of value. There must be a form of value to unite them. But the conditions attaching to both cognition and creation preclude any such unifying principle for either one. Such a principle would have to be a postulate capable of uniting one with the other. At our present vantage point, on high, where both cognition and creation appear beneath us, we are completely alone and abandoned. It is up to us now to take on this final bit of meaninglessness, like death, or like the last of a novice's trials before initiation. But remembering the series of dreams that we shed from ourselves as we ascended to the heights of the activities of cognition and creation, we cannot help thinking that this *is* that last trial of the novice. The very freedom of our decision, through the absence of any criteria of truth, duty, or value, consists in being subordinated to value, and our *gnosis* (immediate knowledge of the spiritual) itself serves as our guarantee that the unity we have postulated actually exists. But cognition has no forms with which to express this unity. For this reason our unity turns out to be an uncognizable symbol, something that is not the product of human hands. "Norm," "unity," "subject"—these are all symbols for this symbol, expressed in metaphysical terms. In the terminology of the various mystical doctrines, it would be the absolute, the abyss, Parabrahman. Creation itself, leading us up the ladder of creation to the heights of theurgy, must scorch us with the triple fire of love, hope, and faith, in order to await in the wilderness the meaninglessness of the true descent of the uncognizable unity. The magic of ecstatic experience would have to combine with the icy cold of gnosis in order for the postulated unity to be changed by free affirmation into the very condition of cognition and creation. We must accept the notion of a symbol as an embodiment. If cognition has not yet become frozen like ice, if the ecstasy of creation has not set us aflame, and if we have already ascended to the heights of the last trial of our novitiate, then the living water of cognition will smother the smoldering coal of creation within us, and this coal will turn the water into steam. In the steam and the ashes, the meaning of existence will perish for us, and the sole answer we will receive will be: "Woe, woe, woe, to the inhabiters of the earth."[44] Here, in the last wilderness of meaninglessness, above the world and above us, the Last Judgment will be accomplished.

We can see now where the value we are looking for has moved to. This value has turned out to lie outside of being, outside of cognition, and outside of creation. But this is because everything we know about being is still not value, and the same is true for everything we know with the help of cognition. Everything we seek in creation has, in and of itself, neither meaning nor value. What about our everyday life? But science reduces this to a collection of meaningless specks. And these specks? But they are no more than games played by our cognition. And what about this cognition? But this is to be found in the concept of duty. And duty? But duty lies in creation. What, then, about creative form? But the value of creative form lies in an understanding of the process of creating something. What about the creation of forms? But this consists in the act of creating oneself. And this act of creating oneself? But this consists in the transformation of oneself into an image and a likeness of the gods. And the gods? But they are emblems of something else. In what, then, does this "something else" consist?

At this point all our dreams flit away: being, science, cognition, art, religion, ethics, theosophy—everything slips by. Everything has value only to the extent that it in some sense refers to us. We are left in absolute desolation, immersed in a Nirvana of nonbeing. And, according to the degree of our immersion, the silence around us sends us a voice: "I am THAT."[45]

The unity of life lies in the process of our immersion in it.

And the unspeakable profundity of our life becomes suffused with sounds, colors, and images only in proportion to the degree to which we cause the zones of cognition and creation to intersect.

The crucial passage at which humanity now stands is this: the clock of life is now, through cognition, creation, and being, striking noon, when the depths of the heavens are illuminated by the sun. The sun has risen and has long been dazzling us. Cognition, creation, and being are forming dark spots in our eyes. And now cognition is tearing the dark spots away from our eyes and is saying to us in its own language: "I do not exist at all." Creation is also tearing the dark spots from our eyes, and it, too, is saying: "I do not exist at all." And, finally, everyday life is tearing the dark spots from our eyes and saying: "I do not exist at all."

It is up to us to decide whether there really is something that exists.

It is our inclination to say, "Nothing exists." But we are not blind: we hear the music of the sun, which now stands in the very midst of our soul, and we see its reflection in the mirror of the heavens. And we speak, saying: "Thou art."

9

At the heights of both cognition (A_3)[46] and creation (C_3) we are obliged to postulate some unity (B) for which both the metaphysical unities (A_3) and the unities of the images of creation (C_3) are symbols. The metaphysical unity cannot be determined by a norm of cognition, by cognitive form, or by the forms of scientific methodology. On the contrary, it is the metaphysical unity that determines *them*. The unity of creative forms, in turn, cannot be determined by the image of the Muse, by the forms of symbolization, or by the forms of images and their contents. But this unity is expressed as B. B is a symbol determined in terms associated with both cognition and creation. Conversely, cognition and creation, being defined by means of the symbol B, are symbols of this symbol. For this reason we term the symbol B an embodiment. To broaden the sense of this we may represent the symbol graphically as a triangle whose angles correspond to the following points: cognition, creation, and their postulate (A_3BC_3). In the center of this trinity are located the value and meaning of life. Figure 1 shows just how much more profoundly this symbolic triangle reveals the meaning and value of being than is commonly supposed. Let us examine this diagram.

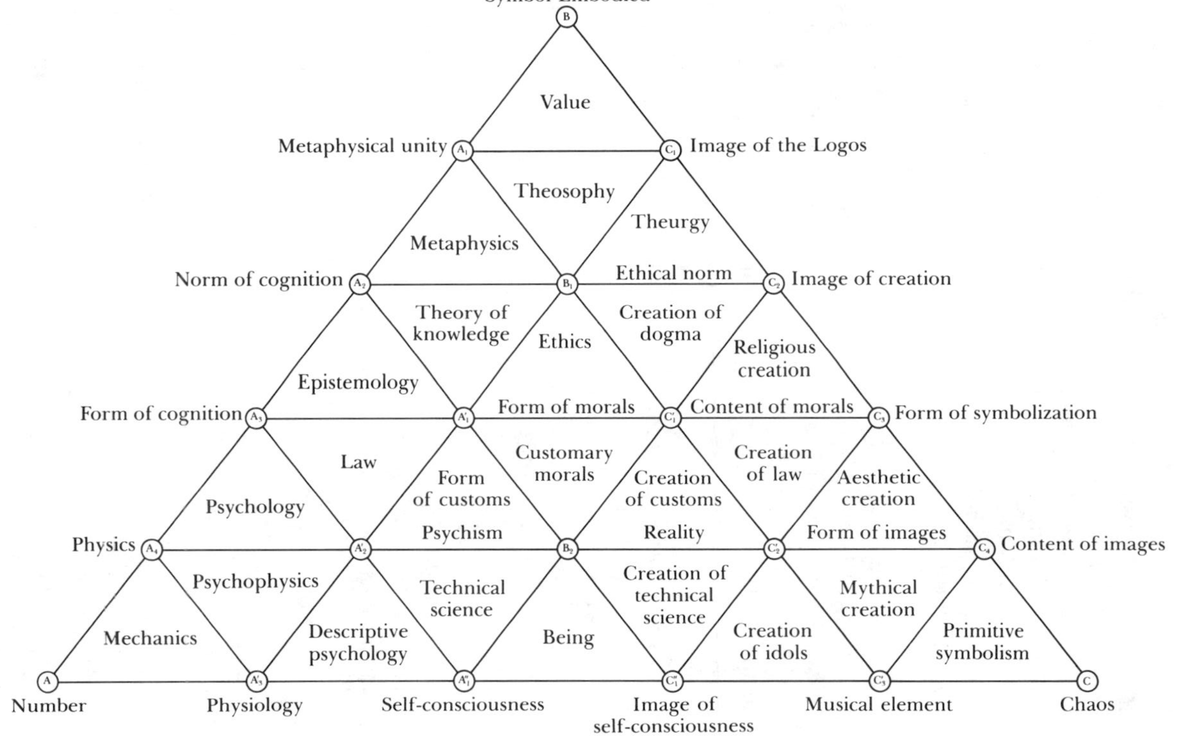

Symbol Embodied
B
Value
Metaphysical unity
A1
C1
Image of the Logos
Theosophy
Theurgy
Metaphysics
Norm of cognition
A2
B1
Ethical norm
C2
Image of creation
Theory of knowledge
Ethics
Creation of dogma
Religious creation
Epistemology
Form of cognition
A3
A'1
Form of morals
C'1
Content of morals
C3
Form of symbolization
Law
Form of customs
Customary morals
Creation of customs
Creation of law
Aesthetic creation
Psychology
Physics
A4
A'2
Psychism
B2
Reality
C'2
Form of images
C4
Content of images
Psychophysics
Technical science
Creation of technical science
Mythical creation
Mechanics
Descriptive psychology
Being
Creation of idols
Primitive symbolism
A
A'3
A''1
C''1
C'3
C
Number
Physiology
Self-consciousness
Image of self-consciousness
Musical element
Chaos

Figure 1

Triangle A_1BC_1 lies four steps above science and two above theory of knowledge. This implies that the symbol of value is a premise of a premise [that is, two steps removed] of theory of knowledge. The symbolic trinity (A_1BC_1) crowns another triangle (A_3BC_3), at whose base angles lie epistemology and religious creation. This implies that the value of activity unites the fire of religious creation and the icy coldness of epistemological investigations: theory of knowledge, ethics, theology [*creation of dogma* on the diagram], metaphysics, theosophy, and theurgy constitute intermediate links leading us to a theory of symbolism. Of these intermediate links leading us to the symbol, it is the theory of knowledge, ethics, and theology that have been most fully elaborated in our day. The construction of an epistemological metaphysics of unity and the construction of a theosophy lie in the future, as does any sort of theurgical creation. It is for this reason that a theory of symbolism in our time is possible only when considered as a future prospect. It is important to define theoretically the place occupied by metaphysics, theosophy, and theurgy in relation to theory of knowledge, ethics, and theology. Only when we have done this can we graphically define the position of value with respect to the theories just mentioned. A theory of value cannot be constructed on the basis of scientific doctrine, ethics, and theology. On the contrary, a theory of value predetermines these disciplines.

Triangle A_3BC_3 is symbolized by the following three triangles: A_1BC_1, $A_3A_2A'_1$, and $C_3C_2C'_1$. The second and third of these, in turn, are symbolized by two other triangles: $A_3A_2A'_1$ is symbolized by $AA_4A'_3$ (mechanics) and $A''_1B_2C''_1$ (being). $C_3C_2C'_1$ is symbolized by $A''_1B_2C''_1$ (being) and C'_3C_4C (primitive symbolic creation).

For the first triangle, this implies that epistemology, through the form of cognition and the form of morals, predetermines being, knowledge, and cognition. A whole series of cognitive groups arises in between epistemology and being: psychophysics, descriptive psychology, general psychology, law, form of customs, technical science.[47] This implies that all these cognitive groups enter into the competence of epistemology.

The triangle of religious creation predetermines being and primitive symbolic creation [*primitive symbolism* on the diagram]. The intermediate links here are the various types of creation: creation of myth, creation of idols, technical creation, creation of customs, law, and forms of art [*aesthetic creation* on the diagram].

The symbolic unity appears to us from the very first as a triunity, and then as three triunities: these three triunities then are repeated three times, forming a pyramid of triangles (triads), all derived from symbolic unity.

The altitude, intersecting the pyramid up through the middle of the upper triangle, shows graphically at which state of activity the dualism between cognition and creation ends. A theory of symbolism must take holism as its point of departure, and for this purpose it is necessary for such a theory first to locate theoretically the place of this holism, in order to deduce from it all the activities represented in the form of systems of subordinated and coordinated triangles. Each triangle in the figure governs the triangles beneath it. Thus aesthetic creation governs primitive creation of symbols [*primitive symbolism* on the diagram], mythical creation, and creation of idols. Religious creation governs all of these forms of creation in addition to the following forms of creation: technical, customs, and law. It also governs being. Theurgical creation [*theurgy* on the diagram] has the power to change not only all these activities together with religion, but also psychology, the technical sciences, customary morals, theology, and ethics. As far as the activities over which metaphysics holds sway, it is sufficient to list all those activities listed beneath it in the figure. Thus, the activities subordinated to theurgy but not to metaphysics are: primitive symbolism, mythical creation, aesthetic creation, creation of law, and religious creation. But metaphysics also governs activities that theurgy does not, namely: theory of knowledge, epistemology, psychology, and so on. Ethics, for example, is in a position of dependence on both metaphysics and theurgy. This is why, in the field of ethics, we remain doomed to dualism until the Symbol crowns the pyramid of activities. This dualism will be reflected in the psychology of our feelings, in the technical sciences, in the forms of customs, and in the creation of these forms. It will be reflected in customary morals as well as in the very experience and consciousness of being.

We have derived all of this from our diagram, which serves as an emblem for our whole theory of symbols. By looking at the diagram to which we have referred, we get a thorough idea of how a theory of symbolism should be constructed.

10

Unity is Symbol.

But here we must stop. How do we define the Symbol in metaphysical terms? The metaphysical definition of the Symbol must be our immediate task (in our diagram metaphysical unity is a part of the symbol triangle).

First of all, symbolic unity is the unity of what we call, in the theory of knowledge, form and content.

Symbolic unity is the unity of form and content.

This definition of unity is still relative, though, just as the very concept of Symbol is relative. Let us pause for a moment and consider the character of relative concepts.

To begin with, we generally assume that concepts reflect a given reality to be represented. If this is the case, then truth is the coincidence of the object with its representation. Relative concepts are to be distinguished from real concepts. Real concepts, in the process of representation, coincide with objects of reality, whereas relative concepts do not coincide with any object of reality. Instead they appear to be no more than the product of the aimless play of concepts that have been severed from their objects. If this is so, then relative concepts must be distinguished from real concepts in a truly fundamental way. Real concepts reflect something that bears truth. In relative concepts this does not occur. In this sense, to call something a relative concept is to call it a false concept. And if the concept of the Symbol is relative, then in forming a class of symbolic concepts, we are separating ourselves from both reality and the truth. The world of symbols is, then, a world of fiction. Every act of symbolization is merely the false designation of existing objects in terms that correspond to nothing. In this light, symbolism appears to decompose the world of reality.

The proposition, "Unity is Symbol," then, is equivalent to the proposition, "Unity is that which does not exist." We are left in the midst of a plurality of flux, where we can truly say, "All is flux" (πάντα ῥεῖ).

These, in any case, are the traditional attacks on symbolism. Every attempt to formulate a theory of symbolism, in fact, has come up against these simple judgments.

Fortunately, however, such judgments are simply not true.

The fact is that the relation between relative concepts and real concepts is one of dependence and not one of opposition. Either real concepts are a class of relative concepts, or relative concepts are a class of real concepts.

A relative concept does not rest directly on the object being reflected. Between the concept and the object there is a whole series of transitional concepts. These concepts are real concepts. If we accept this, then relative concepts are actually *indirect* real concepts.

But our intellectual processes are by no means restricted to direct real concepts. Any scientific theory, for example, would certainly be a classification of real concepts, or even just one type of such concepts—those bearing on reality. But the basis of the classification cannot be a concept bearing on reality. And even if the basis of the classification consists in an arrangement of such concepts bearing on reality in a certain order, and so appears to be real itself, at the same time it is relative, since there is no object in reality to which it corresponds. If this underlying concept serves as the basis for a classification of concepts bearing on reality, then it is a true concept. But a true concept is one that corresponds to a real object. If no such object exists in reality, then truth is not the coincidence of the object with its representation, or the object is not an object of reality, or, finally, the basic concept underlying the classification is a false one.

If this is so then the basic concept underlying any classification of real concepts is a relative one.

Furthermore, we have seen the necessity of applying theory of knowledge to a treatment of scientific concepts. Epistemological concepts are not based on reality. On the contrary, they are the very premises for the emergence of the process of representing reality. The basis for any scientific classification, however, does rest on an assumption of reality as a premise. Theory of knowledge, in fact, is a kind of controlling lever that takes reality and turns it over and over. An epistemological concept, since it is a relative concept, predetermines experience, and the organization of experience subsequently gives rise to a whole class of concepts bearing on reality. In this light, relative concepts begin to appear more "real" for the reasoning consciousness than concepts [directly] bearing on reality. Relative concepts now turn out to be a sort of distinct class of real concepts. Or, to put it differently, concepts that at first were termed real actually work out to be indirect, relative concepts.

Seen from this point of view, general concepts in science as well as concepts of the universal in theory of knowledge prove to be symbolic concepts. Theory of knowledge must be abstracted from any kind of psychologism. All concepts bearing on reality, however, are psychological concepts. But in the historical [that is, genetic] process whereby concepts are formed, all concepts are obtained from reality, and in this sense they are psychological. Epistemology, although it makes use of psychological concepts ("form," "norm," and so on), strives nevertheless to give these concepts a specific significance not to be found in psychology, attempting to mask the true, psychological significance of the concepts with this meaning. In this sense epistemology is purely relative. Epistemology is indispensable, however, because it predetermines all the experimental sciences. For this reason the relative concepts of epistemology designate something that is not to be found in reality. Relative concepts bearing on reality are emblematic concepts. Emblematic concepts lie at the foundation of both real concepts and those to which we originally referred as relative. The givenness of the world of reality and that of the world of consciousness combine to unite reality and consciousness into an image of immanent being. Emblematic concepts concern not only consciousness and external being but also the data of these two realms considered in their content. Normative concepts, which through their connection with ethics rest on images, and which in turn deduce the methodical concepts of science, create a bridge between the world of images and the world of terms. The emblem takes on the aspect of an allegory when it implies a certain unity between images and metaphysical terms. And the emblem becomes a normative concept when it predetermines a certain system of concepts. In both cases the emblem constitutes the unity of the systems in question. In metaphysics and in ethics the emblem becomes allegory. In theory of knowledge it is a norm. An allegory is a connection with a consciously selected system of images that has an established order of its own. A norm is a connection between cognitive forms. But we have already seen that the norm and the image of value are mutually conditioned. An allegory is a metaphysical interpretation of this image. The emblem is any schema by means of which a norm becomes an allegory.

But between the image of reality, understood as an image of value, and the imaginal concept (allegory),[48] there is still no single, unifying principle. An image of all reality, given in an abstract term, is a metaphysical concept. This reality, which is given to us in an image of value, is the manifest Image of world unity.

A concept that is comparatively less abstract than others is an image. Various degrees of concreteness exist among concepts. Concepts can be more or less imaginal, for instance. Scientific concepts would be one extreme in this category. And yet I can take a system of strictly scientific concepts, replace it with a system of more imaginal concepts, and still express scientific concepts with both. In this sense an allegory would be a concept that brings together relative, scientific, and epistemological concepts on the one hand, and images of reality on the other (thus, the image of chaos may be a negative allegory for endlessness, whereas "endlessness" itself as an image is an allegory of the number series). Allegorical concepts do not simply take the relative concepts of science and cause them to revert back to the concepts of reality from which they are historically, genetically formed. On the contrary, allegorical concepts actually make relative concepts more distant from concepts bearing on reality. Still, however, allegorical concepts are derivative concepts that come from groups of images bearing directly on reality. In this sense allegorical concepts are indirect images, but they are not relative concepts. A relative concept unites within it features of a reality given in concepts with features of images that are not always given in reality. Or, to put it another way, an allegory arbitrarily unites images of reality into a complex not given in reality. This complex is, then, the image of a new reality, and this reality is distinguished from reality as given to us in precisely the same way as value is distinguished from being. This is why the transformation of images of reality (the process of creation) is either a precondition for allegory or the imaginal derivative of allegory. Allegory rests on both cognition and creation. But creation cannot rest exclusively on cognition, just as cognition cannot rest exclusively on creation. Allegory can be reduced to emblem. Thus the emblem, that is, the schema,[49] proves to be the basis for the classification of relative, real, and allegorical concepts. *All three are emblematic concepts.*

An emblem is always an emblem of some unity. The top of any classification of emblematic concepts must be occupied by a concept that can derive the emblematism of the concepts itself from unity. For this unity is not, in and of itself, an emblem. Instead, it is what inspires our understanding to construct a system of emblematic concepts. We saw above that the unity in question cannot be metaphysical in character. Consequently, the very concept of metaphysical unity is an emblem.

For this reason, the very concept of unity is given in emblematic terms. This emblem of emblems, as the absolute limit of any construction of concepts, we will call, speaking from the point of view of cognition, the Symbol.

It is in this sense that we say, "Unity is Symbol."

Given this, we henceforth renounce any right whatsoever to define unity in terms of science, psychology, theory of knowledge, or metaphysics. Any definition of the concept of the Symbol as a relative concept is bound to be relative itself. Such a definition can be constructed only in terms of relative concepts. The concept of Symbol as unity, however, is the very condition for the existence of an emblematism of concepts. Both relative concepts and real concepts are mere subtypes of emblematic concepts.

11

Symbolic unity is the unity of form and content.

First of all, it needs to be said that this is a relative definition. What we are doing is projecting this unity onto the plane of metaphysics, where we see already that the object of true cognition is at the same time a cognitive product. Cognitive products are the same as contents of cognition. The subject of cognition can be identified with form. We also see that the subject of cognition is supra-individual. As a result, the products of the subject, in the genetic development of individual cognition, are the *objects* of this cognition. The supra-individual subject emerges in the reasoning consciousness. This is why this emergence of the subject as a reasoning consciousness is really an act of self-limitation. By means of this self-limitation the product of the supra-individual subject appears as an object. It is possible to consider ourselves, then, products of activity. Our development consists in a process of raising ourselves to the level of supra-individual consciousness by means of the transformation of products into objects (that is, to use the language of the mystics, a process of discovering in ourselves the genuine "I"). In any case, the moral imperative requires such a relation between us and cognition, by stipulating the very conditions for cognition and by normatively predetermining its form. But this predetermination is possible only if it is purposive. And if we are speaking of purposiveness in its true sense, then we must assume from the beginning that the cognition of the subject is our end, while the cognition of the object is merely a means to that end. But if this is so, then there is a certain reciprocal action between the subject and the object. The elements of content (that is, the means) already contain within themselves an element of purposiveness (that is, form), and the converse is also true. Form and content are merely two manifestations of a certain unity. The reader will excuse a tiresome reference to the philosophy of Fichte and Schelling, but it should be pointed out that this philosophy has a profoundly ethical, rather than directly epistemological, force to it. No metaphysics can manage without acknowledging this philosophy. The necessity of such a metaphysics, of course, is a postulate of theory of knowledge.

In epistemology and psychology, however, such a relation between form and content is impossible. Epistemology and psychology both take givenness as their point of departure. For the former, givenness is the material of cognition and cognitive principles, whereas for the latter, givenness is of the physical and psychic order.

Theory of knowledge constructs contents (objects) from cognitive forms. But then its form is found to be hanging in a void. For, through the representation of form as norm, theoretical reason becomes practical reason, and the idea of reason becomes an ideal. The ideal is an essence adequate to the idea, that is, something that encloses form and content in an indissoluble unity. The demand for unity leads to a metaphysical definition of unity as containing form and content.

But we are already aware of the relativity of such a definition. We also know that it will be groundless from an epistemological point of view. At the same time, however, we know that what we call the "reality" of a scientific definition is yet more relative than the definitions we have just mentioned. We are aware that epistemology itself is epistemologically groundless. It is a case of curing like with like. But if we are curing like with like, then we recall that the metaphysical "like," as it were, is unavoidable, that it determines the very search for value in the Other. And we accept this metaphysical component as an emblem that draws us closer to the *Symbol.*

Thus we understand the unavoidability of the metaphysical problem. We understand, too, the unavoidability for metaphysics of eternally revolving on the same circle of contradictions from which the only exit lies in the direction of the concept of the Symbol.

We can see just how broad and how alluring the metaphysical systems of the past are. We also see the resulting bankruptcy in metaphysics. But we are obliged to accomplish the passage, so injurious to the self-respect of our reason, through metaphysics and beyond, recalling all the while that the gates that will lead us into freedom and salvation are narrow indeed.

12

Symbolic unity is the unity of a series of cognitive acts in a series of creative acts. A metaphysical definition of this series, however, soon results in a division of the unity.

It is exactly the same unity that crowns our "ladder" of creation, appearing to us in the image and likeness of man. This is why the ladder of human creation ends with the likening of man to this unity. To use the language of religion, creation leads us to an epiphany, or actual manifestation of the deity. The World Logos takes on the Image of man. The very height of creation is indicated in the words of the Apocalypse: "To him that overcometh will I grant to sit with me in my throne, even as I also overcame, and am set down with my

Father in his throne" [Rev. 3:21]. And this is why, in defining theurgy from the point of view of metaphysics, we say that the purpose of metaphysics is to manifest metaphysical unity in a human image (or Image), to transform the word (principle) into flesh (that is, into the content of our activity). In the language of icons this means: to transform the Word into Flesh. This is how the apostle speaks of it: "In the beginning was the Word, and the Word was with God, and the Word was God" [John 1 : 1]. And further: "That which was from the beginning, which we have heard, which we have seen with our eyes, which we have looked upon, and our hands have handled, of the Word of life" [1 John 1 : 1].

On the ladder of creation, where the Symbol is manifested as Flesh, metaphysical definitions appear beneath theurgical practice.

As soon as we attempt to represent emblematically unity on the order of cognition or on the order of creation it appears to us as a duality. The very expression, "The Word made Flesh," dooms us to duality. Any general judgment about unity is impossible, since every judgment consists of a subject and a predicate, and in the judgment, "The Word is Flesh," the verb "to be" serves as a copula: duality presupposes unity. And unity, therefore, inevitably splitting and becoming duality, reveals the initial *triad* of unity. Triplicity, in fact, is the initial determination of unity. It is the symbol of this unity. And the reason we call symbolic unity "Symbol" is that we represent it as a triad.

This triad (To Be, Word, Flesh) is a Symbol. What is affirmed in the Symbol is the unity of Word and Flesh. From this it is metaphysically comprehensible that, as Rickert maintains, in every judgment we encounter four elements: (1) a subject, (2) a predicate, (3) a copula, (4) a categorical imperative (affirmation).[50] The judgment, "The Word is Flesh," in essence assumes the form: "Let the Word be Flesh." An original unity is symbolically indicated in the "Let it be." Only subsequently does the unity become a duality: "Word—Flesh."

Any judgment is an emblem of symbolic unity (Let it be), of duality (Word—Flesh), of triplicity (The Word will be Flesh), and of quadruplicity (Yes: the Word will be Flesh). In the last judgment the copula *to be* connects unity (Yes) with duality (Word—Flesh). *To be* relates at once to "Yes" (Yes, it is) and to "Word—Flesh" (the Word is Flesh).[51]

This is why, from the point of view of the metaphysics of unity, it becomes clear that Rickert's theory of knowledge recognizes three constitutive forms of cognition: the norm (Yes), the category of givenness (to be), and a transcendental form (Word—Flesh).[52] It is also clear why both the forms of cognition given to us (word, principle) and the images of reality given to us (flesh) can be transcendental forms. The norm, the category of givenness, and the transcendental forms are merely necessary emblems for a theory of knowledge, symbolizing, respectively, unity, duality, and triplicity. But these are symbols. The whole symbolics of unity that we encounter in Fichte was an attempt to include this unity in the jurisdiction of metaphysics. The *Identitätsphilosophie* of Schelling also involved a renunciation of duality. The metaphysics of Hegel established a triplicity in the form of the law of dialectical development. The foundations of the metaphysics of Fichte, Schelling, and Hegel are fully understandable. But the actual theses of these systems, that is, regarded as purely metaphysical systems, doomed the endeavors of these three men to complete failure. For instead of trying to grasp the symbolism of each metaphysics, they took each symbolism and derived it from metaphysics. As a result of this reversal, they could not help appearing monstrous in the light of both science and creation.

It was precisely in the same fashion that, taking the summit of each creative symbolization (Epiphany) for something real in and of itself, and asserting, through cognition, that this new reality belongs to the world of being (when in fact this reality is "real" only for creation), certain thinkers broke the theurgical unity down into a norm of symbolization (that is, of religion) on the one hand, and a norm of morals on the other. Seen in this light, theurgy divides into three fields: the creation of religious symbols (religion), the assertion of these symbols as dogmas (theology), and ethics.[53] Attempts to systematize the first of these fields led to all kinds of teachings about the divine Sophia, or world soul, and the various other emblems of gnostic philosophy. The second field has been reduced to quibbling over the "Filioque."[54] And the third field has become an area for teaching the norms of conduct.

In the same fashion, too, the inevitable failures attending upon every attempt to establish some form of metaphysical unity had the effect of definitively dividing metaphysics. And it was only because metaphysics was indispensable for providing the connections between the different cognitive forms that it was eventually modified and broken down into epistemology, theory of knowledge, and ethics.

The field of ethics has thus, on the one hand, been placed in a position of dependence on creation: ethics assumed the guise of creation. On the other hand ethics could be seen as predetermined by cognitive norms, and thus could be considered as a particular variety of cognition. Ethics has been cut in two by the schism between cognition and creation. Symbolic duality predetermines ethics.

The symbolic triunity in its dualism splits into two triunities: metaphysics and theurgy. In the case of the former triunity, cognitive symbolism constitutes a triad under all the emblems (unconscious—will—representation; or unity—subject—object).

In the case of the second triunity, the symbolism of creation is reflected in various ways: I—thou—he; I—God—world; body—soul—spirit.

But each of the two triunities inevitably breaks down into a new triunity: metaphysics subdivides into epistemology, theory of knowledge, and ethics; the theurgical triunity splits into religious symbolics, dogmatism (theology), and ethics.

Epistemology. Here we have a triune emblem (form of cognition, content of cognition, and norm). With Kant, for instance, this emblem assumes the following form: cognitive activity, the Categories, and the synthetic unity of apperception.

Theory of knowledge. Here the emblem of the triunity takes a different form: norm of cognition, norm of conduct, norm of morals.

Ethics. Here the emblem of the triunity is form of morals, content of morals, norm.

Theology. Here the triunity takes the form: content of morals, norm of conduct, norm of religious creation (triunity).

Religion. Here we have the following emblem: content of morals, form of creative symbolizations (summit of art), norm of creation (or Holy Spirit, Son, Father). Characteristically, religion and art coincide precisely in the form of creative symbolizations. Apollo Musagetes serves as the emblem for the religious symbol of "the Son."[55]

If we turn now to our graphic representation of the pyramid of emblems [see figure 1], then we can understand the necessity of symbolizing the upper triangle by means of a number of other triangles described by the figure: the sum of triangles constitutes the first large triangle. The large triangle is the symbol of our triunity. But triunity is a symbol of unity, and unity appears to us in the guise of a symbol. Thus, whether we treat it in terms of cognition or in terms of creation, it is still in the language of symbols that we are speaking of unity. This is the sense in which we must understand the judgment: "Unity is Symbol."

Until we are able to find the areas belonging to meaning and value within the limits of this triangle, all forms of symbolization will be purely relative, and we will thus have the right to address them with a "No."

And when the forms of cognition, having fettered science on all sides, attempt to place the freedom of our activity in chains as well, then we respond once again with a "No" to every epistemological treatise. And if we wish to justify this "No" in a language comprehensible to epistemology, then we simply say that epistemology finds its ultimate, complete form in theory of knowledge. But when the norm prescribes a purposiveness for our practical and theoretical reason, then we say "No" to this purposiveness too. The very form of the denial of purposiveness is a clear indication of the fundamentally metaphysical bases underlying any theory of knowledge.

It is precisely thus that we deny the meaning of ethics, that is, by pointing to its dependence on creation, on the one hand, and on metaphysics, on the other.

In this way, too, our freedom denies religion and theology. And when anyone speaks to us in dogmatic terms of the Father, the Son, and the Holy Spirit, then we proclaim a triple disavowal of these names. We disavow the name of the Father, because the Father is in the Son. We disavow the Son, because He is in the Holy Spirit and in Truth. We disavow the Holy Spirit too, because the Holy Spirit is in us, and because everything contains within itself the One Image, which is always coming toward us: in us and around us.

But we answer "No" to this Image as well, just as we say "No" to all metaphysical unities. And at that point we find ourselves in an absolute desert, where we make our choice between our "No" and our "Yes, it is."

Having chosen the "Yes, it is," one acquires the gift of seeing, with the radiance of one's own sight, the range of this "Yes" through all the lower triangles. Having chosen the "Yes" and maintaining a skeptical attitude, one begins to understand what metaphysics means by all its relative unities and what creation means when it asserts: "To him that overcometh will I grant to sit with me in my throne, even as I also overcame, and am set down with my Father in his throne" [Rev. 3:21]. And all the different kinds of dogma and all the different disciplines grow iridescent with a thousand rainbow colors. In every color there sings a triumphant "Yes, yes, and yes."

In finding this affirmation, I do not at the same time lose the right to *deny* and ridicule all dogma in cases where dogma affirms itself as value. But my sole dogma is not a dogma of cognition. And it is also by no means a trinity. Neither the "Word made Flesh" nor the "Flesh made Word and Sight" (many-eyed Seraphim) can become a dogma for me.[56] My dogma consists in one thing: "Yes, yes, and yes."

When I wish to develop this dogma, I have the right to add: "Yes, yes—it is." And further, when I measure out the stream of time over which I have risen, I see that even in time *this will be*. And I say with a smile, "Yes, yes—it will be." And when I measure with my glance the distant past, I see the coming splendor of all surrounding reality. In the present is contained all the millennial past of mankind. This past speaks to me in the smiles of those about me, it smiles to me in history, in the relics of religion and art—it is my past. And I answer to it, "Yes, yes—this was."

More than this I do not require.

As for what will be, what is, and what was—this is the language of emblems. The dogmas speak to me in this language, and I answer them with my "Yes."

Once I rise in the realm of my secret bliss, my spirit founders in the center of the summit. It is surrounded by the sides of a triangle, and the lines of time describe a circumference around this triangle. What *was* in the beginning now becomes what *will be*, just as what *will be* becomes what *was* in the beginning: a blinding light permeates everything.

Figure 1 now takes on a different appearance: we saw that the small triangle at the summit was symbolized by the large upper triangle, which in turn split into the two large lower triangles whose base angles overlap in the area labeled "being." We have already described the upper triangle: it contains epistemology, theory of knowledge, ethics, theology, religion, metaphysics, theurgy, and theosophy. Value appears at its top.

In the process of ascent towards Value, the meaning of everything that is not Value was devalued. Now, however, the summit has become the center and illuminates everything that had previously appeared to be empty. We know already that in this region form and content are indivisible. In order to leave the triangles of metaphysics and theurgy in a position where they are joined with the triangle of Value, while at the same time joining the norm of cognition with that of creation into a symbolic unity, we may now arrange the three lower triangles [immediately underneath the triangle of Value] so that they surround the upper triangle [that is, the triangle of Value].

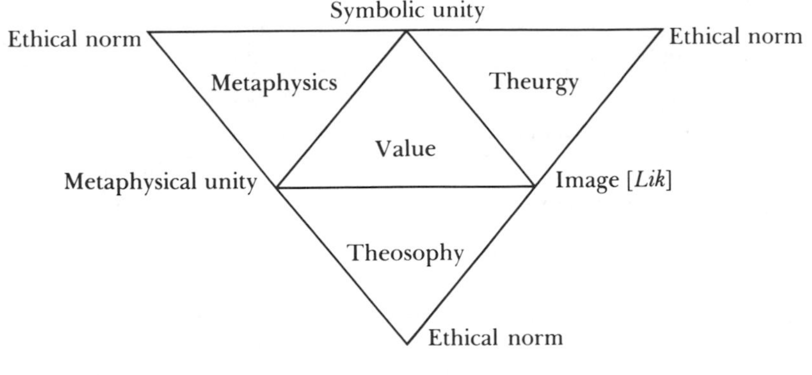

Figure 2

The new figure (see figure 2) is significant. At each of the points of the new triangle lies the ethical norm. This is because, in figure 1, one angle of each of the triangles of theosophy, theurgy, and metaphysics met at the point designated "ethical norm." The ethical norm is the common factor found in theurgy, theosophy, and metaphysics. Thus, by arranging the triangles in accordance with our rules (namely, that the norms of cognition and creation must coincide), we obtain a new triangle, all of whose points correspond to the ethical norm, and whose angles form the areas of metaphysics, theosophy, and theurgy, while the center of the whole triangle is Value. We will call the emblem thus obtained an ethical emblem. The meaning of this emblem is that ethics is an external determination of Value, or, conversely, that Value is an internal determination of ethics. That one of the angles whose vertices are designated "ethical norm" should enclose the area of theurgy demonstrates that ethics is simply the external form of several essentially creative activities. And in so far as religion and theurgy are premises of artistic creation, aesthetic value may take on an ethical form.

If we turn back now to figure 1, we see that ethics and theosophy share a common point. But, recalling the dual character of ethics (ethics as a symbol of cognition, ethics as a symbol of creation), we may now make two triangles out of the triangle of ethics and place them on either side of theosophy, one representing the metaphysical dimension of ethics [ethical cognition], the other, the theurgical [ethical creation]. Proceeding thus, we obtain figure 3.

If we examine this new emblem, we see that it forms three triangles ($a_1 b_1 c_1$, $a_2 b_2 c_2$, $a_3 b_3 c_3$), which intersect each other at three

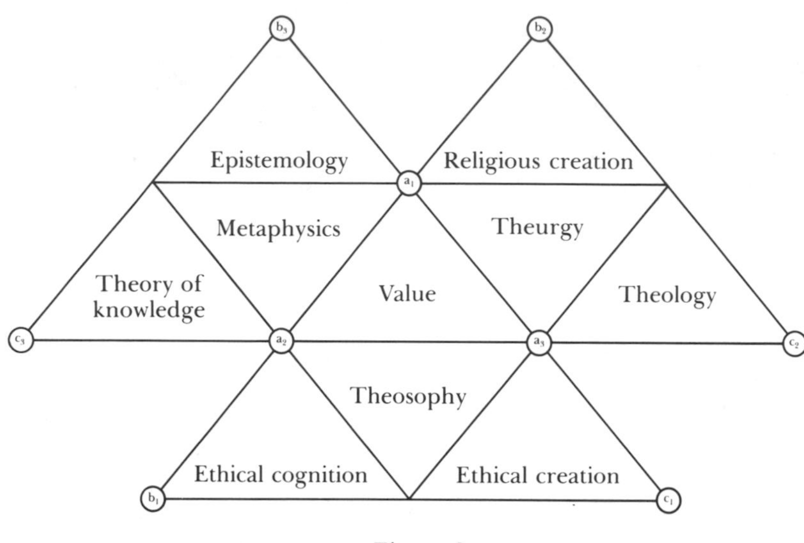

Figure 3

points $(a_1 a_2 a_3)$. The area $a_1 a_2 a_3$ is a triangle at whose center lies Value. This signifies that Value illuminates three areas of activity: cognitive, ethical, and creative. The triangle of cognition $(a_3 b_3 c_3)$ leads to Value by way of metaphysics. In this sense it is possible to speak of metaphysical value as one variety of symbolization. Similarly, the religious area $(a_2 b_2 c_2)$ leads to Value, but by way of theurgy, and one may speak in the same sense of theurgical value. Theurgy is one of the various means for symbolizing value. Finally, one may speak of ethical value, which is symbolized by theosophy. The triadic quality of this area is symbolized in psychology, seen, that is, as comprising the triad of activities of consciousness: mind, feeling, will. Continuing with our schema, we may say that the mind is the emblem of cognition, feeling is the emblem of religion, and will is the emblem of ethics. Such an arrangement is adopted by our triangles, which designate the locus of the highest activities of cognition and creation when they are represented in the light of a unifying principle. If we examine figure 3 carefully, we see that it contains three pairs of triangles inverted with respect to each other, with the apex of each triangle resting on the base of its pair.[57] We may now say that the Symbol is expressed in symbolizations, and, in the present case, metaphysics, theosophy, and theurgy are such symbolizations. In asserting that the Symbol is [expressed] in symbolizations, we may shift the area of the symbolizations (for instance, theosophy) so that it coincides in part with the area of the Symbol. In this case we get three six-pointed stars.[58] It now also becomes clear why the six-pointed star occupies such an important place among the mystical emblems. In our diagram the six-pointed star designates the appearance of symbolic unity in the symbolizations.

We have seen that it is possible to speak of Value as being relatively expressible in cognition, ethics, and religion.

If we now treat theurgical creation in the same manner as we have treated Value, we may orient all the triangles lying beneath theurgy [in figure 1] so that they now surround theurgy, just as we had previously placed theurgy in one of the positions surrounding Value. If we were to proceed thus, we would obtain a figure analogous to figure 3, but where theurgy would occupy the area of intersection of the three areas of creation: aesthetic, ethical, and custom. And its values, incidentally, would be symbolized in dogmatism, religious creation, and ethics. Religious creation would then be the nerve center of aesthetic creation. And further, if we were to arrange the primitive forms of creation around aesthetics, we would see that it is possible to speak of aesthetic values.

The pyramid of cognition and creation (see figure 1) would then appear as a system of all the different kinds of symbolization. Or, to put it figuratively, symbolic unity, illuminating from within all the different types of activity, transforms these activities into series of values.

The aim of a theory of symbolism is this: first, to identify the theoretical locus, as it were, from which to construct a system, and, second, to form, on the basis of the most fundamental concept of Value, a series of methodical values.

Our task consists quite simply in demonstrating convincingly that a theory of symbolism cannot be constructed solely from the natural sciences, from psychology, or from theories of knowledge, law, or custom. Nor can such a theory be derived from mythical creation, aesthetics, ethics, or religion. And finally, a theory of symbolism cannot be the same thing as metaphysics, theurgy, or theosophy.

What, then, is a theory of symbolism?

13

When I use the word *terminology* I refer to a science of terms (although such a science does not exist). A science like this would trace the genetic development of terms (Eucken,[59] as a matter of fact, was interested in terminology) and classify them. It would also acquaint us with the rules for using the terms in question. The great majority of theoretical debates involve not the meaning of ideas, but the meaning attached to them by terms. And the great changes in philosophical systems are really for the most part changes in terminologies. A term that is clear in the beginning will suddenly become obscure as the conceptual apparatus becomes more complex. The same term at that point requires a reclarification. Our grandfathers, for instance, read Kant and understood what he meant. But we, after reading the Critiques several times over, are still disputing the terminological meaning of "thing-in-itself." In fact, if the very essence of the development of philosophy did not lie in terminology, then Natorp would never have taken Plato and turned him into a good Cohenist.[60] Let us, however, ignore the problem of terminological ambiguity for the present and attempt to understand what Leibniz meant by his "Monadology."

Here is what Leibniz says: "[1.] The Monad, of which we shall here speak, is nothing but a *simple* substance, which enters into compounds. By 'simple' is meant 'without parts.' . . . [3.] Now where there are no parts, there can be neither extension nor form nor divisibility. These Monads are the real atoms of nature and, in a word, the elements of things. . . . [9.] Indeed, each Monad must be different from every other . . . [11.] . . . the natural changes of the Monads come from an *internal principle*. . . ."[61]

We will not bother to direct our attention to the terminological meaning of the concepts "substance," "atom," or "element." Let us inquire instead what Leibniz meant to say. The Monad is something without extension, without divisibility, and without parts. It is obvious, then, that what Leibniz means by Monad is unity. And we have already seen that such a unity is related to symbolic unity. The Monad is unity.

On the other hand, Leibniz speaks of the internal principle of the Monad. If Monads are *individua simplicissima*, then the internal principle of each Monad must be the norm of its change. If the Monad has an internal principle and if it changes, then by virtue of this very fact it is not of primary simplicity, for when we speak of the internal principle of the Monad, we are implying something that is *not* the internal principle: we are speaking of a duality. Consequently, Leibniz's Monad is not the end point of all divisibility, for there is a unity that precedes and predetermines it. Monads, then, are individual complexes, all determining an internal principle. The internal principle of the Monad is symbolic unity. Its place, to refer to our diagram [see figure 1], is at the top of the pyramid. It is the sum of all the triangles in that diagram. The internal principle may also be defined thus: it is the macrocosm in the microcosm and vice versa. The internal principle of Monads defines the Monads. Monads, which may be defined by unity, enter into various kinds of relationships with each other. The internal principle of Monads, once we define it, demands a diadic emblem, which is to say that, as the norm of Monadic change, this principle is also the norm of relationships between two Monads.

Let us return now to figure 1. Two lines spread out from the top of the triangle, graphically depicting the Monadic manifestation of unity. Symbolic unity emerges as both diad and triad. Each triangle in the pyramid forms a triad. But any one of the Monads, far from destroying triads, may be included in yet more complex groups of Monads. Thus the metaphysical interpretation of the Monad as the unique essence of cognition is an indication of the tendency of the Monad to exist in a more elaborate complex. A Monad, for instance, can become part of the composition of a tetrad. The ethical interpretation of the Monad as the unity of ethical activity defines it as forming part of a hexad, and so on.

But in our understanding of unity as Symbol, we have already overstepped the limits of any monadology. On the contrary, the very concept of the Monad as an indivisible essence may be derived from the concept of the Symbol.

The judgment, "Unity is Symbol," is a synthetic judgment. The judgment, "Symbol is unity," however, is an analytic judgment, since the concept of unity [in the predicate] is already contained in [the subject] "Symbol." Similarly, the concept of "something" is contained in the concept of Symbol.

Starting from the concept of Symbol, we can clearly understand the symbolic notions of the ancient religions. The Hindu conception of Parabrahman, for instance, as the causeless cause of all being, comes quite close to our concept of Symbol. The Parabrahman is the "THAT" and "THIS," Avidya and Vidya. "THAT" is the nonexistent, and from its emanation arises Brahma. "THIS" is "the Self," "one only" (cf. Symbol as "unique"). "THIS" does not create anything (cf. the position of symbolic unity above the various types of creation in figure 1). The noncreating unity can be identified with the first Logos. From the first Logos descends the second Logos (form is metaphysical unity, Purusha) and every kind of content (Prakriti). From the second Logos descends the third Logos, identified with the norm of cognition (Mahat) and with the World-Soul. This hierarchy of three Logoi is to be found in the teaching of contemporary occultists.[62]

As the disciple ascended the ladder of creation, after passing beyond Yoga, he would attain the ability to merge internally with Alaya (Soul of the World), since Alaya, though internally changeless, alters nonetheless in various zones of being. This is the teaching of Aryasanga. The highly developed Yogi would then be able to exist in a state of Paranishpanna, that is, absolute perfection. At that point his soul would be called Alaya, and he would become Anupadaka, that is, without origin, and would embody with his image the manifested Logos in the world.[63]

How often we have seen in history that the symbol has been represented by means of relative images! For some image-content inevitably seems to enter into any concept of the symbol because of the intervention of various artistic means of representation. The Symbol cannot be given without symbolization. This is why we embody it in an image. The image, embodying the Symbol, is called a symbol[64] only in a more general sense of the word. God, for example, is such a symbol, when seen as an existing something. (One cannot, however, say of the Symbol that it exists or does not exist, just as it is impossible to make such statements about a norm of ethical duty. From the point of view of Eastern philosophy, the idea of a thing may cease to exist, but the *thing* does not thereby cease to be. How strongly Rickert would agree with this view!)

The reality created by God is a symbolic reality. It cannot be said of this reality that it ever actually manifests itself in our own reality. One can, however, say simply that it *is*. At the same time one cannot say that this reality is the same thing as being, for in saying this we would be regarding the Ought as predetermined by being, whereas theory of knowledge leads to the opposite view.[65] And finally, one cannot say of symbolic reality that there is simply no such thing, for in that case value would not predetermine the Ought.

We must surmount all forms of the areligious, but we must also surmount all forms of the religious. The character of this surmounting of the forms of religious culture is that of religion sui generis. The imaginal expression of this religion lies in eschatology. The religion of the Symbol is in this sense the religion of the end of the world, the end of the earth, the end of history. Christianity attains this religion of the end in the Apocalypse.

14

Concerning symbolic reality it can be said that it is "something." This "something" in our sense is the Tao of Lao-tze.[66]

An epistemological analysis of immanent being (the content of consciousness) depicts being to us from the point of view of its concrete irreducibility: being in this sense is something individual and irrational. But this in no way signifies that it is unconscious. For concreteness and individuality also characterize the world of reality if we regard reality from outside the methodological forms of science. In theory of knowledge it is constitutive forms that predetermine reality.[67] For Rickert these forms are: the norm (yes), the category (to be), and the transcendental form. But reality may not be understood as essence. "The question of the essence of the content of reality," says Rickert, "is actually no question at all, since reality does not have just one content."[68]

These words contain an extremely important point that determines the whole character of reality. We have defined symbols, from the viewpoint of metaphysics, as the unity of form and content. Symbolic content, which shows us diversity in the individual, is located in the conflict between the different contents of immanent reality. Immanent reality appears new in every individual complex. From this point of view, the world is a collection of individualities. The temporal form of individual content is called an "instant." The instant emerges, not as the farthest limit of the divisibility of time, but as a concentration of moments united by the individual unity of content. This unity flows by us as a self-enclosed world. The process of immersion in this world is the process of experiencing. To experience the instant is to experience an individual process that is enclosed from all sides.

"Whoever wishes to become familiar with the content [of reality]," says Rickert, "in so far as this content is represented in the absence of the content of concepts from the individual sciences and, consequently, in the absence of methodological forms, must attempt simply to *experience* as much of that content as possible."[69] These words contain yet another extremely important point that determines the essence of individual content: our own experience turns out to be that essence. But if we order our experiences, we can place them in a single, continuous series. If we then delve into an individual experience, we see that our experience proceeds along a series of steps that disclose themselves to us as a single, individual complex. This process of delving into an experience condenses it, as it were: the experience becomes more acute, it becomes possible for us to infect others with it. The depth that is experienced becomes noticeable from outside as a force. An individual experience becomes individual-collective (as do the experiences of artists or poets). An individual-collective experience may subsequently become a universal experience (the experience of Christianity, for example). This is because it is easier to comprehend the surface of an experience after having first delved into it and explored its depth. For this reason the depth of an experience emerges as its force. Whole groups of individualities, gliding along the surfaces of experienced content, while these surfaces from within enter the sphere of influence of the individual, find themselves drawn into the individual process. Any individual experience strives for universality. The unity of individual processes becomes the symbol of a whole series of unities. And the individual experience becomes a sort of norm for a whole series of experiences. This "experienced norm" is one type of creative value. The individual becomes a symbol of value. Such an individual must always tend towards his own norm. He recreates his own person. The experienced instant embraces the individual's entire life. His own image precedes him in the past and continues along up to each experienced instant. And in the future a certain unknown Image stands before him and penetrates into his soul. The farthest limit of the individual's union with the Image becomes the limit of his experience. The eternal "I" is experienced in the personal "I": "Ye shall be as gods," says the Book of Genesis.[70]

The eternal world-"I", from the point of view of theory of knowledge, is merely an allegory for the supra-individual subject. Thus religion, when examined from the point of view of theory of knowledge, is experience in immanent being of the supra-individual. God thus becomes a symbol for the subject.

"And now I am no more in the world, but these are in the world, but I and He are one."[71] Such will be the words of one who has transformed the instant into eternity.

15

Aesthetic experiences properly speaking are those in whose form images are taken from immanent being and actualized in some material substance. The various art forms arise in a state of dependence on the material [in which they are to be actualized]. The relation between the forms of aesthetic creation and those of religious creation is equivalent to the relation existing between constitutive and methodological forms. The former (religious forms) are the forms of individuals, whereas the latter are universal forms. Aesthetic and religious forms are combined in the mystery play. On the one hand, the mystery play contains a synthesis of universal forms. On the other hand, the form of experience in the mystery is the form of the individual. The form of the individual *becomes* the individual here in the stricter sense of the word, that is to say, it becomes the person. Between the individual and the aesthetic form, we observe a series of transitional stages. The individual may be the norm of aesthetic creation, as, for example, in Greek sculpture. Furthermore, in drama there is an underlying myth, that is, a chain of events that overtake the individual. But the individual carries this chain (the norm) within himself, and in this sense the individual controls his own destiny.

A mystery play is really a form of expanded drama. At the same time, our individual life, in light of attempts to define it from the point of view of aesthetics, is an expanded mystery play. Our life is thus an object of aesthetic symbolization. But it is also an object of religious symbolization. Aesthetic symbolization breaks our life down into forms of art, whereas religious symbolization exposes the life given to us as the irreducible content of some form. Both types of symbolization are predetermined by a creative norm.

The Symbol may also be defined in epistemological terms, and in that case it appears as the norm of [all] symbolization. Symbolization in religious creation is connected with individual conduct. The norm of symbolization is at the same time the norm of conduct. This is why, if we speak of the Symbol in the relative terms of normative philosophy, we can construct judgments about it in the three formulae of the categorical imperative. In [*The Groundwork of the*] *Metaphysic of Morals*, Kant asks how pure reason can be practical, but says, "Human understanding is utterly powerless to explain this, and all our efforts and pains to find an explanation are in vain."[72]

The content of the imperative is not dependent on its formulation. This content is symbolic to the extent that any content of immanent being is symbolic, and, in fact, any content of immanent being in our sense *is* at the same time symbolic content. We will not elaborate on how the heteronomy of the will is already implied in the definition of practical reason as will, something Simmel has pointed out.[73] The relation between Kantian morals and Nietzschean morals is by no means a relation of opposition.

Theurgic symbolization in and of itself knows no moral norms in the Kantian sense, since its norm is the Image of the Symbol. Its goal is to approach this Image. It is in this tendency that the morals of theurgic creation lie. In saying "morals" I am mindful of expressing myself with the help of emblems, which, in turn, are predetermined by the Symbol.

But the norms that actualize the theurgic tendency [to approach the Image] necessarily coincide with the forms of morals, expressed, that is, in the three Kantian imperatives. The norms of morals lie in freedom, but freedom exists only in the Symbol. Symbolization, that is, the linking of experiences in an instant, is expressed in images (symbols). From the point of view of cognition, symbolization is "causality through freedom."[74] Symbolization occurs at the point where cognition has overstepped all possible restrictive boundaries, that is, at the point where it has turned back to itself. In the forms of knowledge, in the forms of cognition, and in the norms of practical reason, the definition of freedom is heteronomous. We are within our rights in applying the term *heteronomous*, which Kant uses for the will, to symbolization.[75] For symbolization rests on experience, but experience ultimately goes back to the same unity as reason does. But this heteronomy of freedom is in fact autonomy when we are speaking of attempts to define it either in terms of practical reason or in terms of creation. Only in the Symbol does one find freedom. The relation to reality, as well as to symbolic reality, is what provides the maximum of freedom. This maximum of freedom subordinates the norm to the very Image towards which creation is directed. The concept of the Symbol as some sort of unity is necessarily connected with the understanding of the Symbol as the very principle of autonomy. This is why the emblem of ethical duty, related, as it is, to Value, becomes at the same time an emblem of freedom. This is the reason that the words of a certain young theoretician of symbolism are so arresting: "The Symbol, 'I want,' turns into 'I must,' but 'I must' also turns into 'I want.'" In deriving all the types of cognition as emblems of values, I discover in cognition the very source of autonomous cognition. In precisely the same way, if we understand all the different types of creation as symbols of different values, we discover the source of autonomous creation.

The Symbol is the limit of all cognitive, creative, and ethical norms: the Symbol is, in this sense, the limit of limits.

16

Our quest for the meaning and value of life has in every instance proved vain, so long as we failed to perceive that it could never be fruitful in any cognitive sphere. We then undertook to search for meaning in the next sphere beyond, and this too turned out to be fruitless. The ladder of our ascent grew ever taller. Everything that lay behind us appeared dead. And once we reached the summit of the pyramid in our diagram, we were convinced that the entire pyramid of knowledge was dead. Only at the summit of [the scale of] cognition did it become clear that the meaning and value of our activities lay in the creation of life. But if we wish to experience the life we have identified as our own, we encounter nothing but chaos, and every creative effort just spreads more chaos. And when we wish to secure a foundation on an image of the embodied cosmos, such as the Image, we see that the beauty of this Image is merely the foam on the crest of religious creation. Turning then to religion, we see that it arises out of an aesthetic need. Religion is the foam on the crest of the wave of aesthetics, as it were. Turning to the element of beauty, we see in turn that the beautiful is merely the foam on the crest of the dark wave of primordial creation. And finally, primordial creation is the foam on the crest of chaos. If we stand on the steep heights of cognition and use cognition to define creation as something we must experience, we see that the Images of this creation are like the play of the sun's rays on the ocean of future chaos. We find ourselves ineluctably constrained to hurl ourselves into the chaos of life if we do not wish to freeze to death on the steep, icy heights of cognition. Value now begins to bare its chaotic countenance. Such has been the first trial of our novitiate. If we do overcome, if we do hurl ourselves fearlessly into the eddy of the swirling Maelstrom, we will see that some force will come and bear us up anew: we will see that the chaos of experience is not chaos at all: it is cosmos.[76] The musical element in the world resounds in the roar of the chaotic waves of life. This element is the content of some force that impels us to create beautiful images. It then begins to appear to us as though some image were presenting itself to us in a kind of visitation in the depths of the whirlpool of life and beckoning us to come to it. If we follow where the image beckons us, we are out of danger: our novice's trail has been successfully completed, and the first stage of our initiation is over.

Thus begins our ascent along the order of creation. The image, beckoning us ever higher, slips away from us every time we come close to it. We surpass the creative order by means of the creative order itself; and then we land on the summit of theurgical creation. But there the image, beckoning us to itself, turns out to be nothing more than a norm, and the starry heavens turn out to be a ceiling.

Once again we perish, this time in creation, just as we previously perished in cognition, for creation has turned out to be dead, just as cognition was. We find ourselves now at the threshold of our second initiation.

We have already passed the point of no return: we have passed beyond the pyramid of cognition and the pyramid of creation. Out here there is nothing to support us. Life on earth flies by in front of us, and we recall everything we ever learned with our cognitive faculties and everything we ever created. It is now up to us to say to our past either "yes" or "no." Here we remember that the life of the universe was symbolically reflected to us in our quest for meaning and value. It is within ourselves that we will find the force to say to this life "yes" or "no."

If we say "no" we are ruined. If, on the other hand, our entire being, in spite of the senselessness of it, in defiance of that "common sense" that so readily persuades us of the senselessness of actions, proclaims "yes," then the light of the last affirmation will flare up before us, and we will hear the eternal Hosannah of the universe.

The second trial is over, and we have successfully completed our second initiation.

Now, as we gaze behind us, we see dead life. All the names for things have flown away, and all the different kinds of creation have crumbled into dust, even as we were standing at the threshold. Now, as we stand in the temple, we must, like Adam who was created before all other men, give names to things. We must, like Orpheus, make the stones dance with the music of words. As we stand now on the magic halo of truth and value, we see nothing but death surrounding the halo. Only dead things are in front of us. But when we give names to these cherished dead we restore them to life. The light that bursts from the triangle at the summit of the pyramid begins now to penetrate through to everything below. Everything that had been killed in cognition and creation is now summoned back to life in the Symbol.

Now, like magi, we descend the pyramid, and wherever we step, right is restored: the right for cognition to be cognition, and the right for creation to be creation.

The dead pyramid has now become a living pyramid. Knowledge of life, the ability to resurrect, takes the initiate to the third stage.

Descending to the realm of theosophy, we give theosophy the right to establish a parallel between the emblems of metaphysics and the symbols of creation. Both kinds of emblems are emblems of value.

Descending to the realm of metaphysics, we can now illuminate all the different kinds of metaphysical unity. We require only one thing: that metaphysical unity should properly derive the norm of cognition and the norm of ethics, since it is in effect a bridge, allegorically joining the norm of theoretical cognition and the norm of ethical cognition. We may now orient metaphysics around these norms and this unity. It is here that the conviction arises that one and only one kind of metaphysics is possible, namely one that acts to predetermine both our cognition and our conduct.

Descending further to the realm of epistemology, we see that symbolic unity, after creating an emblem of this unity for metaphysics, derives a new emblem for epistemology. It is the norm of cognition that becomes the emblem of value in theory of knowledge, breaking down into either forms of cognition or forms of morals. The norm of cognition in theory of knowledge becomes a unity joining theoretical and practical reason. And thus all the existing kinds of epistemological constructions must, from the point of view of a theory of value, be oriented around the schema indicated in figure 1. The norm of cognition must serve as this schema, predetermining both cognitive and moral categories.

Descending once again to the realm of psychology, we see that symbolic unity, after creating emblems of this unity for metaphysics and epistemology, constructs a new emblem for psychology. The emblem of value in psychology is cognitive form, which joins the psychical and the physical (internal and external) in a concept of immanent being. Psychological unity breaks down into the physical interpretation of psychical factors on the one hand and the internal [that is, psychical] interpretation of physical manifestations of the organism on the other. This psychophysical monism comes close to our psychological schema, which, as in all our schemas, is a triad (form of cognition, the psychical, the physical). But psychophysical monism is a postulate of parallelism. What we are illuminating here is the right of psychology to become psychophysics. From the point of view of a theory of value, *all* types of psychological construction must be derived from a unity and oriented around a psychological schema.

Descending further to the realm of exact science, we see that symbolic unity, after creating emblems of this unity for metaphysics, epistemology, and psychology, derives a new emblem for mechanics. The emblem of value for the exact sciences is the principle of the physical interpretation of nature, combining number, as a means of measuring (measuring time, that is), and the physiological process of life. This is why a schema of the exact sciences consists in an examination of the processes of life through measuring them, in time, in physical (or mechanical) terms. All the different types of exact science (botany, zoology, physiology) are defined by their dependence on physical and mathematical constants.

Each emblem derived from Value presents itself to us as a triadic schema, very much like what is shown in figure 1.

A theory of symbolism, after determining the locus of unity (namely, as that of the Symbol), must then deduce from this unity a whole series of emblematic disciplines. Within the limits of each of these disciplines, we find relative conclusions regarding the meaning and value of being.

In precisely the same fashion, we descend the ladder of creation and see that symbolic unity in theurgical creation shows us the Image of divinity [Image of the Logos in figure 1] itself. The Symbol gives its own emblem in the Image and Name of the Living God. In theurgy this Image is the emblem of value. In conformity with the triadic quality of each scheme, the Image appears as a unity predetermining both the norm of conduct [ethical norm in figure 1] and the feminine element [image of creation in figure 1] in religious creation. This element is symbolized in the image of the Eternal Feminine, Sophia, or the Heavenly Church. All the different kinds of theurgical creation must be oriented by cognition within a theurgical schema and must be examined in their relation to the symbols of Sophia and the Logos. Thus we see that, from the point of view of cognition, it is possible to speak of norms of theurgical creation. We must not forget, however, that, in so doing, we are speaking the language of emblems.

Descending now into the realm of religion [religious creation in figure 1], we see that symbolic unity, after giving theurgy an emblem of this same unity, derives a new emblem—this time a religious one. This emblem is none other than the image of Sophia-[Divine] Wisdom [image of creation in figure 1] seen as the principle uniting man with the unities. The Church becomes the emblem of value in religion, the Church, that is, seen as the bond between believers (the Church is, as it were, an image of the Divine Sophia). But even this unity takes on the appearance of a duality, since it breaks down into the content of our moral experiences [content of morals in figure 1] on the one hand and the form of religious symbolizations [form of symbolizations in figure 1] on the other. All the religions can be oriented in accordance with their relation to religious unity. In fact, the relation between experience and symbolization as well as the relation of both to the unity that lies at the source can serve as a schema for such an orientation. The triadic quality of this schema in and of itself gives rise to the notion of the triadic principle of the divinity, where the Father is unity, the Son is the form of external manifestation of the unity [that is, the form of symbolizations], and the Holy Spirit is the content of religious forms [that is, content of morals].

As we descend into the realm of aesthetics, we see that symbolic unity, having given its emblem to theurgy and religion, constructs a new emblem for aesthetic creation. If we define this type of creation from the standpoint of the very highest form of creation, we see that the religious Symbol of the Son is reflected, in aesthetic creation, in the image of both Apollo (the form of the image) and Dionysus (the content of the image). The image of the Divine Sophia, however, is reflected in the form of the Muse. The relation between the Muse and Apollo in aesthetics is the relation between the feminine element of theurgic creation (Sophia) and the masculine (the Image of the Logos). If we define the emblem of aesthetic creation from the standpoint of cognition, then we cannot help deducing that this emblem is equivalent to the unity of the various forms of symbolization. In aesthetic creation the emblem of value is the form of symbolization. It appears, nonetheless, as a duality, since it breaks down within the artistic image, existing as both form and content of that image [form of images and content of images in figure 1]. The unity of the form and content of the image is the schema by which any aesthetics is constructed. We must, then, orient our various systems of aesthetics around a schema, which is to say, around a norm of aesthetic construction.

As we descend now to the content of images that captivate us so much in art, we see that symbolic unity, which has given emblems to theurgy, religion, and art, derives a new emblem for primitive creation. Here the content of images is the unity of world chaos [chaos in figure 1] and the musical element of the soul. This unity breaks down into a duality, namely, the spirit of music on the one hand and the imageless chaos of being that surrounds us on the other. The image lies over the abyss of chaos, closing it off from us as if with a shield. But the image and its content join together with the chaos, or so primitive creation is described from the point of view of a higher form of creation, namely, aesthetic creation. From the point of view of cognition, however, primitive creation is defined as a law that controls the sources of all other kinds of creation. Those mute physiological processes governed by the rhythm of our blood as it circulates in our veins arouse within us the urge towards activity. We take this tempo of our blood and redirect it into the creation of images. In primitive symbolism the emblem of value is the content of the image.

Thus we have explained the pyramid of cognition and creation in light of the concept of value. At the base angles of the pyramid lie chaos and number, which governs chaos. In number and chaos our paltry being is torn apart. Only symbolic unity can restore both value and meaning to being. To change being in any way is to raise it higher.

Let us now take a quick look at the pyramid of emblems. The position of any triad in this pyramid is preestablished by a unity. If we call this unity by an absolute name, then we reduce all the different kinds of cognition and all the different kinds of creation to the emblematics of pure meaning. Any time we attempt to ground our entire life within the limits of a single given triad, we get nothing but a series of relative concepts and relative creations. But owing to the weakness of our cognition, we [tend to] regard relative concepts concerning cognition and creation as real concepts.

It is for this reason that, within the limits of our cognition, we always turn unity into the Symbol.

The first definition of unity is the definition of it as Symbol.

Thus the emblematics of pure meaning is divided into three parts: in the first part the theoretical locus is derived that lies at the base of our system of emblems. In the second, the emblems themselves are deduced independently of the paths we have chosen to ascend in order to reach them. But it is only in the third part that we can systematize all the emblematic loci of cognition and creation into any given discipline. Here we might, for example, create a system of creative values within the methods of a mechanical world view. It is not difficult to see that theurgic, religious, aesthetic, and primitive creation within the confines of a mechanical world view would [in relation to each other] begin to look somewhat like the mutual conversion of different forms of energy. We might also create a system of creative values within the confines of psychology, and here it is not difficult to see how, in the end, we would get a classification and system for correlating creative experiences. We might give an epistemological foundation to our system of creative values. Then, as it is easy to see, we would obtain a theory concerning the forms and norms of creation. Or we might create a system of creative values within the confines of metaphysics, and it is not difficult to see how this system would take on the appearance of a theory of the metaphysical essences that predetermine creation. This is essentially the same thing as Schopenhauer's theory of ideas in art. Finally, we might create a system of creative values that begins from the very idea of Value, and here it is not difficult to see that this system would be an emblematics of pure meaning, that is, a theory of symbolism.

And conversely for cognitive values. We might create a system of cognitive values using the images of primitive symbolism. It is not difficult to see that we would get, as a result, cosmologies and ontologies where metaphysics, epistemology, psychology, and mechanics would adopt mythological images. Such was the philosophy of the ancient Greeks, for example, the school of the physicists. We might create a system of cognitive values using the images of aesthetic creation. It is not difficult to see that all the constructions of metaphysics, knowledge, and psychology would then be explained as aesthetic phenomena of cognition. The world would then appear to us as an aesthetic phenomenon. This, for example, is the basis of Nietzsche's theory of Greek culture, which he sees as the product of a confluence of two creative forces. We might also create a system of cognitive values using terms from religious symbolism. It is not difficult to see that the result of our labors in this case would be all the different kinds of gnosticism and all the different types of scholasticism. The whole Alexandrian period of Greek culture is tinged with gnosticism, and the Middle Ages are replete with scholasticism. We might systematize the cognitive values by employing the images of theurgical creation. In this case we would obtain a variety of forms of magic, Kabalism, alchemy, and astrology. Finally, we might create a system of cognitive values by starting from the concept of value itself. It is not difficult to see that the resulting system would be a system of symbolism.

A theory of symbolism sanctions all the different kinds of value. All such a theory requires is a firm orientation. The emblem of value within the limits of any given triad must not conflict with the emblem of the same values within the limits of any other triads. The emblems may not be moved outside the limits of the schema. The level of any of the different values is determined by the position of the triad relative to the fundamental triad, that is, the triangle at the top.

17

Contemporary epistemology ultimately goes back to problems whose solution is precisely the starting point in the construction of a theory of symbolism.

In the representation of being as a form of judgment, in the assertion that any given judgment must be actualized not as something true, but as something obligatory [that is, based on the Ought], in the way truth coincides with the Ought and with Value, we have already abandoned the strict grounds of epistemological analysis.[77] Theory of knowledge here comes very close to the metaphysics of unity.

Let us pause for a moment to consider the nature of the judgment, "Truth is Value."

The Freiburg school of philosophy joins the following two judgments with the one we have just mentioned:[78]

"Truth is the Ought."

"The Ought is Value."

From which it follows:

"Truth is Value."

What concerns us here is a whole range of questions to which the Freiburg school has no answer.

First, in the judgment just cited, where is the subject and where is the predicate? The judgment might also be read in the reverse order: Value is truth.

Second, is this judgment a synthetic or an analytic judgment, in the Kantian sense, that is, is the relation of the predicate to the subject that of something already included in it, or is the predicate something entirely separate from the subject?

Third, if the judgment, "Truth is Value," is an analytic one, does this mean that the concept of truth is a concept belonging to the subject, so that the predicate is already contained in it, or is the reverse true, that Value is a concept belonging to the predicate and truth is already derived from *it*?[79] In the former case Value is one attribute of truthfulness among others. In the second case truthfulness is an attribute of Value.

Fourth, the judgment, "Truth is Value," may also be formulated thus: "The Ought is Value." Or it may take the form: "Truth is the Ought." How are these three judgments related to each other in content? We know besides that the Ought is the norm of these judgments. The judgment, "Truth is the Ought," is a judgment asserting the Ought itself. The content of this judgment consists in no more than the assertion of a norm for all other assertions. The content of this judgment is the very norm of judgments in the category of givenness. A strange picture results. An epistemological prius (yes) for all givenness is subsumed under givenness (to be). The norm of givenness becomes a mere transcendental form. The category "to be" can never be attached to a norm (Ought). In the present case, however, it is.

Here we ought to point out that a judgment asserting the very norm of all assertions cannot have a strictly epistemological character. Here the transcendent norm, by means of the category of givenness (to be), is necessarily asserted as something existing: the only way we can conceive of a transcendent norm is as a metaphysical reality. In this judgment, the Ought turns into a metaphysical unity. The judgment, "Truth is the Ought," regardless of what the subject and predicate are taken to be, becomes an assertion of existence: "Truth—is," "The Ought—is." This is what we think when we state, "Truth is the Ought." On the basis of these same judgments, we must also assert, concerning Value, that "Value—is." Regardless of the character of a judgment (that is, whether it is analytic or synthetic), we always formulate it as a statement of existence. An extremely important conclusion concerning all epistemological judgments follows from this: namely, that every single epistemological judgment presents itself to our cognition as a metaphysical judgment. The quality that is peculiar to metaphysical judgments is their ontological character. When we recognize the ontological problem as something that cannot be proved with the aid of theory of knowledge, what we are in essence doing is endowing our own cognition with being: cognition is thus already ontology.

The first epistemological objection that will be raised to what I have said is this: the norm of the Ought, in the end, is no more than the norm of a judgment asserting the *existence* of the Ought. From an epistemological point of view, the objection is justified. But then the necessity of formulating basic epistemological judgments in a metaphysical form is a prius for any epistemological analysis.

So either we must renounce any formulation of epistemological judgments, or, in formulating these judgments, we must recognize that we are asserting the norms of content themselves in the form of the contents of consciousness.

In driving out any kind of psychologism from the word, we are endowing the word itself sui generis with being. The word becomes Logos. Logical activity itself is sui generis ontology. All attempts by theory of knowledge to reject all content come down to one thing, namely, that the forms of a theory of knowledge become contents in any attempts to articulate them (that is, to express them with the aid of judgments). The emblematism of epistemological concepts is particularly striking here. On this basis we may affirm theory of knowledge as a metaphysics, that is, acknowledge its ontological character.

But are we not then reverting to psychologism here? Do we find ourselves constrained to derive our theory of knowledge from content, just as Lipps, Stumpf, and others would want it?[80]

It is well worth our while to stop and consider this question.

When we use the terms *psychologism* and *psychological*, we must firmly agree on a definite, clearly established sense in which we understand them. Otherwise none of our definitions of terms will have any meaning whatever. When we say psychology, then, we must clearly understand whether we mean a science that investigates the processes of mental life, whether we mean a science of the mind, or whether we have in mind a description of our mental life in symbolic terms.

If by psychology we mean a science that investigates the processes of mental life, then, first of all, the form of such psychological investigations is a methodological form, and methodological forms of knowledge are predetermined by the connection between them. Epistemology, in deriving these same forms from the cognitive reality that is given to us, thereby permanently narrows the field of scientific-psychological methods. And if theory of knowledge leads us to think that its own conclusions are predetermined by the content of judgments concerning epistemological concepts, this does not signify that the content of these judgments is in any way the content of psychological experience, seen, that is, as scientific experience. And second, even if this were so, the concept of a process of mental life would place us under an obligation to establish the concept of process as a term. And in this case, either the concept of process becomes an allegorical image of the indissoluble unity of experience (indissoluble by science, that is), or it assumes the character of a formula. This formula would contain, among other things, the concepts of work and force. Now the concept of force, implying as it does a concept of activity, leads us to causality, understood as a dynamic underlying principle (in the Kantian sense). And in this case we find ourselves once again safely moored in the haven of theory of knowledge. Thus in adopting the point of view of epistemology, we arrive at psychology, but in rendering our psychological concepts more intelligible, we arrive right back at the epistemological premises of psychology.

If by psychology we mean a science of the mind, then any metaphysics becomes at the same time a science of the mind. On the other hand, mind and science are mutually contradictory concepts, for the concept of mind is necessarily associated with one type of givenness, namely, psychic content experienced as "I," whereas the concept of science is necessarily associated with another type of givenness, namely a mode of investigation. But a *mode of knowledge* is clearly a *givenness* that is incommensurable with any psychic content. Moreover, in following this course we find ourselves replacing the term *psychological* with the term *psychic*, and thus, with one stroke of the pen, we reduce the significance of the work of Locke, Hume, Herbart, Beneke, Fechner, Bain, Wundt, and others to zero.[81]

If, finally, we mean by psychology a description of content, then this description will have a purely symbolic character. "The contents of consciousness," says Lipps, "cannot be defined; all one can do is substitute other expressions for them: the contents of consciousness are what is immediately discovered or experienced, the immediately present, what I have in mind; the 'images' that I have."[82] Lipps distinguishes three types of cognition: cognition of things, which has its origin in sense perception; cognition of the "I," that is, the internal perception of this "I"; and cognition of other [individuals]. But where is the unity of psychology as a science in a theory involving three different incommensurable types of cognition? A psychology like this must ultimately fall apart, for the psychology of sense perception inevitably turns into association theory, that is, exposes itself to the very same reproaches [as association theory]. A psychology of the second type is really a sort of mysticism, where the criterion of simplicity and irreducibility is the "I," that is, something that in psychology is always defined as being complex; and a psychology of the third type is really a theory concerning the perceptions of other "I's." This is where Lipps develops his theory of *Einfühlung*. But the theory of *Einfühlung* is really in its own way a theory of symbolism.[83] Lipps's [*Leitfaden der*] *Psychologie* is an important accomplishment, but it is not so much a *Psychologie* as it is an *Einfühlungslehre*. If Lipps chooses to take mysticism and symbolism and call them psychology, then psychology as a scientific discipline simply crumbles. Psychology becomes not an "-ology," as it were, but simply a matter of intuition. We acknowledge that Lipps's point of view is important, but his is a point of view that presupposes that closed cycle of theory of knowledge to which we referred earlier. In short, Lipps's point of view, compared with experimental psychology (understood as a science), is in effect the point of view of mystical realism.

Thus none of the three senses in which psychology may be understood takes the point of view at which we had arrived in asserting the dependence of epistemology on the content of basic epistemological judgments.

We would do better to call this point of view epistemological metaphysics. It is distinguished from any other metaphysics in the following ways: its content consists of basic epistemological judgments, its form is the principle of purposiveness, and its final conclusion consists in recognizing in any logical judgment the character of ontological being.

18

In the preceding section we established an extremely important principle: that basic epistemological concepts are possible only if their own existence is posed as a condition.

"Truth—is."

"The Ought—is."

"Value—is."

The connection between these concepts is the category of *givenness*. But the metaphysical condition for this category is existent unity. When we say "existent," we mean a certain kind of being that is beyond our imagination. It is in this sense that we assert that *unity* is *Symbol.*

This symbolic being, reflected in theory of knowledge as a categorical imperative of judgment ("So be it, so shall it be, so shall it have been"), is the metaphysical connection between the three forms of assertions of givenness: givenness as based in truth (cognition), as based in the Ought (ethics), and as based in Value (creation).

These three concepts exist in a relation of mutual coordination. To determine the character of this relation of coordination, we must explain the nature of the relation between the concepts of the Ought and truth on the one hand, and the concept of Value on the other.

The truthfulness of a judgment is the criterion of its entire theoretical significance. The Ought is the norm of truthfulness. The judgment, "Truth is the Ought," is a synthetic judgment. The judgment, "The Ought is truth," however, is an analytic judgment because the concept of the truthfulness of the Ought is already contained in the concept of the Ought itself. It remains to be determined how things stand with the judgment, "The Ought is Value."

If cognition did not have an emblematic character and *only* an emblematic character, we would be thoroughly bewildered by any analytic judgment. But we have seen that the primacy of the formation of basic epistemological judgments lies in asserting them as ontological judgments. The epistemological judgment in this case is asserted as a metaphysical (that is, emblematic) reality. The assertion of an epistemological judgment as something existing and real cannot be identified with the assertion of all judgments as obligatory. It is the judgment's symbolic being that asserts the judgment as obligatory. The value of a judgment lies in its being, not in its obligatory character.[84] Let me repeat: the being of a judgment is a transcendent being. The Gospel text expresses the imaginal essence of this being: "In the beginning was the word, and the word was with God, and the word was God." It is this being of the judgment, the being that is found in the symbol that we term its *value*.

It is clear now that the judgment, "The Ought is Value," assumes the following form: "Value is the Ought," that is, "Value" is the subject of the judgment, and the Ought is its predicate. With the reverse reading the judgment becomes synthetic.

The ontology of basic epistemological judgments assumes the following form: there is only Value in these judgments, and this Value emerges in both the Ought and truth. The Ought and truth are attributes of Value. We obtain the following hierarchy for the basic judgments of epistemological metaphysics:

The Symbol is unity.

Unity is Value.

Value is the Ought.

The Ought is truth.

The first judgment lies at the base of epistemological metaphysics.

The second judgment is the condition for givenness in this metaphysics.

The third judgment places this metaphysics at the basis of theory of knowledge.

The fourth judgment is a basic epistemological judgment.

All four judgments are analytic judgments: if we recall the process by which the concept of symbol is formed, we must conclude that the concept of unity is already contained in the Symbol. The concept of Value is contained in the concept of symbolic unity, when, in virtue of the limitations of cognition, we endow this concept with being. The concept of the Ought is already contained in the concept of Value. Finally, truth is contained in the Ought.

On the other hand, in the process of forming the concepts, these judgments are synthetic.

19

If we reject any kind of psychologism from the content of a judgment, we find ourselves obliged to assert something equivalent to the being of our judgments as their form. Transcendental logic at this point in its investigation begins to appear to us as a kind of organism that creates being itself. When we say "organism," we are carrying over into logic something known to us in the world of being. What we are doing is openly constructing an emblem. But then cognition can never get on without emblems. Cognition acquires (in and of itself) a closed meaning. It becomes Logos. The content of judgments, like the content of our being, is unified by the category of givenness. This is essentially the world pneuma of the Stoics. And the form itself of judgments is the Logos of Heraclitus, that is, the law of all things, animating the world and identical with the world in content (being as the form of judgments). Certain features of Stoicism have necessarily been revived in contemporary theory of knowledge, in the face of a metaphysical understanding of its purposes. In the teleology of the Freiburg school, we recognize the Stoic theory of the purposiveness of all things. This purposiveness, according to S. N. Trubetskoy, "derives from the idea of the universal Logos and is developed by the Stoics as well as in the traditions of Attic philosophy."[85]

The idea of a symbolic unity that breaks down into duality is expressed in Pythagorean philosophy in the theory of the two world principles: unity as the active principle, and duality as the principle of matter. Essences are the products of unities and dualities. Thus the metaphysics of unity is replaced by a metaphysics of number. Unity is occasionally equated with the monad: "[the] point, by fluxion, creates the line, the line, by fluxion, makes the plane, and it in turn . . . generates the three-dimensional body."[86] And further: "Unity symbolizes a point, duality, two points, and consequently the line connecting them as well."[87]

This emblematism can be connected with the symbols of folk religion. The Orphic hymns unwittingly betray a confluence of traits from the philosophy of the Stoics, the Pythagoreans, and Heraclitus on the one hand, and religious symbols on the other. Professor Novosadsky has quite correctly observed that the bases of the allegorical representation of divinities nonetheless are not the same for the Orphics and the Stoics.[88] The Stoics reduce the divinities to mere abstract forces (the emblematism of concepts lies at the basis of the image). The Orphics, on the other hand, regarded these forces as emanations of the godhead (the image of symbolization for them lies at the basis of the logical emblem). The common point between Orphism and Stoicism is in their idolization of matter seen as a symbol. Here we have a clear case of the distinct heteronomy of cognition and creation. The creation of life in the mysteries is a prius of all cognition (in the Orphic view). World reason, as the source of cognition, is a prius of all creation (in the Stoic view). The point of departure for both schools (Stoics and Orphics) is the same: being as a symbol of cognition (Stoics), and being as a symbol of creation (Orphics).

We can clearly understand the process by which the metaphysics of the Logos arises simply from our need to overcome the antinomy of cognition: this metaphysics seems to solve the problem of cognition. In asserting the norm (yes), the category of givenness (to be), and the transcendental forms as the constitutive forms of cognition, the Freiburg school ineluctably finds itself propounding the metaphysical doctrine of the Logos.

But how, then, does the metaphysics of creation, which spurs the logical image itself (Logos) into activity, arise?

To answer this question we must return to Rickert.

Rickert opposes constitutive to methodological forms of cognition. The methodological form is the general form of logical activity. The analysis of the methodological forms is related to the purposes of general logic. General logic also examines the means for applying the logical forms to the individual sciences. The particular form of a judgment depends on the category (in the Kantian sense) under which a given content is thought (for example, if we employ the category of quantity we obtain numbers).

On the one hand we have in front of us a series of scientific methods. This series ends in the extra-experiential postulate of sequence. Any such postulate amounts to a condition of the sequence of experience. Any such postulate worked out by logic can also appear as the product of the pure activity of reason. The categories of reason are at the same time methodological forms, that is, general forms of cognition. These categories are, in short, the rules of scientific experience. But experience[89] and the activity of reason cannot be derived: both are given. And experience cannot be given without the category that conditions it. The condition of experience is *given* for experience. In both cases it is givenness we are dealing with.

The constitutive forms of cognition, on the other hand, are the forms of just this givenness. And if the methodological form is a general form, then the constitutive form, that is, the form of givenness, is, by opposition, the form of "the general." But it is also the form of "the individual," since "the individual" and "the general" fall under the same category: both are given.

How are the general and the individual given?

They are given by means of the norm (affirmation), category, and form.

The area of competence of theory of knowledge is above all that of the deduction of constitutive forms. The area of competence of science is the application of methodological forms.

In theory of knowledge the content of every method is deduced from the form (of the method). If, however, we do away with all scientific method in the deduction of the constitutive forms, then we will regard the content of these forms as their immanent being. "The general" and "the individual" thus appear to us not as forms but as contents. The world of being is a world of contents. There are as many contents as there are forms. Form is to be understood here as image. One image is replaced by another. We experience images as something irrational, irreducible.

Immanent being, like chaos, is opposed to the constitutive forms of cognition. These forms assert chaos in givenness just as they assert the methodological forms of the sciences. The form of the image and the form of the method that derives the content of the image are now independent of one another. The value of scientific thinking disappears, and the world of images, like chaos, adheres to our eyes.

The methodological forms of cognition are like a bridge between the content of cognition and its constitutive form. In reverting to these forms, cognition derives them from itself. Cognition turns out to be a thing-in-itself. The bridge between cognition and the world of content crumbles. Content becomes a thing-in-itself.

The methodological forms of cognition are derivatives located, as it were, between the content of cognition and its norm. The norm and content are things-in-themselves. As soon as the derivative character of scientific knowledge becomes clear, cognition becomes the Logos. Those contents that have not been worked out in methodical forms, however, appear as a multiplicity of individual essences. These contents, opposed as they are to any norm, are a mere chaos of essence until we have experienced them. As soon as we begin to experience them, it appears as if the world were filled with "gods, demons, and souls." Chaos, once experienced, ceases to be chaos. When we experience something, it is as though we were allowing these contents to pass through us. We become the image of the Logos, which organizes chaos. We give chaos an individual order. This order is by no means a logical order. It is the order of the flow of experienced contents in us. The epistemological cognition we are familiar with flickers out here. Instead, we cognize in experiencing. This type of cognition is not cognition at all—it is creation. And the first act performed by creation is the naming of contents. In naming contents we turn them into *things*.[90] In naming things, we transform the formlessness of the chaos of contents into a series of images. We unify these images in a single whole. This wholeness of images is none other than our "I." Our "I" summons gods out of the chaos. A god is the very core of my "I," hidden from me, and forcing me to erect both a pyramid of symbols and a symbolic image of myself in the image and likeness of a man ascending to the summit of the pyramid. The word *wherefore* has no place here.

This creative activity in its initial stages is pure fetishism: all the contents are things-in-themselves. They strive to enter my soul. As things-in-themselves, these contents *are* souls. The designation of contents as souls is the first act of my creative activity. In experiencing my first content I say, "I am." In experiencing a series of contents I say, "There is a God." In saying this I create a myth. Out of myth arises history. The first contemplation of chaos is time. The contemplation of contents as things-in-themselves is space. This is why in a logical order this first contemplation is reflected as sequentiality, whereas the second contemplation is a positing of contents. Space is the positing of contents. All this represents stages of descent into the abyss of chaos, which is opposed to the norm of cognition (seen as Logos). Thus, all this represents stages of descent of cognition into creation. The first experience of cognition, its first content in creation, is the creation of the "I." "I am"—this is the first unconscious prattling of the newborn. In experiencing a whole series of contents, I perceive order in their flow. All contents, when they pass through me as positings in sequentiality, become a content dictated to my infantile "I" by some other "I." I say, "There is a God." The world for me is a fairy tale. The infantile "I," obeying some unknown command, creates a mythology. The world appears. The history of the world appears, too. Thus the world comes into being through creative activity. Theogony gives rise to cosmogony. ϑεός now appears as κόσμος. Chaos has created all varieties of religion, of reality, and of objects of reality.

At the summit of creative activity, my infantile "I" already contains within itself the seething sea of contents. It recognizes its own creation. It becomes Logos.

It is only from the heights of logical cognition that the view of chaos unfolds before us, that we are given the right to experience chaos. Chaos becomes a criterion of reality.

It is only in the hollow of the chaotic spout that chaos itself becomes an image and likeness of logical cognition. Cognition is permeated with chaos. Chaos turns out to be the very reality of cognition.

Hence either everything is mere flux in an eternal dream, and there is nothing, neither chaos, nor Logos, nor cognition, nor creation; or chaos and Logos are dreams of reality. But this reality cannot be defined in a dream. The image of a dream is the very wholeness of logical reality that predetermines the reality of being. And the other image of the same dream is the wholeness of creation, drawing logical reality itself in images and, by means of this same reality, predetermining reality.

If this is so, then reality is merely a Symbol in the language of our dreams.

Metaphysics leads us to the very same conclusion.

Value predetermines truth. Value is also contained relatively in truth. Truth is a symbolic concept. It is a symbol of Value. But truth, understood as that to which judgments are obligated, transforms the flux of the world into a flux of syllogisms. The world is then one enormous syllogism. But a syllogism is not the same thing as Value. What, then, must Value be?

Value cannot be defined by means of the Ought. Value is the mere fact that Value *is*. In saying that it *is*, we are asserting its existence. Value determines the being of cognition. An image of Value can only be an emblem. Cognition is just such an emblem. On the other hand, being is something that is not cognition. Noncognition [that which is not cognition] is immanent being. Or, from the perspective of experienced contents, noncognition is creation. Creation is an emblem of Value. Value unites within itself two extreme emblems. As a union of emblems, Value is a Symbol.

We do not call the Symbol by the name of the absolute and unconditional. The concept of the absolute and unconditional is easily replaced by the concept of the relativity of all being and all cognition. Creation, too, is easily replaced by the relativity of being. The relativity of creation, however, is actually an emblem. Furthermore, in calling the Symbol absolute and unconditional, we easily identify the absolute and unconditional with divinity. In the concept of the Symbol, the divinity is actually conditioned by symbols.

1. *The Symbol is unity.*
2. *The Symbol is the unity of emblems.*
3. *The Symbol is the unity of emblems of creation and cognition.*
4. *The Symbol is unity in the creation of contents of experience.*
5. *The Symbol is unity in the creation of contents of cognition.*
6. *The Symbol is unity in the cognition of contents of experience.*
7. *The Symbol is the unity of cognition in the creation of the contents of this cognition.*
8. *The Symbol is the unity of cognition in the forms of experience.*
9. *The Symbol is the unity of cognition in the forms of cognition.*
10. *The Symbol is the unity of creation in the forms of experience.*
11. *The Symbol is unity in the creation of cognitive forms.*
12. *The Symbol is the unity of form and content.*
13. *The Symbol is disclosed in the emblematic series of acts of cognition and creation.*
14. *These series are emblems (symbols in the figurative sense).*
15. *The Symbol is cognized through emblems and imaginal symbols.*
16. *Reality approximates the Symbol in the process of cognitive or creative symbolization.*
17. *The Symbol becomes reality in this process.*
18. *The meaning of cognition and creation lies in the Symbol.*
19. *As we approximate cognition of any meaning, we endow every form and every content with symbolic being.*
20. *The meaning of our being is disclosed in a hierarchy of symbolic disciplines of cognition and creation.*
21. *The System of symbolism is the emblematics of pure meaning.*
22. *This system consists of a classification of [acts of] cognition and creation under a hierarchy of symbolizations.*
23. *The Symbol is disclosed in acts of symbolization. That is where it is both created and cognized.*

These are the premises of any theory of creation. The Symbol is a criterion of Value for any metaphysics as well as for any theosophical or theurgical symbolics.

20

We must now distinguish the *concept* of the Symbol (the Symbol being taken as the limit of all possible acts of cognition and creation) from the following:

1. *The Symbol itself (the Symbol is unknowable, uncreatable, and any definition of it must be relative)*
2. *Symbolic unity*
3. *Normative cognition of Value*
4. *The methodological concept of Value*
5. *The image of the Symbol (Image)*
6. *The central Symbols of religion*
7. *The symbolic images of our experience*
8. *Artistic symbols*

The Symbol itself is certainly not a symbol. Both the concept and the image of the Symbol are symbols of this Symbol. With respect to these symbols the Symbol is an embodiment.

The concept of symbolic unity must in turn be distinguished from the synthetic unity of self-consciousness (epistemological unity), from the Category of unity,[91] and from the numerical emblem (one). Epistemological unity, the Category, and the numerical emblem are emblems of the metaphysical concept of the Symbol as unity.

The concept of the Symbol is not yet a concept of Value. The concept of Value is a normative concept. Or, to put it differently, the concept of Value breaks down into a series of methodological concepts. Thus the value of a methodological concept lies in its epistemological truthfulness. The value of an epistemological concept lies in the degree to which it rejects psychologism. The value of a normative concept lies in the Ought. The value of the Ought lies in something that *conditions* the Ought. This condition of obligation is the concept of Value as Symbol.

The image of the Symbol rests in the manifest Image of a certain principle. This Image appears in various forms in religion. The purpose of theory of knowledge as regards religion consists in reducing the central images of religion to a single Image.

Finally, we use the term *symbol* for the images of our experience. When we say "image of experience," we mean the irreducible unity of the processes of feeling, willing, thinking. We call this unity a symbolic image, because it cannot be defined in terms of feelings, will, and thinking. This unity, though, is embodied in each instant individually. We also call an individual image of experience a symbol. We catch the individual rhythm in the changes in our experiences and embody both this change and the change of instants. The images of experience arrange themselves in a certain order relative to each other. We may call this order a system of experienced symbols. In continuing the system, we see that it embraces our very life. And this life, which is comprehended in rhythmic images, we call our individual religion. The rhythm of the relation of our experience to the experience of others broadens the individual understanding of a religion into a collective one. It is easy to see a religious foundation in this process of cognition that Lipps calls *Einfühlung*. And if *Einfühlung* lies at the basis of aesthetic experiences, then by the same token, artistic creation receives its illumination in religious creation.

21

Finally, the expression of an image of experience in various plastic and rhythmic forms leads us to the construction, from one kind of material or another, of schemas expressing the union between the image of appearance and the image of experience. These material schemas are artistic symbols. The artistic symbol is thus an extraordinarily complex sort of unity. It is the unity of disposition of artistic materials. When we study the various means of artistic representation, we distinguish in them, first, the material itself, and, second, technique, that is, the disposition of material. The unity of the means is the unity of disposition, and this predetermines choice [that is, of materials]. Furthermore, the artistic symbol is the unity of experience embodied in the individual image of the instant. Finally, the artistic symbol is the unity of these unities (that is, the unity of experience in the techniques of the art in question). The artistic symbol, given to us in an embodied form, is the unity of the reciprocal action of form and content. Form and content here are only *means*. The embodiment of the image is itself an end. And for this reason, if we analyze the artistic symbol from the point of view of its form, we will see nothing more than a collection of relative definitions. Form in the crude sense is already predetermined in the symbol by the artistic technique employed. The artistic technique is predetermined by the conditions of space and time. The elements of space and time are predetermined by the form of the creative process. The form of the creative process is predetermined by the form of individual experience. This experience is given by means of the norm of creation. If we analyze the artistic symbol from the point of view of its form, we obtain a collection of forms and norms that recede into the depths of the unknowable. The apparent content is merely the order followed in the breakdown of form. The content of the artistic image turns out to be an *unknowable unity*, that is, a symbolic unity.

And conversely: if we take the apparent content as our point of departure, we begin to see that this content consists of our own vague emotional state but that the form of creative vision, that is, the image that arises in our mind, depends on it. Moreover, the very choice of spatial and temporal elements, that is, the choice of rhythm and the means of representation, are predetermined. Rhythm and the means of representation both represent a subdivision of content. When we speak of, say, the pyrrhic feet in Pushkin's iambic verse, we are in essence speaking of the particular qualities of Pushkin's artistic emotion. Moreover, the very form of creation is predetermined by rhythm and technique. For example, in the literary arts the form is predetermined as, say, lyric, drama, or novella. In addition, the *emotion* of the content determines the form of the artwork. If I work in ceramics, for instance, instead of composing verses, it is because my emotions are such that ceramics expresses them better than the pen. When we take the apparent content as our starting point, it is useless to look for form. The clay we were working with sets the limits beyond which content cannot proceed. Form turns out to be the unknowable unity of my work, that is, the symbolic unity. The artistic symbol is above all emotion rendered by representational means. And conversely: the means of representation is given in emotion.

A great many views in aesthetics assert that form and content in art are separable. These views are groundless, as long as the form and content of an artistic image are taken as real, and not relative, concepts. Systematic definitions of art are formal and consequently one-sided. Aesthetics must elaborate its own method, basing its efforts on the pursuit of the indivisible wholeness of artistic images. It was the symbolist school in poetry that proclaimed the unity of form and content in the images of art. This slogan fully conforms to the premises of a theory of symbolism.

"Form is given in content." "Content is given in form." These are fundamental aesthetic judgments defining the symbol in art.

On the basis of the judgments set forth in section 17, we may conclude that both these judgments are deductive. They are both deduced from the judgments, "Form is content."

Is this, then, a synthetic or an analytic judgment?

If we take *content* as the subject,[92] then the judgment, "Form is content," becomes an analytic one, since the concept of form is derived from that of content. This implies that the work carried out on the *material* [the content] on the one hand and the work devoted to *representing* the image of fantasy [the form] on the other are united by the content of the creative process. But in investigating the processes of creation, we find ourselves confronting a dilemma: does this investigation consist in description or in analysis? In other words, is the process of creation an object of scientific investigation or is it an object of artistic description? In describing images of experience that arise in the mind out of some nameless content, I am creating them. Aesthetics in this case is creation. Or perhaps I may arrange these emerging images in the order in which they emerge. In this case aesthetics would have to concern itself with the classifications of images of creation. A classification without some sort of principle, though, is impossible. When, however, we examine the processes of creation, we are looking at only the form of these processes, and moreover, we are examining them with the help of various methods. This sort of investigation gives us a series of terminological definitions that aesthetics must follow as a sort of raw material, but nothing more.

If we now take *form* as the subject of the judgment above, we turn the statement, "Content is form," into its opposite, "Form is content." In this guise, too, the fundamental judgment of the aesthetics of symbolism is an analytic one, since here the concept of content is derived from that of form: the work devoted to representing the image [form] and the work carried out on the material [content] are united in the fundamental form of the material of creation, whatever it may be. This form is the relation of the material to the elements of space and time. But in studying the elements of space and time in various artistic forms, we once again confront a dilemma: does our task consist in a study of the geometric and rhythmic proportions of forms, or does it consist in a classification of forms in a spatial and temporal order? In the former case we obtain a series of terminological definitions from mathematics, mechanics, and psychophysics. In the latter case we describe the very form of symbols in the order of their appearance, and nothing more. In the former case aesthetics becomes a problem in applied mathematics and mechanics. In the latter case aesthetics becomes ethnographics and history of art. In both cases the real meaning of aesthetics is lost.

The judgment, "Form is content," is a symbolic judgment. If form is predetermined by content, then we are obliged to look for content outside of art. If content is predetermined by form, then we can never find a common form for the arts. The aesthetics of the symbolist school must seek its basis outside of aesthetics.

Without an elucidation of its relation to a theory of symbolism, such an aesthetics can have no true meaning. Still, however, the slogans propagated by it can only enrich and deepen the slogans of the psychological aesthetics of the recent past.

The adherents of the symbolist school, as well as its opponents, continually confuse a great many concepts, and the result is the complete chaos we distinguish in their polemical articles.

The concept of the Symbol as limit, for instance, is confused with the concept of the symbol as image.

We propose the following nomenclature: defining the symbolic image as the unity of experience given to us in some medium of representation, let us call this unity the artistic symbol. The unity of experience, on the other hand, which takes the form of an image in our mind, we will call the symbolic image of experience. Now it is certainly possible for the symbolic image of experience *not* to be given in a medium of representation. It is an image of our mind and as such occupies a place in a system of similar images. A consciously developed system of symbolic images of experience is a religious system. It finds its completion in religion.

The symbolic image of experience is closer to religious symbolism than to aesthetic symbolism. The image of experience is not an artistic symbol, but it enters into the artistic symbol. In entering into this symbol, the image of experience must not be seen as forming part of a system of experiences, but must be seen as separate. Starting as the means leading to the end, it then becomes the end itself. This is why the view of art as purposiveness without purpose underscores the degree to which artistic creation is conditioned by religious creation.[93]

We propose to call the various means of representation, taken as a unity (for example, the mutual conditioning of rhythm, literary instrumentation, and the material of artistic tropes), *style*, as distinguished from stylization. In the disposition of these elements, there is an unintentional unity whose definition is entirely symbolic. This unity is not the artistic symbol, although the artistic symbol, too, enters into it.

If we call the image of experience an artistic symbol, then we will fall into error, as long as we explain experience in terms of feelings, will, or cognition. We wish to explain what this unity signifies. But when we interpret the image of experience in rational terms, we transform the image into an allegory, that is, into an analogy between the image and its meaning in terms of reason.

We must understand once and for all that an allegory is not a symbol.

Finally, we will use the term *emblem* for artistic and other symbols when they are defined in terms of cognition. The very definition of the Symbol in terms of cognition, as a unity not given to us, we will call an emblem.

It is customary to confuse symbolism as a creative activity with symbolism as a system of thoughts allowing in principle for the formation of symbols. Some people think of symbolism as a method, but this is not true. The theory of symbolism is a theory that constructs a great many methodological disciplines as emblems of the Symbol. Another reason why the theory of symbolism is not just a method, is that it actually proposes an emblematism of all the different cognitive methods and retains for each one the right to be what it is. The theory of symbolism, relative to art and religion, is a theory of creation. This is its more restricted definition. In fact, *symbolism is creation itself*.

It is also customary to confuse symbolism with symbolization, and so we must, in a word or two, characterize the terminological difference between these concepts.

Creation has certain definite zones through which it passes while remaining invariable in its inner tendencies. Primitive creation is thus the unity of rhythmic movements in the primordial chaos of feelings. This unity has as its form the musical element of the soul, that is, rhythm. This type of unity is expressed in the symbolic image of experience. The symbolic image of experience, extracted from the soul and embodied in the material of representation, gives us a more complex unity, namely the artistic symbol. The attempt to give life to this complex unity, in order that the symbol may begin to speak the language of human acts, leads to a yet more complex unity, namely the unity of the religious symbol. This is accomplished in such a way that the artist himself and those surrounding him become artistic forms. Forms of conduct then appear as a form of artistic creation of life, and the aesthetic symbol becomes an image of content. The indivisible unity of form and content here is religion. Moreover, the religious symbol, that is, the beautiful life of man, which is taken as the norm of all behavior, takes the unity of human nature and turns it into the dualistic image of the God-man. Thus we arrive at theurgic creation.

We see here that the height to which creation can reach is determined by the scope of ever larger spheres of human activity. Primitive, artistic, religious, and theurgic creation are all stages of the same creation. When creation is defined from the standpoint of unity, we call it symbolism. When we seek to define any particular zone of that creation, we call that zone symbolization.

And so:

The Symbol is given to us in symbolism.
Symbolism is given to us in symbolizations.
Symbolization is given in a series of symbolic images.
The Symbol is not a concept, nor is symbolism.
The Symbol is not a method, nor is symbolism.

22

Here we will stop. Our task has been to indicate at least the reference points for a future system of symbolism. Such a system will, of course, have to take these reference points into account. Otherwise it will always be threatened by some form of dogmatism or other. How this future theory of symbolism will come to terms with the antinomy between cognition and creation only the future can tell. Undoubtedly the theory will face a fatal pair of alternatives: on one side, the necessity of basing theory of knowledge in metaphysics, while deriving metaphysics from creation; on the other, the necessity of using theory of knowledge to check the rectitude of its construction. Is it possible for a theory of symbolism to be a theory in the proper sense of the word, or must its purpose consist rather in the theoretical rejection of all theory? In the second case, a theory of symbolism would amount to a simple enumeration of a variety of types of creation. Or else it would serve as the basis for a particular type of creative experience. In this case the theory of symbolism would be a new system among all the existing systems of Hindu philosophy: Vedanta, Yoga, Mimamsa, Sankhya, Vaisheshika, and others.[94] Most likely of all, a theory of symbolism would not be a theory at all, but a new religious-philosophical doctrine predetermined by the whole course of development of Western European thought. Vladimir Solov'ev has pointed out the turn in consciousness of European humanity towards the East, in his *Crisis in Western Philosophy*.[95] As eminent a scholar of Hindu philosophy as Deussen has also recognized the tremendous significance of this philosophy.[96] Solov'ev's error lay in identifying the turning point in the development of European thought in the unpersuasive metaphysics of Hartmann. The fact is, however, that the turning point in the development of European thought really becomes apparent in the inability of contemporary Kantianism to find a way out of dualism while still leaving the epistemological base of its investigations untouched. All efforts to escape from dualism are either metaphysical or psychological. Theory in the epistemological sense of the word ceases to be theory the minute we introduce a metaphysical, psychological, or ethical element into the theoretical constructions of reason. On the other hand we are inclined to ask ourselves the following question: can the theory remain a theory as long as a condition of its very possibility is the necessity of acknowledging a dualism between the noumenal and phenomenal worlds? Instead of determining how any given theory is justifiable, we must ask what a theory must be: must it, on the one hand, derive the conditions of the possibility of experience from a single cognitive principle, or must it, on the other hand, describe the process, internally experienced and ineluctably a part of us, whereby we construct all possible theories? In this case *theory* must retain the meaning contained in the Greek word: it must be divine (*ϑεός* [god]) vision (*ὁράω* [to see]).[97] But here the following objection will be raised: the theory of symbolism, seen as a system of mystical and aesthetic experience described and set forth in an orderly fashion, turns into a special type of descriptive psychology. If we used the term *psychology* loosely, we might almost call the theory of symbolism a neopsychology of the future. But it is dangerous to play with the prefix *neo-*, since it always contains a certain unknown. In calling the description and enumeration of the processes of symbolization a psychology of the future we risk introducing an even greater confusion into our concepts than if we simply call this enumeration a theory. It would be strange indeed to call the teachings of Saint Seraphim of Sarov, Saint Isaac the Syrian, or Shankaracharya, "Treatises in Psychology."[98]

I can think of no reason why we should not refrain from calling a classification of creative processes a theory.

On the contrary: if contemporary epistemologists concur in thinking that a theory can be a theory only if it is derived from fundamental epistemological premises, then the construction of such a theory can only underscore the needlessness and even harmfulness of such a theory for anything living and active that gives meaning to our life. Contemporary epistemologists, amiably flirting with [the meaning of] life while at the same time wishing to remain thoroughly consistent, openly acknowledge, with a sort of good-natured comic spirit, the tragedy they are living through: namely, that they are always stretching their hands out towards this thing called the value of life, whereas epistemology itself guarantees them this value, but not until they have first extinguished life! All these details concerning the difficulty of their position do not, however, disturb the epistemologists' good humor. For all they need to do is to think one of two things: either the tragedy of cognition is simply fictitious, and cognition is not capable of backing up its position of primacy; or else this flirtation with all the possible meanings of life is a dangerous flirtation. What is more, the advocates of epistemologism are all afflicted with a persecution mania: wherever they go it seems that the grim specter of psychologism is in hot pursuit. The neo-Kantians all attempt to dispel any kind of psychologism and complain that all epistemological concepts have a psychological meaning. Rickert is an example of this. Finally, there are some (disciples of Cohen) who see even in Rickert nothing more than a "miserable psychologist." In fact, even the High Priest of Epistemology, Cohen, has been accused of psychologism.

The epistemologist who is consistent must, out of fear of committing heresy, declare his true faith early on, and through the only means possible: absolute silence. Every judgment, once uttered, casts the speaker into the abyss of psychologism.[99]

Silence is the sole escape for the epistemologist who wishes to remain thoroughly consistent. The only other possibility is to utter a jest about his own awkward position in this world of psychologism.

I do not see any reason not to inquire into the meaning the epistemologist assigns to the words, *theory*, *theoretical*, *pure sense*.

Can it be that any theory that takes into account the groundlessness of epistemology in treating the question of the meaning and value of being is already an "impure theory?"

23

Every art is symbolic—present, past, or future. Where does the meaning of contemporary symbolism lie? What has it given us that is new?

Nothing.

The symbolist school has done nothing more than to reduce to a common factor all the statements by artists and poets maintaining that the meaning of beauty lies in the artistic image and not solely in the emotion that the image arouses in us. And not in a rational interpretation of this image, either: the symbol cannot be reduced to emotions or to discursive concepts. It is what it is.

The symbolist school has greatly extended the limits of our conception of artistic creation. It has shown that a canon of beauty cannot be treated academically. There is no single canon, like romanticism, classicism, or realism, that must be *the* canon. The symbolist school sees all three trends as different expressions of a single creativity. This is how a romantic, fantastic element suddenly burst the bounds of realism in recent times. Conversely, it is also how the bloodless shades of romanticism were given flesh and blood in the symbolist school. But symbolism has also burst the bounds of aesthetic creation, underscoring how closely the domains of religious creation and art adjoin. A powerful stream of Eastern mysticism penetrated into the otherwise closed world of nineteenth-century European art, for instance, and, under the influence of this mysticism, the Middle Ages were suddenly resurrected. The novelty of contemporary art lies precisely in the enormous quantity of past material that has all at once emerged before us. We are experiencing today, in our art, all ages and all nations. The life of the past is actually rushing by right before us.

This is because we are now standing on the edge of a great future.

1909

THE ART OF THE FUTURE

We can distinctly see the path that the art of the future will follow as it develops. Our conception of what that path is arises out of an antinomy we perceive in contemporary art.

The existing art forms are rushing headlong towards disintegration. The degree of differentiation among them is infinite, something to which the development of technical skill has contributed greatly. The notion of technical progress is increasingly replacing the notion of the living meaning of art.

At the same time, however, the various art forms, in all their diversity, are beginning to merge with each other. But this tendency towards synthesis is not expressed in any dissolution of the boundaries separating adjacent art forms. The tendency towards synthesis is expressed rather in various attempts to arrange these art forms around one form that is taken as the center.

Thus we have seen the emergence of music in a position of primacy over the other arts. Thus we have also seen the emergence of an attraction to the mystery play and to a synthesis of all possible art forms.

But as much as music corrupts its adjacent art forms, it also nurtures them in another respect. A false penetration into the other arts by the spirit of music is an indication of decline. But this sort of decline captivates us, and therein lies our sickness. A soap bubble just before bursting displays all the colors of the rainbow. The rainbow carpet of exoticism keeps both plenum and void concealed behind it. And if art of the future were to construct its forms by imitating pure music, then it would bear the character of Buddhism. Contemplation through art is a means: it is a means for catching the summons to vital creation. In art subsumed by music, contemplation would become an end in itself: it would transform the contemplator into an impersonal spectator of his own experiences. The art of the future, having become immersed in music, would permanently arrest the development of all the arts.

If art of the future is to be understood as art consisting of a synthesis of today's existing forms, then wherein lies the unifying principle? One might certainly clothe oneself in the garb of an actor and say one's supplications at the altar. At the same time the chorus might perform dithyrambs composed by the finest lyric poets of the time. Music will accompany the dithyrambs, and dance will accompany the music. The finest artists of the time will create an illusion around us, and so on, and so forth. But what is this all for? Is it simply so that we may transform a few hours of our lives into a dream, only to have the dream destroyed again by the intrusion of reality?

"But, then, what about mystery play," will come the response.

But the mystery play had a living, religious meaning. In order for the mystery play of the future to have the same meaning, we would have to carry it outside the limits of art. It would have to be something designed for everyone.

No, it is not in a synthesis of the arts that the principle of the art of the future is to be sought!

The artist is first and foremost a man. After that he is a specialist in his craft. Perhaps his creation even exercises a certain influence on his life. But the conditions of his craft that accompany his creation limit that influence. The contemporary artist is tied to his own art form. To require him to sing, dance, and paint pictures, even if he took great pleasure in all the different types of aesthetic refinement, would be impossible. It is consequently also impossible to require of him a tendency towards synthesis. Such a tendency could be expressed only in a kind of wild rampage, a return to the primitive forms of a distant past. And besides, creation in its primordial form, as it developed naturally, led art to precisely the complexity of forms that we have today. A return to the past would thus merely lead that past right back to the present again.

A synthesis of the arts based on a return to a distant past is impossible. So is a synthesis of the arts based on a mechanical reunification of existing art forms: a reunification like this could only lead art to a lifeless eclecticism. The temple of art would thus become a museum for the arts, but the *Muses* of that *mus*eum would be wax dolls and nothing more.

But given the impossibility of either an external unification or a return to the past, we still have before us all the complexity of the present. Is it then possible to speak of an art of the future? Such an art would perhaps simply be a complication of the present.

But this is not the case.

In the present age the evaluation a work of art receives is closely associated with the special conditions of artistic technique that produced the work. No matter how great the artist's talent, it is always linked ultimately to the whole technical past of his art. The moment of knowledge, of study in an art has come increasingly to condition the development of talent. The power of method and its influence on the development of creation are increasing not by the day, but by the hour. Individualism of creation in our age is more often than not an individualism of work methods. This individualism thus represents merely an advance in the methods of the school with which the given artist is affiliated. Individualism of this type is merely specialization. It stands in direct opposition to the true individuality of the artist himself. The artist, in order to create, must first of all *know*. But knowledge has the effect of decomposing creation, and the artist thus risks falling into a vicious circle of contradictions. The technical evolution of the arts makes the artist a slave. It is impossible for him to reject the technical past. The artist of the present day becomes increasingly a scholar. And in the process of this transformation, the last remaining purposes of art disappear from his view. Technical progress has thus brought the proper domain of the arts much closer to the domain of knowledge. Art is now the concentration of a particular type of knowledge.

What happens, then, is that the cognition of a method of creation puts itself in the place of creation. But creation precedes cognition: it creates the very objects of cognition.

By including creation among the existing art forms of today, we are condemning it to a position under the power of method. Creation thus becomes cognition for its own sake, without an object. Is not "objectlessness" in art the living credo of impressionism? And once "objectlessness" is installed in art, then the method of creation becomes an object in and for itself, and this carries with it as a consequence the most extreme form of individualization. To find one's own method becomes the goal of creation. Such a view of creation must inevitably lead to a complete dissolution of the art forms, a state where every individual work of art is its own form. In art, under conditions like these, inner chaos takes over.

If it is possible to build a new temple on the ruins of the old one that has apparently collapsed, we may not erect the new temple on the atomized forms in which today's forms were molded. The old forms must be discarded. In this way we divert the issue of the purposes of art from an examination of the products of creation to the processes of creation themselves. The products of creation are mere ash and fused rock. The processes of creation, however, are like flowing lava.

Has not mankind's creative energy gone wrong in choosing the path on which the forms that captivate us so much today were constructed? Should we not rather analyze the laws of creation themselves than concur in an art that appears to us in forms like these? Do these forms not represent the distant past of creation? Is it necessary for the creative flow of today to plunge into life by way of all those petrified steps in the scale of art forms, the highest of which is music, and the lowest, architecture? For, once having identified these forms, what we have done is to turn them into so many different technical means, thus freezing the life out of creation. We turn creation into cognition, turn the comet into its own sparkling tail, which barely illuminates the path that creation takes when flying through space. Music, painting, architecture, sculpture, poetry—all this is nothing more than a past now out of date. Now, in the rock, the paint, the sound, and the word, a process of reforming the life that was once living but is now dead has been accomplished. Musical rhythm is the wind blowing across the sky of the soul. And as it courses through this sky, which languishes warmly in expectation of creation, musical rhythm, that "voice of delicate cold," has already thickened the clouds of poetic myths. And myth has veiled the sky of the soul, begun to sparkle with a thousand colors, and fused into stone. The creative flow has created a living cloud myth. But the myth has hardened and disintegrated into colors and stones.

The world of art has arisen like a mortuary temple of living creation.

By consolidating the creative process in form, we are in essence commanding ourselves to see flowing lava in ashes and fused rock. This is why our perspective on future art is so hopeless. We are ordering this future to be ash. We are at the same time putting creation to death either by combining its fragments into one heap (synthesis of the arts) or by dividing the forms ad infinitum (differentiation of the arts).

In both cases it is the past that is reborn. In both cases we find ourselves at the mercy of the cherished dead. The glorious sounds of a Beethoven symphony, the victorious sounds of Dionysian dithyrambs (Nietzsche)—all this is no more than a collection of dead sounds. We think at first that these are tsars, clothed in "fine linen,"[1] but in fact they are merely embalmed corpses. They approach us to fascinate us with death.

In art, in life, things are much more serious than we think. The abyss over which we have been hanging is deeper, darker than we had supposed.

In order to escape from the charmed circle of contradictions, we must cease speaking of everything, whether it is art, cognition, or our very own lives.

We must forget the present. We must recreate everything, and in order to do this we must create ourselves.

And the only slope on which we may still clamber is ourselves.

At the summit our "I" awaits us.

Here is the answer for the artist: if he wishes to remain an artist but not cease to be a man, he must become his own artistic form.

Only this form of creation still holds out the promise of salvation.

Here lies the path of the art of the future.

1907

THE ESSAYS

THE SCIENTIFIC AESTHETIC

THE PRINCIPLE OF FORM IN AESTHETICS

1

In art there must be a principle governing the manner of presentation. The form of art is just such a principle. Every art requires an external means of expression. The question then arises whether there exists a norm that is common to [all] the forms of expression of the various arts. In other words, is there some principle by which the existing forms of art can be placed in a systematic order? If it were possible to discover such an order through natural means, the forms in which art presents itself to us could then be derived from a single norm. This norm, since it is not given, would provide an underlying basis for the existing forms of art, prescribing purely formal ends for them. This formalism, by identifying the ends of art, would preserve art from any tendentious encroachments on it while at the same time representing artistic expression as possessing a certain orderliness, or *cosmos*, and not just a meaningless *chaos*.

When we speak of the *form of art*, we do not speak of something that is distinct from content. The indivisible unity of form and content is a canon of aesthetics, or must be if aesthetics is to escape the tutelage of scholastic dogmatism. When we speak of the form of art we refer to a way of looking at any given artistic material. A study of the techniques by which a creative symbol is embodied in artistic material yields a natural series of general conclusions arranged in groups. These groups are the forms of art. When we study the means by which form acts upon us, we are talking about the content of a given art. In this case, form and content are merely methodological devices for examining a given artistic unity. The unity in question is the symbol. When one speaks of the symbolism of any given artistic embodiment, one may not speak of the relation between form and content as one of opposition. Form cannot be separated from content, and vice versa.

Disputes among learned scholastics in the Middle Ages concerning *substantia* and *accidens* have led recent scholars to the necessity of understanding these concepts in a formal manner. The theory of work and energy proposed by physicists, for example, removes the opposition between substance and accident. To put it differently: the latest research has given a [purely] formal sense to the concept of substance. Substance has been reduced to a law, namely that of causality. Something similar is going on in the arts as well. I am thus obliged to make the following qualification: when I speak of the forms of creative expression, I use the term *form* in a relative sense, as a convenient means of combining the designation of several different methods for examining a given artistic symbol.

When we speak of a norm of presentation of the phenomena of beauty, we refer to a single order in which the existing forms of art may be systematically arranged. The "plan" that predetermines each form of art, and that cannot be determined by that form, is the norm. The existing forms of art are restrictions on the universal norm of creation. These restrictions create the individual conditions for each form of art. I may study a painting as a form of individual creative expression. Or I might study the general conditions that determine that form qua painting, relating it to the art of painting, which is to say the generic form embracing the entire class of [individual] paintings. The conditions for study would vary accordingly. If I am discussing a given painting from the first point of view, I will examine the technical devices the creator used to distinguish his picture from those belonging to various other schools of painting. If, on the other hand, I adopt the second point of view, I will approach the question differently: I will ask instead what determines the given artistic form (qua painting). I will direct my attention to the necessary, a priori conditions of the art of painting, that is, the spatial elements that give the paint the capacity to represent reality on a plane surface. An aesthetics constructed in accordance with the first point of view will be an empirical aesthetics. It will limit itself to elucidating and classifying the given forms of art. An aesthetics constructed in accordance with the second point of view, however, will seek the laws by which the given forms are of necessity constructed and derived from the necessary elements of space and time.

Only in the latter case can aesthetics free itself from the various encroachments on it from all sides: from various unprincipled and sharp-witted aesthetes, from those trends that seek to place art in the service of any number of tendentious causes utterly foreign to it, and from the empirical sciences. Only then can aesthetics become an independent, formal discipline whose sole task is to preserve [artistic] creation from both principled and unprincipled encroachments. The purpose of the present article is to set out a projected path by which aesthetics may free itself from all the foreign, tendentious elements imposed on it, regardless of the cause these elements serve: aestheticism or the public at large, individualism or universalism, idealism or realism, mysticism or positivism.

2

In the existing forms of art, reality is divided [into separate aspects]. No art form can embrace reality in all of its aspects. When we study the various means by which artistic creation embodies its material, what we are really looking at is a process of differentiation. Some forms of art, for instance, will more completely render the elements of spatiality; others, temporality. Sculpture and architecture, on the other hand, deal with three-dimensional spatial representation.

Architecture represents the correlation of masses, sculpture the correlation of forms. Painting involves the abstraction of three-dimensional representation: it is the fate of painting to be restricted to the plane surface. But painting gains a certain richness of representation from this abstraction. Because of this abstraction, it elevates color to a position of primacy. Music is confronted with a reality from which all visual elements have been abstracted. It represents change in experience, but without seeking the corresponding visual forms. Time is the essential formal element of music, elevating the meaning of rhythm to a position of primacy. Poetry unites the formal conditions of both temporal and spatial forms of art by means of the word. The word represents in a mediated fashion. This is the weakness of poetry. But the word represents not only the form of the image but the shift from image to image as well. This is the strength of poetry. Poetry is a mediated form of art, but the range of areas it can represent is very broad. Poetry can change spatial features into temporal features, and vice versa.

3

Spatial elements, which always appear in inverse proportion to temporal elements, determine the ranking of the various forms of art.[1]

Music

In music temporality is expressed in rhythm. There is no spatial aspect. Space is expressed in music only by vague analogies. The pitch and strength of a tone might perhaps be seen as analogous to the density and dimensions of physical masses. The quality of a tone is perhaps analogous to color. But these analogies do not give rise to any truly essential conclusions. In music, rather, we are presented with a purely ideal space. Consequently, the images evoked by music are also purely ideal. If art is symbolic, then the purpose of its images must be to combine the ideal and the eternal in the elements of the final product. But the images evoked by music are already perfect and complete: that is why music, which is a temporal form, is able to exert such an influence on the spatial art forms. It is also why it is possible to find the spirit of music in the fundamentally nonmusical forms of art, where it is potentially present. Music is thus the latent energy of creation. The fewer the formal means used to "convert" this energy, the more perfect the form of the image. Time is the form of inner sense, and this is why music, which is a purely temporal form, expresses symbols that appear especially profound to us. Music deepens everything it touches. It is the very soul of all the arts. This is the reason why the fundamental requirements we place on art are so clearly outlined in music. A symbol is the union of experience with the form of an image. But such a union, if it is possible, may be attained only through the form of inner sense, that is, time. This is why every true symbol is necessarily musical, that is, necessarily idealizes empirical reality more or less, depending on the degree to which it is abstracted from the real conditions of space.

Poetry

In poetry the element of temporality, pure rhythm, is overgrown with images, so to speak. This is how the Apollonian vision arises from the depths of the soul. Only music can reveal to us that the visible world is really a veil cast over the abyss. Poetry views the visible world musically, like a veil over an unspoken mystery of the soul. This kind of view is a musical one. Music is the skeleton of poetry. If music is the common trunk of all creation, poetry is its leafy crown. The images of poetry, which grow out of rhythm (which, in turn, is free of images), limit rhythmic freedom, so to speak, burden it with visibility. The musical theme then becomes myth. If poetry burdens music with images, then conversely music, thanks to poetry and through poetry, is able to permeate the visible world. In poetry we deal with images and their changes. The consequence is a significant complication in the formal elements of the art. This complication can be seen in the mediating nature of images. Poetry's mediated form of representation makes it easy to overlook the images of the poetic myth in favor of the causal connections between them. If myth grows out of rhythm, so to speak, then the complication and subsequent breakdown of myth leads to the emergence from it of elements that bear no direct relation to art. Myth exists as a kind of parasite on a free musical theme, and tendentious ideas do the same to myth. All this has the effect of distancing the elements of pure art from art's original basis in music. This distancing in turn has the effect of complicating the formal elements of art. The music of creation now becomes a kind of distant background, and the form of the image is elevated to a position of primacy. Only occasionally is poetry's homeland (the musical element) revealed in its form.

Painting

A full representation of the visible world is rendered in a mediated fashion in poetry. Spatiality in poetry is only half-embodied. The greater realizations of the visible spatial world in art are always accompanied by an accumulation of artistic material [that is, the material dimension of art]. There is an intention realized in this material, however. Sound in and of itself is less material, whereas paint and marble are entirely material. In realizing a condition of spatiality, we are treating form in the narrow sense. The introduction of the material necessary for the embodiment of this form (in the narrow sense) is accompanied by a breakdown of the visible world, first into representation by color, and second into representation by form. The introduction of the material—paint—itself (the empirical element) for the purpose of realizing ideal poetic images in visual form implies spreading these images over a plane surface. Moreover, it fixes them to the surface, that is, limits their freedom of movement in time by fixing the one single moment of time that is represented. If poetry is cut off from the purity of rhythmic movement because of myth, painting too, by catching just a single moment of mythic action, excludes the underlying musical qualities of the thing represented. The elements of poetic symbolization that are immediate (freedom in time) here become mediate (physical restrictions of the plane). Conversely, the elements of symbolization that are mediately represented in poetry (the existence of the image in space) are given immediately in painting (the presence of the image represented in a plane). Here the element of spatiality occurs in inverse relation to the element of temporality.

The Art of Form (Sculpture, Architecture)

A more faithful embodiment of the visible world than that achieved by painting is possible only if those images that painting imprints on a plane surface are now carried out into space. This process breaks down the very moment of representation of the image, selecting from it only certain forms. If the musical theme associated with Siegfried, for example, is full of images depicting Siegfried's heroic exploits, a painted representation, on the other hand, can do no more than fix one or several moments of Siegfried's life. Sculpture can give us an image of Siegfried himself at the given represented moments by abstracting, for example, elements from the landscape in which the image in question occurs. But any such moment that painting captures from myth splits apart once it is removed from the plane and rendered in three-dimensional space. The center of gravity moves from color to form, and any diversity of color in the image will fade or will often be absent altogether. Rhythm in the proper sense of the term is thus replaced by so-called harmony of form. This harmony, which rests on the purely mathematical laws of correlation of masses, presents a remote analogy to the mathematical basis of musical rhythm. One might say that music contains potentials of space, and architecture potentials of time.[2] In music, what is actually given is a sequence of rhythmic impulses; in architecture, it is the position of mass.

4

If spatiality occurs in inverse relation to temporality in the various art forms, then we can recognize as the *norm* for investigating increases and decreases in temporal and spatial elements a natural order governing the arrangement of existing art forms. Such an order establishes a relation of dependence between the given art forms and the formal conditions of sensible intuition, namely space and time. In so deriving the place of a given art form from the space-time relation it presents, aesthetics first becomes a science of forms. It is not our purpose here to deduce the general norms of such a science. Instead, what interests us is the path that must be followed in order to liberate aesthetics from the grip of dogmatism.

The elements of space and time are the necessary formal elements of all types of art. The conversion of these formal elements from one to another may follow upon an examination of the existing forms of art. If we can establish as a fact that such a conversion of elements takes place, then there must be laws governing this conversion, laws, that is, of conversion of art forms. If time or space is the transcendental form of art, and if we can establish that an increase in elements of time entails a decrease for elements of space and vice versa, then the law of conversion of formal elements is a special case of the law of conservation of the universal norm of the creation of forms. The law of conservation of the universal norm of the creation of forms is the law of conservation of creation.

Every art form is defined, first, by the formal laws of space and time, and, second, by the material that goes into its formation. In the second case we are concerned with the material substance of form. Substance, or matter, is a necessary condition for the formation of an empirical form. The general laws governing matter necessarily influence the laws governing the formation of art forms. The laws governing matter, as established by theoretical chemistry and physics, may be easily extended for our purposes: they are convenient models that serve the purpose of concentrating our attention on the requirements we must make on the study of the formal principles of art.

This is why the law of conservation of the formal elements of artistic images presents such a clear analogy to the law of conservation of matter. This latter law is the basis of theoretical chemistry. But the law of conservation of matter is really only a corollary of the law of conservation of energy.

We may expect in advance that the formal principle governing the status of form in art will be analogous to the energy principle we just mentioned. The purely external features of the aesthetic principle present a clear equivalence to the energy principle. In art, form and content compose an indivisible unity. Energy, for its part, unites *substantia* and *accidens*. *Accidens*, then, would correspond to the content of art, which is derived from the form of creation. This form, in turn, which makes the individual art form, is analogous to *substantia*. The indivisible unity [in art] is the symbol. The symbolic principle may thus be easily compared with the energy principle. In fact it is quite possible to elucidate the symbolic principle in terms of the energy principle, and vice versa. The inseparability of form and content is an entirely formal principle. The law of conservation of form serves as a regulating factor and a more complete elucidation of the formal basis of symbolism. This basis is expressed in the law of inseparability of form and content. And this latter law arises as a consequence of an epistemological examination of art. On the other hand, the law of conservation of form is necessarily linked to the law of conservation of creation. The law of conservation of creation is one of the fundamental laws of formal aesthetics.

5

For the present exposition of the fundamental formal law, I will use an analogy. The elements of theoretical chemistry will serve as the elements of this analogy. These elements are intended to construct a model for a future aesthetics. The construction of models is accepted under the broad patronage of science in general, and for this reason I find nothing paradoxical in my use of them.

Mass is energy in a resistant form. This definition of mass has the advantage of introducing unity and proportion into our understanding of the phenomena surrounding us. Only in static definitions are we concerned with a definite mass as such. But, as we know, the moment of stasis is really a special case of dynamic relations. Saying that mass is resistant energy is equivalent to indicating the dynamic basis of any theory of mass.

An art form often owes its embodiment to substance. Substance, which is expressed in terms of mass, can be defined dynamically. The formal principle of art must therefore be ultimately based in a dynamic principle. The quantity and velocity of motion must constitute a fundamental dimension of art. But the formula expressing velocity introduces the factor of time. Time is thus a necessary constituent of the formula expressing velocity. But it is also both the form of inner sense and the formal condition of all symbolization. It is thus a necessary condition for the perfection of an artistic production. The perfection of any form is contingent on this ultimate reduction to time. But the purely temporal art form, as we have said, is music. For this reason we may say that the degree of perfection in artistic form is determined by the spirit of music. The material of artistic production, seen in this light, is thus resistant music [that is, as mass is equivalent to resistant energy]. In this sense, the process by which rhythm becomes permeated with space can be defined as the process of converting pure music into resistant music. Resistant music thus latently absorbs the spirit of pure music. That is to say that it is potentially charged with the energy of music. The process of converting spatial into temporal elements is the discharge of the spirit of music into pure music. The element of time, which is indispensable for the dimension of motion in music, is immediately given in rhythm. From these considerations alone we can already see the dominant significance of music in a system encompassing the other forms of art. The perfection of the other forms of art is determined by the degree to which they approximate music.

In contemporary physics one may speak of the "density" of energy. The density of energy and the density of matter are inversely proportional.

The material of representation in art, that is, form in the literal sense, corresponds to matter. The method of arranging this material is conditioned by an *internal effect.* To this internal effect there corresponds an *attitude of mind, experience,* which has provoked a crystallization of creativity. This attitude of mind is the form of expression for the internally experienced creative effect. Creative effect in this sense is the sole content of artistic form. We may then speak of an inverse relation between the quantity and density of the material of artistic representation on the one hand, and the density of energy in the arrangement of this material on the other. Density of energy is defined as the degree of approximation to music.

If we assign an equal quantity of energy to materials of different density, we will obtain an unequal effect. This effect, as it were, stands in inverse proportion to the quantity and density (intensity and resistance) of material, and in direct proportion to the quantity of work expended by us. Work is here defined as the capacity to transmit a certain creative effect to a listener, spectator, or reader. In other words it is defined as the perfection of symbolization. This is why work carried out on form always stands in direct proportion to the internal effect, so that the form of the symbol is already a symbol itself.

Here we see a direct necessity to identify the formal laws of aesthetic symbolization with the supreme law of theoretical physics. But such an identification is possible only where we know that the quantity of both the internal and the external forces of creation is a constant. In creating external obstacles to the embodiment of the internal effect (through either the quantity or the density of the material), I must diminish proportionately the internal energy of creation, assuming, of course, identical conditions of space and time.

6

The law of conservation of creative energy may be formulated as follows:

The quantity of general effort required to overcome stasis in the material of creation is constant. By increasing the external effort through complication and accumulation of the material used for a given form, we diminish the internal energy of creation, and vice versa. Here the correlation is the same as that between potential and kinetic energy in any given mechanical configuration. And in the same way that, in energetics, we are constantly concerned only with the forms of kinetic energy, arriving at the notion of potential energy by inference and viewing it as a mere supplement [to a more fundamental concept], so, in the energetic conception of art forms, we always begin by examining patterns of regularity in an artistic arrangement of a given set of material used in that form of art and proceed from there to the idea of energy of creation, something that is *not* given. Thus we perceive a certain regularity in the arrangement and evolution of temporal and spatial features in certain given art forms. We see that the aesthetic power of the form lies in the simplicity of its expression. We infer from this either that it is impossible to speak of norms in the arrangment of forms, or that only the concept of internal energy of creation is capable of providing us with a rigorous classification of art without doing art any violence. By allowing the concept of internal energy of creation, we are drawing an inference from an unconscious general premise concerning the norms of creation. This premise, once we recognize it as the indispensable condition for any discussion of a system of aesthetic forms, is none other than the law of conservation of creative effort. The law of conservation of creative effort—which sets up a necessary connection between the form of art and the form of creation, as well as setting up a connection, through the common norm of creation, among the various forms of creation—will permanently lead us away from the realm of static, dogmatic, and metaphysical definitions of beauty and into the realm of dynamic definitions. There, by means of differential and scientific symbols, we can represent as an indissoluble unity the *work* of creation together with the *work* exhibited in the effect the creation has on its perceivers. And, just as the laws of this unity may be at least relatively defined by graphic, but not by logical, means (like certain mathematical symbols), these same laws, since they remain purely formal, present the truest and most successful model for representing the rules and laws of internal symbolization. But in refuting and shattering all outspokenly metaphysical views on art, the energetic model still leaves completely open the question of the symbolic means for evaluating artworks, and consequently a vast expanse of space is opened up for both creative freedom and subjective criticism.

If the methods of formal aesthetics were fully elaborated, they would serve effectively as heavy artillery, relentlessly and definitively smashing petty incursions into creative freedom.

7

The law of equivalents could well find expression in a formal aesthetics.

The possibility of drawing parallels between probable aesthetic principles of the future and principles of energy enables us to outline our analogy more concretely.

Let us imagine a statue of gigantic proportions. Let us also select one of Pushkin's greatest poems. Now let us imagine for a moment, entirely abstractly, the possibility of measuring the effect produced by each of these two artworks both on us and on others. (At present no real means for performing such a measurement exists, but it is possible in theory.) It is possible, let us say, that the effect from contemplating the statue will be stronger than that produced on us by Pushkin's poem.

If in both cases the elements of the comparison are correlated with the intensity of artistic expression, then do we not find a violation of the principle outlined above? For in that case an example of a less perfect art form (sculpture) would be affecting us with greater intensity than the corresponding form of a more perfect art (poetry). If we seem to see here a violation of our law, we must, however, recall that it is necessary to consider a quantity and an intensity of creative effort for an *equivalent* quantity of the form being compared. A poet using a smaller quantity of external effort (kinetic creative energy) in the creation of his artwork will transfer his effort to charging the poetic image with *internal* creative energy. The [total] quantity of energy is always the same: this is entailed by the principle of conservation of creative work. Conversely, the sculptor working on an equivalent amount of material will expend a greater quantity of kinetic creative energy. If the quantity of his external effort [kinetic creative energy] happens to be four times greater than that of the poet, then the poetic work will affect us with four times the intensity. If, however, the sculptor uses an amount of material sixteen times greater than the equivalent material used by the poet, and if the amount of time for embodying the material is also sixteen times greater, since the sculptor, in any given unit (t) of time, is expending a quantity of internal creative energy equivalent to that in the poetic creation, then a certain equality will occur. If the effect on us of the sculptor's work is expressed by the symbol $8/4$, then the poet's effect will be expressed thus:[3]

$$\frac{8 \cdot 4}{4} = 8, \text{ or } \frac{8}{4} \simeq 8.$$

For an amount of material sixteen times greater than that used in the poetic work, we get:[4]

$$\frac{8 \cdot 16}{4} > 8.$$

The greater strength of effect always appears to be on the side of sculpture,[5] because in practice we habitually fail to take into account the law of equivalents.

The most pressing task of the future exact science of aesthetics is to discover the true bases for this law, which for now has been arrived at purely a priori.

8

If we successively raise the numerator of the fraction $8/4$ by increments of 1, we get:

$$\frac{8+1}{4}, \frac{8+1+1}{4}, \frac{8+1+1+1}{4}, \text{ and so on.}$$

This shows an increase in *tension* in creative energy.

By repeating the whole fraction $8/4$, we may raise the quantity of creative energy in the following fashion:

$$\frac{8}{4}+\frac{8}{4}+\frac{8}{4}+\frac{8}{4}=\frac{32}{4}.$$

The quantity of creative effort in the creation of large-scale artworks is higher than artistic tension.

Artistic tension, on the other hand, plays a greater role in the creation of smaller-scale artworks.

While composing large-scale artworks, Ibsen, for instance, attempted at first to expend a certain quantity of energy

$$\left[\frac{a}{b}+\frac{a}{b}+\frac{a}{b}+\frac{a}{b}=\frac{4a}{b}\right],$$

but then, through corrections in his manuscript, heightened the *tension* of the expended effort:

$$\left[\frac{4a}{b}, \frac{4a+a_1}{b}, \frac{4a+a_1+a_2}{b}, \frac{4a+a_1+a_2+a_3}{b}, \ldots\right].$$

This is how Goethe wrote *Faust*.

9

An artistic image arouses in us a definite mood. This mood is achieved through the application of a certain creative effort. It is immaterial whether we attain the expression of this mood through an increase in quantity or through an increase in tension.

Thus creative effort expended to express the power (intensity) of the mood is, as it were, inversely proportional to the effort used to increase its tension.

Quantity and tension of mood occur in inverse proportion to each other.

Thus for any Q, Q_1, Q_2 (quantity), and T, T_1, T_2 (tension), we have:

$$\frac{Q}{Q_1}=\frac{T_1}{T}, \text{ or } QT=Q_1T_1=Q_2T_2=Q_3T_3=\text{Constant}.$$

This relation between the quantity and the tension of mood presents a perfect analogy to the gas law of Boyle and Mariotte,[6] which has played such an important role in physics and theoretical chemistry, namely:

$$pv=p_1v_1=p_2v_2=\text{Constant}.$$

The inverse proportion between the volume of a gas and its pressure serves as a convenient model for characterizing the equally regular relation between the quantity of mood aroused and its tension under equal creative efforts applied to equal material.[7]

10

The analogy pointed out above is actually only a special case of a much broader analogy existing between the established [physical] laws of matter and the not-yet-established laws of exact aesthetics. This broader analogy comes directly out of the formal principle adopted above.

The laws governing changes of state in matter are analogous to the laws governing the change of spatial and temporal elements in art.

A change of state in physical bodies is parallel to a change of form in art. [In physics] the rate of acceleration of molecular motion is accompanied by a successive increase in the quantity of overall motion. Perfection of artistic form (in the broad sense) is [by the analogy] measured by the overall quantity of motion.

Motion is change over consecutive moments of time, and this, as it happens, is the basis of rhythm.

1. The solid state of bodies is analogous to the forms of architecture and sculpture.

These are the three-dimensional art forms. They possess elasticity and volume. The relation of light to shadow, that is, the combination of convex and concave surfaces, plays an important role here. This alternation of unequally illuminated surfaces gives the eye the impression of a solid body in space. The reason for the difference in illumination is inequality in the diffusion of light corpuscles.[8] Fluctuations in light constitute "motion" in sculpture and architecture. This is where the spirit of music appears, bringing these forms closer to musical forms. One can even speak of the "rhythm" of light diffusion. This rhythm then forms harmonies, as it were, out of the unequally illuminated surfaces. This is the source of the notorious harmony of forms.

It should be recalled that the quantity of motion here is counteracted by the inertia of mass. A diminution in mass in sculpture corresponds to an increase in quantity of motion, although the character of motion here is different. One can also speak of muscular tension, the energy of poses, and so forth.

The spirit of music increases. Sculpture is a more perfect art form than architecture.

2. The liquid state of matter corresponds to painting. A liquid has no form. It adopts the form of its container and also spreads out over a plane surface. The molecules of liquid substances move about each other freely, although all mutual attachment has not yet been dissolved.

The painter, representing images on a plane, does not require a great quantity of inert mass in order to embody his intentions. A decrease in inert mass here results in a complication in light fluctuations through color fluctuations, since color is more important than light in painting. It also results in a simplification (a kind of dissociation, as it were) of space (since one dimension is lost).

3. Poetry corresponds to the transitional state of matter between liquid and gas, namely the vaporous state. The laws governing the vaporous state of matter consist of those governing the gaseous state but are limited and complicated by the laws governing liquid substances.[9] Poetry is the transitional art form between the temporal form (music) and the spatial forms. Matter, essentially obliterated in poetry, is expressed here only in the form of material images. Such images are abstract, ideal. A decrease in matter here is accomplished by an increase in quantity of motion (myth, rhythm, temporality).

4. The final art form, music, corresponds to gas. As a substance approaches the gaseous state, its molecules are capable of reaching ever greater velocities. Music is the art of pure motion.

There is no discontinuity between the solid, liquid, and gaseous states of substances. Nonetheless, all substances appear to us only in these few states and not in an infinite multitude of different physical states.[10]

The same is true in art. We group the forms in which it appears into the traditional categories: architecture, sculpture, painting, poetry, music. Some forms of art are clearly transitional (drama, bas-relief).

Art forms, like species in the animal kingdom, may interchange as they develop. But the fundamental forms of art all have one unifying principle: the simplicity of the indivisible unity of the experienced Symbol. Its form of expression is symbolization.

11

Given a stationary level of creation *t*, if we establish an inverse proportion between *Q* (quantity) and *T* (tension), then any increase in creative tension [overall effect, t, or the product of Q and T] will be accompanied by an increase in tension of mood aroused [T]. This also implies that for a constant tension of mood [T], Q will rise in direct proportion to overall creative tension [t]. Designating increases in tension of mood by X, X_1, X_2, etc., we have:

$$\left.\frac{X}{X_t} = \frac{Q}{Q_t}\right\} \text{for } X = 1 \left.\right\} Q = \frac{Q_t}{X_t}, \text{ and, since } X_t = t,$$

$$Q_t = QT, \text{ or } \frac{Q_t}{Q} = t.$$

The following relation also holds:

$$\frac{Q_t}{Q_{t\text{-}1}} = \frac{Q_{t\text{-}1}}{Q_{t\text{-}2}} = \frac{Q_{t\text{-}2}}{Q_{t\text{-}3}} = \alpha = \text{Constant.}$$

α is the coefficient of increase in Q for any increase in overall creative volume [t] by an arbitrary theoretical unit.

We have, then, the following equation:

$$Q_t = Q_0 + Q_0\alpha t.$$

Applying the distributive law, we obtain:

$$Q_t = Q_0\,(1 + \alpha t).$$

This formula is analogous to the formula expressing Charles's and Gay-Lussac's law:[11] $pv = p_0v_0\,(1 + \alpha t)$, where α is the coefficient of expansion of gases.[12]

12

The laws governing the gaseous state of matter are analogous to the laws governing the harmonic (musical) state of [artistic] form. The gas laws are the simplest and most general laws of theoretical chemistry. Any complications and restrictions invariably involve a shift to laws governing other states of matter, vaporous, liquid, and solid.

The musical state of form is the simplest and most intensely perceived artistic state of the visible world. This is why the capacity of the art object to return to a condition of music is a fundamental capacity of aesthetic effect. This capacity is none other than symbolization.

One good reason for the necessity of returning to a condition of music, that is, to the symbolization of experience, is the simple necessity of defining α. "α" is the coefficient of increase in quantity of creative effort for a relative increase in creative volume. But this is, in the end, required by the extension of our analogy: the laws of Boyle and Gay-Lussac are, after all, gas laws, but with analogies to the laws of music. Any condensation of forms (that is, an increase in the element of spatiality) must a priori violate the principle of regularity mentioned above. Such a violation occurs in sculpture, painting, and architecture: one cannot conceive of a building, a statue, or a painting of minuscule dimensions and at the same time without any violation of harmony. It is as though it were always easier to embody a state of mind showing greater tension, in spite of the decrease in the quantity of material requisite for embodying the artist's intention.

If the quantity of tension is seen as analogous to temperature [in the gas laws], then the quantity of creative effort is analogous to the quantity of heat. When this quantity increases, it raises proportionally either the tension of the mood produced by the artistic material or, if the degree of tension remains constant, the quantity of material. We have already seen that we expend more effort to increase the tension where the overall mood is constant than to increase the overall mood, where the tension remains constant (here there is undoubtedly a connection with the psychophysiological law of Fechner).[13] But a perfect analogy presents itself in the area of heat in physics; thermal heat capacity under constant pressure (C_p) is greater than under constant volume (C_v).

Having adopted the similarity between various principles of energy and various principles of aesthetics as the basis for an analogy between the formal laws of aesthetics and the formal laws of matter, I could extend the analogy endlessly in all its details. Although this analogy certainly does not penetrate to the very essence of aesthetics, it nonetheless provides, from without, a sketch of the autonomous development of the principle of form in aesthetics, and it does so rather completely. Serious theoreticians of art in the future will have to become involved in this field if they wish to abandon the kind of groundless daydreaming and mindless prattle that is forever imposing foreign purposes on art.

1906

LYRIC POETRY AND EXPERIMENT

1

Exact science is unlimited in its competence. It covers every conceivable type of object. It is said that the boundaries of exact science are delineated not by any group of objects, but by the sharpness of the visual angle[1] for each of these many groups of objects. The degree to which this visual angle is defined depends on the method of investigation.

Exact science connects various methodological groups on the basis of the techniques of investigation employed, and not on the basis of the objects themselves. It establishes connections between methods that, in some determined fashion, are distinct from other methodological connections. The objects so connected are essentially a matter of indifference. Ethnography, for example, is a science showing a definite connection with both philology and natural science. This implies that in an ethnographic investigation, I can approach a single group of objects with two different methods. The results of such an investigation, which might occasionally be contradictory, are incommensurable in the absence of a critique of the objective significance of the two methods employed. Let us suppose that I have before me a vase of a certain shape, with an ornament and various hieroglyphic inscriptions. I can determine the time and place the vase was cast, first by analyzing the inscriptions, second by analyzing the ornament, and third by analyzing the form, that is, the vase's sagittal and tangential sections. In the first instance, I would be approaching the analysis from the point of view of a philologist; in the second, from that of an art historian; in the third, from that of a naturalist, since I would be applying to an ethnographic object methods borrowed from comparative anatomy (something, incidentally, that is practiced successfully by ethnographer-naturalists).

If the investigative techniques I just mentioned lead me to three conflicting results, this does not mean that they are faulty, so long as I have a clearly elaborated theory concerning the vase's inscriptions, its ornament, and its sections. Investigative methods are complicated and relative. A great many different methods exist whose results do not coincide, though each is exact in its own right. Critiques of these different methods also exist. Only one thing is true, however, and that is that the class of objects of investigation is always the same.

It would seem unnecessary to repeat this elementary truth, and yet the occasion does arise when one must. Is it possible for aesthetics to have its own method of investigation? Or is it obliged to borrow methods from other fields?

Let us consider, for example, Pushkin's poem, "The Prophet."[2] How shall I approach the task of analyzing it? Clearly, I can analyze the poem in either of two ways: first, from the point of view of content, and second, from the point of view of form. Now, even if I leave aside the whole epistemological question of form, content, and their mutual relations, even if I restrict my understanding of form and content to the purely naive senses of these concepts, I will observe nonetheless that considerable ambiguity attaches to them. Content may signify, first, the ideational content of "The Prophet"; second, the experiential content as expressed in the form of images; and third, the image of the prophet as he is presented in the poem. If I choose the first option, I may analyze the idea of "The Prophet" (*a*) from the point of view of Pushkin as an individual, (*b*) from the point of view of the history of ideas, (*c*) from the point of view of the social and class conflicts of Pushkin's era, (*d*) from the point of view of comparative ideology (analyzing the *type* of the prophet in various poets), or (*e*) from the point of view of various moral, philosophical, theological, and even mystical systems. The same multitude of investigative techniques greets us when we attempt to analyze the experiential content and the form of the image. Five investigative techniques multiplied by three different senses of content in "The Prophet" give fifteen possible methods for analyzing the content, plus all the different possible arrangements and combinations of these methods.

Similarly, when I turn to an analysis of the form of "The Prophet," I may understand by form, first, the aggregate of means of representation that give relief to the image of the prophet; second, the arrangement and combination of words (verbal instrumentation [*instrumentovka*]); and third, meter and its individual application (rhythm). Any arbitrarily indicated means for analyzing form breaks down into an infinite multitude of investigative possibilities. For instance, the aggregate of means of representation may be pursued from the following points of view: (*a*) the poet as an individual, (*b*) the poet's historical era, (*c*) his nationality, (*d*) his situation, (*e*) the history of art, and so forth. The results of our investigations of the form and content of "The Prophet" will be incommensurable with each other. They will depend entirely on the methods employed.

I may appraise "The Prophet" from the point of view of history, sociology, meter, style, and so on. A poem may express a great idea while being utterly unmusical to the ear, and vice versa. What, then, are the criteria for establishing its significance? What exactly *is* lyric poetry?

It is customary to say that lyric poetry is one form of poetry in general, and that poetry is one form of art. But is there such a thing as a science of art forms? And what, moreover, is science? A given science is an aggregate of investigative techniques brought to bear on a given set of objects. But, as many will hasten to point out, the objects of scientific investigation are unlimited. Consequently, an artistic object (beauty) must be, among other things, an object of scientific investigation.

We have seen how in one object of investigation several different scientific methods may intersect (for instance, ethnography, psychology, and so forth). The same is true of beauty, which we may approach from a variety of points of view. But among the various scientific groups of approaches, two primary tendencies emerge in the construction of methods: the tendency to group objects on the basis of their origin (the genetic method) and the tendency to group them according to their end or purpose (the teleological method). In the first case we obtain sets of laws; in the second, sets of value judgments. The sets of value judgments are what forms the group of human sciences, whose defining basis lies in norms of value. In the first case we are speaking of the group of so-called exact sciences, whose basis lies in the norms and forms of cognitive activity. The relation between norms of value and norms of cognition is the single most complex question confronting theoretical thought today.

Some people maintain that aesthetics is a science. Others maintain that it is not. Sciences have been defined according to the objects of their investigation. But they have also been defined according to their methods. The goal of any given science is defined now as a series of varied investigations on a particular collection of objects for the purpose of decomposing this collection under the science's methods. A tendency exists to derive the object from the method. At the same time, the exactness of any given method arises from its ability to establish a definite connection among the objects of one group but not among those of another. This exactness is what has made it possible to separate method from object. The possibility has thus arisen to expand indefinitely the object of methodological investigation. This second way is the path of development of exact science. It has led to the elaboration of a whole theory of methodological construction. And this task, in turn, is what has raised the question of the possibility of deriving the very objects of investigation from the methods of investigation.

If aesthetics is understood as the science of the beautiful then its domain is the beautiful. What is the beautiful? This is either a metaphysical question of the same order as that concerning the end and value of beauty, or a positive question (what does mankind consider beautiful?). In the first case we are confronted with the task of constructing a metaphysics of beauty. In the second, we are confronted with an aesthetic experiment involving the set of all monuments of beauty in the world. The goal of an exact aesthetics is to analyze artistic monuments and derive rules that define and determine those monuments. The goal of a metaphysical aesthetics is to discern the one, true purpose and end of beauty and, by means of it, to probe the aesthetic experience of mankind. But the uniformity of such an aesthetic is intimately connected with the uniformity of metaphysics. And how is a single metaphysics possible? It is possible as a necessary condition of a theory of knowledge. And if an ideal theory of knowledge pretends to universality, then its metaphysics will be both universal and obligatory. But the construction of a universal and uniform metaphysics is a task that can hardly be accomplished by mankind in the present age. And this is why it is impossible to establish norms for aesthetic values. Aesthetics is impossible as a human science.

But is it possible as an exact science?

In fact, it *is* entirely possible.

For only in such a case can aesthetics do away with all universally binding value judgments. Its task then becomes the derivation of principles that will provide connections between the empirical hypotheses of aesthetic investigations. Its hypotheses will result from a process of induction from empirical laws.

What is the material of investigation in the area of aesthetics? If aesthetics is possible as an exact science, then its material of investigation must be its own: it is the form of the arts that must serve as that material. For instance, in lyric poetry this form is no more than words that have been arranged in particular phonetic, metric, and rhythmic combinations and that constitute a certain combination of means of representation. This, then, is the empirical dimension of the branch of aesthetics that investigates the laws of lyric poetry.

The objection will be raised that in any lyric poem the categories of image, experience, and plot must also be considered. But image, plot, and experience may be examined from the point of view of form. There may exist a historical account of both the formation of plot and the inception of an image. Thus the jurisdiction of formal aesthetics as a science is much wider [than one might have supposed]. But the laws governing the inception of images (any regular or taxonomic distribution of symbols and experiences) may also be studied from a point of view that is *not* wholly aesthetic. They may be examined using applied mythology, psychology, sociology, and so forth, depending on the method we have chosen to approach our object of study. The object of study here is the same for a whole range of disciplines. But the exactness of the method is tied to the degree to which the object is clearly defined. Every exact science has arisen through a process of limiting the object of investigation and discovering a connection sui generis between its objects. This connection sui generis between objects subsequently separates off from its object to become *method*. Only then is the class of objects able to expand indefinitely. Take the example of botany: originally the term *botany* applied primarily to the taxonomy of plants. Later on, however, separate areas of study were demarcated for the forms of plants (morphology), the anatomical structure of plants, their functions (plant physiology), and their various species (taxonomy).

Through this process of limiting, plant physiology grew to be a self-sufficient whole. This is where the role of physical-chemical processes became evident, for it was the physiological method that enabled botany to approach the ideal of the exact sciences. The very diversity of physical-chemical processes revealed the possibility of elucidating not only the anatomy of plants but their morphology and all the rest as well. Taxonomy and morphology in the original sense thus became the applied fields of botany as an exact science, and plant physiology became its center.

Has aesthetics developed as an exact science? Has the same limiting of objects of investigation taken place here as in the exact sciences? No, for aesthetics has always been an applied field, never an independent one. Aesthetics has been a separate heading in turn under metaphysics, psychology, sociology, theology, linguistics, physiology. A complete chaos of methods has reigned in aesthetics since time immemorial, just as people from time immemorial have evaluated works of art, have done nothing else but evaluate them, and have done so, moreover, in spite of their complete incapacity ever to discover any norm of evaluation beyond personal taste, the authority of others, or concurrence with some dogma that bears no relation whatever to aesthetics as an exact science. People have always talked about what art ought to be but always forget what art is. The existing forms of art all came about in one particular way and in no other. Perhaps the art that exists now is not art at all, and perhaps the art of the future will create new forms that will correspond to some notion of what art should be. Still, the conception of what art is did not arise before the fact of its existence but after. And it is for this reason that the facticity of the material of art (that is, of its forms) gave rise to the question of what this material is. And so it was that the material came to be studied. The object of aesthetic cognition was defined.

The complexity of the objects of this type of cognition and the multiplicity of viewpoints from which to examine such objects gave rise to such confusion in the aims and methods of aesthetics as to prevent it from existing as an exact science even to this day. But aesthetics cannot be an exact science: it can only be a system of sciences. Physics is not botany, and botany is not ethnography, but all three are possible as separate fields of natural science. Similarly, we have music, we have painting, we have the dramatic arts, and we have lyric poetry. We may conceive of a science of counterpoint, of perspective, color, rhythm, and style. But it is the system of these separate sciences, all united by their diverse relations to the material of sounds, colors, words, and other means of representation, that would constitute the sphere of exact aesthetics. Even now attempts are being made in certain fields of aesthetics to find and express scientifically the principles governing the formation of artistic material (for example, in music and painting). In other areas, however, the study of forms (anatomy) is often a forbidden occupation: people simply disdain it. The idea of a composer who has made his way through counterpoint theory is entirely normal. But a poet immersed in the study of questions of style and technique is a virtual monster in the eyes of the Russian public. The music academies and the academies of fine arts all enjoy the patronage of the public. But the very thought of the possibility of an academy of poetry stirs only derisive laughter. Illiteracy, in fact, is a virtue for a poet in the eyes of the public. A poet or a writer must be an ignoramus. All this is indicative of the absurdity of the attitude, in European society in part and all through Russian society, towards questions relating to poetry and literature; the subtlest and most deeply tormenting problems of style, rhythm, and meter are simply absent—all these are viewed as a mere luxury. But then even Leibniz's discovery of differential calculus in his age was a luxury and nothing more (the practical application being discovered only later). For that matter all the interests of pure knowledge are a luxury. But they are what motivates the development of applied knowledge.

It seems almost disgraceful to repeat such an elementary truth concerning questions of aesthetics, but the occasion does arise when it must be repeated. An abstract interest in poetic forms is an idle one not only in the mind of the public but also in the minds of the majority of art critics, writers, and sometimes even literary scholars in Russia today. The majority of literary scholars, utterly unfamiliar as they are with the natural sciences (and with the exact sciences in general, for that matter), attempt to create a surrogate for scientificity in their researches by subordinating poetry and belles lettres to one form of dogmatic ideology or another, one that might perhaps be appropriate in other fields of knowledge, but that is utterly out of place among the problems of pure aesthetics. This is why the idea of aesthetics as a system of exact, experimental sciences is so heretical for the literary scholars (since they are almost completely unfamiliar with scientific experiment). And the notion of aesthetic experiment is for them a total absurdity. Instead of this, a science of literature for the literary scholars is, even in the best of cases, a history of images, plots, and myths, or simply history of literature. And, depending on whether they subordinate the history of literature to history of ideas, history of culture, or sociology, the grim fact remains that aesthetics as a science continues to be saddled with sociology, history, and ethnography. On optimal and very rare occasions, aesthetics is thus saddled with philosophy (after all, the problem of value in the arts persists, and philosophy more than other disciplines is equipped to assess the self-sufficiency of beauty).

But even this entails the disappearance of the possibility of, say, poetics, metrics, or stylistics as exact sciences.

On the other hand, everything that has been most valuable in the elaboration of aesthetics has been given to us by investigators in the natural sciences (Fechner, Helmholtz, Ostwald, and many others).[3] But even these investigators did not organize their research around aesthetics, but around other sciences that, even though exact, were only obliquely related to aesthetics.

Aesthetics as a system of sciences is a complete void today. A great deal of conscientious experimental work will be necessary to fill the void. Dozens of unassuming laborers will have to dedicate their lives to a great deal of tedious work so that aesthetics as a system of sciences may rise up out of what have until now been mere presumed possibilities. Today aesthetics is like the poor donkey that is obliged to carry any young fellow who happens by. The youth may bridle aesthetics with any method he wishes, and aesthetics will appear before him as the dutiful implement of sociology, morals, philosophy, or, for that matter, any personal calculations and tastes. How much more honest and simple, then, not to take those judgments of artwork that do appeal to personal taste and camouflage them with the tawdry rouge of objectivism. The fact that literary criticism, that is, the applied field of literary theory, stoops in the press to the fabrication of clear and frank speculation, the fact that great legions of speculators, on the strength of their numbers, are directing the public opinion of thinking people is indicative not only of the venality of the press but also of the complete bankruptcy of the legislators of today's literary theories: their theories, which allow one to "elaborate" a work of literature in any direction one wishes, have given rise today to nothing more than pure literary speculation.

Has the hour arrived when each of us who loves art is obliged to withdraw into the solitude of his study, when artists and investigators in the area of aesthetics must resign themselves to being in a position like that of medieval martyrs, suffering for knowledge and creation so as not to be burned at the stake of public disgrace? The official quasi aesthetics in sway will pay these martyrs no heed. And the profligate criticism of today either crucifies them or corrupts them.

As we enter an era distinguished by a massive rise in interest in the arts, the more superficial this interest becomes, the more pressing the urge becomes for people dedicated to art to flee into the catacombs. It was, after all, out of the catacombs of thought that all the Copernicuses have stepped into eras in which the great Savonarolas were ambling through the public squares, surrounded by throngs of people. As regards art today, Savonarola would sooner join forces with brigands than with artists or disinterested researchers.

2

If it is possible to conduct scientific investigations in the field of lyric poetry, then the starting point of such an investigation must be concrete material in the form of the lyric works of various peoples from ancient times to the present day. The lyric poem itself, not abstract propositions about what it ought to be, must underlie our investigation. But where exactly does the initial path of our investigation lie? We have already seen that the field of study concerning the content of either the image or the experience, as given in our experimental material, actually comprises many different methodological investigations whose center is not aesthetics but some adjoining scientific discipline (physiology, psychology, linguistics, ethnography). What is necessary is to find a starting point for our investigation that will concern lyric poetry and only lyric poetry. If we free a poem from all ideational content (seen as not entering the field of formal, and consequently exact, observations), then only form will be left, that is to say, only the means of representation: images, words, their combination and arrangement. In this way our task is narrowed and becomes more distinct. But words, their combination and arrangement, and, for that matter, the combination and arrangement of all means of representation do not completely delineate the jurisdiction of the science of lyric poetry we are seeking. For, on the one hand, studying the laws of combination and modulation of means of representation constitutes a more advanced development of the theory of literature, uniting lyric poetry and literature into a single whole in this one area. On the other hand, the study of words and their arrangement encroaches on the fields of philology and linguistics.

Is there any well-developed theory of literature? The question is debatable. Theory of literature has not been constructed on a sufficient quantity of analyzed material. It is also not sufficiently experimental as a discipline. One cannot call it an exact science, since it is primarily a descriptive and not an experimental science. Philology, too, is a descriptive science in this sense. But all modern exact sciences have undergone a stage where they were primarily descriptive: botany, psychology, and zoology were all initially descriptive sciences (the taxonomy and morphology of plants and animals, descriptive psychology). Taxonomy reached greater levels of depth and gave way to anatomy (comparative anatomy of animals and plants). The study of anatomical structure is already a first step towards explaining the taxonomically classified material. Description always gives way to explanation, as Rickert has said.[4]

But as far as works of lyric poetry are concerned, there have been no attempts at good, honest descriptions. It simply goes without saying that the finest works of [literary] art (say, the lyrics of Pindar or Goethe, Gogol's prose) have not been truly described at all. We read Pushkin or Gogol, just as we read Goethe, and are utterly incapable of explaining how the enchantment we experience is expressed by these artists in their manner and style, in the very thing, in short, that constitutes the concrete, visually or aurally sensible flesh of their creation. It also goes without saying that we do not read Goethe: we read *around* him. It is only later, after reading a literary work for the tenth time, that we accidentally discover its hitherto unknown beauties.

Art criticism, such as it is today, simply passes these beauties by. This is why all the preaching about content in art concerns not content as something revealed through form but a kind of naked, rationalistic content. No matter how we attempt to manipulate this type of content, our manipulations will never set aesthetics on the path towards exact science—such manipulations are not even capable of educating our aesthetic tastes.

Some philologists maintain that philology is the science of slow reading. The art of seeking a meaning in works of poetry is certainly an art of even slower reading. For every word, every punctuation mark arises not accidentally but by slowly crystallizing into a whole as complex as the very world that we call the lyric poem. We glide over a poem with our eyes and thus glide right by it. Poets tend to be more attentive to poets than do others. But the aesthetic experience of each poet develops slowly, throughout his life. In the process of developing this experience, and also the experience of reading, even the most careful and thoughtful of poets will invariably discover whole new Americas. The poet's experience dies with the poet, but his readers remain in a blissful state of ignorance, not knowing how to read or what to interpret. Any major poet can form an entire school, not only because he has an immediate influence on others, but also because his working quarters unwittingly become a kind of forum for stylistics: for only he can provide answers to complicated and difficult questions of form that arise for all those who value beauty.

If we wrote down everything that poets have to say on questions of form, we would have an immense quantity of material for the purely scientific treatment of the area of aesthetics dealing with lyric poetry. How surprised the teachers of literature would then be to see that all the verbiage on poetry they have produced for generation after generation contains not the hundredth part of the kind of scientificity that would immediately impress us if we had before us the commentaries of poets on other poets.

What does it mean to describe a work of literature? To describe means to give a commentary. Every lyric work demands a basic commentary. In commenting on a poem we are decomposing it, as it were, into its constituent parts and looking carefully at the means of representation, at the choice of epithets, similes, and metaphors in order to characterize the content. We feel the words and look for their mutual rhythmic and sonorous relations. In thus reorganizing the analyzed material into a new whole, we often can no longer recognize a familiar poem at all. Like the phoenix, it arises anew out of itself in a more beautiful form, or, conversely, it withers away. In this way we come to recognize that a comparative anatomy of poetic style is truly necessary, that it is the ultimate stage in the development of a theory of literature and lyric poetry, and finally that it represents a *rapprochement* between these two disciplines and the various fields of scientific knowledge.

Let us take as an example a poem by Nekrasov (an excerpt from "Death of a Peasant").

U dóma ostávili krýšu.
K sosédke svelí nočevát'
Zazjábnuvšix Mášu i Gríšu
I stáli synká obrjažát'.

Medlítel'no, vážno, suróvo
Pečál'noe délo velós':
Ne skázano líšnego slóva,
Narúžu ne výdano slëz.

Usnúl, potrudívšijsja v póte!
Usnúl, porabótav v zemlé!
Ležít, nepričástnyj zabóte,
Na bélom sosnóvom stolé.

Ležít nepodvížnyj, suróvyj,
S gorjáščej svečój v golováx,
V širókoj rubáxe xolščëvoj
I v lípovyx nóvyx laptjáx.

Bol'šíe s mozóljami rúki,
Pod"jávšie mnógo trudá,
Krasívoe, cúždoe múki
Licó—i do rúk borodá.

[They left the coffin lid by the house.
They sent to a neighbor's to spend the night
Shivering Masha and Grisha,
And began tending to their son.

Slowly, solemnly, sternly
The mournful deed was done:
Not a needless word was spoken,
Outwardly no tears were shed.

He has gone to rest, having sweated his life in toil!
He has gone to rest, having worked the soil!
He lies, free of care,
On a white pine table.

He lies motionless, stern,
A burning candle at the head of the bed,
He wears a broad linen shirt
And new bast sandals.

His large, callused hands,
Having toiled hard,
His beautiful face, which knows no suffering,
And a beard down to his hands.][5]

What does it mean to describe this poem? Does the poem not describe itself? The fact is that it does not, if we examine it from the point of view of content. I may analyze the excerpt according to its ideational content: the idea of the excerpt is the grandeur of the dead peasant laborer surrounded by the "slow, solemn, stern" efforts of his dear ones to pay their last respects to him. The stern image of death hovers over him. I may also analyze the ideational content of this excerpt from the point of view of the individual poetic creation of Nekrasov. In this case I would have to connect the excerpt given here with one of the dominant ideas of Nekrasov's creation, namely, the idea of poverty in the Russian countryside and the Russian peasant's life of toil. The doleful grandeur of this life is revealed in death. The purpose of the analysis in this case would be to single out all the essential signs of this idea in this poem and then connect them with the essential signs [of the same idea] in all the parallel passages in the poetry of Nekrasov. Such a task would certainly be most venerable, but the conclusions to be drawn from this procedure would bear more on the characteristics of Nekrasov's view of the countryside than on the characteristics of the traits inherent in his poetry. The individuality of Nekrasov's view of the countryside might equally well be set forth in a scientific or publicist form. In fact, the accuracy of Nekrasov's views might be more compellingly demonstrated by means of statistics. And the techniques of the publicist, which do not necessarily exclude the persuasive means of statistics, would serve as a far more powerful weapon than poetry. Why, then, set forth this ideational content in amphibrachs with rhymes and the other attributes of metrics? When I analyze the excerpt from the point of view of its ideational content I am not dealing with Nekrasov the lyricist, but with Nekrasov the publicist. In other words, when I use this method of analysis I lose sight of the poet.

I may also connect Nekrasov's view of the Russian countryside with the ideologies of the time, compare his description of the countryside with those of Ogarev and Nikitin.[6] I might perhaps link Nekrasov's ideology with the social conflicts of his era. I might look at the element of sentimentalism and romanticism in Nekrasov's brand of populism and elucidate his psychology by referring to the psychology of the "penitent noble landowner," or the psychology of the "intelligentsia." This is where a sociological analysis of the excerpt would enter the scene. I could thus illuminate such expressions as: "He lies, free of care, / On a white pine table," or, "He has gone to rest, having sweated his life in toil," by referring to them as traits of Nekrasov's sentimentalism and pessimism, Nekrasov being thus seen as a representative of the liberal intelligentsia cut off from the people. I could then illuminate this pessimism by mentioning how alien to Nekrasov the proletarian world view was. In addition, I might compare the peculiarity of Nekrasov's depiction of a funeral with depictions of funerals by (*a*) Russian lyric poets, (*b*) European lyric poets of the nineteenth century, or (*c*) major lyric poets of all eras. The attitude towards death in world poetry is certainly a theme for a respectable work of many hundreds of pages. This work could even serve as a mere introduction to a whole series of other no less respectable (even more respectable) works: "The Attitude towards Death in Nekrasov, in Lyric Poets of the World, in Kant, Hegel, Fichte, Schelling, Schopenhauer, Hartmann, Nietzsche, and so on." Beside the names of Kant and Schopenhauer one could have, if one wished, the names of Boehme, Eckhart, or (depending on one's point of view) Vasily the Great, Saint John Chrysostom . . .[7]

The question is, what then remains of the poet Nekrasov? It is unclear why the poet set forth his views on the death of the Russian peasantry in amphibrachs using the rhymes: *kryšu* [lid]—*nočevat'* [spend the night]—*Grišu*—*obrjažat'* [tend], and so on. The objection will be made that the ideational content in poetry has a particular form in which it is embodied. In that case the amphibrachs, the rhyme, the choice and disposition of words would clearly constitute such a form of embodiment. In order to gain an understanding of the relation of form to content, we must first understand form and content themselves in lyric works. But the constitutive elements of form are never studied at all. These are what we must describe.

Let us overlook the purely ideational content of this excerpt and focus our attention instead on the experiential content. But the experiential content in a poem is the relation of the form of an idea to the form of the image that embodies that idea. The idea of the given excerpt is this: the grandeur of the death of the poor peasant laborer and the grandeur of those around him who share in the experience of his death. The images in the given excerpt are these: the children of the deceased, who are suffering from the cold and who have been brought to a neighbor's house; the coffin lid by the cabin; the deceased lying in the cabin with his callused hands and broad, full beard, wearing bast sandals and a linen shirt, encircled with candles. This is what is depicted. Here again we might do as we did with the ideational analysis and give the characteristics of Nekrasov's images in connection with images of death in other lyric poets. It is possible to conceive of respectable scholarly works in this area as well. Such works would be tied in with the history of images, myth, and plot. All historians of poetry, critics, and professors of literature have dealt with and continue to deal with images, plots, and ideas, but this is not a purely aesthetic field of study. It is instead a questionable field involving many different methodologies. For an aesthetic description, what counts is not what is depicted and what expresses the thing depicted, but how the thing is depicted and how the depicting is done. This "how" is to be sought in the words and sounds of the poem.

In which aspects of the words and sounds is the image in question given?

Here is the first quatrain:

U dóma ostávili krýšu.
K sosédke svelí nočevát'
Zazjábnuvšix Mášu i Gríšu
I stáli synká obrjažát'.

[They left the coffin lid by the house.
They sent to a neighbor's to spend the night
Shivering Masha and Grisha,
And began tending to their son.]

The meter of the poem is amphibrachic: ◡–́◡|◡–́◡|◡–́◡|. The words must be composed in such a way that the resulting configuration of accented and unaccented syllables will produce a succession of one long for every two short syllables. Monosyllabic conjunctions and prepositions are all unaccented. Words of two syllables will always carry an accent. Three-syllable words, however, are the most suitable for use in meters like the dactyl, the anapest, and the amphibrach. In fact it is these words that must form the skeleton, so to speak, of the amphibrach. Depending on the actual distribution of the accents (that is, *nočevát'*, *narúžu*, *skázano*), three-syllable words allow for the proper combination of dissyllabic and monosyllabic words to make the free use of the amphibrachic rhythm possible: *k sosédke* (three-syllable) *svelí* (two-syllable) *nočevát'* (three-syllable). A combination of two-syllable and four-syllable words is also possible: *usnúl, porabótav v zemlé* just as a combination of two dissyllabic words is possible: *pečál'noe délo velós'*. A combination of three monosyllables or the combination of many monosyllables and dissyllables together gives the amphibrach (and the anapest and dactyl as well) a certain heaviness: for example, the verse, "No mné ty ix skážeš', moj drúg" (six monosyllables and one dissyllable), is heavy and unmusical. The following verse is also heavy: "Ty s détstva so mnóju znakóma."

No mné ty ix skážeš', moj drúg!
Ty s détstva so mnóju znakóma.
Ty vsjá—voploščënnyj ispug,
Ty vsjá—vekovája istóma!

[But to me you will speak of them, my friend!
We have known each other since childhood.
You are fright incarnate,
You are age-old weariness!][8]

I cite the strophe in its entirety to illustrate how the absence of three- and four-syllable words in the first two verses makes these lines heavy by comparison with the third and fourth lines. This is because the accumulation of monosyllabic words, each of which, depending on its position, may or may not carry an accent, slows the line down and eliminates the contrast between accented and unaccented syllables. "No mné ty ix skážeš'" can also be read, "No tý mne ix skážeš'" or "No íx ty mne skážeš'." The words *ix*, *ty*, and *mne* can either carry an accent or not carry one. In those meters where the foot contains three syllables, it is advisable to avoid such words.

As we analyze the first strophe of our excerpt from the point of view of metrics, we observe that the meter here does not disturb the ear:

U dóma ostávili krýšu.
K sosédke svelí nočevát'
Zazjábnuvšix Mášu i Gríšu
I stáli synká obrjažát'.

[They left the coffin lid by the house.
They sent to a neighbor's to spend the night
Shivering Masha and Grisha,
And began tending to their son.]

Only the end of the third verse, "Mášu i Gríšu," is metrically suspect, since it presents a combination of a monosyllabic conjunction with two dissyllabic words.

But if we compare the first strophe with the second, we see that the second reads more easily. The second strophe seems more rhythmic because of its metric uniformity:

Medlítel'no, vážno, suróvo
Pečál'noe délo velós':
Ne skázano líšnego slóva,
Narúžu ne výdano slëz.

[Slowly, solemnly, sternly
The mournful deed was done:
Not a needless word was spoken,
Outwardly no tears were shed.]

The first strophe contains three monosyllabic, seven dissyllabic, four three-syllable words, and one four-syllable word. The total number of words is sixteen.

The second strophe contains two monosyllabic, five dissyllabic, five three-syllable, and two four-syllable words, which is to say that the second strophe reads more easily because of a more successful combination of words. The total number of words is fourteen.

In addition, the second strophe shows a certain symmetry in the arrangement of words. Thus the first and second verses of the second strophe begin with four-syllable words (*medlítel'no, pečál'noe*). The third and fourth strophes show an inverse symmetry in the first two words (ne skázano *líšnego, narúžu* ne výdano). The penultimate words in the last two verses are symmetrical, since both contain three syllables with the first one accented (*líšnego, výdano*). And finally, the second words in the first two verses are symmetrical with respect to accent (*vážno, délo*). These are all details, but the sum of these details is what determines symmetry of structure.

The third strophe is even more symmetrical in word arrangement:

> Usnúl, potrudívšijsja v póte!
> Usnúl, porabótav v zemlé!
> Ležít, nepričástnyj zabóte,
> Na bélom, sosnóvom stolé.
>
> [He has gone to rest, having sweated his life in toil!
> He has gone to rest, having worked the soil!
> He lies, free of care,
> On a white pine table.]

Here we observe symmetry, not only in the arrangement of words by syllable and accent, but also in the grammatical forms of words. To begin with syllables and accents: the middle of each verse is occupied by three-, four-, and five-syllable words (*potrudívšijsja, porabótav, nepričástnyj, sosnóvom*) flanked by dissyllabic words (*usnúl, usnúl, ležít, bélom, póte, zemlé, zabóte, stolé*). Grammatical forms: the first three verses are composed of a verb (*usnúl, usnúl, ležít*), a participle or gerund (*potrudívšijsja, porabótav, nepričástnyj*), and a noun (*póte, zemlé, zabóte*). The final verse, however, ends with a noun and begins with two adjectives that contrast with each other and define the noun (*stol*): "Ležít . . . / Na *bélom, sosnóvom stolé*." The adjective *bélyj* [white] defines the color, giving a visual image, whereas the adjective *sosnóvyj* [pine] defines the material and perhaps even the smell of the table. In addition, the first and second verses begin with the same verb, *usnúl* [has gone to rest], whereas the third begins with the verb *ležít* [lies], that is, a verb in the present tense, instead of the past. This is a case of parallelism, but parallelism with a contrast (he has already *gone to rest,* but is *lying* there before us). Moreover, the repetition of the verb *usnúl* right before the prefix *po-* (*po-trudívšijsja, po-rabótav*) gives a certain phonetic charm to the entire strophe, just as do the alliterative words of the final verse, "na sosnóvom stolé" [on the table of pine]. A felicitous accumulation of like vowels and consonants frequently calls attention to the energy of literary instrumentation. Here are some examples of accumulation of vowels: "V minútu žízni trúdnuju" [In a difficult moment of life], i-u-u-i-i-u-u-u; "Est' síla blagodátnaja" [There is a beneficent force], e-i-a-a-a-a-a-a, where, of course, the syllable *go* is pronounced *ga.* Sometimes a succession of vowels corresponds to the meaning, as for example in Tyutchev: "Téni sízye smesílis'" [The bluish shadows have formed pools]—here the high vowel [i] is dominant; "Cvét—poblëknul, zvúk—usnúl" [The color has faded, the sound has died away]—here the low vowel [u] dominates.[9] The fading away of the color corresponds to the lowering of vowel sounds from the high [i] to the low [u] by way of the intermediate [e]. Here are two examples of accumulation of consonants: "Krugóm krutyé krúči" [All around steep precipices]; "Smetáet sméxom smért'" [With laughter sweeps death aside].

The combination of greater rhythmic symmetry and lightness with a symmetry of meaning and word arrangement to form a single harmonious whole in the third strophe of the excerpt from Nekrasov affects us in such a manner that the whole strophe appears more successful both phonetically and in terms of its images.

The parallelism that began in the third strophe is continued in the fourth:

Ležít nepodvížnyj, suróvyj,
S gorjáščej svečój v golovàx,
V širókoj rubáxe xolščëvoj
I v lípovyx nóvyx laptjáx.

[He lies motionless, stern,
A burning candle at the head of the bed,
He wears a broad linen shirt
And new bast sandals.]

If we compare the third strophe with the fourth, we observe that they share the same parallelism. From the total of eight verses, the first two begin with the verb *usnúl* [has gone to rest], following which it is determined *who* has gone to rest and *how* he has done so ("having sweated his life in toil," "having worked the soil"). In conformity with the past tense, these determinations of who and how have a more abstract character. The third verse introduces a present tense, *ležít* [lies], and right afterwards, in the fourth verse of the third strophe, a concrete image appears ("ležít . . . / Na bélom sosnóvom stolé" [he lies . . . / On a white pine table]). The fourth strophe turns out to be a continuation of the parallelism of the verb *ležít.* Here we find the two adjectives *nepodvížnyj* [motionless] and *suróvyj* [stern]. The adjective *nepodvížnyj* renews the parallelism of the first, second, and third verses of the third strophe (except that the corresponding words there were participles and gerunds). One expects a noun after "motionless," just as two verses above, but the parallelism breaks off with the appearance of a second adjective, "stern," as in the immediately preceding verse. The only difference here is that the preceding verse had *begun* with two adjectives, while this one *ends* with them. Nor is there any inverse symmetry, since the verse begins with a verb, *usnúl* [has gone to rest], instead of beginning with a noun. And even this verb is a repetition of a previous word, namely the one that opened the third verse of the third strophe. The verse, "Ležít nepodvížnyj, suróvyj," is connected in a distinctive way with the verse, "Ležít, nepričástnyj zabóte," and in an equally distinctive way with the verse, "Na bélom sosnóvom stolé." This last verse is doubly symmetrical, since it contains a synthesis of two rhythmic motifs. Finally, the two adjectives, *nepodvížnyj* and *suróvyj*, are of a different order from *bélyj* and *sosnóvyj*: the first two have a way of appealing to our imagination (we ourselves are called upon to imagine the stern and motionless countenance of the dead man), whereas the second two are *given* to our imagination: here we have merely to evoke with our imagination an already existing representation of a white table made of pine wood.

One can see how many immediate perceptions are aroused in the first verse alone of the fourth quatrain. We have given this description only to demonstrate what great craftmanship can be discerned in the form in which this verse is written, and also to demonstrate that Nekrasov may be considered a poet solely because he wrote it like this. But to return to our description: the fourth strophe continues the depiction of the image of the deceased man begun in the previous strophe. The image becomes increasingly concrete: "Ležít . . . / S gorjáščej svečój v golovàx" [He lies . . . / A burning candle at the head of the bed]. This verse juxtaposes a participle [*gorjáščej* (burning)] with two adjectives [from the preceding verse], but the participle modifies another word. Nonetheless, the three grammatically related words at the end of the first verse and at the beginning of the second in the fourth quatrain show an inverse symmetry with the three adjectives at the end of the third quatrain [that is, *nepričástnyj, bélyj, sosnóvyj*] and also with the three adjectives in the third and fourth verses of this fourth quatrain: "V . . . rubáxe *xolščëvoj* / I v *lípovyx, nóvyx* laptjáx" [*linen* shirt / And *new bast* sandals].

The verse: "S gorjáščej svečój v golováx" [A burning candle at the head of the bed] is interesting in another respect. The expression *v golováx* [at the head of the bed] is colloquial: one frequently says, for example, *poduški v golovax* [pillows at the head of the bed]. An expression like this lends a commonplace quality, a certain coziness to the thing expressed. When one says "candle" in the singular, one generally means a candle for domestic rather than for mortuary use, since not one, but three candles are normally placed around the coffin at the head of a dead person. Instead of saying "candles by the head," Nekrasov uses the expression, "candle . . . at the head of the bed." The symbol of death acquires from this usage an everyday, domestic, and almost cozy character. By using the expression, "candle at the head of the bed," Nekrasov introduces a delicate and barely perceptible impressionism into the description of death. Furthermore, the two [s] sounds in the second verse, "s . . . svečój" [with . . . a candle] create an assonance with the [s] sound of the adjective *suróvyj* [in the previous verse]. The third verse, "V širókoj rubáxe xolščëvoj" [He wears a broad linen shirt], shows a partial symmetry with the previous verse if only because, like the preceding verse, it contains a new brush stroke that gives us a concrete image of the dead man. This stroke is accomplished by means of the preposition *v* [in] (in the preceding verse it was the preposition *s* [with]); the three-syllable adjective *gorjáščej* [burning], accented on the second syllable (in the corresponding position in the preceding verse there is also a three-syllable adjective, *širókoj* [broad]); and the noun that this adjective modifies, *rubáxe* [shirt] (the preceding verse had the noun *svečój* [candle]). In the third verse, as in the first verse, we encounter two adjectives, but their placement is different here: the first verse of this strophe reads, "Ležít *nepodvížnyj, suróvyj*," whereas this one reads, "V *širókoj* rubáxe *xolščëvoj*." The following verse, "I v lípovyx, nóvyx laptjáx" [And new bast sandals], like the two preceding ones, introduces a new and even more concrete feature into the image of the dead man and does so, moreover, by means of entirely analogous verbal material (the preposition *v* [in], two adjectives, and a noun), but verbal material that is arranged somewhat differently. Like the preceding two verses, it opens with a preposition and an adjective but follows this adjective with a second one, thus showing an arrangement identical to that of the fourth verse in the third strophe ("Na bélom sosnóvom stolé"), inversely symmetrical with the first verse of the fourth strophe ("Ležít nepodvížnyj, suróvyj"), and analogous in verbal material to the immediately preceding verse ("V širókoj rubáxe xolščëvoj"). After the preposition, the fourth verse proceeds like the previous two verses, namely with a three-syllable adjective, but the stress is different here (*lípovyx* being accented on the first syllable). Also interesting here is the literary instrumentation of vowels and consonants: (1) vowels—note the occurrence of the [related] sounds [i] and [y]; (2) consonants—note the alliteration (*lipovye . . . lapti*); (3) combination of vowels and consonants—note the identical declensional endings of the two adjectives (*líp-ovyx*, *n-óvyx*), even though the two adjectives are not stressed on the same syllable. The instrumentation in this verse may be contrasted with that of the preceding verse, "V širókoj rubáxe xolščëvoj," where, through a combination of sounds, the consonants create an impression of waviness and rustling associated with the feel of linen. The fourth strophe gives a strikingly delicate, impressionistic description of the circumstances surrounding the dead man, a description, moreover, that proceeds from the general to the concrete: the detail of the sandals' being new and made of bast has an extraordinary way of bringing the image of the dead man closer to us.

The third and fourth strophes constitute a single whole. They both paint a picture of the dead man's clothes and the surroundings of the coffin. They are united by their parallelism and joined together also by the single sentence that begins in the second half of the third strophe and then occupies the entire fourth strophe. Both strophes are made up of combinations of nouns, adjectives (including participles and gerunds), and verbs, all arranged in a complex symmetry. Designating nouns by *a*, adjectives by *b*, and verbs by *c*, we arrive at the following schema:

c b a
c b a
c b a
b b a

c b b
b a a
b a b
b b a

If we could compose a series of similar diagrams for all the poems of Nekrasov and compare these with diagrams for other poets, we would be able to discover the empirical laws of word arrangement peculiar to each poet. In this way description and observation would lead us into the field of aesthetic experiment.

If we now designate monosyllabic words by *a*, dissyllabic words by *b*, three-syllable words by *c*, four-syllable words by *d*, and five-syllable words by *e*, we obtain the schema representing the Nekrasov excerpt:

First strophe	*Second strophe*	*Third strophe*	*Fourth strophe*	*Fifth strophe*
abdb	dbb	beab	bdc	cdb
cbc	dbb	bdb	cbc	dbb
bdab	accb	bdc	ccc	dcb
abbc	cacb	abcb	acbb	baaac
15	14	14	13	14

If we examine this excerpt from the point of view of word economy, then we may say that rhythmically the most successful strophe is the fourth, and the least successful is the first.

Arranging the strophes now by symmetry of grammatical forms, we obtain the following schema:

aca	bbb	cba	cbb	baa
acc	bac	cba	baa	bba
baa	cba	cba	bab	bba
cac	bca	bba	bba	aaa

Examining the excerpt from the point of view of symmetry, we conclude that the most symmetrical strophe is the third, after which, in descending order, come the second, the fourth, and finally the first and fifth.

If we combine the two schemas into one, we conclude that the most rhythmic strophes are the first, third, and fourth. But an immediate impression of ease of reading had already struck us in these strophes even without our analysis.

Let us consider some additional strophes of Nekrasov (also in amphibrachic trimeter) and schematize the word pattern:

dbb		aaaabaa			
abcc	16	ababc	20	abbab	11
abcb		aadc		aaacaa	
abbac		aadc			

The reader will conclude a priori that this example of amphibrachic rhythm will sound heavier than the previous selection. And this is in fact the case:

> Slučájnaja žértva sud'bý!
> Tý glúxo, nezrímo stradála,
> Tý svétu krovávoj bor'bý
> I žálob svoíx ne vverjála,—
> No mné ty ix skážeš', moj drúg!
> Tý s détstva so mnóju znakóma.
> Tý vsjá—voploščënnyj ispúg,
> Tý vsjá—vekovája istóma!
>   Tót sérdca v grudí ne nosíl,
>   Któ slëz nad tobóju ne líl.

> [Chance victim of fate!
> Silently, unseen, you have suffered,
> To the world of bloody struggle
> You would never entrust your complaints,
> But to me you will speak of them, my friend!
> We have known each other since childhood.
> You are fright incarnate,
> You are age-old weariness!
>   He has no heart in his breast
>   Who sheds no tears for you!][10]

Can it be an accident that figurative qualities in words so clumsily combined are almost completely lacking? Can it be an accident that the content itself holds together better in the more completely elaborated form of the previous excerpt?

Earlier we touched on the question of vowel-consonant combinations and contrasts. If we now arrange the vowels in order of their height (using, for the sake of simplicity, *a* for *ja*, *u* for *ju*, *o* for *ë*, and *i* for *y*), we obtain the diagram of the excerpt cited above from "Death of a Peasant" [shown in figure 4].[11]

The broken line in the diagram characterizes changes in vowels. If we were to study this curve and establish a mean curve of vowel shifts in Nekrasov, then we could, for example, compare this curve with the mean curve for Pushkin. And such a study and comparison might very well lead to an empirical law. Then from the totality of such laws, we would be able to delineate the fields of experimental stylistics, rhetoric, and lyric poetics. But experimental fields like this do not exist today. Instead, everyone continues to write

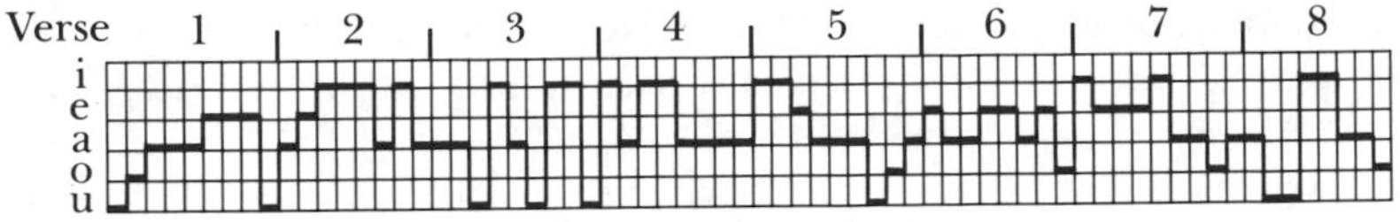

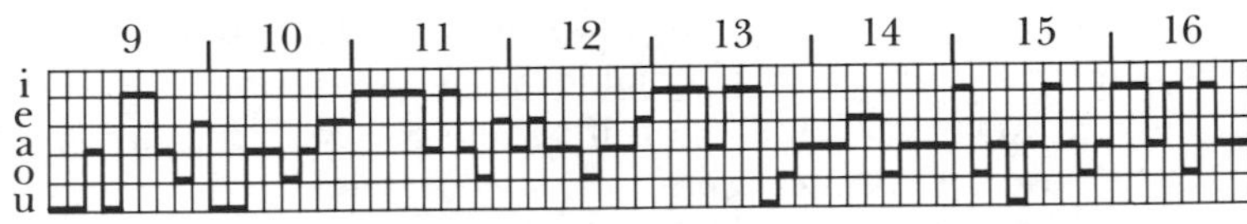

Figure 4

about how Nekrasov was the poet of civic grief, how Pushkin was a national poet, and how Fet was the poet of butterflies. For dozens of years the critics have been burdening experimental aesthetics with methods utterly foreign to it or, in the best of cases, have been occupying themselves with pouring from an empty vessel into a void.

At long last, however, there is a field where experimentation with verse is quite simple, but where the results can be extraordinarily rich. I am speaking of rhythmics.

3

One of the tasks of contemporary poetics is to establish an exact definition of rhythm: to define, that is, the area of rhythm in poetry, its boundaries, and its connection with music on the one hand and with poetic meter on the other. This is the most urgent task facing researchers in the area of Russian poetry. The only people who have been working in this field today in Russia are poets, musicians, and Professor F. E. Korsh.[12] In the West, though, we are seeing more and more exemplary work being done on versification, rhythm, and meter.

The first pressing task consists in precisely differentiating between rhythm and meter. Strange though it may seem, these two areas continue to this day to be blurred and confused. Rhythm is the actual expression of the natural melody of the poet's soul (the spirit of music); meter is the precise, crystallized artistic *form* of rhythmic expression. I once had occasion to talk at length with a well-known musical theoretician, S. I. Taneev,[13] who was studying the rhythmics of *byliny*.[14] I was forced to concur with him that, without any knowledge of the musical laws of rhythm, it is hardly possible to follow the genesis of metrics. Taneev is of the opinion, for example, that a certain musical regularity underlies the *bylina*, that consequently any verse may be rendered in musical notation (where each syllable would appear as a half note, quarter note, or eighth note and where the sum of syllables in any two consecutive verses would give an equal number of musical measures), and finally that the enormous rhythmic freedom that characterizes the creation of verses in the *bylina* is due precisely to this. And yet, he maintains, this freedom does not allow such creation to be totally arbitrary: any syllable in any verse may be either stretched (say, to a half note) or accelerated (say, to a quarter note or eighth note), but only on the condition that the acceleration never extend as far as the sixteenth note, for the sixteenth note in reading will create an impression of dissonance. If we write out several verses of a *bylina* in musical notation, we will see that a connection exists between the rhythm and the word stress. The natural accent almost always falls on syllables that are pronounced more slowly. It is also worth noting that, among all the possible rhythmic modulations of the *bylina*, for example:

or

,

we also find the following one:

,

that is, one with the following metric notation:

⏑–⏑–⏑–⏑–.

We see thus that the Russian iambic tetrameter is already to be found in the *bylina* as a special case of a more general tendency towards rhythmic regularity. The same is true of the amphibrachic trimeter, which would be represented rhythmically something like this:

.

We may ask, then, whether the amphibrachic trimeter and the iambic tetrameter are not mutually convertible metric forms, that is, whether it is possible to write a verse that could, with appropriate changes in the rhythm of one's reading, theoretically follow an iambic pattern *or* an amphibrachic pattern. Theoretically this is indeed possible. And here is the reason: a pure iambic rhythm in sustained form does not exist anywhere in the Russian language. Instead, in almost every case we will find a combination of iambs, paeons, pyrrhees, spondees, and so forth. For example:

> Kak démony gluxonemýe
> Vedút besédu mež sobój.
>
> [Like demons deaf and dumb
> Carry on a conversation with each other.][15]

The meter of these two verses is iambic (relatively). But they may also, de facto, be written thus:

∪–|∪∪|∪∪|∪–|∪
∪–|∪–|∪∪|∪–|

The first verse is thus a combination of two paeons (a second paeon and a fourth paeon)[16] or else a combination of iambs and pyrrhees. In order to make clear that the verse is iambic, it is necessary to force an accent vocally on two syllables that are accented only relative to the rhythm of the whole. If when we read these two verses, we make only a single forced accent on the third foot, but read the second foot without accent, then we get amphibrachic trimeter.[17]

In the first instance we would have two forced vocal accents:

> Kak dé—moný—gluxó—nemýe.

One arrangement of vocal accents would thus bring the rhythm of one's reading closer to amphibrachic trimeter:

∪ – ∪ | ∪ – ∪ | ∪ – ∪
Kak dé mo | ny glú xo | ne mý e
Be sé du | ve dút mež | so bój.[18]

The other arrangement of vocal accents brings the rhythm of reading closer to iambic tetrameter:

∪ – | ∪ – | ∪ – | ∪ – | ∪
Kak dé | mo ný | glu xó | ne mý | e
Ve dút | be sé | du méž | so bój. |

But in *fact* the first of these two verses is read:

Kak dé—mony gluxone—mýe.

That is, it is *neither iambic nor amphibrachic.*

Is it possible that we have here a combination of metric forms? Certainly. But what is the point of introducing into our study of metrics forms that are meaningful only relative to Greek prosody and that make true rhythmic sense only in a language whose poetry is musically constituted in iambs, trochees, amphibrachs, and so on? In Russian prosody the only meters that are formally permitted are the iamb, trochee, dactyl, anapest, and amphibrach. But an artificial cultivation of, say, the trimeter, does not always create a natural impression on the ear of the listener. Demonstrating the rhythmic modulations of the iamb by speaking of "paeons" is only using metrics to compound the problems of metrics, since in so doing one forgets that the metric form itself expresses a rhythm that has become crystallized. The rhythm of folk songs is a natural expression of the individual pathos (or spirit of music) peculiar to the people who sing them. How then, for example, can traditional metrics explain the rhythmic meaning of the introduction of a single anapestic foot into an otherwise iambic verse of Tyutchev?

◡ – | ◡ – | ◡ – | ◡ –
O, kák na sklóne nášix lét
◡ – | ◡ – | ◡ ◡ – | ◡ – | ◡
Nežnéȷ my ljúbim i suevérnej!

[Oh, in our declining years,
How much more tenderly and superstitiously we love!] [19]

The second verse could also be notated thus:

◡–|◡–|◡◡◡|◡–|◡.

If we explain this verse formally, as a combination of iambic feet with one anapestic foot, our explanation will say nothing. For in that case every selection of words would be a complex whole formed from a variety of meters. For example, the sentence, "Ósen' stojála tëplaja" [The autumn was warm], is a combination of a trochee, an amphibrach, and a dactyl. The boundary separating poetry from prose is obliterated altogether in a case like this, for, when applied thus, what purpose do rules of prosody serve? Now the objection will be raised that introducing all the complexity of Greek metrics into the Russian language is a necessity and that only by doing so can we hope to explain the laws of metrics. But the problem is that it is impossible to take ancient Greek versification as a whole and apply it to Russian. Even as early a Russian author as Lomonosov characterized Russian prosody—and rightly so—as syllabo-tonic rather than metric.[20]

Thus from the point of view of metrics, it is difficult to justify Tyutchev formally in the verse, "Nežnéj my ljúbim i suevérnej," and yet the irregularity is appealing to the developed ear. Why? Is it completely arbitrary? Absolutely not, for this deviation from the accepted rules of metrics has a vital rhythmic meaning if we represent Tyutchev's verse in musical notation:

The verse is here notated as occupying two measures, without sixteenth notes.[21]

The same verse represented in musical notation but with sixteenth notes would produce a harmonically unpleasant impression and destroy the rhythm in iambic tetrameter just as in amphibrachic trimeter.

The examples cited above clearly show that one of the most serious, purely experimental problems in aesthetics has never been addressed at all.

I have decided to use iambic tetrameter for these studies, and we will see that the modest materials involved in this task touch on a number of theoretical problems concerning form. Starting with the notion that the Russian iambic tetrameter is, in the end, very far from being truly iambic but is rather a combination of iambs and other meters, and at the same time not wishing to burden our attention with all the forms of Greek metrics, we have chosen provisionally to use the term *half-accent* for deviations from the regular vocal accent in iambic feet.

Thus the verse, "Moj djá|dja sá|myx čé|stnyx prá|vil" [My uncle of most steadfast principles],[22] is quite close to pure iambic because of the coincidence of accents and long syllables in each word. The verse, "Kogdá|ne v šút|ku zá|nemóg" [When he took seriously ill],[23] however, deviates from the normal pattern, because the word *zanemóg* must take a forced secondary accent on its first syllable in order to conform (*zánemóg*). Still, when we read the verse we naturally pronounce the syllable *za-* short instead of long, and in this way the iambic verse assumes the following form:

$$\cup - | \cup - | \cup \cup | \cup - |,$$

that is, formally it is a combination of iambs and a fourth paeon, or [three] iambs and a pyrrhee. We say, then, that the third foot of the second verse of *Eugene Onegin* has one relative accent, or half-accent.

Half-accents may [also] occur on the second foot, on the first, on both the first and third, or on both the second and third. Thus within the limits of iambic tetrameter as a metric form, we will get a number of rhythmic deviations peculiar to each poet. It becomes possible in this way to represent the rhythm of a given poet (the indefinable music of his verse, so to speak) visually and graphically, and to use graphs to study the peculiarities of the poet's rhythmic deviations. The graphic method of recording rhythm as we are proposing it is as simple as can be [see figure 5].

The poem itself appears in the first column.[24] The second column shows the succession of accented and unaccented syllables (or long and short, speaking relatively). If we examine the second column verse for verse, we will see that in many feet the typical iamb, $\cup -$, has been replaced by a pyrrhee, $\cup \cup$. We will call pyrrhic feet, feet with half-accents. In the third column we have marked the position of these feet with a black dot and connected the dots with lines. By this [method] we can show that a series of consecutive verses that deviate from the normal iambic tetrameter forms a certain rhythmic (and individual) tempo. It now becomes possible to study and classify the graphic figures generated by the dots and lines and thus obtain a clear picture of the graphic lines of various poets by comparing them. Such a comparison is particularly apt if done on a large scale. The relation between the figures and the intervals between them (standing for regular iambic verses), as well as between the figures themselves, marks the rhythmic individuality of the poet within the bounds of a given metric form. As our experiment shows, the elements constituting the graphic-line diagram (namely the [geometric] figures and the dots) are the same for all poets. But the number of elements present and the manner of combining them are peculiar to each poet. The same is true of melody; any melody is composed of the same intervals: fifths, thirds, octaves, and so on. But what makes a melody individual is the particular manner of combining these intervals.

Our graph now enables us to assess visually the relation between the total number of metric verses (empty) and the total number of

Figure 5

Dă, já ne Píndar: mné strašnéj	——	◡—	◡—	◡—
Vsegó—toržéstvennaja óda,	◡—	◡—	◡◡	◡—
Berëzovec i jubiléj	◡—	◡◡	◡◡	◡—
Roždén'ja kónskogo zavóda.	◡—	◡—	◡◡	◡—
Kogdá b slová v stixáx moíx	◡—	◡—	◡—	◡—
Ložílis' výpukly i kóvki,	◡—	◡—	◡◡	◡—
Vstaváli rázom by iz níx	◡—	◡—	◡◡	◡—
Kopýta, šéjki i golóvki.	◡—	◡—	◡◡	◡—
Sledjá za káždoju čertój,	◡—	◡—	◡◡	◡—
Znatók ne proxodíl by mímo,	◡—	◡◡	◡—	◡—
Ne vosxitívšis' krasotój	◡◡	◡—	◡◡	◡—
Ljubímca íli Ibragíma.	◡—	◡—	◡◡	◡—
Já, lávry oglasjá tvoí	——	◡◡	◡—	◡—
I vsé stjažánnye nagrády,	◡—	◡—	◡◡	◡—
V zavóde kónskom Ilií	◡—	◡—	◡◡	◡—
Našël by zvúki Iliády.	◡—	◡—	◡—	◡—
No ètix zvúkov-to i nét,	◡—	◡—	◡◡	◡—
I já, gremét' bessíl'nyj ódu,	◡—	◡—	◡—	◡—
Liš' poželáju mnógo lét	◡◡	◡—	◡—	◡—
Tebé i tvoemú zavodu!	◡—	◡◡	◡—	◡—

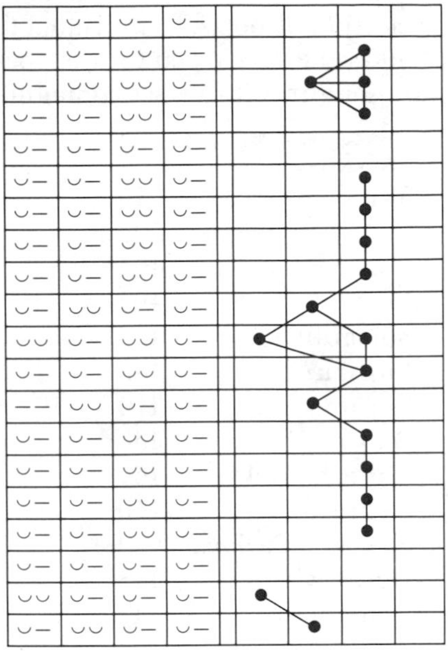

(Fet)

[Truly, I am no Pindar: more terrifying to me
Than anything is the solemn ode,
Berëzovets, and the anniversary
Of the foundation of the stud farm.
If only the words in my verses
Would come out vivid and malleable,
Then there would rise up from them all at once
Hooves, necks and heads.
Following closely each characteristic,
An expert would not pass by
Without admiring the beauty
Of Lover-boy or Ibrahim.
I, in proclaiming your laurels
And all the prizes you have won,
Were I to find myself in a stud farm in Ilium,
Would find the strains of the Iliad in which to sing.
But these strains escape me
And I, powerless to thunder forth in an ode,
Will simply wish you and your farm
Many years!]

rhythmic verses (containing dots). This relation, as statistics show in a selection of poets, is individual for each poet. Thus out of a total of 596 verses recorded for the poets listed below, we obtain the following figures for verses containing half-accents:[25]

Yazykov	527	Lomonosov	424
Tyutchev	519	Sluchevsky	429
Fet	505	Zhukovsky	422
Baratynsky	493	A. Tolstoy	419
Mey	492	Bogdanovich	419
Sologub	489	Polonsky	410
Pushkin	486	Bryusov	407
Lermontov	479	Maikov	400
Blok	468	Neledinsky–Meletsky	395
Merezhkovsky	461	Kapnist	377
Nekrasov	450	Dmitriev	376
Karolina Pavlova	450	Batyushkov	374
Derzhavin	448	Gorodetsky	362
Benediktov	447		

Our graph also allows us to see the frequency of occurrence of half-accents on each foot. In the Fet poem just analyzed we can see that the total number of half-accents (eighteen) are distributed thus: none on the fourth foot (the fourth foot does not customarily contain a half-accent in iambic tetrameter); thirteen on the third foot; three on the second; two on the first. We may say in advance that the third foot is the dominant position for half-accents in all poets (speaking always of the iambic tetrameter). Arranging the poets now by period, we obtain a statistical chart representing frequency of occurrence of half-accents by position in the verse (out of 596 verses) [see p. 253]. This table is extremely valuable in that it shows us the essence of a rhythmic revolution in Russian poetry. It begins with Zhukovsky and continues with the whole Pushkin group.

Before Zhukovsky the figures for half-accents on the second foot in our selection of poets are 139, 139, 114, 100, 100, 109, 112, that is, all more than 100.

After Zhukovsky the figures fall well below 100 for the Pushkin group: 52, 33, 47, 13, 4.

Conversely, the figures for half-accents on the first foot before Zhukovsky are 13, 46, 24, 54, 25, 36, 35. After Zhukovsky they are 90, 110, 101, 126, 164. Thus the frequency of half-accents on the

	Half-accents		
	1st foot	*2d foot*	*3d foot*
Poets before Zhukovsky			
Lomonosov	13	139	273
Derzhavin	46	139	263
Bogdanovich	24	114	271
Ozerov	54	100	226
Dmitriev	25	100	251
Neledinsky-Meletsky	36	109	258
Kapnist	35	112	230
Batyushkov	28	33	313
From Zhukovsky to Tyutchev			
Zhukovsky	90	52	280
Pushkin	110	33	341
Lermontov	101	47	321
Yazykov	126	13	388
Baratynsky	164	4	325
From Tyutchev to the Modernists			
Benediktov	59	24	343
Tyutchev	115	62	342
Karolina Pavlova	107	72	271
Polonsky	96	43	284
Fet	139	34	330
Maikov	77	24	299
Mey	123	17	352
Nekrasov	81	42	347
A. Tolstoy	83	13	323
Sluchevsky	74	32	323
Merezhkovsky	86	16	359

second foot decreases beginning with Zhukovsky, while the frequency of half-accents on the first foot increases.

Here is an example of a verse with a half-accent on the second foot:

> Zlatýe stëkla risovála
> *Na lákovom polú moëm.*
> (Derzhavin)
>
> [Drew golden glass panes
> On my lacquered floor.]

Here is an example of a verse with a half-accent on the first foot:

Ne pój, krasávica, pri mné
Ty pésen Grúzii pečál'noj:
Napominájut mné oné
Drugúju žízn' i béreg dál'nyj.
(Pushkin)

[Sing not, O fair one, to me
Your songs of sad Georgia:
They remind me of
Another life and distant shores.]

A comparison of the italicized lines leads us to the conclusion that the verse, "Na lákovom polú moëm," reads more slowly than the verse, "Napominájut mné oné." The verse by Derzhavin is in more of an andante tempo, whereas that of Pushkin is an allegro.

The ode and solemn epistle of the eighteenth century are distinguished rhythmically in Russian poetry by an abundance of half-accents on the second foot.

Greater liberty and simplicity of manners, the style of friendly, humorous epistles, a new freedom in the mastery of forms at the beginning of the nineteenth century were all reflected in rhythm as well, through an abundance of half-accents on the first foot of the iambic verse (or, to put it differently, the use of the second paeon gave way to the use of the fourth paeon in the first hemistich of the iambic verse; instead of this pattern: ◡–◡◡, poets began using this one: ◡◡◡–).

But this rhythmic modification of the iambic meter still does not necessarily indicate that there is an *improvement* in the meter. If this verse was superior in the Pushkin school, this fact was reflected not in the transfer of the half-accent from the second to the first foot, but rather in the increase in the overall number of half-accents (largely because of the increase on the third foot) and in the configuration of half-accents in consecutive verses, which generated a greater variety of rhythmic figures. It would be difficult to say which tempo is more perfect, andante or allegro: both are good. Everything depends on the rhythmic theme, on the instrumentation, on the relation of elements of form to the image, and so forth.

Now that we have characterized the reform in iambic meter, let us pause for a moment to consider Batyushkov as an example of a poet standing on the border between two eras. We will see that his iambic rhythm is entirely characteristic. The overall quantity of half-accents on the second and the first feet (in proportion to the number of verses in the sample) is: 28 (first) and 33 (second), which is to say that in his use of the pattern ⏑–⏑⏑, he is fairly closely following the practice of the eighteenth-century poets, while in his use of the pattern ⏑⏑⏑–, he is already foreshadowing the Pushkin school.[26] It is, of course, impossible to infer from this that either Zhukovsky or Pushkin was consciously attempting to modify the Russian iambic. To the extent that this modification was the replacement of one rhythm with another, it was the era that was influential rather than any individual.

If we look at the graphic figures in the chart representing the Fet poem [figure 5], we see that they are formed by joining points together with straight lines both in the same verse and in consecutive verses. As a result we get geometric figures in some places, whereas in others we get broken lines consisting of angles, triangles, and so forth. Similar tables on a larger scale would show us a series of figures (angles, rectangles, rhombuses, squares) formed by the mutual relation of two or more [consecutive] verses containing feet with half-accents. We have attempted to classify these figures and study them statistically so that, after the rhythmic sense of each figure has been explained, we may define the individual character of each poet's rhythm by examining the figures and statistical charts for his work. As an example let us consider the figure resembling a roof in the Fet poem. 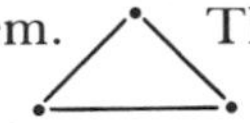 This figure is generated because the first of the two verses in question contains a half-accent on the second foot (⏑–⏑⏑) and the second verse contains two half-accents (one on the first, the other on the third foot) or two fourth paeons (⏑⏑⏑–|⏑⏑⏑–). Here are the two verses that correspond to the figure:

Znatók ne proxodíl by mímo,
Ne vosxitívšis' krasotój.

In the first of the two verses, the rhythm seems to stumble intentionally, with the result that the verse is read more slowly. In the second verse, the rhythm speeds up considerably. The rhythmic effect is thus that of a *ritenuto* followed by an acceleration.

This pattern may be entered on our statistical chart under the rubric of figures formed by half-accents on the first, third, and then second foot. Zhukovsky among other poets is especially fond of this pattern as well as the reverse, depicted graphically by an inverted roof 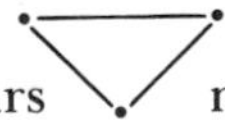 (that is, acceleration followed by a *ritenuto*). But it appears most frequently in Derzhavin, Tyutchev,

Karolina Pavlova, and, among the contemporary poets, Blok, Vyacheslav Ivanov, and my own work.

Another pattern, depicted graphically as a square ⁞□⁞, belongs to the group of figures formed from half-accents on the first and third feet [in two consecutive verses]. This one is particularly harmonious for the ear:

Kak zasvetlévšaja ot Mèri
Peredzakátnaja zarjá.

(Blok)[27]

This pattern consists of four consecutive fourth paeons over two consecutive verses:

◡◡◡–◡◡◡–‖◡◡◡–◡◡◡–.

Examples of "roofs":

Dlja róskoši, dlja négi modnoj
Vsë ukrašálo kabinét.

(Pushkin)

Goré, kak božestvá rodnýe
Nad usyplënnoju zemlëj.

(Tyutchev)

Kogdá že čerez šúmnyj grád
Ja probirájus' toroplívo.

(Lermontov)

Borólis' za naród tribúny
I imperátory za vlást'.

(Bryusov)

Elénu, usledívšij s výsi
Mír rastočájuščij pred néj.

(Vyacheslav Ivanov)

Examples of "inverted roofs":

Nečelovéč'imi rukámi
Žemčúžnyj raznocvétnyj móst.

(Zhukovsky)

I nad mogíloju raskrýtoj
V vozglávii, gde grób stoít.

(Tyutchev)

Examples of "squares":

Ne vospeváj, ne slavoslóv'
Velikoknjážeskoj porfíry.

(Fet)

Trë́x pokolénij krasotú
Dóč' korolévy sovmestíla.
(Fet)

Ne udručënnyj tjagotóju
Dúx glubiný i vysotý.
(Blok)

I otražénija očéj
Mné ulybálisja blagíja.
(Fedor Sologub)

Tý nezamétno proxodíla,
Tý ne sijála i ne žglá—
Kak nezažžënnoe kadílo,
Blagouxát' tý ne moglá.
(Fedor Sologub)

The last example is characteristic: here we find eight fourth paeons over four verses, forming a "ladder":

Figures of the "roof" type are almost completely lacking in Baratynsky, who is a typical case in that his graph shows a maximum of half-accents on the first foot (164) and a minimum on the second (4). Baratynsky is thus rhythmically the opposite of the pre-Pushkin poets.

The "roof" is a favorite figure of Zhukovsky, who frequently joins together two such figures to form a rhombus,

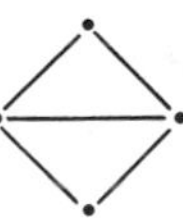

or a "cross,"

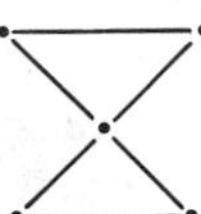

The square is often used by Pushkin, Lermontov, and Yazykov. In our own age it can be found most frequently in Fedor Sologub's *Fiery Circle*.[28]

A great many different figures are formed by [patterns of] half-accents. They can be classified as simple, complex, symmetrical (longitudinally or transversally). The most effective rhythmic figures are those whose graphic designs are symmetrical: the "roof," the square, and their combinations in the rhombus and "cross" are examples of symmetrical figures. As far as the rhythmic line itself is concerned, a broken, zigzag shape is an indication of rhythmic richness, while a simple line is an expression of rhythmic poverty. In the patterns outlined below, it should be pointed out that an abundance of dots not joined together by lines indicates that a true rhythm has not yet emerged. The same holds for any accumulation of empty spaces containing no figures. Rhythmic complexity and richness are indicated not by the total number of half-accents, but by the total number of figures formed from the broken line on the graph. Thus, for example, seven consecutive verses with a half-accent on the third foot generate an extended straight line without a single geometric figure (Aleksey Tolstoy's rhythm is like this). Another sample of seven verses might, however, generate a whole system of figures (as is the case with Pushkin, Tyutchev, Baratynsky).

[Figure 6] shows examples of poor rhythms. Here poems by Aleksey Tolstoy, Kapnist, Benediktov, and Pushkin in his Lyceum years have been analyzed.[29]

I consider these rhythms poor. The length of simple rhythmic lines in Aleksey Tolstoy and the accumulation of dots unconnected by lines indicates, in the first case, a uniformity in the type of deviations Tolstoy makes from the iambic meter, and, in the second case, the great number of metrically correct verses that often force the rhythm and give the poetry a wooden dryness. Observe how much richer is the rhythm of the fifteen-year-old Pushkin! Pushkin's rhythm describes a broken line, where we find angles, right angles, a "roof," and a figure—very characteristic of Lomonosov and Derzhavin—resembling the letter *M* (formed by a pattern of half-accents on the second and third feet). The abundance of right angles already looks ahead to the later Pushkin. Not only are the [broken] rhythmic lines long, not only is there a great quantity of half-accents, but isolated, unconnected dots are almost completely lacking: where Kapnist has five and Benediktov has six, Pushkin has only one. The rhythmic samples I have analyzed represent selections I purposely chose (from material available to me) as intrinsically characteristic of each author's rhythm.

So much is clear: a dot occurs in any case where there is a half-accent (acceleration) in the midst of metrically regular verses. But rhythm is always a relation, or ratio. If the ratio of metrically regular feet to accelerated feet is high (say, 17/1), then the ear does not notice the irregularity in tempo enough [for it to make a difference]. With an abundance of irregularities that occur close to-

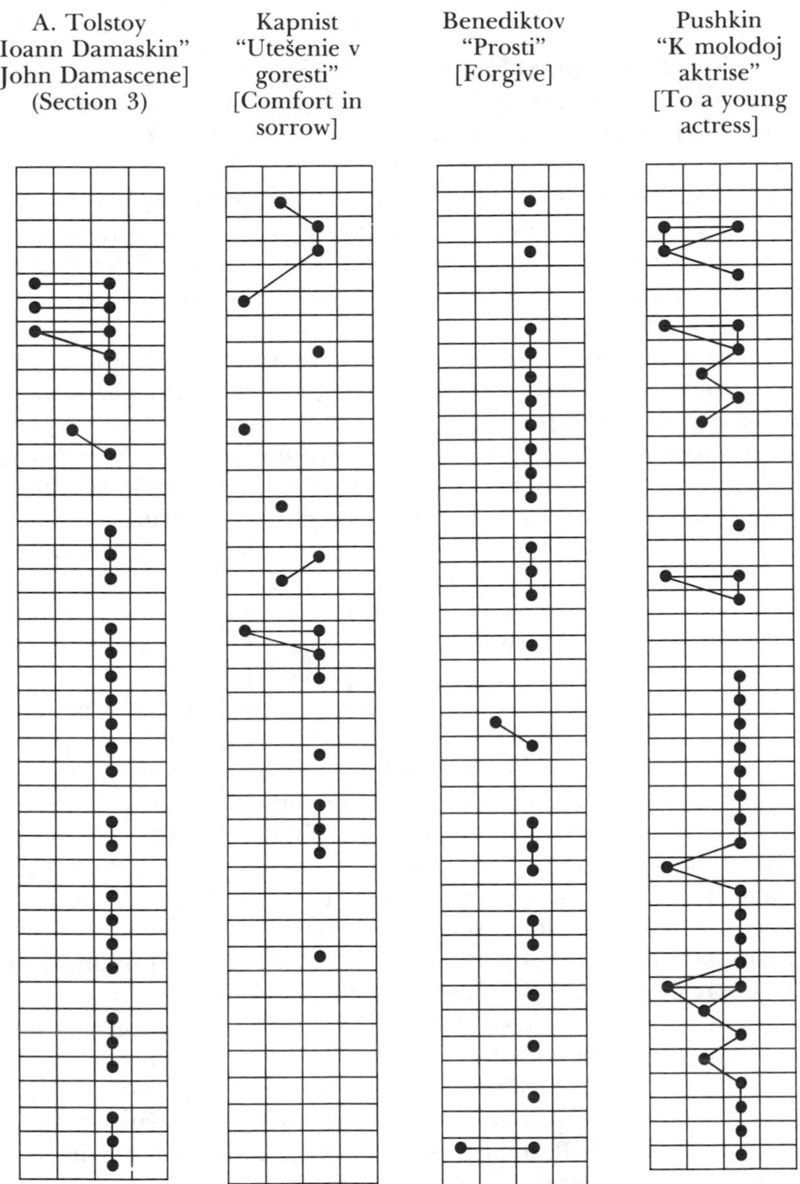

Figure 6 Poor Rhythms

gether, however, the rhythmic ratio (taking each irregularity separately) will be smaller (say, 3/1, 4/1, 5/1), and the total number of irregularities will be higher. Our experiment proves that density in patterns of half-accents generating geometric figures is characteristic of the rhythm of our best poets. We may conclude provisionally that rhythm is the relation of two meters, occurring by turns, the one tending towards acceleration, the other towards deceleration. For the iambic tetrameter, these meters are the double fourth paeon and the triple amphibrach.

What is true of iambic tetrameter is also true of trochaic tetrameter, except that there, instead of second and fourth paeons, we have first and third paeons.

Comparing the examples of rich rhythms [in figure 7] with the examples of poor rhythms [in figure 6], we see that the rhythmic figures for the rich rhythms are distinguished by greater complexity. The lines here are broken rather than straight, and simple figures join together here to form a series of complex figures. The selections analyzed were chosen with a view to presenting a clear visual characterization of the individuality of each rhythm. The resulting graphs are thus typical for the mature Pushkin, Tyutchev, Baratynsky, and Derzhavin. Also characteristic is that the complexity of the graphs is so much greater for the truly renowned poets, whereas the rhythmic line of third-rate poets is strikingly poor.

Let us compare the young Pushkin with the mature Pushkin. The rhythmic lines of the mature Pushkin are more broken and irregular than those of the young Pushkin. The young Pushkin is quite close to Derzhavin in the shape of several of the curves in his line. The young Pushkin shows relatively few half-accents on the first foot, whereas this figure increases in the mature Pushkin. If we compare the curve of the mature Pushkin with that of Tyutchev, we observe a significant resemblance. Nonetheless, there are differences. The number of half-accents on the second foot is greater for Tyutchev. In this regard one might say that the rhythm of Tyutchev represents an attempt to restore the loftiness of Derzhavin's rhythms that was lost with Pushkin and his school. Tyutchev's rhythm resembles that of Derzhavin also in the accumulation of "roof" figures (Derzhavin has 14 in 596 verses; Tyutchev has 13). If we now compare Tyutchev's rhythmic line with that of Baratynsky, however, we are immediately struck by how different the two are. Although both lines are broken, Baratynsky's is distinguished from Tyutchev's by the sharpness of its angular breaks, and this is caused by the complete absence of half-accents on the second foot. The characteristic "roof" figure is thus also lacking in Baratynsky. What strikes me

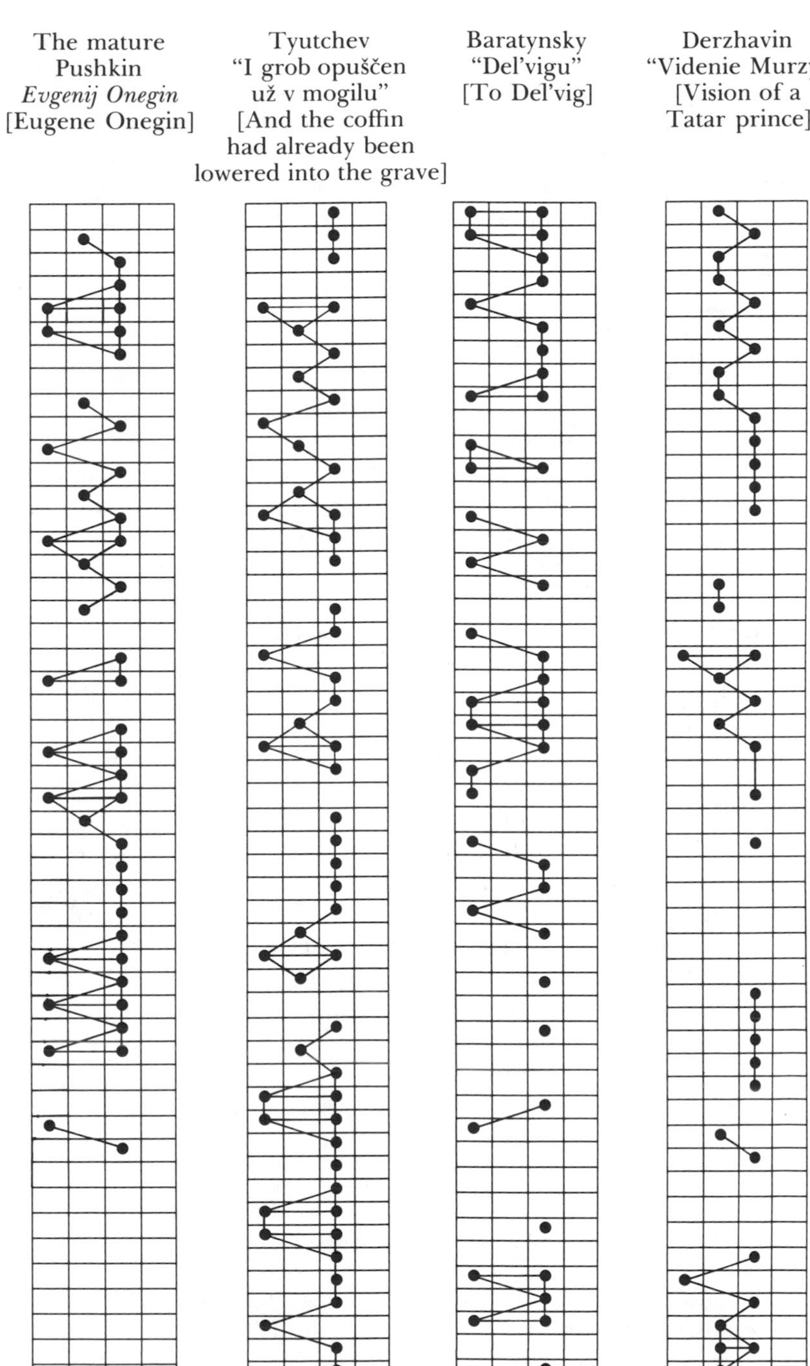

The mature
Pushkin
Evgenij Onegin
[Eugene Onegin]
Tyutchev
"I grob opuščen
už v mogilu"
[And the coffin
had already been
lowered into the grave]
Baratynsky
"Del'vigu"
[To Del'vig]
Derzhavin
"Videnie Murzy"
[Vision of a
Tatar prince]

Figure 7 Rich Rhythms

in Baratynsky's line after a superficial observation is its tendency towards symmetry. There are hints everywhere at a complex symmetry, but true symmetry is lacking. And after all, is this not the way in which Baratynsky plays with parallelisms in the disposition of his words? Baratynsky's parallelisms more often than not are artfully disguised.

In the course of my investigation, I attempted to define all the characteristic changes in rhythmic line, assigning to each one the name of a [geometric] figure. I then enumerated these figures on a statistical chart, together with the ones I mentioned above, and grouped them under a variety of different rubrics. Each figure on the chart formed one column. The number of occurrences of each figure for the poet in question was then entered in the appropriate column over the total number of verses [in the statistical sample]. Thus, for example, the figure I have called an "acute angle" occurs in Baratynsky 47 times over 596 verses, while in Lomonosov it occurs only once in the same number of verses. In Bryusov the figure occurs 8 times (in the period of his *The Garland*);[30] in Fet, 35 times; in Pushkin, 21 times; and so forth. The comparatively rare figure that I have termed the "small triangle" occurs only once. We can thus see that every poet has his own favorite figures. But what rhythmic meaning does a given figure have? This is not the place to list all the figures and analyze each one separately. Let us say simply that the rhythmic meaning of a figure depends both on the number of dots that form it and on the position of the feet on which the dots fall. Thus on certain feet a half-accent will slow down the general flow of the verse, whereas on others it will speed it up. Any figure is a typical concentration of decelerated and accelerated vocal accents relative to normal iambic meter within the confines of that meter. If a poet accumulates so many half-accents that a reading of the half-accented feet accelerates the meter excessively, the result will be cacophonous. As an example of such cacophony, let me cite a line of my own poetry written in this way in order to follow a rare pattern, but nonetheless included in my book, *Ashes*:[31]

Xot' i ne bez predubeždén'ja.
[Though not without prejudice.]

What is curious about this? Three consecutive feet here contain no accent, and one must read "Xotinebezpredube-" all in one breath before the vocal accent is heard, "-ždén'ja."

But since it is impossible to pronounce this verse without any accent [before the fourth foot], an accent tends to fall of its own accord on the word *bez*. As a consequence, the word *bez* is highlighted, even though no *logical* accent falls on it.

Among the regular types I have observed in my study of the rhythmic meaning of the geometric figures I have been discussing are the following: (1) the most harmonious to the ear are those figures whose half-accented feet, by virtue of proximity, appear in the graphic diagram as symmetrical or doubly symmetrical (doubly symmetrical meaning that they show an axis of symmetry along both a longitudinal section and a cross section); (2) as far as concentrations of figures go, the most harmonious to the ear are concentrations of symmetrical figures that are asymmetrical with respect to each other.

Figures, or rhythmic patterns, are divided into those formed by half-accents on (1) the second and third feet; (2) the first and third feet; (3) the first, second, and third feet. Or, to put it differently, if we regard the first and third feet as the outer feet and the second as the middle foot, groups of figures can be divided into those formed by half-accents on both one outer foot and the middle foot, on two outer feet, or on all three feet.[32]

On page 264 is an interesting statistical chart showing the total number of all three groups occurring in a sample of 596 verses for a selection of Russian poets.

Once again we see a decrease in the figures in the first group beginning with Zhukovsky, while, conversely, the figures in the second group rise beginning with Zhukovsky. The figures in the third group do not change markedly.

And with Batyushkov, just as previously, the figures in the first column follow those for poets of the subsequent period, while the figures in the second column follow those for poets of the preceding period.

We have already seen that the total number of half-accents does not coincide with the total number of geometric figures. In order to obtain a clear notion of rhythmic richness, let us now divide the total number of half-accents by the total number of geometric figures for each poet. The result will indicate the average number of half-accents required to generate a rhythmic pattern. Rhythmic richness will be defined, then, in inverse proportion to the average number of half-accents required to generate a geometric figure.[33]

We thus obtain the following results: for Tyutchev we find a rhythmic pattern occurring for every 1⅓ half-accents. From this we may conclude that Tyutchev is rhythmically the most interesting of all the Russian poets. After him come: Zhukovsky (1¾), Pushkin (2), Lermontov (2), Baratynsky (2), Fet (2). We may also conclude

	1st Group	*2d Group*	*3d Group*
Poets before Zhukovsky			
Lomonosov	122	6	26
Derzhavin	75	29	68
Bogdanovich	89	17	25
Ozerov	50	40	31
Dmitriev	75	18	44
Neledinsky-Meletsky	65	25	44
Kapnist	73	15	26
Batyushkov	16	7	13
From Zhukovsky to Tyutchev			
Zhukovsky	23	136	102
Pushkin	19	172	53
Lermontov	30	144	58
Yazykov	6	214	27
Baratynsky	3	224	15
From Tyutchev to the Modernists			
Tyutchev	37	200	78
Benediktov	4	56	12
Karolina Pavlova	44	83	66
Polonsky	17	107	39
Fet	17	150	66
Maikov	13	92	19
Mey	17	198	32
Nekrasov	23	99	40
A. Tolstoy	3	98	3
Sluchevsky	11	85	14
Merezhkovsky	6	121	24

from this that the rhythm of [Lermontov,] Baratynsky, Zhukovsky, and Fet is on a par with that of Pushkin in richness. After this come Yazykov (2⅓), Polonsky (2½), and Karolina Pavlova (2⅔).

After this comes a whole series of poets who show only one rhythmic pattern for every three half-accents. Such, for example, are all the poets who come before Zhukovsky (with the exception of Batyushkov): Lomonosov, Derzhavin, Bogdanovich, Dmitriev, Ozerov, Neledinsky, Kapnist. Nekrasov also belongs in this category of rhythmically poorer poets. Even poorer than the members of the preceding list is Maykov (3½).

Particularly poor from a rhythmic standpoint are A. Tolstoy (4) and Sluchevsky (4), and a poet of truly exceptional rhythmic poverty is Benediktov at 6¼. As for Batyushkov's rhythm, the figures would require a detailed discussion, and for this reason we have purposely omitted them.

Among contemporary poets, Aleksandr Blok and Fedor Sologub are exceptionally rich from a rhythmic standpoint (both showing figures of 2).

We may, then, with sufficient justification roughly divide Russian poets into four rhythmic categories. The first category appropriately includes the greatest of the Russian poets (from which we may conclude that our method is accurate). The four categories are

I. Tyutchev, Zhukovsky, Pushkin, Lermontov, Baratynsky, Fet.
II. Yazykov, Polonsky, Karolina Pavlova.
III. Poets of the eighteenth and early nineteenth centuries and Nekrasov.
IV. Maikov, Sluchevsky, A. Tolstoy, Benediktov.

If we compare the statistical figures of more recent poets with the corresponding figures for poets of an earlier era, we find ourselves in a position to define quite precisely a rhythmic affinity between a more recent poet and an earlier one, and we find that our statistical results often confirm and help explain the immediate judgments of our personal taste. In this way we can establish a rhythmic genealogy of poets. For example, the iambic tetrameter of Valery Bryusov of the period of *The Garland* has very distinct affinities with the rhythm of Pushkin's Lyceum poems (but not the mature Pushkin) and also with the rhythm of Zhukovsky (though it is less rich). Our work in correlating rhythms consists in a simple collection of statistical graphs. Since this mechanical task has pointed up a connection between Bryusov's rhythm and that of Pushkin's Lyceum poems, we recall that the period during which Bryusov was working on the Lyceum poems of Pushkin coincides approximately with the period of composition of *The Garland*. His closeness to Zhukovsky, on the other hand, in the rhythm of his "Orpheus and Eurydice" is amply explained by the dedication of that poem to Zhukovsky, and so forth.[34]

In the same way the rhythmic genealogy of the iambic tetrameter in Sologub's *Fiery Circle* would connect the author with Baratynsky and Fet. The rhythm of Fet, peculiarly refracted through Baratynsky, is the basis for the development of the iambic rhythm of Sologub.

The auditory peculiarity of a pyrrhic (half-accented) foot is a function not only of the foot itself, but also of the word[s] within the foot. If such a foot occurs between two regularly accented feet, then the interval between the two long syllables consists of three short ones. For example:

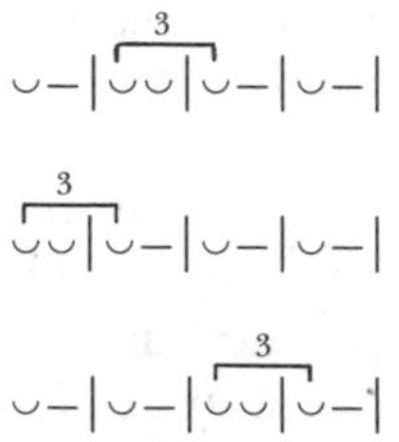

(3 over ⌣⌣|⌣)
⌣–|⌣⌣|⌣–|⌣–|

(3 over ⌣⌣|⌣)
⌣⌣|⌣–|⌣–|⌣–|

(3 over ⌣⌣|⌣)
⌣–|⌣–|⌣⌣|⌣–|

The rhythmic character of the half-accented foot differs sharply depending on whether the three [consecutive] short syllables occur in one word (for example, *ótoropi*) or two. In the second case the position of the break between the two words is very important: it can occur after just one short syllable (for example, *svjatája / krasotá*) or after two (for example, *volnénie / moë*). In the case where all three short syllables occur in one word of four or more syllables, it is important to know whether the accent occurs *before* the three short syllables (as in *ótoropi*) or *after* (for example, *otobrazít'*). Either of these words could serve to form a half-accent on the second foot of a line of iambic tetrameter, but the rhythmic character of the verse would alter accordingly. Here is an example of the first type:

> Poxrústyvaet v nóč' valéžnik.

Example of the second type:

> Dušá potrjasená mojá.

In both cases the second foot is a pyrrhee, but the rhythmic character is different. In both cases the pyrrhic foot strives, as it were, to cut the line in two with a pause, but in the first case the pause comes before the vocal accent, whereas in the second it comes after. Let us put the two lines together:

> Dušá potrjasená mojá . . .
> Poxrústyvaet v nóč' valéžnik.
> Ja vnóv' odín . . . Sryváju já
> Moj néžnyj, golubój podsnéžnik.
>
> (A. Bely)

> [My soul is shaken . . .
> The windfallen branches crackle in the night.

I am once again alone . . . I tear off
My delicate, light blue snowdrop.]

In this quatrain the rhythmic contrast occurs not because of a change in position of half-accented feet, but because of a change in the position of the accent in the word. Both verses contain a second paeon (⏑–⏑⏑). What, then, do they have in common?

Here are some examples of different kinds of word division in verses containing a half-accent in the second foot:

Ugrózoju | krivítsja rót. (3)

V resnícax | stekljanéjut slëzy. (3)

There is a total of four possibilities for a pyrrhee on the second foot [that is, where only one major word division occurs between the first and third feet]:

a. Dušá | potrjasená mojá.
b. V resnícax | stekljanéjut slëzy.
c. Ugrózoju | krivítsja rót.
d. Poxrústyvaet | v nóč' valéžnik.

Finally, if the three consecutive short syllables include two monosyllabic words or occur in two words where one is dissyllabic and the other monosyllabic, then still another case arises [that is, where there are two or three word divisions between the first and third feet].

e. Xot' í | ne | bez | predubeždén'ja.

The same five possibilities exist for a half-accented first foot.

a. | Ispepeljájuščimi dén'.
b. I | razol'ëtsja nad lugámi.
c. Pered | otčíznoju moéj.
d. Peredo | mnój javílas' tý.
e. I | nad | obrývami otkósa.

And for a half-accented third foot:

a. I mné kričát | izdaleká.
b. I nad pribréžnoj | polosój.
c. I nad pribréžnoju | kosój.
d. Ispepeljájuščimi | dén'.
e. I pered útrom | pered | snóm.

A total of three possible half-accented feet in a line of iambic tetrameter gives fifteen possible rhythmic modifications. In verses containing half-accents in both the first and third feet, the number of possible variations is equal to the product of four and five, or twenty. And if we take into account that half-accents on both the second and third feet add another ten possible variations, and spondaic feet another five, we see that the sum of possible rhythmic modifications in one verse of iambic tetrameter is equal to fifty (and this is a minimum).

Keeping in mind the method set forth above, we may now substitute letters [representing variations in word division] for dots in our diagrams. [See figure 8.]

If we now examine the pattern of half-accents in relation to the letters, we see that *b* and *c* are more common than *a* and *d* in iambic tetrameter, pentameter, and hexameter. Of these two, *b* is the more common.

1. When a pyrrhee occurs on the first foot of any iambic meter, it is usually of the *a*, *b*, or *e* type; *c* and *d* are extremely rare. I have encountered one *d* type in a half-accented first foot—in Pushkin: "Peredo mnój javílas' tý" [And before me you appeared] ("Kern").[35]

2. A pyrrhee on the second foot of a line of iambic tetrameter in Pushkin is almost always of the *b* type, less often of the *e* type. The *c* type is quite rare in Pushkin, but common in Derzhavin, Lomonosov, and others. My own iambic tetrameter follows Derzhavin and Lomonosov, a peculiarity of mine that I have never wished to resist. Baratynsky's lyric poetry has almost no pyrrhees on the second foot, whereas for Tyutchev they are quite common. In Tyutchev's case we find all the variations from *a* to *e*.

3. The *b* type decidedly predominates in pyrrhees on the third foot. Such is the case in general for Tyutchev, although he has poems with a preponderance of *c* types in this position, for example, "Pervyj list" [The first leaf] and "Ženeva" [Geneva]. In Tyutchev's "Živym sočuvstviem priveta" [With a lively sympathy of greeting], in fact, there are two instances of the *c* type in the first foot. In Baratynsky, the *b* type predominates in the third foot. The *c* type, however, occurs in this position in all poets without exception. Sometimes the pattern corresponds to the content of a poem, as, for example, in Baratynsky's "Vesna" [Spring]. In the third strophe of this poem there begins a description of a naiad, during which there is a series of four consecutive verses all containing a *c* type on the third foot. When the description of the naiad gives way to a de-

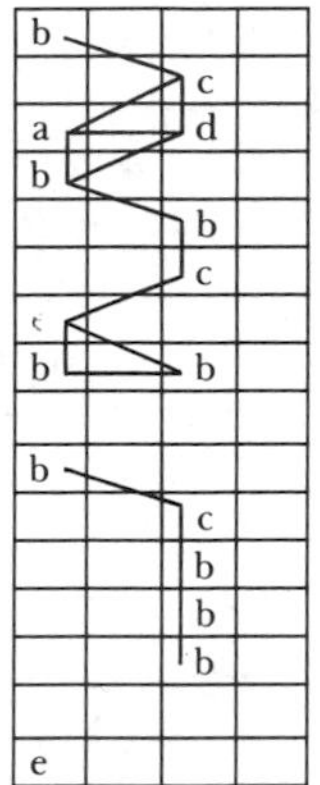

Figure 8

scription of the raptures of the spirit, however, the series of *c* types at the same time gives way to a series of *b* types.

4. Interestingly enough, in iambic hexameter *only* the *c* type can occur on the third foot, since if, for example, a *b* type occurred in that position the hexameter would assume the form of a trimeter.

5. Finally, spondaic feet are characteristic of iambic meters, as, for example, in the following verse by Baratynsky:

> Ní žít' ím, ní pisát' eščë ne nadoélo.
>
> [They had not yet grown weary of either living or writing.]

That is:

— —|— —|◡—|◡—|◡◡|◡—|◡.

We could prolong our foray into metrics, rhythm, and versification indefinitely, but we will stop here.

The examples we have cited demonstrate that the experimental method is indeed both possible and fruitful in this area, but it is still entirely a thing of the future.

4

We deny the existence today of any true criticism in the area of poetry known as lyric. Tendentious criticism is already a thing of the past. Tendentious criticism never produced a single major poet. Historical criticism is theoretically possible, but if it did exist, it would undoubtedly be based on a description of lyric forms and images. True description of this type does not exist, and so neither does historical criticism. Aesthetic criticism today is also lacking. At its best, this type of criticism rests on a small quantity of forms to be analyzed. As a result, it is usually mere personal taste that determines judgments in this area. Finally, there is impressionistic criticism, which is not criticism at all. It is nothing more than a kind of lyrical improvisation. To be sure, such improvisation is occasionally valuable: it is interesting to know about the lyrical impressions that poets, writers, and artists have of other writers and poets. But lyrical outpourings of delight and anger from the pens of mediocre pamphleteers can never be of any interest to those who truly esteem poetry. In fact, outpourings of this sort usually turn into cheap advertising, or pretexts for settling personal accounts. Impressionistic criticism as it exists today, having once made its way into our newspapers, has served only to corrupt our taste.

Lyric poetry still awaits its own criticism. Only experimental criticism can ever be such a criticism. We have seen that such a form of experimentalism is possible in studying form in a work of lyric poetry. But many years of assiduous work are still necessary for experimental criticism to emerge fully. The basis of this criticism must be a carefully elaborated notion of meter. For we still do not know just what Russian meter is and how it is distinct from other meters. Anything we might have to say about meter is thus purely conjectural. No theory of Russian meter exists. Like any other scientific theory, a theory of meter would have to be founded on experiment, and such experiment is possible only with a clearly delineated and classified body of material. In this case the material would be the great monuments of our poetic tradition from the *byliny* to the poetry of the present day. This body of material is, of course, immense, and it would be necessary to describe it variously from the point of view of meter, verbal instrumentation, style, and means of representation.

We have seen, on the basis of numerous examples, that there are certain conditional designations for the various metric forms that are accepted as standard, but that the Russian language has the capacity for creating word combinations that, without ceasing to be verses, do not fit any of the standard metric forms. Such deviations from standard meter must also be described, studied, and classified. Indeed, a theory explaining such deviations would lie at the very basis of any theory of rhythm in Russian verse. The laws of deviation would be the very laws of poetic rhythm. Such laws would then have to be compared with the laws of musical rhythm. Who can tell? Perhaps it is only at that point that we will have at our disposal a proper theory that will enable us to deal critically with both old and new lyric forms of poetry.

Here, for example, is a short poem by Baratynsky:

Vzgljaníte: svéžest'ju mladój
I v ósen' lét oná plenjáet,
I u neë letún sedój
Lanítnyx róz ne poxiščaet;
Sam pobeždënnyj krasotój
Gljadít—i pút' ne prodolžáet.
("Zenščine požiloj, no vse ešče prekrasnoj")

[Behold: with youthful freshness
Even in the autumn of her life she is captivating,
And the grey-haired, airy sprite of old age
Has not stolen away the rosy glow in her cheeks;
But, overcome himself with her beauty,
He looks—and cannot continue on his way.
(To an elderly, but still beautiful woman)]

Alliterations and assonances in this poem are concealed. But if we analyze the poem carefully verse by verse, we begin to see that the entire thing is constructed on [e] and [a]. [e] predominates at first, then [a]. The resoluteness and cheerfulness of the closing words seem to be connected with the open vowel [a].

That there is in fact alliteration here can be demonstrated by emphasizing the alliterative sounds:

Vzg*l*ja*n*í*t*e: svéžes*t*'ju *mlad*ój
I v óse*n*' *lét* o*n*á p*l*e*n*jáe*t*
I u neë *let*ú*n* se*d*ój
*L*a*n*í*tn*yx . . .

There are three groups of alliterations here: (1) those on [l], (2) those on nasal consonants ([m] and [n]), and (3) those on dental consonants ([d] and [t]). Thus for twelve consonants that are not clearly alliterative, there are twenty-three that are clearly alliterative (or twice as many alliterative as nonalliterative).

In Baratynsky's poem, "S. D. P.," the first strophe goes like this:

*Primán*koj *l*áskovyx *r*ečéj
Va*m* ne *l*išít' *m*e*n*já *r*assúdka!
Ko*néčno* *mn*ógix vý *mil*éj
*N*o vás *l*ju*b*ít'—*pl*oxája šútka.
Va*m* *ne* *n*už*n*á *l*ju*b*óv' *m*ojá . . .

[By the enticements of tender words
You will not deprive me of my reason!
Certainly you are kinder than many,
But loving you is a bad joke.
You do not need my love . . .]

Let us examine the instrumentation of these verses. (1) The nasal consonant [n] predominates; furthermore, it occurs in conjunction with [m] five times. (2) If we read through the first two verses, we can see a symmetrical pattern in the distribution of alliterative sounds as well: in the first verse we find "*l*áskovyx *r*ečéj," corresponding to "*l*išít' *r*assúdka" in the second. In addition to this, in the first verse we find the group [mn] occurring before [l] and [r], and in the second verse we find the same group occurring *between* [l] and [r]. We see thus a kind of capricious regularity in the distribution of sounds. (3) In the fourth verse [lb] and [pl], two liquid-labial groups are related to each other by means of a labial group. The general instrumentation scheme here is such that a nasal sound runs through all the verses, as if accompanying the melancholic mood that the words are imbued with. In conjunction with this nasal sound appear the liquids and liquid-labial groups. The whole quatrain [that is, excluding the fifth verse cited] is revealed in the word *Primánka*, in which all the verbal instrumentation elements of the entire quatrain come together: the labial [p], the liquid [r], and the nasals [m] and [n].

As the poem progresses, the melancholic tone gives way to one of gloomy determination and anger, and the melancholic instrumentation ([m], [n], and [l]) correspondingly changes: dental consonants are introduced, trumpetlike, and these, in turn, with the appearance of a [z] sound, give way to sibilants in the following extremely caustic verse:

Ja *sost*jazát'*s*ja ne *d*erzáju.

[I dare not compete.]

It is clear that the content of experience in this poem is harmoniously joined with the verbal instrumentation. The force of this content is heightened by its reflection in the choice of sounds. If we could find the correspondence here between the instrumentation and the rhythm, then we would be in a position to represent the inexpressible charm of the lyric (its music) in a clear form. But no theory of rhythm exists, just as no theory of instrumentation exists, and we are consequently doomed to mere dilettantism.

From the study of the rhythmic skeleton of the words, from the study of verbal instrumentation, which provides the skeleton with musculature, we ought to proceed to the question of word choice. Word choice is an individual matter for every poet, and there ought to be dictionaries for each poet. But such dictionaries do not exist. Only in the work of the scholar Aleksandr Veselovsky on Zhukovsky do we find a timid attempt to investigate the individual style of the poet.[36] After all, it is the poets, more than anyone else, who have always enriched the language—and continue to do so—with archaisms and neologisms.

Only when we have all these things at our disposal will statements bearing on the form of lyric poems have weight and value. Only then will we be able to create a bridge between the form of lyric images and their experiential and ideational content.

1909

TRANSLATOR'S NOTES

BELY AS THEORIST

1. *Petersburg*, trans. Robert A. Maguire and John E. Malmstad (Bloomington: Indiana University Press, 1978).

2. *The First Encounter*, trans. Gerald Janeček (Princeton: Princeton University Press, 1979). *Andrei Bely: Complete Short Stories*, trans. Ronald Peterson (Ann Arbor: Ardis, 1979). "The Magic of Words," in *Symbolism: An Anthology*, ed. Thomas G. West (London and New York: Methuen, 1980), pp. 120–43.

3. Vladimir Nabokov, *Strong Opinions* (New York: McGraw Hill, 1973), p. 57.

4. *St. Petersburg*, trans. John Cournos (New York: Grove, 1959). *The Silver Dove*, trans. George Reavey (New York: Grove, 1974). *Kotik Letaev*, trans. Gerald Janeček (Ann Arbor: Ardis, 1972). For an account of Bely's reputation outside of Russia and the dissemination of his work in foreign translation as of 1975, see Gleb Struve, "Andrey Bely Redivivus," in *Andrey Bely: A Critical Review*, ed. Gerald Janeček (Lexington: The University Press of Kentucky, 1978), pp. 21–43.

5. The most complete bibliography of Bely's noncreative writings is Georges Nivat, "L'oeuvre polémique, critique et journalistique d'Andrej Belyj," *Cahiers du Monde Russe et Soviétique* 15 (1974): 22–39. Nivat lists everything he has discovered except for public lectures and individually published poems. A total of 328 items in Nivat's list are not full-length books, and of these, roughly three hundred could broadly be described as writings on aesthetics and criticism (although this means including such things as book reviews and obituaries of contemporary authors). In addition, there are eleven full-length books and all the essays appearing in *Symbolism*, *The Green Meadow*, and *Arabesques*. These last total 89, but a great many had appeared in periodicals and are duplicated on Nivat's list. A

more recent bibliography is the one compiled by Olga Muller Cooke and Ronald E. Peterson, "Andrej Belyj: A Bibliography since 1964," *Newsletter of the Andrej Belyj Society* 2 (1983): 18–21. This list is an update of a bibliography by Anton Hönig in his study of Bely's novels, *Andrej Belyjs Romane: Stil und Gestalt* (Munich: Fink Verlag, 1965), pp. 114–17. Cooke's and Peterson's bibliography adds three new items to Bely's corpus that could arguably be called aesthetics and criticism.

6. *Masterstvo Gogolja: Issledovanie* (Gogol's craftsmanship) (Moscow and Leningrad: Ogiz, 1934).

7. "Gogol," in *Twentieth-Century Russian Literary Criticism*, ed. Victor Erlich (New Haven: Yale University Press, 1975), pp. 33–50. (Translation of "Gogol'," in *Lug zelenyj* [The green meadow] [Moscow: Al'cion, 1910], pp. 93–121.)

8. *Simvolizm* (Moscow, 1910; rpt. Munich: Fink Verlag, 1969); *Lug zelenyj*, see note 7; *Arabeski* (Moscow, 1911; rpt. Munich: Fink Verlag, 1969).

9. *Načalo veka* (The beginning of the century) (Moscow and Leningrad: Gosudarstvennoe izdatel'stvo xudožestvennoj literatury, 1933), p. 9.

10. *Načalo veka*, p. 115.

11. V. M. Žirmunskij, "Formprobleme in der russischen Literaturwissenschaft," (Problems of form in Russian literary scholarship), *Zeitschrift für slavische Philologie* 1 (1925): 119. For an account of the relations between Bely and Zhirmunsky see Thomas R. Beyer, Jr., "The Bely-Zhirmunsky Polemic," in *Andrey Bely: A Critical Review*, ed. Gerald Janaček (Lexington: The University Press of Kentucky, 1978), pp. 205–13.

12. Žirmunskij, "Formprobleme in der russischen Literaturwissenschaft," p. 130.

13. Roman Jakobson, "Retrospect," in *Selected Writings*, 5 vols. (The Hague: Mouton, 1979), 5:569–601.

14. Jakobson, *Selected Writings* 5:569.

15. Jakobson, *Selected Writings* 5:588.

ON THE ESSAYS THEMSELVES

1. *Petersburg* (Petersburg, 1916; rpt. Letchworth: Bradda Books, 1967), p. 55. The best critical treatment of *Petersburg* (in my view) to appear in English contains an excellent discussion of the thematic relation between the world of concrete appearances and the transcendent realm in Bely's novel. See Vladimir Alexandrov, "Unicorn Impaling a Knight: The Transcendent and Man in Andrei Belyi's *Petersburg*," *Canadian-American Slavic Studies* 16 (1982): 1–44.

2. See Anton Kovač, *Andrej Belyj: The "Symphonies" (1899–1908): A Critical Re-Evaluation of the Aesthetic-Philosophical Heritage* (Munich: Peter Lang, 1976), passim, for a discussion of Nietzsche's place in the development of Bely's literary style and philosophical outlook.

3. Aleksandr Afanas'evich Potebnja, *Iz zapisok po teorii slovesnosti* (Notes

on the theory of literature) (Kharkov, 1905; rpt. The Hague: Mouton, 1970).

4. "Mysl' i jazyk (filosofija jazyka A. A. Potebni)" (Thought and language [A. A. Potebnya's theory of language]), *Logos* 2 (1910): 240–58.

5. See Aleksandr Afanas'evich Potebnja, *Iz lekcij po teorii slovesnosti* (Lectures on the theory of literature) (Karkov, 1894; rpt. The Hague: Mouton, 1970), p. 123.

6. Potebnja, *Iz lekcij*, p. 130.

7. Potebnja, *Iz lekcij*, pp. 124–25.

8. See Šklovskij, Viktor, "Voskrešenie slova" (The resurrection of the word), in *Texte der russischen Formalisten*, ed. Jurij Striedter (Munich: Fink Verlag, 1969–1972), 2:4.

9. For the relationship between Shklovsky and Potebnya, see Daniel Laferrière, "Potebnja, Šklovskij, and the Familiarity/Strangeness Paradox," *Russian Literature* 4 (1976): 176–98.

10. "Apokalipsis v russkoj poèzii" (Apocalypse in Russian poetry), in *Lug zelenyj* (Moscow: Al'cion, 1910), p. 230.

11. Stéphane Mallarmé, *Oeuvres complètes* (Paris: Pléiade, 1945), p. 364.

12. *Simvolizm*, p. 484.

13. *Meždu dvux revoljucij* (Between two revolutions) (Leningrad: Izdatel'stvo pisatelej, 1934), p. 377.

14. Heinrich Rickert, *Der Gegenstand der Erkenntnis: Einführung in die Transzendentalphilosophie* (The Object of cognition: Introduction to transcendental philosophy), 2d ed., rev. and enl. (Tübingen and Leipzig: Mohr, 1904). In Russian: *Vvedenie v transcendental'nuju filosofiju. Predmet poznanija* (Kiev, 1904).

15. *Načalo veka*, p. 257.

16. *Načalo veka*, p. 115.

17. For instance in volume 1 of Husserl's *Logische Untersuchungen* (Logical investigations), where, curiously enough, the author, without mentioning Rickert by name, refers to all theories of logic based on a *Bewusstsein überhaupt* as being relativistic. See *Logische Untersuchungen* (1900–1901; rpt. Tübingen: Max Niemeyer Verlag, 1968), 1:124.

18. On the crucial distinction between *emblem* and *symbol*, see sections 10, 15, and 16 in "The Emblematics of Meaning" and my discussion of section 16.

19. See the chapter "Symbolism and the Iconic Imagination in Bely" for further discussion of this concept.

20. *Načalo veka*, p. 114.

21. *Simvolizm*, p. 286.

22. *Simvolizm*, p. 298.

23. V. M. Žirmunskij, *Vvedenie v metriku* (Leningrad, 1925; rpt. Munich: Fink Verlag, 1971), pp. 33–45. Also in English translation, as *Introduction to Metrics*, trans. C. F. Brown (The Hague: Mouton, 1966), pp. 37–48.

24. Boris Unbegaun, *Russian Versification* (Oxford: Clarendon Press, 1956), p. 158.

25. Vladimir Nabokov, *Notes on Prosody* (London: Routledge & Kegan Paul, 1964), p. 14n.

"SYMBOLISM AS A WORLD VIEW"

1. *Nietzsche Werke*, ed. Giorgio Colli and Giorgio Montinari (Berlin: Walter de Gruyter, 1972), 3–1 : 128. My translation.

2. Eduard von Hartmann (1842–1906). German philosopher, author of *Philosophie des Unbewussten* (Philosophy of the unconscious) (1869).

3. *Godmanhood*. The references in this paragraph are to Vladimir Solov'ev's *Čtenija o Bogočelovečestve* (Lectures on Godmanhood) (1877–1881).

4. Nietzsche, see note 1.

5. *The duality in critical philosophy* . . . Bely seems to mean that the duality between the appreciation of the masses for art and that of the elite few is analogous to the critical duality between common human understanding and revealed truth, implying that the "elite few" have access to a realm of ideas that are transcendent with respect to ordinary understanding.

6. *little ones*. The phrase occurs four times in Matthew (10:42, 18:6 [repeated in Mark 9:42], 18 : 10, 18 : 14). It refers to Christ's disciples, who are compared here to the little child that Christ has called and set in their midst (18 : 12). Bely is paraphrasing 18 : 10: "Take heed that ye despise not one of these little ones; for I say unto you, That in heaven their angels do always behold the face of my Father which is in heaven."

7. *blue prison*. From a poem by A. A. Fet, "Pamjati N. Ja. Danilevskogo" (To the memory of N. Y. Danilevsky).

8. Nietzsche, *Also sprach Zarathustra*, "Die stillste Stunde," in Part 2, *Werke*, 6–1, pp. 183–84. My translation; emphasis in original.

9. *Like demons* . . . From Tyutchev's "Nočnoe nebo tak ugrjumo" (The night sky so gloomy).

10. See note 11.

11. Nietzsche, *Also sprach Zarathustra*, "Die sieben Siegel," in Part 3, *Werke*, 6–1, p. 286. My translation.

12. *Lev Shestov* (1866–1938). Russian philosopher and critic, often grouped with Vasilii Rozanov and Konstantin Leont'ev as one of the "conservative critics" at the turn of the century. Shestov was a Nietzschean and something of an existentialist. His best-known work in the West is undoubtedly his *Dostoevskij i Nicše: Filosofija tragedii* (Dostoevsky and Nietzsche: Philosophy of tragedy) (Petersburg, 1903). Bely wrote a short piece on him in 1909 that was included in the collection *Arabeski*.

13. The quotation is from Maeterlinck's philosophical essay, "Le Réveil de l'âme," the second essay in the collection *Le Trésor des humbles* (1896). Bely has reordered Maeterlinck's thoughts to suit his own purposes here: the second sentence he quotes is actually part of Maeterlinck's opening sentence, and the first sentence in Bely's text appears a couple of pages later. I

have restored the remainder of this sentence (in brackets) for the sake of clarity. See *Le Trésor des humbles* (Paris: Mercure de France, 1917), pp. 29, 31. My translation.

14. See note 6.

15. Jeremiah 23:29: "Is not my word like as a fire? saith the Lord; and like a hammer that breaketh the rock in pieces?" Bely's phrase does not correspond perfectly to this passage, since he uses the verb *drobit'* (smash, crumble—a word that occurs only once in the Russian Bible) instead of *razbivat'*, which corresponds to the English "breaketh" in the cited passage. But it is clear that Bely has the verse from Jeremiah in mind, since the context there is a diatribe against false prophets and since the sense otherwise fits completely.

16. Bely cites the source of this passage, which he has quoted more completely in the previous paragraph, as Leviticus 26:4. The passage in Leviticus, in fact, is the source of the passage Bely quotes, but is worded slightly differently. In the form Bely uses, the passage unquestionably comes from 2 Corinthians.

17. *Otto Lilienthal* (1848–1896). Aeronautical engineer who was among the first to work with gliders.

18. Nietzsche, *Also sprach Zarathustra*, "Von der grossen Sehnsucht," in Part 3, *Werke*, 6–1, pp. 275–76. My translation.

19. The two verse passages are slightly modified and rearranged extracts from Bely's poem, "Zolotoe runo" (The Golden Fleece), written in April of 1903 and subsequently included in the youthful collection *Zoloto v lazuri* (Gold in azure), which first appeared in 1904.

"THE MAGIC OF WORDS"

1. *Every act of cognition arises from a name* (Vsjakoe poznanie vytekaet uže iz nazvanija). The words that have been translated as "act of cognition" and "name" are both verbal nouns in Russian, denoting the act, or more precisely the *result* of the act of cognizing (*poznat'*) and naming (*nazvat'*), respectively. Thus the suggestion is much stronger in the original Russian that the act of naming (and its result, a name) precedes the act of cognizing, or acquiring knowledge (and *its* result, presumably a truth).

2. *Imaginal speech.* The Russian *obraznyj* is the adjective corresponding to *obraz* (image). Bely uses it frequently to mean "rich in images," "characterized by images," or simply "pertaining to images." I have used "imaginal" to avoid cumbersome circumlocutions.

3. From Tyutchev's famous poem, "Silentium!" (1830).

4. *Antoine Fabre d'Olivet* (1768–1825). French philologist and poet involved in the movement to resurrect Provençal language and culture, also author of *La Langue hébraïque restituée* (1815), which Bely cites in a footnote to this paragraph. In that footnote Bely quotes the passage in which d'Olivet

discusses the derivation of the Hebrew name for the divinity. The second part of d'Olivet's book consists of the Hebrew text of the first ten chapters of Genesis with a scholarly commentary, followed by a "literal" translation into French. The passage Bely cites (without page reference) is taken from d'Olivet's note to Genesis 2:5, in which the name Ihoah, as d'Olivet prints it, appears. See *The Hebraic Tongue Restored*, trans. Nayan Louise Redfield (New York and London: Knickerbocker Press, 1921), p. 68n.

5. *Senzar.* A legendary primitive language in which an equally legendary book was written and from which, according to mystic tradition, the basic mystic writings of various religions, from Judaea to China, were derived. Helena Petrovna Blavatsky mentions this book in the introduction to *The Secret Doctrine*: "Tradition says that it was taken down in *Senzar*, the secret sacerdotal tongue, from the words of the Divine Beings, who dictated it to the sons of Light, in Central Asia, at the very beginning of the 5th (our) race; for there was a time when its language (the *Sen-zar*) was known to the Initiates of every nation. . . ." (*An Abridgment of The Secret Doctrine*, ed. Elizabeth Preston and Christmas Humphreys [London: Theosophical Publishing House, 1966], p. xxx). In a note on the present paragraph, Bely paraphrases this discussion from *The Secret Doctrine* (without citing his source) but muddles the facts as Blavatsky presents them.

6. *Aleksandr Afanas'evich Potebnya* (1835–1891). Russian philologist and linguist. Potebnya's research focused on the problem of the "inner form" of words and the relation between this inner form and forms of thinking. His firm grounding in linguistics has made him an important figure in the history of modern criticism as a precursor to the Russian Formalists (some of whom took an exaggeratedly antagonistic stance towards aspects of his theories). *Aleksandr Nikolaevich Afanas'ev* (1826–1871). Russian folklorist, known for his *Poètičeskie vozzrenija slavjan na prirodu* (Poetic views of the Slavs on nature) 3 vols. (Moscow, 1865–1869) and above all for his anthology *Narodnye russkie skazki* (Russian Folktales) 3 vols. (1855–1863).

7. Cited from Afanas'ev, *Poètičeskie vozzrenija*, 1:319 (Bely cites the source in a note in the text).

8. The next three examples are taken from the work of Vladimir Dahl, *Poslovicy russkogo naroda* (Sayings of the Russian people) (Moscow, 1862), pp. 885, 896, and 873. All three examples appear in the section entitled *Mesjaceslov*, a list of months and days with their ecclesiastical significance.

9. This passage comes from the *Russian Primary Chronicle* (Laurentian Text), for the year 992. The pun rests on the resemblance between the name of the city (*Perejaslavl'*) and the phrase "won glory" (*pereja slavu*). I have used the English translation of Samuel Hazzard Cross and Olgerd P. Sherbowitz-Wetzor, *The Russian Primary Chronicle. Laurentian Text* (Cambridge, Mass.: The Medieval Academy of America, 1973), p. 120.

10. *Communication.* The dictionary definition of *obščenie* is "intercourse." The word carries the general notion of mutual relations and exchange between people, something that "intercourse" does not quite convey. Al-

though "communication" is perhaps too specific for the meaning intended, I chose it because it seemed closer than any of the other possibilities.

11. *Purposiveness without purpose.* See note 42 to "The Emblematics of Meaning."

12. *Eduard Hanslick* (1825–1904). Viennese music critic, known primarily for his outspoken distaste for Wagner and for his defense of an "autonomist" aesthetic theory of music, that is, the formalist theory that music does not have a "subject," cannot represent anything (hence his opposition to Wagnerian opera), and has no purpose outside its own formal properties. These ideas he developed in his best-known work, *Vom Musikalisch-Schönen* (The beautiful in music), published in 1854. It is in this work that Hanslick discounts the notion that music can have an aim (*Zweck*) beyond the beauty inherent in its own formal laws. The "odd" coincidence Bely speaks of concerning Hanslick and Kant is not so odd when one considers Hanslick's thorough schooling in aesthetics and his mention of Kant on the first page of the final chapter of *Vom Musikalisch-Schönen*, where he identifies him as an advocate of the idea that music has no subject. Hanslick's treatise appeared in Russian in 1895 (Moscow), as *O muzykal'no-prekrasnom*, translated and with a foreword by the musicologist G. A. Laroche.

13. "Von dem Schematismus der reinen Verstandesbegriffe" (The schematism of the pure concepts of understanding), in the *Kritik der reinen Vernunft*, B 176/A 137–B 187/A 147. The content of Kant's argument in this section is of no importance to Bely here, since all he is saying is that *any* such theory is bound to be a "mere verbal exposition and nothing more."

14. *Cognition here becomes ignorance.* In Russian the resemblance of the words for cognition and ignorance reinforces Bely's point: "Poznanie okazyvaetsja neznaniem."

15. Aleksandr Afanas'evich Potebnya, *Iz zapisok po teorii slovesnosti* (Notes on the theory of literature) (Kharkov, 1905; rpt. The Hague: Mouton, 1970).

16. Potebnya, *Iz zapisok*, p. 406, from a section on "Xarakter mifičeskogo myšlenija" (The character of mythical thinking).

"THE EMBLEMATICS OF MEANING"

1. *Jan van Ruysbroeck* (1293–1381). Dutch mystic. The work that had such a profound influence on Maeterlinck was his *Die Chierheit der gheesteliker Brulocht* (*The Spiritual Espousals*, in English translation), which Maeterlinck translated into French from a German version in 1891, as *L'Ornement des noces spirituelles*.

2. The letters *K* and *P* in the formula stand for *kinetic* and *potential* energy, respectively.

3. Bely uses the terms *emblem* and *emblematic* in a rather vague sense through much of the essay. A more rigorous definition of these terms

(both as they are distinguished from "symbol" and as they are related to the title of the essay) will emerge later in section 10 and again in sections 15 and 16.

4. The reference is to Herbert Spencer's *System of Synthetic Philosophy* (*First Principles of Biology, Psychology, Sociology, Ethics*) (1862–1892), in which the author, among other things, attempts to derive the idea of evolution from the principle of conservation of energy. Bely, incidentally, follows a similar course in his "Principle of Form in Aesthetics" (in this volume), where he uses the same principle to elaborate a theory of aesthetic creation with results that could scarcely be called more successful than Spencer's.

5. Bely uses "theory of knowledge" (*teorija znanija*, or, on occasion, *teorija poznanija*) in the specific philosophical senses equivalent to "epistemology," that is, the field of philosophical study that investigates the nature of man's cognitive faculties.

6. The Russians have continued to use the word *gnoseology* (*gnoseologija*) where we use "epistemology." I have translated "epistemology" in all cases.

7. *Camille Flammarion* (1842–1925). French astronomer and popularizer of scientific learning. His best-known work was his *Astronomie populaire* (1880).

8. *Limiting methodical concept* (*predel'noe metodičeskoe ponjatie*). By *limiting concept* Bely means concepts that mark the limits of knowledge in a given field, either because they cannot be further broken down or because they cannot be further generalized. For instance, the thing-in-itself, which Bely mentions below, is a limiting concept (*Grenzbegriff*) in Kantian theory of knowledge, because, in Kant's view, even though we can never know the thing-in-itself, or noumenon, the idea of it nonetheless serves to mark for us the limit beyond which our knowledge (*Erkenntnis*) may not proceed. See *Kritik der reinen Vernunft*, B 310–311. *Methodical*, as Bely uses it, means "pertaining to method" not "characterized by method" and refers to the formal, conceptual apparatus of the various scientific and philosophical systems in question. A limiting methodical concept is thus one that stands as an absolute, that transcends, but also, by its nature and position, that limits the system of concepts serving as the structural basis for a field of inquiry.

9. Bely's point here is that broad "limiting" concepts from various fields of scientific and philosophical inquiry can never serve as the basis for a world view because (1) they are too restricted, being relevant only to the field from which they are borrowed, and (2) they lack permanence even in their own field, where the march of progress is forever modifying and replacing them.

10. In this section Bely introduces a pair of concepts that will recur frequently throughout the essay and about which a few words are in order here. *Znanie* and *poznanie* in Russian are both derived from a verbal root meaning "to know." *Znanie* is the more general of the two and is usually translated as "knowledge." Like the English "knowledge," it refers broadly

to the entire content of truths already acquired by, and contained passively in, the mind. It also refers to the act of *knowing* where "knowing" means "possessing truths" or "possessing contents of the mind." *Poznanie*, on the other hand, refers to the act or faculty of coming-to-know a thing and is in most cases best translated as "cognition." In general, *poznanie* cannot refer to a content of knowledge, since it is essentially an epistemological, not a psychological, concept. It is perhaps closer to the German *Erkenntnis* in the philosophical sense of that word than to any English word (the word *cognition* having been pressed into service in English in the nineteenth century largely for the purpose of rendering the German *Erkenntnis* in translations of Kant and his successors). For the most part I have adhered to the rule of translating *poznanie* as "cognition" and *znanie* as "knowledge," even in cases where these translations make for somewhat awkward reading (and where English philosophical language would probably favor another choice of words). In some cases I have changed from this course, as in certain instances where Bely uses *teorija poznanija* rather than *teorija znanija* for "theory of knowledge." In this case, either term is appropriate in Russian, but the phrase "theory of cognition" would be utterly misleading in English, since the field of philosophical inquiry referred to is traditionally called theory of knowledge ("knowledge" in this case being equivalent to *Erkenntnis*).

11. *Cognitive forms*. The context of this and the next section makes it clear that Bely uses this expression to mean the same thing as Kant's Pure Concepts of Understanding, or Categories.

12. *Georg Simmel* (1858–1918). German philosopher and sociologist, variously referred to as a *Kulturphilosoph* or a *Lebensphilosoph*. Author of *Die Probleme der Geschichtsphilosophie. Eine erkenntnistheoretische Studie* (Problems in the philosophy of history: An epistemological study) (Leipzig, 1892), translated into Russian as *Problemy filosofii istorii* (Moscow, 1898).

13. *Rickert*. See "Translator's Introduction, The Essays Themselves."

14. *Theory of knowledge*. One of the places where Bely uses the expression *teorija poznanija* (theory of cognition) instead of *teorija znanija* (theory of knowledge). Both expressions are used in Russian to denote the field of epistemology, or what is commonly called theory of knowledge, and it is not clear that the distinction between the two here is especially meaningful. Bely may have wished to specify a theory that concerns itself exclusively with cognition, as distinguished from theory of knowledge in its general sense, which may cover the contents of knowledge in addition to the processes by which they are acquired.

15. *Knowledge about knowledge*. See my commentary to this section in the "Translator's Introduction, The Essays Themselves."

16. *Formed content*. The use of the word *formed* (*oformlennyj*) is derived from Rickert who speaks of "formed reality" (*geformte Wirklichkeit*), or reality that has already been subjected to the ordering and systematizing activity of the cognitive *forms*. See Heinrich Rickert, *Der Gegenstand der Erkenntnis: Einführung in die Transzendentalphilosophie* (The Object of cogni-

tion: Introduction to transcendental philosophy), 2d ed., rev. and enl. (Tübingen and Leipzig: Mohr, 1904), p. 172.

17. *the aims of cognition as limiting the activity of reason.* Bely here reverts to the sense of cognition (*poznanie*) he employed towards the beginning of this section.

18. *Methodical investigation.* For the meaning of methodical, see note 8. A methodical investigation is simply an investigation into methods. One frequently finds this use of the term *methodical* in epistemological studies at the turn of the century, for example in Husserl's *Logische Untersuchungen* (Logical investigations) (1900–1901; rpt. Tübingen: Max Niemeyer Verlag, 1968).

19. Eduard von Hartmann (1842–1906). See note 2 to "Symbolism as a World View."

20. Causality is one of the twelve Kantian Categories, or Pure Concepts of Understanding. It is grouped under the Categories of Relation.

21. *Transcendent.* In Kant's usage, *transcendent* refers to what lies beyond the reach of ordinary, scientific knowledge (for instance, ideas like God, freedom, and immortality), whereas *transcendental* refers to the sort of knowledge whose object is a priori knowledge itself. The twelve Categories, or Pure Concepts of Understanding, which might be described as strictly *transcendent* because we cannot "know" them in the ordinary sense, are established through a Transcendental Deduction, or logical investigation of the mind's own a priori mode of knowledge. When Bely uses the expression "transcendental unity" it is not altogether clear what he means. In the *Critique of Pure Reason* Kant discusses the "transcendental unity of apperception," by which he means the synthetic unity of consciousness, the principle by which a single consciousness remains one and the same. But if this is what Bely means he certainly does not say so explicitly.

22. *The Ought. Dolženstvovanie* (or the substantive *dolžnoe*) is the Russian translation of *das Sollen* in Rickert's *Der Gegenstand der Erkenntnis.* Translators have hesitated between "the Ought" and "obligation" as an English equivalent for the German term. For instance, the standard English translation of Kant's *Critique of Pure Reason*, that of Norman Kemp Smith, translates it as "the Ought," whereas the standard translation of the *Critique of Judgment*, that of James Creed Meredith, translates it as "obligation." Since no English translation of *Der Gegenstand der Erkenntnis* exists, and since the very few English commentaries on Rickert favor "the Ought," I have followed this practice. For Bely's discussion of Rickert in this and succeeding sections, see the "Translator's Introduction, The Essays Themselves."

23. "Truth is value." See Rickert, *Der Gegenstand der Erkenntnis*, p. 117: "So wird das Wirkliche unter dem Gesichtspunkte der Erkenntnistheorie zu einer besonderen Art des Wahren, und die Wahrheit ist wiederum nichts anderes als ein Wert, d.h. der Begriff der Wirklichkeit stellt sich schliesslich als ein Wertbegriff dar." (In this manner the real, from the viewpoint of epistemology, comes to be a particular type of the true, and truth in turn is neither more nor less than a value, that is, the concept of reality ultimately

presents itself as a value concept.) A synthetic proposition is one in which the predicate introduces something not already contained in the idea of the subject. Thus if Rickert's statement is understood as a synthetic proposition, then truth has not already been defined in such a way as to include the idea of value.

24. Word order is more flexible in Russian than in English, and consequently a sentence like "Truth is value" is easily read with either noun as the subject.

25. *Limiting concept.* See note 8 above.

26. *Harald Høffding.* Danish philosopher and psychologist (1843–1931). Several of his works had been translated into Russian by the date of composition of "The Emblematics of Meaning," among them *Psixologičeskaja osnova logičeskix suždenij* (The psychological basis of logical judgments) (Moscow, 1908).

27. *Tree of Life.* In Jewish mysticism, the tree representing the cosmic force that will prevail in the Messianic era, by distinction with the Tree of Knowledge of Good and Evil, which represents the force prevailing in the world age. The two symbols appear in the *Raya Mehemna*, a section of the *Zohar* (the canonized collection of Kabalistic writings) giving a revolutionary interpretation of the commandments and prohibitions in the Torah.

28. *Adam Kadmon.* Hebrew for "primordial man." *Adam Kadmon* in Kabala is an anthropomorphic emanation of the Godhead, the closest approximation to divinity that is still accessible to man.

29. *Book of Dzyan.* Bely's source is *The Secret Doctrine*, by Helena Petrovna Blavatsky, founder of the theosophical movement. *The Secret Doctrine* was intended as a kind of synthesis of the mystical spirit underlying all the great world religions. The book's purpose, in the author's words, was "to show that Nature is not 'a fortuitous concurrence of atoms,' and to assign to man his rightful place in the scheme of the Universe." See *An Abridgement of The Secret Doctrine*, ed. Elizabeth Preston and Christmas Humphreys (London: Theosophical Publishing House, 1966), p. xx. The *Book of Dzyan* contains essential doctrines, in Sanskrit, of the esoteric teachings of Buddhism, the secret doctrine of the inner initiates among the disciples of Gautama the Buddha, and is therefore to be distinguished from Buddhism, the system of Gautama's *public* teachings. Blavatsky's *Secret Doctrine* is organized around stanzas from the *Book of Dzyan*, and the line Bely quotes here comes from verse 5 of the First Stanza: "Darkness alone filled the boundless all, for father, mother and son were once more one, and the son had not awakened yet for the new wheel and his pilgrimage thereon" (*Abridgement*, p. 22).

30. The quotation is from Mabel Collins, *Light on the Path* (London: George Redway, 1888), pp. 5–6. Collins was a member of the Theosophical Society founded by Blavatsky. She knew Blavatsky, but, in spite of the similarities between the style of her book and that of Blavatsky's own writings, wrote *Light on the Path* largely on her own.

31. *Paul Deussen* (1845–1919). German philosopher, author of many

works on Indian philosophy. His principal work was the *Allgemeine Geschichte der Philosophie, mit besonderer Berücksichtigung der Religionen* (General history of philosophy, with particular consideration of religions) (Leipzig, 1894–1917). Part 2 of the first volume of that work is devoted to the philosophy of the Upanishads. Deussen also edited a critical edition of the works of Schopenhauer, in fourteen volumes.

Vedas, Vedantas, Upanishads. The Vedas contain the prayers and hymns for the earliest stage in the development of Hinduism. Vedanta is one of six philosophic schools associated with Hinduism put forth by the ninth-century A.D. philosopher Shankara, who emphasized the illusoriness of the phenomenal world. The Upanishads are the philosophic texts of Hinduism.

32. *Maya.* In Indian philosophy, "the illusive appearance of the marshalling of events and actions on this earth," as defined by Blavatsky (*Abridgement*, p. 146).

33. *Anupadaka.* "Parentless," in Sanskrit. The term is used to designate, among other things, one who is merged with the Absolute or Universal Spirit. (See Blavatsky, *Abridgement*, p. 28.)

34. *Milesians.* The sixth-century B.C. philosophers, Thales, Anaximander, and Anaximenes, were all from Miletos, a Greek colony in Asia Minor.

35. *Anaximander's "Boundless."* In the philosophy of Anaximander (ca. 610 B.C.–ca. 546 B.C.), *to apeiron* (the limitless or boundless) is the first principle in the genesis of the universe, the origin of the cosmic process that governs all things and to which all things return.

36. *Pythagorean Number.* Bely probably has in mind the following passage from Aristotle's *Metaphysics*, the principal source for our knowledge of the Pythagoreans: "Evidently, then, these thinkers [the Pythagoreans] also consider that number is the principle both as matter for things and as forming their modifications and their permanent states . . ." (quoted and translated by G. S. Kirk and J. E. Raven, *The Presocratic Philosophers: A Critical History with a Selection of Texts* [Cambridge: Cambridge University Press, 1962], p. 237).

37. The imagery of steps and ascending planes in the following pages is taken largely from the work of Annie Besant, a disciple of Blavatsky's and author of *The Ancient Wisdom* (New York and London: Theosophical Publishing Society, 1897).

38. The Sanskrit terms in this paragraph (*Sthula Sharîra, Linga Sharîra, Prâna,* and *Manas*) are taken from Besant, *Ancient Wisdom*, pp. 177ff., and elsewhere. Having earlier defined *Prâna* as "a name for the universal life while it is taken in by an entity and is supporting its separated life" (p. 50n.), Besant gives the following chart of the "Principles in Body" (pp. 176–77):

Principles		*Life*	*Forms*
Atmâ. Spirit		Atmâ	
Buddhi. Spiritual Soul			Bliss-Body
Higher Manas	Human Soul		Causal Body
Lower Manas			Mental Body

Kâma. Animal Soul	Astral Body
Linga Sharîra	Etheric Double
Sthula Sharîra	Dense Body

39. *Buddhi*, in [Blavatsky's] *The Secret Doctrine*, is the vehicle of Atmâ, and Buddha is crowned with this knowledge. Bôdha is the internal understanding of this knowledge. Bôdhi is the name for the trance during which we attain higher understanding [Bely's note].

40. Bely develops these ideas in "The Principle of Form in Aesthetics," included in this volume.

41. *Image*. The Russian *Lik* is difficult both to interpret and, consequently, to translate. It has a number of related meanings, and it is not absolutely clear which of them Bely intends. He has further complicated matters by making an apparent distinction between *lik* (lowercase *l*) and *Lik* (capital *L*). A few of the basic meanings of *lik* are: face, countenance, image, person. It seems to represent an intersection between the meanings of *obraz* (image) and *lico* (face, person). *Lik* also has a number of theological senses, and these appear to be the ones Bely draws on. *Lik* is the term applied to the *image* of the face of a saint (or Christ, the Mother of God, and so forth) on an icon. It can mean simply "image" in the iconic sense of an earthly, concrete approximation of a divine quality. And finally, in the expression *lik spasitelja* (Person of the Savior), it refers to the Person of Christ, that is the corporeal, earthly component of Christ's being. What all these senses have in common is the notion of *kenosis*, or *humiliation*. For a discussion of these terms and their application to Bely's system, see my remarks on Section 16 in the "Translator's Introduction, The Essays Themselves." To distinguish *Lik* from *obraz* I have translated *Lik* throughout as "Image" (capital *I*), and *obraz* as "image" (lowercase *i*).

42. *Purposiveness without purpose*. The famous phrase from Kant's "Critique of Aesthetic Judgment" in *The Critique of Judgment*. Estimations of the beautiful, says Kant in section 15, are based on a "purposiveness without purpose" (*Zweckmässigkeit ohne Zweck*) or on purely formal purposiveness. This is distinguished from the objective purposiveness on which representations of the *good* are based, since in this case there is a determined end (*Zweck*) or purpose in relation to which an object is seen. See *Kritik der Urteilskraft*, B 44/A 43–44. Bely's point is that if we fail to have a transcendent norm in ethics, one that stands outside our purely logical system of beliefs as an absolute, then ethics will become aesthetics, where the norm, or end (*Zweck*), is purely formal, rather than being *determined* as it is in ethics.

43. *Transcendental realism*. In the "Fourth Paralogism of Pure Reason" (*Critique of Pure Reason*, "A" Edition), Kant distinguishes between transcendental idealism (which is the same thing as empirical realism) and transcendental realism (which is the same thing as empirical idealism). Transcendental idealism is defined as the theory according to which appearances are mere representations, not things-in-themselves, and time and space are merely the a priori form of sensible intuitions. Transcendental realism, on the other hand, regards time and space as existing in their own right

and sees appearances as things-in-themselves that exist independently of our sensibility. See *Kritik der reinen Vernunft*, A 369. Bely has mistakenly written "transcendent realism."

44. Rev. 8:13: "And I beheld, and heard an angel flying through the midst of heaven, saying with a loud voice, Woe, woe, woe, to the inhabiters of the earth, by reason of the other voices of the trumpet of the three angels, which are yet to sound!"

45. *I am THAT.* In the final stages of man's ascent to Nirvana, the Hamsa is one who is "beyond the Individual," who realizes "I am THAT." See Besant, *Ancient Wisdom*, p. 307 and 307n.

46. For the discussion in this section refer to figure 1.

47. *Form of Customs. Byt* in Russian, like Latin *mores*, or its French derivative *moeurs*, means "way of life," "manners," "things as they are customarily done." I have translated it simply as "customs."

48. *Imaginal.* See note 2 to "The Magic of Words."

49. A *transcendental schema*, in Kant's formulation, is the mediating factor between intuitions and the Pure Concepts of Understanding, that is, it is the factor that allows intuitions, which are purely sensible, to be subsumed under concepts, which are purely intellectual. (See "Von dem Schematismus der reinen Verstandesbegriffe" [The schematism of the pure concepts of understanding], in the *Kritik der reinen Vernunft*, B 176/A 137–B 187/A 147). The analogy with *emblems* for Bely is that emblems, in his system, are what mediate between a transcendent form of value on the one hand, and concrete, perceptible reality on the other, and that, furthermore, they do so *conceptually*.

50. Rickert does not actually make any statement in quite these terms, although he does apply the expression "categorical imperative" to his concept of the Ought. See *Der Gegenstand der Erkenntnis*, p. 231.

51. The sense of this paragraph is entirely lost in translation. To begin with, in the Russian text, with the exception of the first judgment in the series (unity), the number of words in each judgment corresponds to the numerical degree Bely assigns to it. Thus for duality Bely writes the two words: *Slovo—Plot'ju*. For triplicity, since the future tense of *to be* is expressed with a single word in Russian and since there are no articles, Bely's phrase contains three words: *Slovo budet Plot'ju*. For quadruplicity Bely uses the same sentence as for triplicity, but adds the word *Yes* (*Da*): "Yes, the Word will be Flesh" (*Da—Slovo budet Plot'ju*). Regarding this final judgment (quadruplicity), further clarification is in order. The Russian *da* can mean *yes* or can serve as an optative word like our word *let*. In the preceding paragraph Bely had used the phrase, "Let the Word be Flesh" (*Da budet Slovo—Plot'ju*). The judgment corresponding to quadruplicity, however, has been rearranged and repunctuated so as to return the word *da* to its affirmative sense: "Yes, the Word will be Flesh" (*Da—Slovo budet Plot'ju*). When Bely suddenly introduces the word *yes*, it is because, in Russian, he is being consistent throughout the entire section: from the unity judgment,

"Let it be" (*Da budet*), to his otherwise incomprehensible statement that the verb *to be* relates to "Yes" (*Da*), and to "Word—Flesh" (*Slovo—Plot'*).

52. Rickert defines the three "formal factors" in every act of cognition as follows: (1) the transcendent norm, which is "the form of the Ought or of the object"; (2) the category, which is "the form of the judgment-act, which apprehends the transcendent through recognition and allows the product of cognition to arise"; and (3) the transcendental form, which is "the form of the finished product of cognition and, consequently, at the same time, the form of reality." See *Der Gegenstand der Erkenntnis*, pp. 173–74.

53. Refer to figure 1.

54. *Filioque*. One of the principal points of contention between the Eastern Orthodox Church and Western Christianity is the question of the procession of the Holy Spirit. The Holy Spirit was defined originally as proceeding from God the Father. In the West the Creed was modified in 794, during the reign of Charlemagne, and the Holy Spirit was said to proceed from the Father and the Son (*filioque*). Eastern tradition regards this interpretation as blasphemous, since it implies an earthly component in the source of the Holy Spirit.

55. Musagetes is the epithet applied to Apollo in his guise as leader of the Muses. Apollo occasionally served as an image for Christ among early pagan Christians.

56. *Many-eyed Seraphim*. Bely has confused his angelic orders. The *Slovar' cerkovno-slavjanskogo i russkogo jazyka* (Church Slavonic and Russian dictionary) of the Imperial Academy of Sciences (St. Petersburg, 1867) lists the word *mnogoočityj* (many-eyed) and gives as an example the expression *mnogoočitye xeruvimy* (many-eyed cherubim). The reference is to the long passage in Ezekiel in which the cherubim are described. The passage in question is 10:12: "And their whole body, and their backs, and their hands, and their wings, and the wheels, were full of eyes round about, even the wheels that they four had."

57. Bely refers to the three pairs of triangles formed by grouping each of the triangles $a_1b_1c_1$, $a_2b_2c_2$, and $a_3b_3c_3$ with the central inverted triangle whose points are unlabeled.

58. Bely seems to mean that the triangles in each of the previously mentioned pairs may be shifted relative to each other so as to form a six-pointed star, thus:

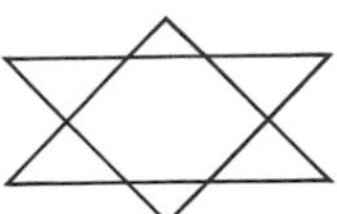

59. *Rudolph Christoph Eucken* (1846–1926). German idealist philosopher, follower of Fichte. Bely, in a footnote, mentions two of Eucken's works: *Grundlinien einer neuen Lebensanschauung* (Bases for a new outlook on life) (1907) and *Der Wahrheitsgehalt der Religion* (The truth content of religion) (1901).

60. The reference is to *Hermann Cohen* (1842–1918), one of the better-known neo-Kantian philosophers of the Marburg school, also teacher of Ernst Cassirer. Bely mentions Cohen's *Kants Theorie der Erfahrung* (Kant's theory of experience) (1871), which he calls simply *Theorie der Erfahrung*, in his novel *Petersburg*, where it is among the bedside books of the hero, a young Kantian idealist-turned-anarchist. Cohen was also known for his *Die Logik der Erkenntnis* (The logic of cognition) (1902) and *Kants Begründung der Ethik* (Kant's foundation for ethics) (1877). *Paul Natorp* (1854–1924) was another member of the Marburg group. The work Bely has in mind, in which Natorp reinterprets Plato by the canons of Marburg neo-Kantianism, is *Platos Ideenlehre: Eine Einführung in den Idealismus* (Plato's theory of ideas: An introduction to idealism) (1903).

61. The quoted passages are from Leibniz's *Monadology*. Bely's selections occur at the very opening of the work. I have followed the English translation of Robert Latta, *Leibniz: The Monadology and other Philosophical Writings* (London: Oxford University Press, 1951), pp. 217ff. Emphasis is in the original. At least two Russian editions of Leibniz's works existed at the time Bely wrote this: *Izbrannye filosofskie sočinenija*, translated by members of the Psixologičeskoe Obščestvo (Psychological Society) and published under the general editorship of V. P. Preobraženskij (Moscow, 1890); and the *Bol'šaja soveckaja enciklopedija* mentions a collection under the same title but with the date 1908. It gives no further details, however.

62. The terminology in this paragraph is taken directly from the Proem to volume 1 of Blavatsky's *Secret Doctrine*, entitled "Cosmogenesis." In those introductory pages, Blavatsky defines the central terms in the system she describes. *Parabrahman*, or *Parabrahm*, is the "collective aggregate of Kosmos in its infinity and eternity, the 'THAT' and 'THIS' to which distributive aggregates cannot be applied" (Blavatsky, *Secret Doctrine*, pp. 6–7). And further, on the notion of "THIS" and "THAT," Bely quotes almost directly: "In the beginning THIS was the Self, one only" (p. 7). Vidya is defined in Blavatsky's introduction as "knowledge, . . . the faculty of cognizing" (p. xxv). The latter part of the present paragraph, concerning the various Logoi, is particularly important since it relates to the process by which, according to the *Secret Doctrine*, the spiritual becomes manifest. Bely appears to have taken his terms from the following summary given by Blavatsky (*An Abridgement of The Secret Doctrine*, ed. Elizabeth Preston and Christmas Humphreys [London: Theosophical Publishing House, 1966], p. 12):

> (1) THE ABSOLUTE; the *Parabrahm* of the Vedantins or the one Reality, SAT, which is, as Hegel says, both Absolute Being and Non-Being. (2) The first manifestation, the impersonal, and, in philosophy, *unmanifested* Logos, the precursor of the "manifested." This is the "First Cause," the "Unconscious" of European Pantheists. (3) Spirit-matter, LIFE; the "Spirit of the Universe," the Purusha and

Prakriti, or the *second* Logos. (4) Cosmic Ideation, MAHAT or Intelligence, the Universal World-Soul; the Cosmic Noumenon of Matter, the basis of the intelligent operations in and of nature, also called MAHA-BUDDHI.

63. The mystical terms in this paragraph come from stanza 1, verse 9 of *The Secret Doctrine*: "But where was the Dangma when the Alaya of the Universe (*Soul as the basis of all, Anima Mundi*) was in Paramartha (*Absolute Being and Consciousness which are Absolute Non-Being and Unconsciousness*) and the great wheel was Anupadaka?" In the commentary that follows, Blavatsky defines the terms appearing in verse 9 as well as others that Bely uses in this passage. *Yoga* is defined as "mystic meditation," *Alaya* is defined in the parenthetical note in verse 9 quoted above, *Paranishpanna* is "absolute perfection," and *Anupadaka* means "parentless," "without progenitors" (Blavatsky, *Secret Doctrine*, pp. 26–27).

64. For the sake of clarity I will note the distinction by capitalizing the word in one case and using a lowercase letter in the other [Bely's note].

65. See the Translator's Introduction.

66. *Tao of Lao-tze*. Lao-tze was the Chinese philosopher (born ca. 600 B.C.) who founded Taoism. Tao, literally "the way," refers to an absolute, cosmic order.

67. The distinction between methodological and constitutive forms (patterned roughly on Kant's distinction between the regulative and constitutive uses of reason) is from Rickert. Methodological forms, according to Rickert, are those that form scientific concepts and that are responsible for organizing and interpreting the material of ordinary, empirical knowledge. Constitutive forms, on the other hand, are those to which "the forms of the Ought, seen as constitutive norms with transcendent value, correspond" (*Der Gegenstand der Erkenntnis*, p. 211). They are thus those that, through the agency of the ethical moment in cognition, normatively *constitute* knowledge.

68. Rickert, *Der Gegenstand der Erkenntnis*, p. 221: "Die Frage nach dem Wesen des Inhaltes der Wirklichkeit ist keine Frage, denn die Wirklichkeit hat überhaupt nicht *einen* Inhalt."

69. Bely continues the same passage he cited above (see note 68): "Wer ihren [der Wirklichkeit] Inhalt kennen lernen will, wie er, abgesehen von dem Inhalt der Begriffe der Einzelwissenschaften, also abgesehen von den methodologischen Formen, sich darstellt, der muss versuchen, möglichst viel davon zu *erleben*" (Rickert, *Der Gegenstand der Erkenntnis*, p. 221; emphasis in the original).

70. Gen. 3:5, where the serpent addresses Eve. The entire verse runs: "For God doth know that in the day ye eat thereof, then your eyes shall be opened; and ye shall be as gods, knowing good and evil."

71. Bely is paraphrasing John 17:11, from Christ's intercessory prayer.

72. Kant, *Grundlegung zur Metaphysik der Sitten*, BA 125: "*wie reine Ver-*

nunft praktisch sein könne, das zu erklären, dazu ist alle menschliche Vernunft gänzlich unvermögend, und alle Mühe und Arbeit, hievon Erklärung zu suchen, ist verloren."

73. *Georg Simmel* (1858–1918). German philosopher and sociologist. Much of his early work focused on moral philosophy, particularly on the heritage of Kant in this area. See his *Einleitung in die Moralphilosophie* (Introduction to moral philosophy) (1892–1893) and his *Kant: Sechzehn Vorlesungen* (Kant: Sixteen lectures) (1903), much of which is given over to a discussion of the will in Kant's ethical philosophy.

74. The reference is to Kant's attempt in *The Critique of Pure Reason* to reconcile the notions of causality in nature and free will in the individual. It is the subject of the next-to-last major heading of the "Antinomy of Pure Reason," entitled, "Solution of the Cosmological Idea of Totality in the Derivation of Cosmical Events from their Causes." The one subsection under this heading is entitled, "Possibility of Causality through Freedom, in Harmony with the Universal Law of Natural Necessity" (Kemp Smith translation).

75. See *Grundlegung zur Metaphysik der Sitten*, BA 74. For Kant, *autonomy* implies a will not based on self-interest, whereas *heteronomy* implies a will that *is* subject to the demands of self-interest.

76. *Cosmos*. *Kosmos* in Greek means "order" and is thus the opposite of *chaos*.

77. In this section and elsewhere I have capitalized *Value* (which translates *cennost'* and the neuter substantive *cennoe*) in those cases where Bely uses it in the absolute sense as the First Principle of his system of emblematics, the term appearing at the top of the triangle in figure 1. In other cases, for instance where Bely refers to Rickert's concept of value, or where he talks about the emblem of value of a particular field, I have written *value*. Bely himself does not make this typographical distinction.

78. *Freiburg school*, or Baden school of neo-Kantianism: its two chief representatives were Wilhelm Windelband and Heinrich Rickert.

79. Bely is essentially asking the same question here as he asks two paragraphs above, namely, which of the two terms of the judgment is to be taken as the subject (since the flexibility of Russian word order permits either reading). The only difference is that here he is specifically concerned with the implications of reading the statement as an analytic judgment, as one, that is, where the predicate is already contained in the idea of the subject.

80. *Theodor Lipps* (1851–1914). German philosopher and psychologist who endorsed a theory of psychophysical parallelism and viewed psychology as the basis of all philosophical investigation. *Carl Stumpf* (1848–1936). A founder of phenomenology, but in a more psychologistic guise than the science developed by Husserl. Stumpf used "phenomenology" in a more literal sense than that in which his successors were to use it. For Stumpf the term designates an empirical science whose object of study is phenomena, which he viewed as the primary data of all experience.

81. *Johann Friedrich Herbart* (1776–1841). German idealist philosopher and psychologist, author of *Lehrbuch zur Psychologie* (Textbook of psychology) (1816) and *Psychologie als Wissenschaft, neu gegründet auf Erfahrung, Metaphysik und Mathematik* (Psychology as a science, with a new basis in experience, metaphysics, and mathematics) (1824–1825). *Friedrich Eduard Beneke* (1798–1854). German idealist philosopher, a proponent of psychology as a science to provide a foundation for philosophy. *Gustav Theodor Fechner* (1801–1887). German physicist, psychologist, and philosopher, known for research into psychophysical parallelism. Author of *Elemente der Psychophysik* (Elements of psychophysics) (1860). *Alexander Bain* (1818–1903). Scottish philosopher and psychologist, also a proponent of the study of the mind as a psychophysical unity. Founder of the periodical *Mind* (1876). *Wilhelm Wundt* (1832–1920). German philosopher and psychologist, one of the founders of experimental psychology.

82. The quotation is from Theodor Lipps's *Leitfaden der Psychologie* (Introduction to psychology) (Leipzig: Engelmann, 1903), p. 1. The original German reads: "'Bewusstseinsinhalte' lassen sich nicht definieren; nur andere Ausdrücke können dafür gesetzt werden: Sie sind das unmittelbar Vorgefundene oder Erlebte, das mir unmittelbar Gegenwärtige oder Vorschwebende; die 'Bilder', die ich habe."

83. This discussion is drawn from chapter 14 of *Leitfaden der Psychologie*, in which Lipps expounds the doctrine most closely associated with his name: that of *Einfühlung*. The three types of cognition Bely lists and a definition of *Einfühlung* are given in the opening paragraphs of that chapter:

> Es gibt drei Erkenntnisgebiete. Ich weiss von den Dingen, von mir selbst, und von anderen Individuen. Jene erste Erkenntnis hat zur Quelle die sinnliche Wahrnehmung. Die zweite die innere Wahrnehmung, d.h. das rückschauende Erfassen des Ich mit seinen Qualitäten, den Gefühlen, und seinen Beziehungen auf Inhalte und Gegenstände. Die Quelle der dritten Erkenntnisart endlich ist die Einfühlung. Zugleich hat diese freilich eine Bedeutung weit über die Erkenntnis hinaus.
>
> Zwei Arten, wie das unmittelbar erlebte Ich, das Gefühls-Ich, auf Gegenstände 'bezogen' sein kann, sind strengstens zu unterscheiden. . . . Die zweite Möglichkeit ist diese: Ich fühle mich strebend, tätig, mich bemühend, Widerstand leistend, in einer Sache; fühle mich beglückt in der Gebärde des Glückes usw., kurz, fühle eine Bestimmtheit meiner unmittelbar als Bestimmtheit des Gegenstandes oder als dem Gegenstand zugehörig. Dies letztere ist "Einfühlung." (*Leitfaden der Psychologie*, p. 187)

> [There are three areas of cognition. I know: things, myself, and other individuals. The first type of cognition has sense perception as its source; the second, inner perception, that is, the retrospective apprehension of the "I" with all of its qualities, its feelings, and its relations to contents and objects. The source of the third type of cogni-

tion is *Einfühlung*. But *Einfühlung* at the same time has a significance that goes far beyond mere cognition.

There are two ways in which the immediately experienced "I," the "I" of feeling, may be "related" to objects, and they must be sharply distinguished. . . . The second possibility is this: I feel myself as striving, active, exerting myself, offering resistance in a certain matter; I feel happy in the very gesture of happiness etc., in short, I feel a determination of myself as immediately being the determination of the object [in question], or as belonging to the object. This is *Einfühlung*.]

84. In this paragraph, "obligatory" is used to translate *dolžnyj*, an adjective that in the present usage corresponds to the noun *dolženstvovanie* (the Ought). Bely frequently uses the substantive *dolžnoe* in a sense equivalent to that of *dolženstvovanie*, and in those cases I have simply translated it as "the Ought." Because of the context, *dolženstvovanie*, which I have rendered elsewhere as "the Ought," is rendered here as "obligatory character."

85. *Sergey Nikolaevich Trubetskoy* (1862–1905). Russian religious philosopher, follower of Vladimir Solov'ev. Trubetskoy described his own philosophy as "concrete idealism." He also wrote a number of works on the history of philosophy, among them his *Učenie o logose v ego istorii* (The doctrine of the logos in history) (Moscow, 1900).

86. The passage is from an account of Pythagorean atomism by Sextus "Empiricus," a skeptic philosopher of the second century A.D. It is quoted in Kirk and Raven, *Presocratic Philosophers*, p. 255. I have used their translation in Bely's text. The entire passage runs: "Some say that the solid body is constructed from a single point; this point, by fluxion, creates the line, the line, by fluxion, makes the plane, and it in turn, by moving upwards or downwards, generates the three-dimensional body."

87. This passage describes the transition in Pythagorean thought from primal unity (the point) to duality (two points defining a line and, consequently, spatial extension). The closest passage I find to the one Bely quotes is the following from Alexander of Aphrodisias: "For since the dyad is the first extension (for the unit first extended into the dyad, so to the triad and the numbers in succession), if we define the line, the Pythagoreans say, we should not call it quantity extended in one dimension, but the line is the first extension" (cited in Kirk and Raven, *Presocratic Philosophers*, p. 252).

88. *Nikolay Ivanovich Novosadsky* (1859–1941). Classical philologist specializing in epigraphy. He taught at the University of Warsaw from 1888–1906, and at the University of Moscow beginning in 1909. The work Bely has in mind is undoubtedly Novosadsky's doctoral dissertation, *Orfičeskie gimny* (The Orphic hymns) (Warsaw, 1900).

89. *Experience*. The Russian *opyt* means both "experience" and "experiment."

90. Cf. Bely's "The Magic of Words."

91. Bely refers to two Kantian types of unity treated in the *Critique of*

Pure Reason: the transcendental (or synthetic) unity of apperception (self-consciousness), and unity as one of the twelve Categories, or Pure Concepts of Understanding (unity, plurality, and totality being the three Categories under the subdivision "Quantity"). The transcendental unity of apperception is discussed in the "Deduction of the Pure Concepts of Understanding," both versions. For the table of Categories, see *Kritik der reinen Vernunft*, B 106/A 80.

92. The reader is reminded that Russian syntax allows the subject and predicate to occur in either order in a sentence like this.

93. *Purposiveness without purpose*. See note 42. The Russian (*celesoobraznost'*), like the German (*Zweckmässigkeit*), contains the word *end* (*cel'*), which Bely has been using in this same paragraph.

94. Bely lists here five of the six traditional Hindu systems of philosophy. The sixth is Nyaya.

95. *The Crisis in Western Philosophy. Against the Positivists* (*Krizis zapadnoj filosofii. Protiv pozitivistov*) was Solov'ev's doctoral thesis in philosophy at Moscow University (1874).

96. *Deussen*. See note 31.

97. Bely is mistaken. *Theory* comes from the Greek root *theā*, which means "vision," "sight." It is unrelated to *theos*, "god." The [*or*] portion of the word does not come from the verb *to see* but is simply part of a suffix.

98. *Saint Seraphim of Sarov* was the religious name of Prokhor Isidorivich Moshnin (1759–1833), a Russian monk widely considered an exemplar of the virtues of Russian Orthodoxy. He is credited with being the first monk to acquaint laymen with monastic traditions. George P. Fedotov includes a section on him in his *Treasury of Russian Spirituality* (New York, 1948; rpt. Belmont, Mass.: Nordland, 1975), calling him perhaps the greatest of the Russian saints and identifying him as the first of the line of *startsy*, or elders, of the type that Dostoevsky depicts in Father Zosima. *Saint Isaac the Syrian* was a seventh-century mystical writer. *Shankaracharya* was a ninth-century Indian religious philosopher who opposed the unreality of the phenomenal world to the Brahman, or world soul, which alone he saw as real.

99. This is a humorous paraphrase of a famous line from Tyutchev's poem, "Silentium!" Bely cites the line in "The Magic of Words." It reads: "A thought, once spoken, is a lie" (*Mysl' izrečennaja est' lož'*).

"THE ART OF THE FUTURE"

1. *Fine linen*. Russian *visson*, from Greek *byssos*: a word that appears recurrently in the Bible, especially in Exodus (25:4, 26:1, 28:5, 28:6, and elsewhere). The English translators in each case used the two-word expression "fine linen" to render the corresponding Hebrew word in the Old Testament and the word *byssos* in the New Testament. It is also the material from which the Order of Saint Vladimir, a decoration worn by the Russian

tsars over their right shoulder, was made. In a poem that Bely mentions and quotes in "Lyric Poetry and Experiment," the poet Derzhavin (1743–1816) describes Catherine the Great as she appears in a well-known portrait and mentions her decoration "Of black-fiery fine linen [*visson*], / Like a rainbow . . ." The poem is entitled "Videnie murzy" (Vision of a Tatar prince).

"THE PRINCIPLE OF FORM IN AESTHETICS"

1. Bely's ranking of the fine arts is borrowed from Schopenhauer. Essentialy the same scheme appears in Book 3 of *The World as Will and Representation.*

2. Given the concentration of terms from mathematics and physics in this passage, it is reasonable to infer that Bely has in mind the mathematical or physical notion of potential as the value of a function (or charge, in physics) relative to a hypothetically given reference point. An electric charge, for example, is measured according to the *potential* energy it has relative to a more or less distant point of reference (such as the earth, or ground). All of which is simply Bely's way of saying that the elements in question (space, time) are not actually in evidence but are latent.

3. $\triangleq$ designates equivalence [Bely's note].

4. The argument is difficult to follow in the form in which Bely puts it. Part of the problem is that, in the mathematical equations toward the end of the section, Bely has arbitrarily chosen the value 8 for the intensity of the poetic artwork but has not said so. His point then would be that, if 8 is the intensity of the poem, $8/4$ would be the intensity of the sculpture, given the same amount of "material" to begin with. For an equal amount of material, $8/4$ is the "equivalent" in sculpure to 8 in poetry, the equivalence factor being, in this case, 4.

So much is clear. The problem now remains to explain the final equation. Since Bely's notation is confusing, and since he has characteristically omitted a number of important steps in his argument, leaving them to the reader to infer, I propose to rewrite the entire argument using a different notation.

The law of conservation that Bely proposes here involves the two notions of "internal" and "external" effort. External effort, as Bely suggests, is the same thing as "kinetic" energy. The terms of the present argument make it clear that *internal* energy is directly proportional to intensity. Let us use the symbol E for external effort and the symbol I for internal effort. The subscripts p and s will designate, respectively, poet and sculptor. Thus E_p will stand for the external effort expended by the poet. By the law of conservation, the product of E and I will always be equal to a constant. Thus:

$$E \cdot I = K.$$

The constant K, as it becomes clear from Bely's argument, is the "material" of creation.

Now, to begin with, Bely says that we are to assume an equal amount of material for the poet and the sculptor. The sculptor, he says, always expends more external effort than the poet. As he has explained earlier, this is in the nature of the art form. Let us say, for the sake of argument, that the amount by which the sculptor's external effort is greater than that of the poet is 4. In this case the intensity of the poet's creation will be four times that of the sculptor. Why? If we are given equal amounts of material, K, then:

$$E_p I_p = K$$

and

$$E_s I_s = K, \text{ or } E_p I_p = E_s I_s.$$

But, as we have said, E_s is four times the value of E_p:

$$E_s = 4E_p.$$

If we now substitute $4E_p$ for E_s in the equation above, we get:

$$E_p I_p = 4E_p I_s.$$

Dividing both sides by E_p, we get:

$$I_p = 4I_s,$$

which, in plain English, means that the internal effort of the poet is four times that of the sculptor. But, since internal effort is directly proportional to intensity of effect, we can also say that the intensity of the poet's creation is four times that of the sculptor's.

The point of Bely's argument is that, even if sculpture inherently presents a higher proportion of external to internal effort than poetry and consequently has a lower intensity of effect, it is still possible to have a sculpture with greater intensity than a poem, provided the "material" in the former is sufficiently larger than that in the latter to offset the proportional factor between the two. For the present case, as we have said, that factor is 4. Let the sculptor's material then be sixteen times that of the poet, says Bely, and we will obtain a net intensity for the sculpture that is precisely four times that of the poem. We have, then, as before:

$$E_p I_p = K.$$

Now, however, the level of material has been raised for E_s and I_s:

$$E_s I_s = 16K, \text{ or } K = \frac{E_s I_s}{16}.$$

Thus:

$$E_p I_p = K = \frac{E_s I_s}{16}.$$

The same proportions hold for E_p and E_s as before, namely:

$$E_s = 4E_p.$$

Substituting $4E_p$ for E_s, we obtain:

$$E_pI_p = \frac{4E_pI_s}{16}, \text{ or } E_pI_p = \frac{E_pI_s}{4}.$$

Dividing both sides by E_p, we get:

$$\mathrm{I_p} = \frac{I_s}{4}, \text{ or: } I_s = 4I_p,$$

which is to say that the internal effort of the sculptor is four times that of the poet. Consequently (since intensity is proportional to internal effort), the intensity of the sculpture in this example is four times that of the poem. In Bely's final equation, the left side is four times the value of the right side.

5. By this Bely means, I think, that our tendency is always to think of a sculpture as having greater intensity than a poem, simply because of its size and its striking physical qualities. But in truth, he implies, this is not so, because, by the law of conservation of artistic effort, which holds that intensity is directly proportional to internal effort but inversely proportional to external effort, and, second, by the inherent qualities of the art forms, namely that sculpture always requires more external effort for a given amount of "material," sculpture always has *less* intensity than poetry, *given equal amounts of "material."*

6. *Robert Boyle*, English physicist (1627–1691), and *Edme Mariotte*, French physicist (1620–1684) who, independently of each other, discovered the law expressing the relation between the pressure and volume of gases. The law holds that the two are inversely proportional or that, given a constant temperature, their product is equal to a constant: pv = Constant. Boyle seems to have been the first to discover the law.

7. Section 9 seems to be Bely's treatment of the aesthetic problem from the perspective of the perceiver, where section 7 treated it from the perspective of the object. Quantity of mood aroused would then be a function of intensity of the object and is thus different from the quantity he speaks of in section 7. There Bely seems to oppose quantity to intensity of creative effort. This use of terms seems to me misguided. The distinction is between two types of creative effort, internal and external, which in themselves can differ *only* in quantity. Intensity, on the other hand, is something belonging to the object and is a function of effort, that is, it is directly proportional to internal effort and inversely proportional to external effort, given equal amounts of material. Quantity of mood, then, is directly proportional to intensity of the object, and tension of mood would seem to be directly proportional to external effort. In other words, tension of mood is the factor that conflicts with simple quantitative intensity. Bely suggests this correspondence in the second paragraph of this section, where he substitutes the expressions power (*moščnost'*) and intensity (*plotnost'*) for quantity.

8. Bely is writing at a time when the wave theory of light—which, at the end of the nineteenth century, had seemed to be established beyond a doubt as fully adequate for the explanation of all observed luminous phenomena—was being challenged by new findings whose explanation required a particle or photon theory. The newly observed phenomena occurred in the interaction of matter with light of high frequencies. Among the scientists reporting these new findings were Philipp Lenard in 1899, Max Planck in 1900, and Einstein in 1905.

9. Strictly speaking, there is no physical distinction between vapor and gas, and it is incorrect to refer to the vaporous state of matter as "transitional . . . between liquid and gas." The term *vapor* is applied either to gases that become liquefied at experimentally attainable temperatures or to those that normally exist in a liquid or solid state. Thus, for example, steam qualifies as a vapor, while hydrogen does not. If Bely makes of vapor a distinct state of matter between liquid and gas, it is undoubtedly because the word *vapor* is implicitly defined with reference to the liquid and solid states, whereas the word *gas* need not be.

10. Bely means that even though there is no chemical difference between the three states of a given substance (ice, water, and steam, for instance, are all forms of the same substance, H_2O), that substance can exist only in one of these three states.

11. Bely writes, "Charles and Mariotte," but this is a mistake, since the law he refers to is clearly the one discovered by J. A. C. Charles, a French mathematician and physicist (1746–1823), and Joseph Louis Gay-Lussac, French chemist and physicist (1778–1850). The law holds that, in a gas kept at constant volume, for any increase in temperature the pressure increases at a rate that is the same for all gases.

12. In the preceding sections Bely has proposed a mathematical proportion to express the relation first between internal and external effort in the aesthetic object, and second between quantity and tension of mood aroused in the perceiver. In the first case he treated the problem of varying both of these quantities by varying the "constant" to which their product is equal (the "material" of artistic creation). He now returns to this problem, using the laws of thermodynamics once again as his model. In the simplest of the gas laws, namely that expressing the inverse proportion between pressure and volume (pv = Constant), the assumption is that one additional factor remains constant, namely temperature. If the temperature is raised, the value of the entire equation is also raised, and it is possible for either p or v to increase while the other remains steady, or for both to increase. The analogous case in Bely's treatment of the aesthetic situation from the perspective of the object was that of raising the amount of material. This is how he was able to raise the internal effort (or, what is the same thing, the intensity) in a sculpture while the external effort remained steady. In section 11 he discusses the same situation from the perceiver's perspective. What happens to the quantity (the intensity) of the mood aroused, he now asks, when the overall effect (t) of the aesthetic experience is raised? The specific relation he seeks in this section is one that

expresses quantity (intensity) of mood (Q) as a function of t for each successive quantum rise in t. The equations he uses in this section are puzzling because, as usual, he has neglected to explain his notation and to supply the necessary steps to complete his mathematical argument. What is important, though, is his conclusion, for he pretends to have discovered a relation between intensity of aesthetic mood and overall aesthetic effect analogous to the thermodynamic relation between pressure and temperature. The relation is, simply put, one of direct proportion, a universal constant being present that determines the rate at which pressure (here, intensity of aesthetic mood) rises with respect to temperature (here, overall aesthetic effect). This constant is Bely's "coefficient of increase for Q," namely α. Bely is not audacious enough to suggest a numerical value for α, but he implies nonetheless that such a value is theoretically discoverable by the science of "exact aesthetics."

13. *Fechner*. See note 81 to "The Emblematics of Meaning."

"LYRIC POETRY AND EXPERIMENT"

1. *Visual angle*: the angle formed by drawing a line from the two extreme points of an object to the eye of the observer.

2. "*The Prophet*:" "Prorok" (1826).

3. *Gustav Fechner*. See note 81 to "The Emblematics of Meaning." *Hermann Ludwig Ferdinand von Helmholtz* (1821–1894). German scientist and philosopher, best known for his work in elaborating the principle of conservation of energy and in physiological optics. *Wilhelm Ostwald* (1853–1932). German chemist, known for his work on catalysis and for studies in the history and philosophy of science.

4. The reference here is to Heinrich Rickert's *Die Grenzen der naturwissenschaftlichen Begriffsbildung* (The limits of concept formation in the natural sciences) (Tübingen: Mohr, 1902), chapter 1, part 6, "Beschreibung und Erklärung" (Description and explanation), where Rickert discusses the distinction between descriptive and explanatory methods in the exact sciences.

5. Nikolay Alekseevich Nekrasov, *Smert' krest'janina* (Death of a peasant), the first part of *Moroz, krasnyj nos* (Red-nose frost) (1863). Bely reproduces section 8 of *Smert' krest'janina*. My translation.

A few words of explanation are in order here concerning the transliterated Russian texts. All accent marks in the Russian texts have been added to indicate which syllable in a word is stressed. In almost all cases the stressed syllable is marked with an acute accent (´) over the vowel. A diaeresis (¨) over the letter *e* indicates that the *e* is pronounced [o] or [jo]. But since it is pronounced thus only when it is accented, the diaeresis is customarily used without an additional accent mark in linguistic notation.

Occasionally a stressed syllable will fall on a metric position that should be unstressed. In such cases I have marked the natural stress but enclosed the diacritical mark in parentheses. For example:

Vsё ukrašálo kabinét.

Here the word *vsë*, which necessarily takes an accent because of the [jo] sound, falls on the first (unaccented) syllable of an iambic foot. Or:

Já, lávry oglasjá tvoí

This line begins with a strong accent on an unaccented position, since *já* (I) is always accented and since it is set off by a comma.

The grave accent (`) over an *e* is not strictly a stress mark, but a mark used in the scholarly transliteration system to distinguish between two similar Cyrillic letters. However, when this letter takes the stress, I have not used any additional marks, since this would be unsightly and confusing. Thus in the following verse from Fet

No ètix zvúkov-to i nét,

the *è* is clearly stressed.

Finally, a note about counting syllables. This is a simple matter, since a syllable in a Russian word contains one, and only one, vowel. The case that might present confusion is the case of two consecutive vowels. Here the reader must remember to read two syllables. Thus the following verse

Tý pésen Grúzii pečál'noj

would be divided like this:

Tý-pé-sen-Grú-zi-i-pe-čál'-noj.

The two *i*'s in *Gruzii* constitute two separate syllables. Similarly, the line

V zavóde kónskom Ilií

is divided thus:

V za-vó-de-kón-skom-I-li-í.

The name *Ilii* contains a total of three syllables.

6. *Nikolay Platonovich Ogarev* (1813–1877). Russian revolutionary poet and publicist. *Ivan Savvich Nikitin* (1824–1861). Russian realist poet.

7. *Vasily the Great* and *John Chrysostom*. Fourth-century saints important in the history of the Eastern Orthodox Church.

8. From section 3 of *Smert' krest'janina*. The poet addresses the Russian peasant woman (that is, as a type). Bely has misquoted the third line of this excerpt, writing *nedug* (illness) instead of *ispug* (fright). I have corrected his error.

9. "Teni sizye smesilis', / Cvet poblëknul, zvuk usnul—" First two lines of an untitled poem (1836) by Tyutchev. Bely misquotes the second line, writing *svet* (light) for *cvet* (flower, color).

10. From section 3 of *Smert' krest'janina*. Bely has misquoted the first line, substituting *bor'by* (struggle) for *sud'by* (fate).

11. Bely for some reason has diagrammed only sixteen of the twenty verses in the extract. It should be pointed out for the nonreader of Russian that unaccented *e* and *o* in Russian are pronounced, respectively, [i] and [a]. Bely has diagrammed his vowels accordingly.

12. *Fedor Evgen'evich Korsh* (1843–1915). Russian philologist, scholar in classical and East Slavic literatures, authority on Pushkin, and known for the application of a comparative-historical method in his scholarship.

13. *Sergey Ivanovich Taneev* (1856–1915). Russian composer, pianist, musicologist.

14. *Byliny* (pl.). A type of epic folksong that developed in Russia between the eleventh and sixteenth centuries.

15. From Tyutchev's untitled poem, "Nočnoe nebo tak ugrjumo" (The night sky so gloomy) (1865).

16. A *paeon* is a metric foot containing four syllables of which three are short (or unaccented) and one is long (or accented). A first paeon is one whose accent falls on the first syllable; a second paeon, one whose accent falls on the second syllable; and so forth. Bely consistently spells the word "paean," explaining in a footnote that he did this in order to emphasize the "genetic connection" of this type of foot to the *paean*, which is a classical hymn of thanksgiving to Apollo. It is difficult to resist the suspicion that Bely simply misspelled the word and added the footnote to mask his error. I have restored the proper spelling.

17. Bely's text includes an example at this point that neither makes sense nor contributes to his argument. I have taken the liberty of omitting it.

18. Note that Bely has rearranged the words in the second verse so that they will fit an amphibrachic pattern.

19. The first two lines of Tyutchev's "Poslednjaja ljubov'" (Last love). Bely misquotes the second line, putting *sil'nej* (more strongly) instead of *nežnej* (more tenderly). I have corrected his text. It should also be noted that, to judge by the rhythmic notation beneath the second verse, he reads a secondary accent on the first syllable of *suevérnej*. His second way of notating the verse (immediately below) shows this syllable as unaccented.

20. Bely writes "metrico-tonic," but the term customarily used in English to describe this characteristic of Russian verse is syllabo-tonic. For an explanation of the term, see the section on this essay in the Translator's Introduction, "The Essays Themselves."

21. We are adhering to S. I. Taneev's explanation here [Bely's note].

22. The first line of Pushkin's *Eugene Onegin*.

23. The second line of the same work.

24. The Fet poem quoted here is entitled "I. F. Ofrosimovu, na jubilej konskogo ego zavoda v sele Berezovce" (To I. F. Ofrosimov, on the occasion of the anniversary of his stud farm at Berezovets) (1888). Bely misquotes the last line. I have corrected his text.

25. The reader will observe that Bely, for some reason, has not used the same list in this chart as in tables 2 and 3. Sologub, Blok, Bryusov, and Gorodetsky appear here but not in the tables, and Ozerov appears in the tables but not here.

26. Bely mistakenly inverts the order of his rhythmic figures in this sentence. I have corrected his text.

27. I have dispensed with translations in the following section. The reader may apply Bely's principles to the Russian examples in order to understand the sense of the geometric figures.

28. *Fiery Circle* (*Plamennyj krug*). A collection of poems (1908) by Fedor Sologub (pseudonym for Fedor Kuz'mich Teternikov).

29. *Lyceum years.* The years (1811–1817) during which Pushkin attended the Imperial Lyceum, newly founded by Alexander I, and during which Pushkin began his literary career.

30. *The Garland* (*Venok*). Collection of poems (1906) by Valery Bryusov that bore the alternate Greek title *Stephanos.*

31. *Ashes* (*Pepel*). Collection of poems by Bely published in 1909.

32. Bely is not really discussing figures here, as he suggests, since figures can be formed only over two or more consecutive verses. His classification here is of single lines of verse containing deviations from regular iambic tetrameter.

33. I have reworded the last two sentences, which are unclear in Bely's original.

34. "Orfej i Èvredika" (1904), one of the poems in the collection *The Garland.*

35. "Kern" refers to a poem written by Pushkin to one Madame Kern. Pushkin did not use the name in the poem, entitling it simply "To * * *."

36. *Aleksandr Nikolaevich Veselovsky* (1838–1906). Russian literary historian. The study Bely has in mind is Veselovsky's *V. A. Žukovskij. Poèzija čuvstva i serdečnogo voobraženija* (V. A. Zhukovsky: The poetry of feeling and sentimental imagination) (1904).

INDEX

Designer: Sandy Drooker
Compositor: G&S Typesetters, Inc.
Text: Baskerville
Display: Baskerville
Printer: Edwards Brothers, Inc.
Binder: Edwards Brothers, Inc.